WILLIAMSTOWN *and* WILLIAMS COLLEGE:

Further Explorations in Local History

WILLIAMSTOWN *and* WILLIAMS COLLEGE:

Further Explorations in Local History

DUSTIN GRIFFIN

ISBN: 978-1-03475-612-5

Designed by Elinor M. Goodwin, Print Shop Williamstown
Set in Perpetua
Printed and bound by Blurb

Cover art:

Detail from map of Williamstown, from *County-Atlas of Berkshire, Massachusetts*, by F. W. Beers (1876).
Courtesy of Williams College Archives and Special Collections.

To Williams College,
with thanks
for inspiring a life of reading and writing
about the liberal arts

CONTENTS

Preface • i

Part 1:
The Town

Chapter 1. Buxton: The History of West Main St.
from Benjamin Simonds to Cole Porter • 3

Chapter 2. Thirteen Galusha Farms • 19

Chapter 3. The History of the Hopper • 37

Chapter 4. E. P. Prentice: Mount Hope's Polymath • 53

Chapter 5. The Hills of Williamstown • 69
i. Northwest Hill • 71
ii. Bee Hill • 83
iii. Stone Hill • 97

Chapter 6. A Layman's History of Williamstown's Trees • 115

Part 2:
The Town and the College

Chapter 7. Enemies of the People:
Political Divisions in Early Williamstown • 131

Chapter 8. The Chadwells of Williamstown • 151

Chapter 9. Williamstown and Vietnam: The War at Home • 163

Part 3:
The College

Chapter 10. Three Eph Generals in the Civil War • 189

Chapter 11. The Resignation of Tyler Dennett • 205

Chapter 12. Political Culture at Williams
on the Eve of World War II • 227

Chapter 13. Frederick Schuman and Max Lerner:
Liberals, Realists, Possibilists • 235

Chapter 14. Clay Hunt • 257

Chapter 15. The "Williams Art Mafia" • 273

Chapter 16. An Architectural History of the
Center for Development Economics (St. Anthony Hall) • 289

Index • 300

PREFACE

This book is a sequel to my *Williamstown and Williams College: Explorations in Local History,* published in 2018 by the University of Massachusetts Press. As in that book, I have assembled a collection of microstudies, or microhistories, each of them focused on a single narrowly defined topic in the local history of Williamstown and its most notable local institution, Williams College. All but one of the essays have been written since 2017, many of them in the COVID-year of 2020. About half have been delivered as public lectures.

The essays are arranged in three sections: those that concern the history of the town; those that treat a topic that involved both town and college; and those that concern some episode in the history of the college. Three of the essays – on the hills of Williamstown – form a linked sequence. Within each section the essays are arranged in rough chronological order. Readers with a particular interest are invited to dive in anywhere.

All of the essays try to tell stories. Broadly speaking, some deal with places (1, 2, 3, 5), some with events (7, 9, 12), and some with people (4, 8, 10, 11, 13, 14, 15). Two of the essays don't fit into these categories: one deals with the history of the town's trees, another with the history of a building. Throughout the book I aspire to appeal not to the specialist but to the general reader, though the long essay about Fred Schuman and Max Lerner may only interest a student of international relations. (Readers who just want an introduction to Schuman and Lerner might be satisfied with the shorter "Political Culture at Williams on the Eve of World War II"). Because the essay on the history of the CDE building aspires to be a complete record, it includes details that may only delight an admirer of its designer, Stanford White.

The stories I tell are based on documentary evidence – old photographs; old town directories; Proprietors' Records in town hall; the *Vital Records of Williamstown to 1850*; the back files of the *North Adams Transcript*, the *Berkshire Eagle*, and the *Williams Record*; property records in the Registry of Deeds in Adams, MA; minutes of Williams College trustee and faculty meetings; manuscript letters and transcripts of oral interviews in the Williams College Archives and elsewhere – and numerous interviews with local residents, as well as some first-person exploration of the various places I describe.

Much of my evidence comes from old maps, including the 1830 *Plan of Williamstown* by John Mills map; the 1843 *Map of Williamstown from Early Surveys* by J. H. Coffin; the 1858 H. F. Walling *Map of the County of Berkshire;* the 1876 *County Atlas of Berkshire, Massachusetts*, by F. W. Beers; the 1894 D. W. Miller *Atlas*; and the 1904 *Atlas of Berkshire County, Massachusetts,* by Barnes & Farnham. Copies of all but the 1830 Mills map and the 1858 Walling map are found in the Williams College Archives, and online in the "Williams College and Williamstown Map Collection" (unbound.williams.edu).

I also draw on early printed histories of the town and college, supplementing and sometimes correcting those accounts: the *History of the County of Berkshire* (1829), the *Gazetteer of Berkshire County* (1885); Keyes Danforth, *Boyhood Reminiscences* (1895); Arthur Latham Perry, *Origins in Williamstown* (1894) and *Williamstown and Williams College* (1899); R. R. R. Brooks et al., *Williamstown: The First Two Hundred Years* (1953).

I am again grateful to the Archives of Williams College and the Williamstown Historical Museum, where much of my research was conducted. Their staffs have been unfailingly generous with their time. I want in particular to thank Lisa Conathan, Sylvia Kennick Brown, and Laura Zepka of the Archives, and Sarah Currie of the Williamstown Historical Museum.

Thanks to the Massachusetts Historical Society for permission to quote from the letters of Theodore Sedgwick in the Sedgwick Family Papers. Thanks to the Williams College Museum of Art for permission to use photographs of several pieces in the museum's collection. And thanks to the archives at Yale for permission to quote from the manuscript letters of Max Lerner in the Max Lerner Papers; to Don Schuman for permission to quote from the manuscript letters of Frederick Schuman; to John Hunt, for permission to quote from the transcription of Clay Hunt's oral-history interview; to the Williams College Archives and Special Collections for permission to quote from the oral-history interviews of Don Gifford, Lawrence Graver, Charles Keller, and Fred Stocking, and from the papers of Tyler Dennett; and to the Yale archives and the archives at the Hoover Institution at Stanford for access to Schuman's letters at Yale and Stanford.

I thank Hank Art, for copies of his published and unpublished work on the history of Hopkins Memorial Forest; Michael and Licia Conforti, for access to a file of records concerning the history of their former house on West Main St.; Jim Galusha, for access to Galusha Family Papers; Peter

Phelps, for access to Phelps family genealogical records; Phil Smith, for documents on the Whelden House on West Main St.; Charles Pardoe, for giving me a tour of the "Cole Porter Estate"; Mark Livingston, for his unpublished 1970 seminar paper at Williams College on Stone Hill and his 1972 *Portraiture of Stone Hill*; Kees Verhuel, for providing a translation of "Poetic Passion," from his *Het Mooiste van alle Dingen: Romeine Essays* (1994); Rob White, and Helena Warburg of the Schow Library at Williams, for securing a photograph of George Chadwell, and Theresa Sawyer, of the Williams College Facilities Department, for a tour of the renovated Center for Development Economics building.

I also thank the many Williamstown residents and Williams faculty and others who shared with me their knowledge of the town and college: Rob Abel, Mike Adams, Mary Anderson, Hank Art, Bob Bell, Peter Berek, Bill Broadbent, Jock Brooks, Adriana Brown, Norman Burdick, Deb Burns, Stewart Burns, Andy Burr, Philip Cantelon, Margo Cardner, John Chandler, Michelle Moeller Chandler, Michael Conforti, Averill Cook, Dean Crawford, Sarah Currie, Carol DeMayo, David Dethier, Joe Dewey, Sam Edgerton, Joan Edwards, Carl and Marilyn Faulkner, Dave Fitzgerald, Bill Flynt, Peter and Marnie Frost, Bill Galusha, Jim Galusha, Jane Gardner, Mary Ellen Geer, George Gelheiser, Racey Gilbert, Suzanne Graver, Bruce Grinnell, Eva Grudin, Allen Hart, Ray Hartman, Hunt Hawkins, Scott Hoover, John Hunt, John Hyde, Bob Janes, Nan Jenks-Jay, Drew Jones, Tim Kaiser, Paul Karabinos, Mike Kennedy, Sanford Lakoff, Jack Lane, Chris Lemoine, Rich Levy, Libby Kieffer, Jim Lillie, Dave Low, Penny Low, Dave Macpherson, Robert McCarthy, Linda McGraw, Doris McNab, Roger Mandle, Mike Miller, Judith Nathan, Virginia Nicklien, Edith Notman, Matt Noyes, Frank Oakley, Dan O'Connor, David Primmer, Larry Raab, Leslie Reed-Evans, Judy Reichert, Allen Rork, Paula Sagerman, Mike St. Pierre, Nada Samuels, Theresa Sawyer, Ed Schofield, Michael Shapiro, Kay Sherman, Dave Simonds, Willard Spiegelman, John Sprague, Mike Steel, David Stern, Lauren Stevens, Bill Stinson, Carl Sweet, Cathy Talarico, Kurt Tauber, Tad Tharp, Anne Tiffany, Paul Tucker, David Tunick, Kees Verhuel, Pam Weatherbee, Cheryl Westall, Arthur Wheelock, Nick Whitman, Eric White, Donna Wied, Bud Wobus, and Marge Wylde. Before he died, Fred Greene told me about debates on the Vietnam war at Williams in the late 1960s.

Special thanks to Bob Bell, Susan Dunn, Sam Edgerton, Gale Griffin, Mark Haxthausen, John Kleiner, Frank Oakley, Theresa Sawyer, Kurt Tauber, and Mark Taylor for reading earlier drafts of individual chapters, and to Charles Dew, Peter Frost, and Allen Rork for reading the entire manuscript.

Specialist readers and future local historians who wish to pursue my topics further may request a copy of my extensive footnotes (documenting my sources, and providing additional detail) at dustinhgriffin@gmail.com.

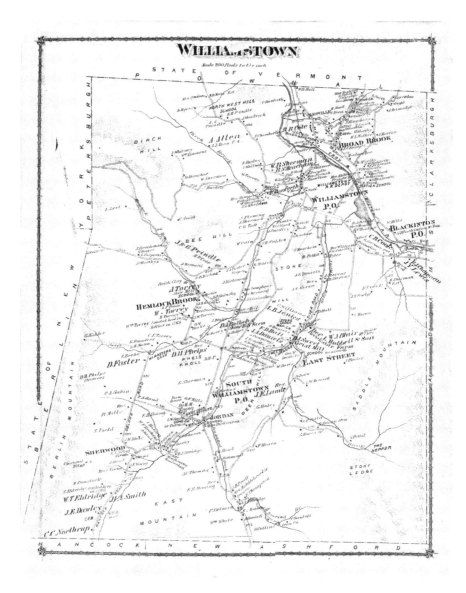

Map of Williamstown, from *County-Atlas of Berkshire, Massachusetts*, by F. W. Beers (1876). Courtesy of Williams College Archives and Special Collections.

PART 1

THE TOWN

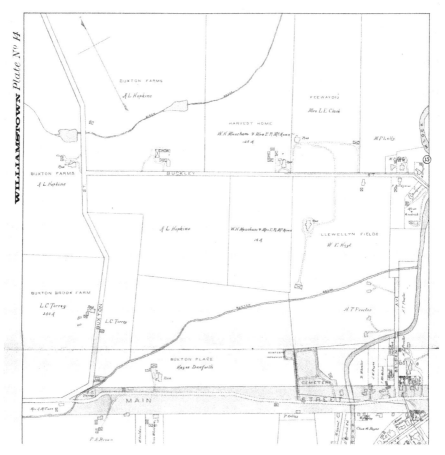

Detail from map of Williamstown, from D. L. Miller, *Atlas of the Towns of North Adams, Adams, Williamstown and Cheshire, Berkshire County, Massachusetts* (1894).
Courtesy of Williams College Archives and Special Collections.

Chapter 1

—⚬—

BUXTON

The History of West Main St. from Benjamin Simonds to Cole Porter

On old town maps you can see that the section of Northwest Hill Rd. between Main St. and Bulkley St. used to be called "Buxton Street." "Buxton" (or "the Buxton District") is the old name for the neighborhood on either side of Buxton Brook, including Buxton Street and the short stretch of West Main St., between Hemlock Brook and Buxton Brook. At various times the street was known as "West Main St." and as "Buxton Way." The hill on the south side of West Main, rising 300' above the two brooks that nearly encircle it, has long been called Buxton Hill. The old one-room neighborhood school on the corner of Main St. and Buxton Street was called "Buxton School." Buxton is the site of the initial settlement of Williamstown, and two of the oldest surviving houses in town. It is the site of the town's first cemetery. The old farms that make up Hopkins Memorial Forest used to be called "Buxton Farms." "Buxton Place" was for more than a hundred years the home of one of the town's leading families. On West Main St. "Buxton Hall" – demolished nearly 60 years ago – was once one of the town's grandest mansions. And a big house called "Buxton Hill" was once the home of the town's most famous summer resident.

The origin of the name "Buxton" is unclear. According to one report, it was given to the neighborhood by a post-Revolutionary settler who called it after a town in Norfolk (England), "for its rugged qualities and the class of people who settled there." But it is just as likely to have been named after the town of Buxton near Portland, Maine, that had recently been incorporated. The history of Buxton is a microcosm of the history of Williamstown: from initial settlement on 10-acre lots along Main St. on either side of Hemlock Brook and what is now Field Park, to the combination of lots into larger farms during the 19th century, to the rise of the summer colony as farms were abandoned and sold off to summer visitors; to the demolition of sprawling mansions and the conversion of large estates in the middle of the 20th century into residential subdivisions. And its social history, the various lives of the residents – subsistence farmers, rich summer people, modest school teachers, professionals and retirees – mirrors the demographic mix of Williamstown. What distinguished Buxton from other parts of town in this history is that it retains the feeling and in some places the look of the original settlement. Westlawn Cemetery still looks like the 19th-century country churchyard that it is. West Main St. has no sidewalks. One of the farms hung on until about 1960 and another survives as a 37-acre estate only a mile from Spring St. But the families who lived along West Main St. for two hundred years have been largely forgotten. Only two names – Benjamin Simonds and Cole Porter – still resonate with Williamstown's residents today. Most of the former residents lie quietly in Westlawn Cemetery.

Early Settlement

As part of the first division of land in 1750 house lots were laid out along the town's first street, 24 of them on Main St. from Hemlock Brook west to Buxton Brook, numbered 11 through 34, the odd numbers on south side, even numbers on the north. At least five "regulation houses" were built near Hemlock Brook – so called because in order to confirm title to their land the original settlers were required to build a house at least 18' x15'. On the north side, lot No. 12, on the west side of Hemlock Brook, belonged to Elisha Higgins (the original proprietor) and later to Dr. Jacob Meack. It was after him that the brook was in the early days called "Doctor's Brook." A regulation house may have been built on the lot. The house, much expanded, is still there, at 1192 Main St. – a regulation house at its core. A little further on the north side of the street was Lot No. 22, belonging to Benjamin Simonds, with a regulation house built in 1752. His daughter, Rachel, born in 1753, was the first child born in Williamstown. The house was later moved across the street, and burned down in 1930. Lot 22 is now part of Westlawn Cemetery. Before 1800 a road was laid out going south from Main St. at Lot 29, at a right angle, heading over Bee Hill. This was part of the old Albany Turnpike, vestiges of which are still visible on the wooded hill west of Thornliebank.

Westlawn was not the first cemetery in town, but began to be laid out shortly after 1762, on the southern part of Lot 12, and even taking up part of the street. Later other lots were added to it. Many of the original settlers were buried here, including Benjamin Simonds and his daughter Rachel, as were other well-known figures from the town's early years, including David Noble and Daniel Dewey.

The oldest surviving house on West Main St. is located at what was once Lot 29 and is now 1385 Main St., a saltbox dating from c. 1766-68, built by Nathan Smith, and now owned by Philip and Susie Smith (no relation). More substantial than the original "regulation houses," it had four rooms downstairs and a loft upstairs. In time, a wood shed was added to the east side of the house, and in the 1830s two rooms were added in back and the front parlor was refitted in what was then the current taste. It was home to the Whelden family for more than a century – from 1826 to 1928 – probably beginning with Salman Whelden, and his son, Samuel G. Whelden, who also lived and farmed there. The house later belonged to Samuel's daughter, Anna (1865-1921), a teacher and a spinster. The last of the Wheldens to live there was another of Samuel's daughters, Elizabeth Kellogg (Lizzie) Whelden (1873-1928). Thanks to a rich uncle, she was an 1879 graduate of Mt. Holyoke who later spent many years as the secretary of the YWCA in Albany and as a teacher and librarian in Williamstown. She was also unmarried. For some time in the 1920s she lived there with her close friend, Margaret Mary Sibley, and left the house to her at her death in 1928. When her brother Willis Whelden died in 1931, he was remembered as the last member of a family "that had been prominently identified with community life for many generations." Many of the Wheldens – including Samuel, Anna, Elizabeth, and Willis – are buried in Westlawn Cemetery.

Lizzie Whelden had at one point hoped to give the house and its contents to the town as a museum, but the town, worried about the costs of maintaining it, declined to accept. Her friend and heir, Miss Sibley, later gave a grandmother clock along with a few dishes and pieces of glass to the House of Local History, now called the Williamstown Historical Museum. They are still part of the Whelden Collection.

The Danforth Farm

Jonathan Danforth (1736-1802) moved to Williamstown in 1775. In 1778 he was renting a house on Lot No. 3 from Benjamin Simonds, where his son, Keyes Danforth, was born. Later he rented a large 7-room house on a 150-ac. farm on the south side of Main St. – "the extreme west lot on Main St" – belonging to David Noble. He then began buying land from Benjamin Simonds on the north side of West Main in April 1787. During the 1790s he built a small 1-story house on Lot #30, on the north side of the street, on the "brink of hill back from Main St., near a spring." This house was moved a couple of times, first out to Main St., and later back again, where it eventually served as a chicken house.

In 1800, when Keyes Danforth married and perhaps needed more room, Jonathan Danforth bought the farm on the south side of the street from David Noble. Jonathan died in 1802, but his son inherited the place. It stayed in the Danforth family until 1863. Keyes Danforth was a farmer, but he also became a major public figure in the village, leader of the local Democratic party, a selectman, a county commissioner, and a member of the state legislature. Although he had no higher education, he was said to have had a clear and strong legal mind, and served as "the poor man's lawyer," providing shrewd legal advice to fellow townsmen . (Of his eight children, three became lawyers and four married lawyers.) In 1822 his son Keyes Danforth, Jr. was born in the old house on the farm on the south side of Main St.

In 1835 Keyes Danforth, Sr. built what his son later described as a "new house" on the north side of West Main St, across from the Whelden House. It was a Greek Revival, the fashionable style of the day. Some circumstantial evidence suggests that he may have added onto a house already there, built c. 1790. Keyes Danforth, Jr. spent his teenage years in the new house, and in 1842 entered Williams College, graduating in 1846, went on to get legal training with an uncle, and began practicing law in Williamstown in 1851. (His seven brothers and sisters had meanwhile all moved away.) His father, Keyes Danforth, Sr., died that same year, and was buried in Westlawn Cemetery. In 1852 Keyes Danforth Jr. married, and four years later had a son, Bushnell. In 1858 he gave 4 acres of land to the town for an addition to Westlawn Cemetery, in order to create a separate Danforth family plot. A new stone was cut for his father – the old stone remained at the farmhouse and is still there today.

Keyes, Jr. and his young family continued to live with his mother in the farmhouse after his father's death, and after *she* died, in 1867, he bought out his siblings' interest. He reportedly took an active interest in the management of the farm. In time he called it "Buxton Place," after the brook that flows along its northern border. In 1868 his wife died, and in 1869, at the age of 47, he married again. He and his second wife had no children. His only child, Bushnell Danforth, graduated from Williams in 1878, where he was captain of the baseball team.

Keyes Danforth, Jr. held many town offices: postmaster, selectman, and town treasurer. He also served twice as a member of state legislature – like his father he was a staunch Democrat – and for 20 years as Acting Treasurer of Williams. He practiced law with his brother-in-law, Joseph White, and had numerous commercial interests in town. He was the co-owner (with Paul Chadbourne, president of Williams) of the former Walley textile mill on Green River from 1879 until it burned down four years later, and owned property on Spring St. In 1885 Keyes Danforth was named justice of the local police court (which dealt with minor offenses), and was henceforth called "Judge Danforth." In his old age, he published sketches in the *Transcript* of his boyhood in Williamstown, collected in 1895 as *Boyhood Reminiscences*.

In 1896, after a fire, Danforth replaced several of his wooden buildings on Spring St. with the three-story brick Danforth Block that survives today. On the ground floor was Judge Danforth's police court. He died the following year, at the age of 75, after being thrown from his carriage on Church St. when his horse shied at an approaching electric streetcar. He is buried beside his father in the big Danforth family plot in Westlawn Cemetery.

After Danforth's death is widow, Caroline, and his son, Bushnell, sold the property to their neighbor, Willis Whelden. Whelden, whose sisters Anna and Elizabeth were living across West Main St., had worked for a year or so as a coachman for Danforth, living in the coach house, and managed to buy the Danforth Farm, probably with a large mortgage. In 1903 (perhaps after a change in his financial circumstances) Whelden sold it back to Bushnell Danforth and his wife, who, with his widowed mother, moved back into the old place. But by 1911 Bushnell Danforth had moved to New York, and in 1912 sold the farm to Alvah K. Lawrie, a wealthy man from Pittsburgh who had been spending summers in Williamstown.

The Lawries

Alvah Kittredge Lawrie – pronounced LOUGH [rhymes with 'cow'] - ree – was born in 1852, in West Roxbury, Mass. (His father came from Edinburgh, Scotland, and made his money in the import business in Boston.) Alvah was one of nine children. A family photo of young Alvah and his brother, Andrew, dressed in the family kilt, suggests that the family retained a strong sense of its Scottish heritage. He attended the Boston Latin School and then Amherst, where he graduated with the Class of 1873. After several stints in business, in the 1890s he joined the Pittsburgh Reduction Co., which later (in 1907) became Aluminum Company of America (Alcoa). Lawrie was general sales agent and elected a director in 1899 and later 2nd Vice President, a more important title than it sounds: there were only five corporate officers. A strong president and a five-person board of directors ran the company.

Lawrie was very close to his siblings, especially his unmarried twin brother, Andrew, his widowed sister, Margaret, and his three unmarried sisters, Mary, Annie, and Amy. Because of ill health, Andrew retired in 1899, and in 1905 bought a big five-bedroom house in Williamstown, together with about five acres, on what was then North St. As an Amherst graduate who now lived in Salem, Andrew would have known that Williamstown was then at the height of its era as a tony summer resort. The 3-story Romanesque Revival house, with a wrap-around porch, had been built in 1887 by Eugene M. Jerome – it's located on what is now Jerome Drive, and is still there today. Andrew and his three unmarried sisters, Mary, Amy, and Annie, spent the summers there. He named the house "Braehead" (the name of a number of country houses in Scotland). The following year – 1906 – Alvah Lawrie bought a half interest in the property, perhaps intending to spend part of his summer there too. He must have enjoyed it, for in June 1910, at the age of 59, Lawrie decided to retire from day-to-day business. He apparently planned to spend more time in Williamstown and devote himself to landscape gardening and golf. (He seems to have retained his title as 2nd Vice President, and continued as an active director of Alcoa until 1933.)

It's amusing to imagine the five unmarried Lawrie siblings – all in their 50s – living together in Braehead. In 1911 things changed: at the age of 60, Alvah married a young woman , Frances Innes, 29 years his junior. She came from two old Kentucky families, descended from Scots who arrived in Virginia in the early 18th century. And he must have decided that Braehead wasn't big enough for him and his wife, and his five siblings. So in 1912 he bought his own place – the old "Danforth Farm" about a mile away. And he sold his half-interest in Braehead back to his brother. For a time Alvah and his new wife lived full-time in the Danforth farmhouse.

In 1914 the Lawrie world changed again: Andrew Lawrie died, as did his unmarried sister, Mary, and "Braehead" was advertised for sale. Amy and Annie then apparently moved in with their other brother, Alvah, in the Danforth farmhouse. That may have triggered his interest in building himself a new house, and in 1915 work began on a three-story stone mansion to the east of the farmhouse, for himself and his new wife – his two sisters, Amy and Annie, remained behind in the Danforth Farmhouse, which they called "Buxton Cottage." Amy and Annie spent the summers in Williamstown and the winters in New York.

Foundation work on the mansion began in April 1915. The cornerstone was laid on June 7, 1915. The exterior walls were built from 7000 cubic yards of yellow sandstone, cut from a ledge along the rail line east of North Adams, reportedly chosen by Lawrie himself. To replace the original driveway gates, large stone piers were built. A stable and large garage near the cottage were built at same time. Work on the house was completed in 1916.

The Lawries called it "Buxton Hall" – a rather grand and even pretentious name, at a time when the big estates tended to be called "Farms." It was designed by an established Boston architect, James Purdon, on the model of a "stately English manor house." (Brooks calls it a Tudor revival.) The footprint of the house was 110' x 25'. It had 15 rooms, including six reception rooms on the first floor, five bedrooms and three baths on second floor, three maid's rooms on the third. The house was featured in two architecture magazines. Outside, on the south side of the house, were formal gardens, with a pergola and a pool. To the east was the view of Williamstown, across a hayfield. On the north was a terrace, looking out on a croquet lawn and then steeply down to Buxton Brook.

Initially the Lawries continued to live full-time in Williamstown. In 1920 he bought the little one-room Buxton School, closed since 1917, as a house for his gardener, Harry Blake. Two Black servants, Jesse and Isidore, ran the house. There was apparently a chauffeur for their big Packard. But Lawrie was getting on in age – he was 70 in 1922 – and by the late 1920s they had bought an apartment on Park Avenue in New York, and only spent the summer in Williamstown, leaving in October. About 1929 Lawrie also bought a plantation in Thomasville, Ga., where he and his wife spent the winter.

The Lawries had no children, but Mrs. Lawrie, who had a number of older brothers and sisters, had many nieces and nephews who visited in Williamstown as children in the 1930s and 40s. Lawrie died in 1936, at the age of 84, leaving a huge estate of nearly $14 million (most of it in Alcoa stock). He left Buxton Hall to his wife (then only 55 years old), who continued to spend her summers in Williamstown. Like her husband, she was a skilled golfer – she won the women's tournament at Taconic in 1934. She was also great gardener, and submitted entries to the annual Williamstown Garden Club show (as did Mrs. Prentice at Mt. Hope), from gardens probably tended by her gardener, who also tended the extensive gardens behind Buxton Cottage, where Amy and Annie became full-time residents in 1944.

Nieces and nephews, with their children and grandchildren, continued to visit Buxton Hall in the summer. One greatgrandnephew, Lion Miles (b. 1934), remembered more than sixty years later (when he had become a Berkshire County local historian) playing croquet on the north lawn, wading in a lily pool at end of south lawn, and helping out with haying in the hayfield to the east. As he recalled, the children were allowed to play in the Large Living Hall and in the Library, where there was a phonograph with lots of 78 rpm records. They walked a mile downtown to Spring St. to go to the movies.

Mrs. Lawrie died suddenly of a heart attack in 1951, at the age of 70. Her sister-in-law, Annie Lawrie, lived on in the Buxton cottage until she died in 1954, at the age of 98. In May 1953 Sprague Electric Co. bought the Lawrie property from Mrs. Lawrie's estate. R. C. Sprague, the president of Sprague, lived on Bulkley St., and knew the Lawrie property well. Management's first plan was to build a research center in the Lawrie mansion, but the Sprague board insisted that any R & D center be located in North Adams. In 1954 William Nolan, Sprague's Treasurer, bought Buxton Cottage and four surrounding acres. During the 1950s the big house stood empty. There was no market for a stone mansion in those years – and most of the great houses in Williamstown had by then been demolished, and others disappeared in the '50s – Elm Tree House at Mt. Hope was the only one left. Neighborhood kids sneaked into the house and played there. They remember that it was very spooky. In November 1960 the house was finally torn down by a local contractor – by then the sandstone of which it was built had turned gray and weathered badly.

The "Cole Porter estate"

The most famous of those who lived on West Main St. is without a doubt Cole Porter, who in the 1940s spent fall weekends at a large estate at 1425 West Main St., on the south side of the street, just east of Buxton Brook. Still commonly known as the "Cole Porter Estate," the property has a more complicated though often misrepresented history. It was once a farm, and the boyhood home of Keyes Danforth, before his father built a larger house across the street in 1835. The young Keyes Danforth remembered that in the 1820s the Williams College president, Edward Dorr Griffin, used to ride his black horse out Main St. and up to the top of the hill behind the farm, from where he could enjoy a view of the village of Williamstown, the Hoosic River Valley, and the mountains beyond it.

While Danforth was living across the street, he converted the old farmhouse in which he had grown up to a barn, and after the barn burned he 1856 sold the 160-acre farm to his cousin, William Danforth, who tried farming for ten years or so, but found he didn't care for it, and in 1865 sold it to Henry Goodrich. Along with his brother, James, he ran the farm for 25 years, but in 1892 the Goodriches seem to have suffered financial reverses, and the farm was sold at public auction to a local banker. (This was at the same time that A. L. Hopkins was buying up failed or abandoned farms in the neighborhood.) Two years later the banker sold the Goodrich farm (with four buildings near Main St.) to Frederic Alden Brown. Brown was a Wall St. banker and an officer and director of several railroads. He announced plans to build a big summer house on what was called "Buxton Hill," with a view of the entire valley. But Brown had long suffered from ill health. He died in 1898, at age 47. The Browns never built a house in Williamstown.

In 1913 Mrs. Brown sold the property, still known as the "Goodrich Farm," to another New Yorker, Helen Jean Aitken (1878-1937), a wealthy unmarried heiress, who had spent summers in Williamstown with her parents. Her father was probably drawn to Williamstown by New York friends. In 1916 (a year after her father died), she built a large two-and-a-half story fieldstone house on the Goodrich Farm, uphill from the farm buildings. (It was thus built in the same year as the Lawrie mansion across the street, and the same year, in fact, that the Prentices began building Elm Tree House at Mt. Hope – a big year for the construction of summer mansions in Williamstown.) In 1916 she bought additional property on Petersburg Rd., including a pasture and a woodlot – increasing the farm from 160 to about 350 acres. A tenant farmer ran the farm for her. A notable local horticulturalist put in her garden and also lived on the estate.

Like her neighbor, Alvah Lawrie, Jean Aitken was of Scottish heritage – her grandfather was born in Scotland. In 1923, when she was forty-five, she married Robert Lewis Paddock, recently retired Episcopal Bishop of Eastern Oregon, where his fiery independence aroused controversy within the church, and led to what has been described as "nervous exhaustion," and to his resignation in 1922. Aitken had met Paddock decades earlier in New York, where he was an inner-city rector and social reformer. She was a graduate of the Masters School in Dobbs Ferry, listed in the social register, but was also a volunteer social worker, and active with the YWCA. Like the Lawries, the Paddocks had no children.

After 1923, unless they were traveling the world, the Paddocks spent winters in New York and summers in Williamstown. They named their Williamstown property "Buxton Hill." The house was managed by a staff of servants. (It's appealing to think that the Paddocks and the Lawries, summer millionaires, lived next door to modest schoolteachers, Anna and Lizzie Whelden.) Gradually, however, the Paddocks apparently became embarrassed by her inherited wealth, and resolved to live more simply and to spend their time giving her money away. She mostly gave to foreign missions and the YWCA, while he, in the 1930s, he began contributing to various leftist causes, both domestic, including the Fellowship of Socialist Christians and the Church League for Industrial Democracy, and overseas, especially the American Friends of Spanish Democracy, of which he became chairman.

In Williamstown they were interested in Harry Garfield's Institute of Politics, which met annually in August in Williamstown from 1921 to 1932, and gave lawn-party receptions for Institute members at their summer villa. They allowed their farmer, after he retired, to remain rent-free in the caretaker's house. Seven photographs of the house, from c. 1930, were donated to the Williamstown Historical Museum by a nephew of the Paddocks. In 1936 they decided that they had just been "playing at poverty" and tried to sell their Williamstown property, but had no takers. In 1937, at the age of 59 Jean Paddock suddenly died of a heart attack, and his death followed in 1939.

Enter Cole Porter. His wife, Linda, acquired the property in October 1940. They reportedly were looking for a country house for weekend getaways from New York, and a friend recommended Williamstown. She redecorated with wallpaper and furniture from their Paris apartment. She also undertook substantial renovations, building a pool and a poolhouse for her husband and his homosexual friends (at a discreet distance from the house), a tennis court, and a greenhouse. She converted a barn into a six-car garage, with a three-bedroom apartment on the second floor. Porter reportedly regarded the main house as "Linda's House," and preferred to spend his time in what he called the "Cottage," a large studio that had been converted from a carriage house, where he worked. Porter reportedly wrote some of the songs for *Kiss Me Kate* (1948) while in Williamstown. The Porters typically spent long weekends in Williamstown, usually in the fall, sometimes together, sometimes separately. In the '40s, with the help of staff from New York, they entertained weekend guests with lavish formal dinners – though apparently the guests (who didn't bring their children) were mostly New Yorkers and show-business types, and did not include college people or Williamstown locals. Their parties must have been as different as possible from the Lawrie family gatherings across the street.

Linda died in May 1954, having expressed a wish to be buried in Williamstown. Porter, however, buried her at his family plot in Indiana. Porter considered giving Linda's house to the college, but in November 1954, only six months after her death, Porter demolished Linda's house, moving the "Cottage" to its foundation, and adding a wing. The big house had been traditional in architectural style and decoration, and well suited for entertaining large groups of guests. The cottage was mid-century modern in style, with big windows, and its interior walls painted white, better suited for working and for gathering a few friends. After Porter's leg had to be amputated in 1958 – the ultimate consequence of a riding accident in 1938 – he preferred to have no more than a single guest in the house, and was reportedly a difficult host. He continued to visit until 1963. When he died in 1964, leaving no descendants, the property, including Porter's Bechstein grand piano, was donated to the college.

Thornliebank

By the late 1950s there was more development on the south side of Main St. In the 19th century much of the land between West Main and Glen St./Cold Spring Rd. was known as the "Sherman Farm." John Sherman sold his land to James Bullock before 1889. Bullock renamed it "Glen Farm" – and later "Yeadon Farm." The hill we now call "Buxton Hill" was then known as "Buxton Cobble." There is a postcard in the Williamstown Historical Museum with a view of Williamstown from Buxton Cobble.) Bullock erected a small observatory on the hill in 1891, but it soon blew down in a windstorm. All the trees on the hill had long been clearcut, and in 1898 Bullock hired a man to plant Scotch and Austrian pines. Some of those pine trees were cut in 1953 to make rafters for the "1753 House" in Field Park. For at least sixty years Williams geology students were taken on field trips to see the quartzite outcroppings on the Cobble.

Bullock's farm was inherited by his son, Anthony, who sold the property in the 1940s to Alex Petrie (1892-1966), president of the H. C. Clark Biscuit Co., in North Adams. Petrie lived in the big white house on the property – on the corner of Glen St. and Bee Hill Rd.

In the 1950s a local contractor, David McNab (Davie) Deans, the one who tore down Buxton Hall, bought land along W. Main St. Deans extended Buxton's Scottish connection – he was born in the village of Thornliebank, near Glasgow, in 1890. In 1958 and '59 he subdivided the land into building lots along Main St. and what he called "Buxton Hill Rd," "McNab Street" (present-day Hawthorne Rd.), and "Hawthorne Court." Access was only via W. Main St. The first houses to be built were along W. Main St. In the early 1960s the neighborhood was known as "Buxton Hill," and what is now Thornliebank Rd. was still a dirt road through a dairy farm pasture, with barns and cows. The "Hill" was partly pasture and partly woods. The land belonged to Petrie, but had long been farmed by Henry George and later his son-in-law Richard Hoar. Later, houses were built on the new streets. In 1965 Bob Jones, a local builder who bought land from Deans, received approval for another subdivision, "Buxton Hill Extension," and house lots were laid out on the upper part of Buxton Hill Rd. Doris McNabb bought two of those lots in 1966 and built a house there in 1975. She still lives there, and remembers that the top of the hill was pasture.

In 1966 Deans sold the first of his building lots on what he called "Thornliebank," then a cul de sac running south from Main St. When he built the house (177 Thornliebank) he reused cut-down joists and other timbers and made the roof out of slate, all salvaged from the Lawrie mansion, and in the living room installed wood paneling from Lawrie's butler's pantry. The fireplace reportedly came from the house that Cole Porter demolished in 1954.

In 1967, a year after Alex Petrie died, his house and farm were sold to Neill and Ann Megaw. Megaw was a professor in the English Department at Williams, and thus an unlikely real estate developer. In February 1968 the Megaws, who had moved into the Petrie house on Glen St. and Bee Hill Rd., laid out a subdivision, to be called "Buxton Hill Meadows," on 27 acres between Glen St. and the Davie Deans subdivision on West Main. The Megaw subdivision was to have access only on Glen St. Later Deans proposed to connect the two subdivisions, extending Thornliebank through to Glen St. This caused controversy. Neighbors on West Main St. worried that through traffic from the south (headed to the race track in Pownal) would cut through from Glen St. to Main St. or Bulkley St. to avoid backed-up traffic at Field Park. Even though the plan was approved, the traffic was apparently not diverted through Thornliebank onto West Main.

Deans only had time to built one more house on Thornliebank before he died in 1968. The Megaws were not able to find buyers for their lots – perhaps potential customers were scared off by the backed-up traffic on Glen St. – and in 1969 they departed for Texas, where Neill Megaw became chairman of the English Department at the University of Texas. By 1971 he had only reportedly sold two lots in the "Buxton Hill Meadows" subdivision – and the bank took ownership of most of the rest, subsequently reselling them at reduced prices. The remainder of Thornliebank was built up over the next twenty years.

The last fifty years

There were other changes on West Main St. in the 1960s. In April 1961 Sprague submitted an application to the town for a subdivision of the Lawrie estate. The property was divided into eleven lots on two streets, named Hill Province Rd. and Laurie Drive – L-A-U-R-I-E – whoever recorded the latter name in town records paid insufficient attention to the pronunciation and the spelling. The first house to be built was on the eastern end of the property, on the brow of the hill, by Sprague executive John Sprague, and his wife Jid, in the early 1960s. They lived there until they moved to Worcester in 1968. Other houses were built in the '60s by other Sprague executives. As a result of this development and the development of Thornliewood and Buxton Hill Rd. across the street, the feel of the neighborhood, though not Main St. itself, became more "suburban."

In 1960 the Nolans added a swimming pool to the old Danforth cottage. They initially called the house "Buxton Hill," and later "Open Gates." In their years the house was more visible from the road. In 1980 the Nolans sold to Wayne and Elaine Wetzel, and in 1983 they sold to Ed and Lynda Scofield, who in turn sold to the Clark Art Institute and its new director, Michael Conforti, in 1994. Each of the owners modified the house in one way or other. A large weaving studio was carved out of the barn by the Confortis. Alicia Conforti restored and improved the gardens into one of the horticultural showplaces in town.

In 1966 the college sold the Cole Porter estate – remember that Porter had donated it to the college – to James (Bing) and Irene Hunter. In 1978 the Hunters gave 176 acres at the back of the estate to the town – it is still known locally as the Hunter Property. They owned the house for 18 years, made it their primary home, added a wing, and entertained there on a grand scale. In the 1980s the house changed hands several times, until 1990 when it was bought by Taylor Briggs – he was a New York lawyer and a Williams alum. After he retired in 1995 he and his wife moved to Williamstown. In 2004, after her husband died, Jane Briggs sold to a New Yorker, Peter K. Davenport, for $2.3m, then the highest sale price in Berkshire County. He tried to run the property as a luxury inn. In 2013 he sold the caretaker's house to two Williams alumni who live in New Jersey, and in 2014 he sold the big house, at a considerable loss, to the present owners, both Williams alums who live in New York. At nearly 37 acres, it remains the largest parcel on West Main St.

In 1967 Phil and Susie Smith bought the old Whelden House, preserving many of its original features, including its basic structure and plain exterior, wide pine floorboards and hand-hewn white oak beams, and making repairs and restorations in keeping with the house's 18th-century origins. The Smiths have lived in the house for fifty years, far longer than the Lawries, the Paddocks, and the Porters lived on West Main St. The Smith house has been there for 250 years. The Lawrie and original Paddock-Porter house lasted few than fifty.

The Lawrie, Paddock, and Porter families are gone too: they had no children, and as summer people they were buried elsewhere. By contrast, although no Danforths remain in Williamstown, many of them are buried in Westlawn, including the Rev. Sinclair Danforth Hart – remembered by many as the Sinc Hart who in his retirement years lived on South St. until he died in 2007. Although not descended directly from Keyes Danforth, Jr., he was the great-great-grandson of Keyes Danforth, Sr. There is even a Danforth connection to the Buxton School. It was founded in New Jersey in

1928 by the greatgrandson of Keyes Danforth, Sr. and his wife – and named after the old Danforth family farm – and moved to the end of South St. in Williamstown in 1947.

I conclude with a memory of another family on West Main St. in the 1960s, in one of four small houses just west of Hemlock Brook, on the south side. Wallace and Alice Howard lived in the second house on the left, a two-story frame and clapboard building, set back from the street, located on 1/4 acre of what was once a larger parcel, and was originally Lot #13. There was a regulation house built there in the 1750s, but it was demolished and replaced by the present building, probably in the late 19th century. (The house is one of four small late-19th century houses.)

I knew Wally Howard in the early 1960s as the custodian at St. Anthony Hall, the Williams fraternity of which I was a member. (It's now the Center for Development Economics, opposite Field Park, and thus a very short walk from West Main St.) Wally was a gentle, kind, and easy-going man who managed to take care of a big fraternity house which wasn't treated gently by the undergraduates, especially on party weekends. What I didn't know at the time is that Wally was a World War II vet – he served in the Pacific with the U.S. Navy and was one of the men who survived when the USS Yorktown, an aircraft carrier, was sunk in the Battle of Midway in 1942. He and Alice raised two children, Kenneth and Janet, in their small 2-bedroom house on West Main St. The Howards lived there from about 1957 until Wally died in 1986. The house has turned over several times since Kenneth Howard sold it in 1989. The "Howard" doorknocker is still on the house. It's now owned by a couple from New Jersey, who use it as a second home, as has happened to a number of houses in town. This is yet another way in which the history of West Main St. reflects the history of Williamstown.

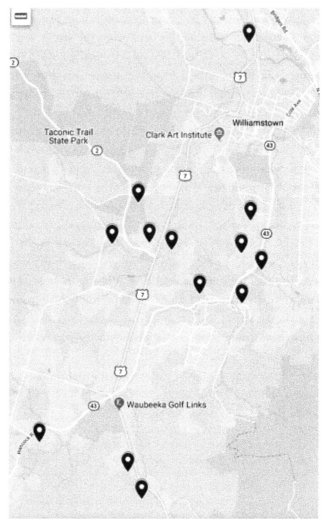

Map showing location of thirteen Galusha farms.

Chapter 2

—ᴀᴦ—

THIRTEEN GALUSHA FARMS

Everybody in Williamstown knows about the Galusha Farm – Fairfields Farm – out on Green River Rd, one of the three surviving dairy farms in town. And many probably know that it was founded by the grandfather of the current owners back in the 1920s. But they probably don't know that members of the Galusha family have been farming in Williamstown since before 1800, and that one Galusha or other, most of them named Daniel, have over more than two centuries run thirteen different farms in Williamstown. To review the history of the Galusha Farms in town is to shed some light on the oft-told but complicated tale of the rise and fall of dairy farming not just in Williamstown but throughout northern New England. And it provides clues about why some dairy farms lasted longer than others.

The first Galusha to buy land in Williamstown arrived here before 1800. Daniel Galusha was apparently born near Boston, maybe in Watertown, Mass., in 1748, and may have spent time in Vermont , where one of his relatives, Jacob Galusha, of Shaftesbury, was later governor. Daniel served in the Revolutionary War, and moved to Williamstown by 1790. That's when the first reliable documentation is found: he appears on the 1790 census as a Williamstown resident. At the age of 42 he married a widow with four daughters – which sounds like he acquired a lot of dependents, and no sons to help out with heavy farm work. But maybe the widow had inherited property and/ or money from her first husband, and by 1791 Daniel and his wife had a son of their own.

The Old Galusha Farm, Part 1

He began buying land in 1798, beginning with a 60-acre lot, the original Lot #25 in the 8th Division, west of what was then called Hemlock Rd. (now Cold Spring Road), bordered on the south by Hemlock Brook and what is now the Taconic Trail. Much of the land was steep and the topsoil was thin. There was water from Hemlock Brook at the bottom of the hill and at least one spring on the hillside. Access to the land was via a farm road up from Hemlock Road – traces of this road are visible in the woods today. He must have built a house not far from the road, but no sign of it remains, not even a cellar hole. He bought another 47 acres in 1806.

He died in 1808, when his son, also named Daniel (1791-1871), was just 17. Let's call him Daniel II. Daniel I's wife presumably inherited the land, and the young Daniel worked it, maybe with hired help. When *she* died in 1833, the land passed to her son, by then 42 years old. The second Daniel also frequently bought property, including land on the east side of Hemlock Rd., and wood lots extending north to the present-day Mezze restaurant, ultimately expanding the farm to 190 acres. He must have prospered – and / or had money from his wife's family to buy land. Other farms in the neighborhood belonged to the Prindle and Hickox families up on Bee Hill Rd. and the Phelps and Sweet families on land further south along Oblong Rd. Over the next several generations of Galushas would marry into all these families.

In 1830 a new road, Torrey's Road, now called Torrey Woods Rd., had been extended from Oblong Rd. down to Hemlock Rd. In the 1840s Daniel II built a new house higher on the hill, with a driveway off the new Torrey's Road, in the fashionable Greek Revival style, 2 ½ stories, with a front porch (similar to the Greek Revival house that survives today on Torrey Woods Rd.). An account book surviving in the Williamstown Historical Museum shows that he bought the lumber for the house – chestnut, cherry, and hemlock – from Giles Torrey, who ran a sawmill nearby.

By then he had two grown sons: the younger of them was Daniel Brown Galusha (1822-1913) – let's call him Daniel III. In 1842 Daniel III married a neighbor girl, and started a family. (That event may have encouraged his father to build the new and bigger house.) Daniel III's children included yet another Daniel (1854-1924) – we'll call him Daniel IV. Daniel III remained on the old farm and helped his father work it. When Daniel II died in 1871, Daniel III inherited the farm.

Galusha Family Papers

A photo from about 1885 shows three generations of Daniel Galushas: Daniel Brown Galusha (Daniel III) and his wife, Adeline; Daniel IV and his wife, Mary. The small boy is Daniel Jones Galusha (Daniel V) and the baby on his grandfather's lap is his little brother, Edward. Two hired men hold the horses.

John S. Galusha Farm, Cold Spring Rd.

Meanwhile, Daniel III's older brother, John Sweet Galusha (1813-66), married young (at age 19) and had moved out of his parents' place to his wife's parents' farm in Fulton County, NY. By 1837 he had moved back to Williamstown and settled on a farm of about 75 acres nearby on Hemlock Road, just downhill from his parents, on either side of Hemlock Brook, probably on land belonging to his father. There was a small 1 ½- story house (25' x 35') near the road. In 1850 he was farming with the help of his first son, Nathan. But it appears that the family, and the farm, did not prosper. For whatever reason, in 1860 their second son, John, was working elsewhere as a day laborer, perhaps to bring in some income. In 1866 John S. Galusha died at age 53. His widow remained there, keeping house, sometimes living with her son Nathan until *he* died in 1873, and then taking care of a grandson. She is named as the owner on an 1876 map. She died in 1883. The farm was later subdivided: today two acres along the road belong to the Bratcher family: the old house is still there, along with an old barn with a big sign on the side saying "Henry E. Bratcher, Carpenter & Builder." The back acres, on the east side of the brook, are part of Herbert Allen's Stone Hill estate, and are still cut every year.

John M. Galusha Farm, Oblong Rd.

In 1862, while he was still working as a day laborer, John Sweet Galusha's younger son, John Marsh Galusha (1841-1931), married a neighbor girl. Three weeks later he enlisted in the 49th Massachusetts and served for a year during the Civil War. Perhaps when he returned, and especially after his father died in 1866, he helped run the family's farm, but by 1870 he had moved out of his mother's place and onto a small 14-acre farm nearby on Oblong Rd., probably left to him by his grandfather, where he built a small 1 ½ story house (only 20' x 24'). He acquired a local reputation as an expert sportsman. His daughter died in 1881 before her 18th birthday, and he and his wife never had a second child. (That's a problem for a farmer, who needs all the free help he can get.) He operated the farm by himself until1926, when his wife's health was failing and they sold the farm and moved into town. She died the next year. He died in 1931 at the age of 90.

After he died the land had several owners, the last of whom sold it to Arthur George in 1945. Art and his wife, Clara, lived on the farm for the rest of their lives. He later established Taconic Stables there, renting horses by the hour, from 1954 to 1974. He also set up the Taconic Riding Academy, a 4-H horse club, where many Williamstown kids learned to ride, along with a riding club for adults (the Hobby Horsemen Riding Club). And he raced horses at the Green Mountain racetrack in Pownal. Today the land – the same 14 acres, with a large field, woods, and the old house and barn on the road – belongs to Jim George. It is no longer farmed, but for years an old retired race horse named George used to graze in the field that you can see from Oblong Rd.

Hickox/Galusha Farm, Bee Hill Farm

Back at the original Galusha Farm, Daniel III had ten children, including five sons. All five became farmers, four of them in Williamstown. The oldest, Lyman (1844-1919), married Sara Jane (Jennie) Hickox in 1866 and moved up to her family's farm, known as Bee Hill Farm, laid out by her greatgrandfather, Stephen Hickox, about 1799, at the top of Bee Hill Rd. In 1870 Lyman and his wife later had moved back downhill into his parents' house, but by 1885 he was again up on the Hickox farm, where there were 18 Jersey cows (for milk) and 32 Merino sheep (for wool) on 246 acres. Although sheep outnumbered cows on Williamstown farms for much of the 19th century, in time dairy cows were more numerous. But there were still so many sheep grazing on Bee Hill Farm in the late-19th or early 20th-century – and perhaps because it was unusual at that time to see so many sheep – that the level high ground (at an elevation of 1200') to the south of the Hickox house on Bee Hill Rd. became known as "Sheep Hill." The name has since migrated a mile or so south and east, and now refers to the steep hillside above the office of Williamstown Rural Lands Foundation.

The Galusha family would operate or own the Hickox farm for the next 75 years, from 1885 to 1960. Lyman continued to run it, eventually with the help of his sons, Chauncey and George, and for a time of his cousin, Daniel V. In 1891 his mother-in-law leased the farm to Lyman, but she retained a right to live in part of the house. In1899 old Mrs. Hickox fell (or maybe, so it was reported in the newspaper, jumped) from a window and died. The lease expired in 1906, and Lyman's wife, Jennie, apparently inherited the property. When she died in 1915, Lyman was still farming. He died in 1919, at the age of 75, and the land passed to his grandson, and in 1937 to his greatgranddaughter, Beulah Bailey Thull.

In 1957 the farm was broken up: Beulah Thull sold the back acres to the state – they became part of the undeveloped Taconic Trail State Park. 3.5 acres along Bee Hill Rd. were separated off as a residential lot. The original farmhouse is still there, owned for many years by former selectman Ron Turbin, and recently sold. The state-owned back acres are hayed by Daniel V's grandson, Jim Galusha, a couple of times a summer.

Mark and Cora Galusha Farm, Green River Rd.

Daniel III's *second* son, Mark Galusha (1852-85), moved out and ran a 75-acre farm a little further away on Green River Rd., across the road from where Col. Prentice would later build the "Million Dollar Cow Barn." After Mark died in 1885, at age 32, his wife Cora owned it. Her name appears on the 1894 town map. In the 1890s her young sons, Charles and Arthur, actively managed it for her. By 1903 Cora apparently moved into town and the farm passed into the hands of her nephew, Harry P. Galusha (one of Lyman's sons), who had been working as a farm laborer for hire in the 1890s. He hung on until 1916, when he sold the land to Colonel Prentice, who was buying up old farms to assemble his Mount Hope estate. Prentice called the house "Cora Cottage." It was an irregular two-story frame house, with a big barn in back, and during the Prentice years was used as the Mt. Hope Farm office. The house and barn are still there today.

Harry Galusha and the Town Farm

Harry Galusha also had another small farm on Green River Rd. When the old mill at Sweet's Corners came up for sale in 1894, he bought it, and in 1895 was operating a cider mill there, and later conducted a sawhill. In 1901, while serving as caretaker for the poor living at the "town farm" at Sweet's Corners, he bought that 33-acre property too. Harry never married, and after selling the rest of his property to Prentice spent his final years as a patient in a state mental hospital.

Frank Galusha Farm, South Williamstown

A *third* son of Daniel III, Franklin Prindle Galusha (1850-1921), also farmed on his own for a while, but did not prosper any better than Harry. In 1874 he was listed in the town directory as a "farmer" in Williamstown, location unknown, probably on leased land on the Hancock Rd. He married in 1876, and was still listed in 1880 as a farmer, but then he must have lost his farm, for in 1885 he was only a "laborer," living on Glen Rd. After his first wife died, he married again in 1893, by which time he was again reported to be farming in town, "in his old neighborhood." But he and his much younger second wife apparently then moved to New Jersey, though he kept in touch with his cousin, John M. Galusha. (They fished together.) He later relocated to Troy, where in 1900 he lived with his sister Grace and brother-in-law, Herbert Dexter Bailey, and with Bailey started a small real estate business, "Galusha's Company," which bought and sold land in Williamstown and elsewhere. But the arrangement apparently did not work out: in 1909 he tried farming again on the outskirts of Troy, and by 1910 had moved to Gloversville, where he was employed as a night watchman at a sawmill. He died in 1921, and was buried back in Williamstown.

The Old Galusha Farm, Part Two

Meanwhile, back at the original Galusha family farm, the *fourth* son of Daniel III, also named Daniel (1854-1924), let's call him Daniel IV, stayed home and helped run his father's farm. He and his wife lived in one half of the house, his parents in the other. In 1885 the 185-acre farm had Merino sheep and 18 cows. They made and sold cheese. His mill down on Hemlock Brook was a major producer of cider. Daniel IV had five children, but one died early, and only one of the four others would marry.

By 1903, his maiden aunts, Abbie and Jennie, who had moved out of the house, moved back in, perhaps to take care of their dying grandmother and elderly grandfather, Daniel III (then 81). Also living at the farm for a time was 26-year-old Daniel V, who in 1906 had married 24-year-old Kate Eldridge (1882-1953), from an old South Williamstown farming family. For his day job Daniel V worked in the post office as a rural delivery mailman. In 1908 Kate kept a diary, which survives in the Williamstown Historical Museum, and provides a vivid first-person account of farming in Williamstown in those days. On New Year's Day 1908 she notes that they began the year with 96 sheep, six cows, three horses and a colt, and some hens. Over the course of the year they sold eggs and apples, bought hay, and took on a hired man for $18 a month.

In 1909 young Daniel V and his wife Kate moved out to their own farm – more on that below. His grandfather, Daniel III, died in 1913, at age 91, and his mother, Daniel IV's wife, Mary, died in early 1915. That left a widower and two unmarried aunts, Abbie and Jennie, in the house. The 190-acre farm, which had pretty much been worked out, passed to Daniel III's children, who then deeded it for $1 to Abbie and Jennie, who needed a place to live and something to live on.

The two sisters lived there, Abbie teaching at the nearby Hemlock Brook School and Jennie helping on the farm and doing the cooking and housekeeping. They kept a few cows and some chickens, and had a full-time hired man to help out. They raised enough food to feed themselves and to sell a little. Henry Bratcher, Jr., who grew up in the neighborhood in the 1930s, remembered Abbie and Jennie driving their buggy down Cold Spring Rd. to deliver milk as well as butter, cheese, and cut-up chickens to local grocery stores. Over the years to make ends meet they sold off parts of the farm. A photo of the farm about 1930, just after the Taconic Trail was put in, shows the house and barns, and an ice house to keep milk, cheese, and eggs cool.

In 1940, when Abbie and Jennie got too old to run their farm – Abbie was 79 and Jennie was 76 – they sold their remaining acres to Henry Bratcher Sr., and moved down to a small house on Glen St. Bratcher quickly re-sold it to Alfred Holt, a writer and a Williams alumnus, who lived in Florida in the winter and spent summers in Williamstown on his "Sunrise Farm." (In May 1971 the old Galusha farmhouse burned down, apparently as a result of arson.) In 1987, after the Holts died, the 95-acre piece west of Cold Spring Rd. was bought by Jim and Joan Burns, and in 1991 56 of those acres were developed by them on a newly-laid-out public road, Old Farm Way. There are now five houses on what was once the old Galusha farm. The biggest of the Galusha barns was moved and repurposed into a two-story barnlike house by Jay and Rachel Tarses. The old farm fields are still kept open, you can find old Page-wire sheep fence in the woods, and an old Galusha stock tank, next to a unused spring house, still overflows.

The Galushas and the old "Andrews Farm"

Back in 1914 Daniel IV, at age 60, who had joined in the agreement to give the old family farm to his unmarried sisters, needed a place for *his* three unmarried children. So in 1914 he bought the 100-acre "Andrews Farm" on North St., along Hemlock Brook – known today as Bonnie Lea Farm. Said to have been "one of the best [farms] in the town," it had previously been owned by Barney Andrews. His granddaughter later said she thought Andrews himself called the farm Bonnie Lea ('beautiful meadow')– though it is likely that it had been given that name much earlier by Williams Professor Albert Hopkins, who liked to assign fanciful names to local places. In any event, in 1914 Daniel IV's three unmarried children moved there. After his wife died the next year, Daniel IV followed them to North St., and lived there with them until he died suddenly from a heart attack in 1924.

The house dated from 1778, and was expanded over the years to six bedrooms. The Galushas kept some cows and a team of horses, and hired help to run the farm for them. Edward (1885-1967) was the bookkeeper and later cashier of the Williamstown Savings Bank, retiring in 1960 after 55 years at the bank. He died in 1967. Belle Galusha (1886-1959), like her Aunt Jennie, was a schoolteacher. Grace (1891-1980) was interested in family history. The Galusha siblings pretty much kept to themselves and lived abstemiously. From

1926 to 1939, to supplement the household's income, the two sisters ran a small restaurant, attached to the house, that they called the Little Blue Tea Room, serving breakfast and dinner. They also rented rooms to overnight guests. Over time the Galushas sold off some of their land. Belle died in 1959, and in 1969, after Edward died, Grace, now left alone, sold the remaining 45 acres to the DeMayo family, to whom she was related by marriage. (Dick DeMayo was Mary Lou Galusha's brother.) In 1991 the DeMayos opened a horse farm, and brought back the old name, Bonnie Lea.

Arthur Galusha and Springside Farm

By the time Daniel IV of North St. died in 1924, his nephew, Mark's son, Arthur Galusha, was the leading Galusha farmer in Williamstown. In 1900 26-year-old Arthur, who had been operating his widowed mother Cora's farm on Green River Rd., bought the 175-acre Thomas Farm on New Ashford Rd, and began breeding Guernseys. In 1902 he bought 80 acres of adjacent property, and called the combined acres "Springside Farm," presumably because it was near Waubeeka Springs. By 1912 he was doing well enough to add a large "piazza" to the old farmhouse, where he lived with his wife and two sons.

Arthur very successfully raised Guernseys until the late 1940s, when the farm passed to his younger son, Walter, who lived there from 1940 to his death in 1979. The farmhouse was then moved from beside Rt. 7 uphill and out of sight of the road. The core of the farm now belongs to Katie Wolfgang and Jonathan Krant. Another 36 acres of old Galusha woodlot belong to Pam Weatherbee, who put a conservation restriction on them.

Fairfields Farm, Part 1

Meanwhile, in 1909 Arthur Galusha's first cousin, young Daniel V, while still living with his father and grandfather at the old family farm, had bought the broken-down 90-acre "Briggs Farm" on Green River Rd. (He apparently had some financial help from his cousin Arthur.) By 1911 Daniel V and Kate had moved there. He kept his post office job and in the first years his main activity on the farm seemed to be as a fertilizer and seed broker, buying from a Boston wholesaler and reselling to dozens of local farmers. By 1916 he was doing well enough to buy a touring car for $450, in which he delivered the mail. After fifteen years of marriage, a son, Daniel Eldridge

Galusha, call him Daniel VI, was finally born in 1921. He proved to be an only child – there's that Galusha family problem again. By 1923 Daniel V too had begun breeding Guernseys at what he was now calling Fairfields Farm, and by 1926, with help from a recent graduate of Massachusetts Agriculture School, was selling Guernsey heifers. Years later Daniel VI remembered that in the early 1930s his father worked at the post office in the morning, and delivered mail in the afternoon. Young Daniel VI helped out on the farm – he later said that he milked five cows before breakfast. Milk was kept cool in the cellar with ice from the ice house – there was no commercial refrigeration on a farm this small. In the town directory for 1928 Daniel V is still listed not as a farmer but as a mail carrier, and in time began delivering milk to local customers along with their mail in his old Ford. But he was still using horses to pull farm wagons. He did not retire from his mailman job until 1937, so it appears that for some years his small dairy operation was not enough to support the family. Like most small dairy farmers, he needed another source of income.

Green Meadow Farm

Arthur Galusha, Daniel V's first cousin, had a much bigger and more successful Guernsey operation. In 1925 he leased and operated George Alfred Cluett's 500-acre Green Meadow Farm, on Gale Rd.[lii] (Cluett, a wealthy shirt manufacturer from Troy, had been raising Guernseys on the farm as a hobby, but in 1925 decided to get out of farming after his dairy herd was infected with TB, and to devote himself to collecting early Federal furniture). Arthur, who had bought 30 cows from Cluett's herd at public auction in 1922, built up a herd of about 140 prize Guernseys on Cluett's Green Meadow Farm. He lived there with his wife and two sons, but still owned and operated his own farm on New Ashford Rd. The Green Meadow barns were located along a farm road that is now Cluett Drive, and the fields were up behind the big house which survives today as Pine Cobble School.

In 1933, when a neighboring farm came up for sale, Arthur Galusha decided to buy it, but continued leasing at Green Meadow at least until 1937. In that year Cluett reclaimed the house and farm, and used it as his summer residence, and to display his furniture collection, until he died in 1955. In 1958 Cluett's heirs gave 178 acres of the property, including the house, to Williams College.

The college arranged to have Daniel Galusha VI move the Cluett barns down Green River Rd. to Fairfields Farm, cleared the farmyards, laid out Cluett Drive on eleven acres in 1960, began selling eight housing lots, and established the Cluett Center for Development Economics in the Cluett house. The college retained about 150 acres of field and woods, and kept the big field behind the house open. It came to be known as Kite Hill, after Williams professor Lee Hirsche, who with his art studio class designed and flew kites there on what he called Kite Day every spring from 1961 to 1975. After the Center for Development Economics moved into town in 1966, the college used the house as an alumni center, but in the 1970s sold the house and 100 acres to David and Joyce Milne. The Milnes set up Highcroft School in the house and grounds, and ran it from 1978 to 1993. And after the Pine Cobble School lost its building on Main St. in a fire, it moved out to the old Highcroft School site and is still there. There is no sign of the old Green Meadow Farm today, but Jim Galusha cuts hay every summer on the open field.

Coronation Farm

While his herd was still at Green Meadow Far, Arthur bought the old 400-acre "Hillside Farm" next door, once owned by Harley Proctor and later by Samuel Blagden. The property included a large 27-room main house. There were also two other houses, four barns, a poultry house, and a spring-fed swimming pool. Over time Arthur bought another 100 acres. With his two sons, he ran a dairy, which he named Coronation Farm, selling milk locally, but the main business of Arthur Galusha & Sons was buying, breeding, and selling prize Guernsey cows: he established a national reputation – in 1936 one of his cows set a world record for milk production. In 1939 a major fire destroyed two of the barns. In the same year Arthur's son Mark was named by Governor Leverett Saltonstall (a Guernsey owner himself) to a three-year term as Director of the Division of Livestock Disease Control in the state Agricultural Department, and later as state Commissioner of Agriculture.

In 1948 Arthur Galusha sold the farm with 130 head of cattle to Walter Hoover, a wealthy Vermont engineer, for the substantial sum of $100,000. Why did he sell? Presumably because he was 74 years old and ready to retire, and neither of his sons (Mark was now a career military officer, and Walter a full-time mechanical engineer) wanted to take over and run the business. In retirement, Arthur did a lot of traveling, and spent the winter in Vero Beach, but retained ownership of a house on the Coronation Farm property. He died in 1953.

Hoover hired a herdsman and continued the dairy business until 1952, when he sold his herd of Guernseys, but kept the farm, returning to his engineering work with his Hoover Transmission Company, which led in 1953 to the invention of a pulley for use in small farm vehicles. He converted his 158' x 22' calf barn into a manufacturing facility, in which he hoped to produce 150,000 pulleys a year, but had difficulty getting a zoning variance, and by 1960 abandoned the project. In 1982 Herbert Allen bought the property, demolished most of the farm buildings, and built a new house. He also restored the old Coronation farm barns along Green River Rd., though they are no longer used for agricultural purposes. But Jim Galusha raises corn and cuts hay on Allen's fields.

Eldridge Farm

The thirteenth and final Galusha farm started out as an Eldridge farm. Until the early 1980s it was still being farmed by James Eldridge III, called "Bert." After Bert, who never married, died in 1983, the 365-acre Eldridge farm and woodlot on the New Ashford Rd. passed to his nearest surviving relative, his nephew, Daniel Eldridge Galusha (Daniel VI), whose mother, Kate Eldridge Galusha, was Bert's sister. In 1990 Daniel VI, who had a strong interest in land conservation, sold part of the property to the commonwealth of Massachusetts. It is now operated by the state's Fish & Wildlife Department. In 1992 he also gave 100 acres of the Eldridge Farm to Williamstown Rural Lands Foundation, which transferred it to the state. In the last thirty years much of the farm's open land on the west side of New Ashford Rd. has been allowed to grow in to encourage wildlife but the Galushas are still haying the fields on both sides of the road every year.

Fairfields Farm, Part 2

In 1939 Daniel VI enrolled in an agricultural program at Iowa State University in Ames, Iowa, but did not finish, and returned to Williamstown to help run Fairfields Farm. By then his father had an International Harvester Farmall- F20 tractor. Other power equipment included a hay baler and a belt-driven stationary hay chopper. In 1941 the family determined that in order to make money from farming they had to have a bigger operation, and began buying additional land. Over the next twenty years they were to acquire another 500 acres of old farm land off of Blair Rd., including the old Sweet Farm, adjacent to the original Briggs Farm on Green River Rd.

Farmers have always had to worry about the weather, but if you farm along a river you have more to worry about. In 1945 17 young cows drowned in a flash flood on Green River. But Daniel V and young Daniel VI soldiered on. In 1946 they bought a Caterpillar bulldozer and used it to build farm roads and ponds, and to clear hedgerows so as to make larger fields. And they prospered. In 1949 Daniel VI, at age 28, married 21-year-old Mary Lou DeMayo, who had grown up on a farm on Henderson Road. Continuing to live at Fairfields Farm, Dan and Mary Lou soon had their first son, James E. (whom we all know as Jim Galusha), born in 1949. Two more boys were to follow, John (born 1952) and Bill (born 1958).

Daniel VI now took over primary management. Daniel V was still involved, but also found time to be a selectman in Williamstown from 1950 to 1957. Producing and delivering milk was still the main business of the farm. At the peak, customers included local schools, Williams College, college fraternities, the old Gym Lunch, and the pharmacies with soda counters on Spring St. In 1952 the Galushas decided to diversify, and established a 200-acre tree farm on their back acres, for timber, maple sugar, and Christmas trees. In 1953 they expanded operations by buying the milk business from Cricket Creek Farm: by the terms of the deal, they bought Cricket Creek's raw Guernsey milk, processed it, and delivered it to Cricket Creek's customers. This added to overhead: the Galushas now had to buy three trucks and hire three drivers for home delivery. Their Guernsey milk was high in fat: customers looked for the cream line at the top of each bottle.

Later that same year Kate Galusha died, and the widower Daniel V moved up to live at the house on the old Sweet farm off Blair Rd. After a couple of years, in November 1955, he married a local widow, Evelyn May Sanderson Hickox, who lived in town. According to Mary Lou, the new Mrs. Galusha did not get along with her husband's son and daughter-in-law. In the 1950s she rented the old Hickox family farm on Bee Hill Rd., the same one that Lyman Galusha had leased back about 1890, and that still belonged to Lyman's greatgranddaughter. Daniel V and his second wife moved into the farm on Bee Hill Rd. and left his son in charge at Fairfields Farm. Daniel V, who had worked on Bee Hill Farm as a young man, remembered it fondly, and it may have been he in who in 1957 persuaded his new wife to try to buy it – a deal was struck but in the end the seller backed out and farm was sold to the state. Daniel V and Evelyn remained as tenants in the old Hickox house on Bee Hill Rd.

Down at Fairfields Farm Daniel VI hired a man to run the dairy operation. He also had plans for improvement. In 1955, when he had 100 Guernsey cows on a total of 600 acres, he signed up with the Golden Guernsey company, which enabled him, once he met new standards, to sell "Golden Guernsey" branded homogenized milk at premium prices. (His cousin Arthur had started selling "Golden Guernsey" milk back in the 1930s). And in 1958 his father transferred to him the title to the original 90-acre Briggs Farm. Two years later, in 1960, Daniel V died of a heart attack on the Bee Hill Rd. farm, at the age of 80, while running after horses that had gotten loose.

At Fairfields Daniel VI now made more changes, both to expand and contract the business. He bought more of the land he had been leasing, but also made a decision to change his herd by cross-breeding from Guernseys to Holsteins, because customers were now increasingly demanding milk with a lower fat content. The economics of dairy farming had also changed with the introduction of bulk milk tanks, replacing the old 40-quart cans. These tanks were expensive, and many smaller farmers could not afford them. With 100 cows, Daniel VI decided that he couldn't justify making the investment. He would continue producing milk, but in 1961 signed up with Crescent Creamery in Pittsfield, which took over the processing and distribution of the milk. Freed from the burden of processing and delivering, Daniel VI now increased his dairy herd.

By 2003 there were 500 cows, and the farm was selling wholesale milk to Agri-Mark Family Dairy Farms in West Springfield. Since 2003 the dairy business has been increasingly difficult for small farmers, as milk prices have remained low and competition from huge industrial farms in the Midwest and California make it difficult for small dairy farms in New England to survive. In 2010, in order to raise cash and to protect the land for future farmers, the Galusha brothers sold development rights on most of their land to the state, under the Agricultural Preservation Restriction (APR) program. That means the land cannot be developed as housing sites. In 2013 Daniel VI, who had stepped back from active farm management, died at the age of 91. Ownership of the farm had already passed to his sons and grandson. In 1980 the oldest son, Jim, had set up an excavation business, and in time Fairfields Farm was being operated by Jim's son, Daniel Jay (b. 1972) – that makes him Daniel VII, but he's called Jay. He has help from his father, and his two uncles, John and Bill, as well as *his* son, James (b. 1995). There are still about 500 head of cattle on the farm, of which 230-240 are milked twice a day and 33,000 pounds of milk (about 4000 gallons) sent every other day to the AgriMark milk processing center, where it is turned into butter and dry milk powder. Most of the acreage is devoted to raising food for the cows, 300 acres in hay, 200 in corn for silage, and another 100 for sorghum. Jay has experimented with "no-till farming" for 90 acres of corn, designed to improve soil by increasing its ability to retain water and nutrients. With his huge equipment, Jim has been doing "custom farming" – spreading manure, planting, and harvesting – for the last five years or so on big dairy farms near Hoosick Falls and Cambridge, N.Y.

But the economics of small-scale dairy farming in Williamstown, and throughout New England, remain challenging. Costs for seed, pesticides, vet bills, insurance, and fuel are higher in New England than for larger farms elsewhere, and milk prices are set by the USDA. The number of dairy farms in Berkshire County continues to decline sharply. There are only two wholesale milk-shippers left in Williamstown – the Chenail Farm on Luce Rd. and the Galushas' Fairfields Farm. More changes are probably coming. January 2019 saw another big change at Fairfield Farm, when Mary Lou Galusha died at the age of 90. She had been deeply involved in the running of the farm for more than fifty years, and lived there for nearly 70.

***

Fairfield Farm is the only one of the thirteen Galusha farms that still has dairy cows on it. It's a local reflection of the familiar story of the decline of dairy farming in New England. But why do some farms survive as farms and others don't? Circumstances vary, and explanations no doubt vary, but there are at least two factors shared by the original Galusha Farm, which lasted 140 years, Arthur Galusha's several farms, which thrived under his direction for nearly 50 years, and Fairfield, which has now lasted nearly 100 years. One is their relatively large size, and the fact that the farmers were able over the years to add acreage and build their herds. Another is that there were sons in the family to help with the farming and eventually to take over the business. And in the case of Fairfields Farm, economic diversification – Jim Galusha's excavating and custom-farming businesses, for example – has been a key factor.

But maybe there's another story that the Galusha farms allow us to tell. As the poet William Wordsworth put it, "Though much is taken, much abides." The dairy cows are gone from twelve of the thirteen Galusha farms, but the farm fields largely survive. Bonnie Lea Farm continues to operate – as a horse farm, with goats and some thirty beef cattle. Hay is still being cut on the hill behind the old Green Meadow Farm. John Marsh Galusha's farm field hangs on intact, even though it is no longer a farm, and can be viewed by those who like to walk along Oblong Rd. John S. Galusha's field can still be seen and enjoyed by those who walk along Stone Hill Rd. and look to the west. The same walker can look to the east and see open fields that were once part of Coronation Farm, even though it is now a substantial private estate. Several old Galusha farms have been conserved, as you can see if you drive up Old Farm Way (part of the original Galusha farm) – or Bee Hill Rd. (part of Bee Hill Farm**)** – or drive down New Ashford Rd., where you can still see some of the fields of the old Springside Farm and Eldridge Farm. Some parts of two of the farms, the original Galusha Farm and Green Meadow Farm, have been divided up into residential lots, but other parts of both of those farms remain open fields. Of the thirteen Galusha farms only Mark and Cora's farm on Green River Rd. has fully disappeared – though the barn remains. So we can lament the decline of dairy farming in Williamstown but can find some consolation in the fact that Galusha cows are still producing milk and that many of the once-farmed Galusha acres still provide peaceful rural landscapes for the cyclist, the hiker, the walker, and to anybody driving along the country roads on the outskirts of town.

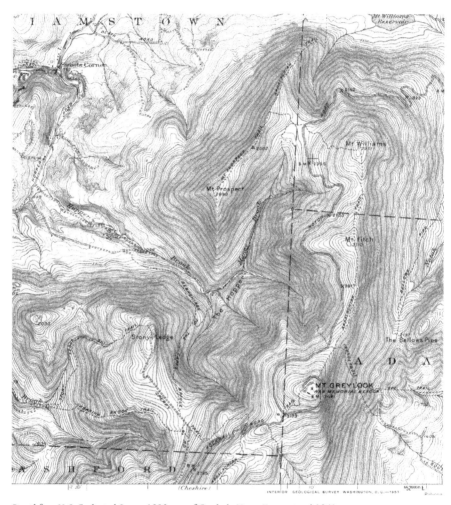

Detail from U. S. Geological Survey 1898 map of Greylock, Mass. -Vt., reprinted 1941.

Chapter 3

—␣—

THE HISTORY OF THE HOPPER

The Hopper is a distinctively rural part of Williamstown, only three miles from Spring St. Like another secluded valley, Treadwell Hollow, it was settled early, but unlike Treadwell Hollow it has been settled continuously. And much of it has remained cleared and contains some fine farmland. It also provides Williamstown's access to the Greylock Reservation and to some of the most rugged topography in town.

When we refer to "The Hopper" we mean one of two things: sometimes the west-facing narrow notch at the northwestern base of Mt. Greylock, hemmed in by Mt. Prospect on the north and Stony Ledge on the south, with steep walls rising more than 1000' on three sides, and a narrow opening on the west side. Its shape reminded some early visitors to the area of a four-sided grain hopper. The Hopper is sometimes called a cirque, a steep-sided geological formation shaped by a glacier, but geologists say it was actually formed by landslides. Its slopes are drained by Bacon Brook and Money Brook, which join to form Hopper Brook. It used to be called the "Inner Hopper" or the "Hopper proper." It's heavily wooded, much of it pretty inaccessible. Three prominent features are: Robinson's Point, with a vista overlooking the Hopper; the March Cataract, a steep 30' falls on Bacon Brook, 1900' above the valley floor; and a stand of old-growth red spruce even higher on the steep slopes.

But sometimes when we refer to "The Hopper" we mean the north-south valley, bounded by Deer Ridge and Mount Hope on the west and carved out by Hopper Brook as it receives water from Potter Brook and turns 90 degrees to the north, flowing more gently down to join the Green River at what we now call Mount Hope Park. There are a few houses along the upper reach of Hopper Rd., but most are built along the lower stretch of the road.

The Hopper might seem to be a throwback to an earlier time, a window on what Williamstown looked like in the distant past. But in fact the area has changed considerably since its first settlement. It was once a remote and lawless place, base for a ring of counterfeiters in the later decades of the 18th century. It was once a dangerous place, the scene of major landslides in the inner Hopper in 1784, 1823,1909, and 1938, significant flooding as recently as 1977, and many house and barn fires. (Rumors circulate that more than one of the fires in the Hopper were not accidental.) It was once felt to be remote enough from town that it was considered a separate hamlet, with its own post office and school. Although it is now the site of several high-end houses on very large lots, it was once a rather raggedy neighborhood, where the town set up "poor farms" in the 19th century. Now there are only three roads in the Hopper – Hopper Road, the private Bressett Rd., and Potter Rd. – but there used to be others: Burchard Rd. that led east from Hopper Rd. up the hillside to an 18th-century house (a road not discontinued until 1979), and a road leading west up to the Mt. Hope property. And there was a farm road leading from the inner Hopper up to what we now call Sperry Rd. in the Greylock Reservation – that road survives but only as the Hopper Trail. Bressett Rd. used to connect to the end of the Hopper Rd. Potter Rd. used to go through to meet the New Ashford Rd., but its southern half has been discontinued for maintenance.

The Hopper Road used to have other names. In the 19th century it was also known as East St. and familiarly known to some as "Shack Street." Hopper Brook used to be thought of as the East Branch of the Green River – probably the reason why Hopper Rd. (along with the whole neighborhood) was once called East St. What we now call Mount Hope Park, at the corner of Hopper Rd. and Green River Rd., was once called Sweet's Corners. More on that later. The Hopper has since the 18th century borne that name, but what we know as Stony Ledge was once called "Bald Mountain" – because of the bare rock outcropping, probably so named by Williams Prof. Albert Hopkins as a pointed contrast to "Greylock" (suggesting gray hair), whose wooded summit is often covered by gray clouds. The southern end of Mount Prospect used to be called Simonds Peak (after Benjamin Simonds).

The most thorough account of the early history of the Hopper is found in Arthur Latham Perry's 1894 *Origins in Williamstown*. A lot has happened in the Hopper in the last 125 years; Perry's account needs to be fleshed out and brought up to date. To do so, this short history tells the story of the people in The Hopper. Actually, five overlapping stories of five fairly distinct groups: 1) those who harnessed the water power of Hopper Brook and built mills, 2) the farmers attracted by the well-watered soil and level ground; 3) hikers and campers drawn to the woods and views surrounding Mt. Greylock, 5) the Prentices, who starting about 1910 bought up land and houses along Hopper Rd. for their employees and until about 1960 ran a major poultry operation, and 5) Williamstown residents and second-homers who for the last fifty years have been drawn to the quiet rural atmosphere along what is in effect a dead-end country road.

Mills and Water Power

The Hopper was being divided into lots as early as the 1750s, when Samuel Taylor bought a meadow lot along the Green River, where the river turns north and Hopper Brook flows into it. The site was soon called "Taylor's Crotch" – 'crotch' is an old word for fork in the river. The river also falls about 5' at that point, enough to power a waterwheel. And in the late 1760s John Krigger and two brothers built a grist mill and saw mill beside the river, designed to serve the new farms along the river and Hopper Brook. Some farmers began to call the site "Krigger's Corners." After two generations the Kriggers were gone, and during the War of 1812 the grist mill was reportedly rebuilt. By that time a few houses had also been built, and the population of the neighborhood began to grow. In 1810 a one-room schoolhouse was built just up the Hopper Brook – it's still there. And a wooden Baptist meeting house was erected just north of the mill. Twenty years later the meeting house was replaced by a stone church – it's still there too, though both it and the school have been converted to houses. Generations of Hopper families attended the Stone Church and sent their children to the school.

Before the middle of the 19th century there were two other mills further upstream on Hopper Brook. Stephen Pettit built a sawmill at the end of the road on the north side of the brook. In 1841 lumber to rebuild a tower on Mt. Greylock was being sawn at the mill. There is a still a cellar hole just upstream of the first bridge on the Money Brook Trail. This may be the site of that old sawmill. Stephen Bacon, whose property bordered Hopper Brook a little downstream, also ran a sawmill, at least briefly. Both mills seem to have disappeared by 1885. (By then waterwheels were being replaced by steam-driven mobile "donkey engines" and later by gas-powered engines.)

In 1879 the grist mills at Krigger's Corners were bought by Daniel J. Sweet. He renamed them Red Mills, ran a general store, and served as postmaster of what became known as Sweet's Corners. There were about fifty inhabitants in the neighborhood, including Sweet, his wife, and eight children. Sweet himself had a local reputation as a poet, publishing humorous and sentimental pieces in the *North Adams Transcript*, and was even listed in a directory of "local and national poets of America," and remembered locally as "the bucolic poet of Sweet's Corners."

He ran the mill until about 1892, when he moved to Pittsfield. Sweet's Corners went into decline. Sweet sold the property to the town for use as a charitable "poor farm." Five inmates who worked the farm were housed in the old Krigger house. (The building was not well maintained, and in 1901 was declared by state inspectors "unfit for occupancy" and was closed and sold. The buyer continued to run a seasonal sawmill.) In 1892 a local lawyer, not the first or the last of land speculators in the Hopper, thought there might be some economic potential in the brook, at a time when Williamstown was feeling the need for additional water supply. He bought 300 wooded acres in the Hopper, thinking that the brook and a millpond might create a reservoir. The post office closed in 1894, and in 1898 the Stone Church was demoted to a mission of the Baptist church in town. The Hopper School closed in 1913.

As he was putting together his estate at Mount Hope, Parmalee Prentice, who needed water for his livestock, bought a spring and spring house on the slopes of Mt. Prospect from Elmer Sweet (son of Daniel Sweet), who owned the surrounding property. Prentice put in a six-inch pipe to convey water downhill and across Hopper Brook and up to Mt. Hope. Mrs. Prentice used to visit the site of the spring annually in the late 1950s. The spring, enclosed by a wire fence, still belongs to the Mt. Hope Conservancy, but the pipe has been shut off, and the spring house apparently not been cleaned out in some time.

Farming in The Hopper

Most of the fifty people who lived around Sweet's Corners were from farm families. And most of the land had been cleared for farming a hundred years earlier. The first houses were built high in the Hopper, where the land is nearly level, well back from Hopper Brook, which was prone to flooding. In 1761 Elkanah Parris built a "regulation house" far up present-day Hopper Rd., beyond the site of the old Haley Farm. It survived until a fire in 1950. In the Fifth division of lots in 1765, the new town laid out thirteen 100-acre lots along Hopper Brook, and a town road to provide access. Along the east side of the north-south section of the road there was good farm land, though most of it was hilly.

In the 1770s Aaron Wright also built high in the Hopper, even further than Parris, on a five-acre lot at the confluence of Money Brook and Bacon Brook. It appears that the house was destroyed by high water in a violent cloudburst in October 1784. It may have been rebuilt. You can still see a cellar hole beside the brook – it may be the remains of Wright's house. About 1780 Samuel Burchard built a house set back from east side of Hopper Rd, on a 100-acre parcel, at the end of a farm road that came to be called Burchard Rd. Another early farmer was William Potter, who built a house at what it now the intersection of Hopper Rd. and Potter Rd., named after him. By 1843 there were eight farmhouses along Hopper Rd. One of them, settled in the 1760s, was by the late 19th century known as the "Lamb Farm," with land on both sides of Hopper Rd., a big two-story wooden house, close to Hopper Rd., built in 1840 – still there, it looks like a roadside inn. John Lamb had some large dairy barns, with solid chestnut beams and flooring; his family lived and farmed there at least until 1910. In the 1880s Lamb was "keeper of the town poor" – some were "kept" on his farm. His two daughters were schoolteachers.

Over time the 100-acre lots were subdivided. In 1885, for example, the Daniels Farm consisted of only 40 acres. George Washington Daniels arrived in Williamstown between 1842 and 1844, and probably built the house at 195 Hopper Rd. He owned his farm at least until 1876. (He was a part-time cobbler. It's unclear whether his cobbler's bench was in his home or in the store at Sweet's Corners.) His daughter married a Lamb. Another daughter, Jeanette (called Jennie), married Levi R. Green, a Civil War veteran. When her father died, Jennie inherited the house on Hopper Rd. She and her husband and then her descendants lived there until 1971.

The farming family who lasted longest in the Hopper are the Bacons. Stephen Bacon bought land in the upper Hopper in 1827, and his descendants still own land there today. Stephen, the first of three Bacons of that name, bought the old Parris house and farm at the end of Hopper Rd. He also bought 1300 upland acres on the level ground east of Stony Ledge from his brother-in-law, Almond Harrison, who had bought them from the original owner, a land speculator. Perhaps as early as 1800 Harrison had put in a farm road leading from the Hopper up to what is now the campground on Sperry Rd. Bacon improved it. It's today's Hopper Trail. The first Bacon, who died in 1849, was long remembered as a teller of tall tales about his prowess as a young farmer. He left land to his son, Stephen, Jr., and to his grandsons. He and his wife, along with more than twenty of their descendants, are buried in the family cemetery on Hopper Rd.

Why did the Bacons last longer than other farm families? Probably because they had more land than other farmers; because it was mostly on level rather than hilly ground; and because they kept producing sons who were ready, willing, and able to take over running the farm. In 1850 Stephen, Jr., age 45, was farming 300 acres, producing mostly oats and Indian corn. He kept 44 cows, 11 sheep, two pigs, two oxen, and four horses. He had a big household, including his wife and eight children, and two farm helpers. In his spare time he built and operated a merry-go-round and a ferris wheel at county fairs and at the Williams College commencement. By 1864 he had sold his upland acres, apparently to the town for a poor farm, which was later called "Bacon's Farm." In 1885 he was still breeding Jersey cattle and farming 700 acres, and leasing land to other farmers.

By 1876 Stephen Jr's son, Stephen Bacon III, then in his early 30s, had his own place on Hopper Rd. When Stephen III died in 1922, the Bacon property was divided. His son, Russell, whom many in town still remember, got an 800-acre parcel. He raised vegetables, apples, and potatoes, and during the season took sweet corn to market in Williamstown early every morning. In 1968 his house was hit by lightning and burned down to the foundation: he spent the rest of his life in a trailer on the property. He liked to tell people that he was "the last piece of Bacon." He was self-consciously a character, declaring that "I've done more damn farming . . . than I ever want to do again." But he was still tending his vegetable garden in his mid-90s. He attributed his longevity to chewing tobacco and enjoying his drink. At the time of his death at 99 he was the oldest inhabitant of Williamstown.

Stephen III's much younger son, Earl, called Carl (1897-1949), inherited the Bacon homestead. Fire was always a danger in the upper Hopper, where the houses were far removed from any reliable water source. In January 1938 fire destroyed a 15'x15' shack on Carl Bacon's farm, home to a 55-year-old Black man named Melvin Brown who made his living as a woodchopper. (His body was found in the ashes the next morning.) In 1940 Carl Bacon was unmarried and living with his mother and his brother Everett, and he was still working the farm in 1949 when he died of heart disease. In 1950, the old Bacon house, empty after Carl's death, caught fire and burned to the ground.

When Russell Bacon died his 800 acres passed to his daughter, Althea, who worked as private secretary to Col. Prentice at Mount Hope. She was married to a Ransford, and at her death in 1996 the land went to their son, Charles (Rusty) Ransford. In 2012 Rusty Ransford, who spent his career as an engineer and real estate developer, applied for permission to host a motorcycle rally on the land. Permission was denied. When he died in 2018 the land went to *his* son Randy Ransford, the 7th generation of Bacons to own it.

The Haley family took over the other Bacon farm in 1951. By then Haleys had already been living in the Hopper for almost ninety years. The first of them was George Washington Haley, a farmer when he enlisted in the Civil War. In 1864 he and his wife bought (or maybe built) a house at the corner of Hopper Rd. and Potter Rd. It's still there today. It was his daughter, Jennie Haley, who married a Bacon in 1895. Another daughter married a Bratcher, and this daughter got the little Haley house when her father remarried and moved away. (Bratcher worked at Mt. Hope for 28 years, taking care of Prentice's apple trees.) Their son, George R. Haley, established a home on Cold Spring Rd. And George R. Haley's son, George W. Haley, bought the Bacon Farm from his cousin Everett in 1951. He also bought a tractor – until the late 1940s plows in the Hopper were pulled by horses or oxen. Haley, with help from his sons, ran the farm for more than twenty years.

After George Haley died in 1974, the farm in the Hopper as well as the homestead on Cold Spring Rd. were inherited by his wife, Mary, and when *she* died in 1980 the land on the Hopper Rd. went to her son Robert and the family homestead to her son, Richard. The Hopper
farm was then run by the two Haley brothers. In 1982 Robert put 367 acres of the farm into a state run forest-management program – the so-called "Chapter 61" – to reduce property taxes.

The Haleys farmed the land in the Hopper until the late 1980s, when they found that the economics of farming were no longer sustainable. In 1988 Robert Haley sold his dairy cows, and in 1991, after receiving a few phone calls from real estate developers, he sold 465 acres to the Greylock Reservation, and thereby conserved them. Through a leaseback arrangement his brother Richard, along with Richard's son, Richie, and his nephew, Carl Sweet, continued to cut hay on 45 acres and to raise some heifers – they are still there over the winter, and in the summer down on Stone Hill behind the Clark. Richard Haley was still cutting hay in 2010 on his 1952 tractor. After he died, his son and nephew carried on with the calves and the hay. Robert Haley still owns 28 acres on the north side of Hopper Rd, and his niece owns a small house on an adjacent lot. Two cellar holes are all that remain of an old storage barn and corn silo.

A few other farms survived into the 20th century. The old farm at the end of Burchard Rd. passed through several hands until it was bought by young Dudley Ward (1882-1968) in 1908. Ward had spent three years at Williams, but did not graduate. He married a local girl, Betty Green, who had grown up on Hopper Rd. They lived full time at his farm until she died of cancer in 1925. He was still running the farm in 1942, along with a riding stable, the Jerdana School of Horsemanship. By then he had married a much younger and glamorous woman, Charlotte Dunham, a noted hunter and expert rider. In the spring of 1942 she was riding on Prentice's Mt. Hope estate and while cantering on the Cobble, behind Elm Tree House, was thrown from her horse and died from a fractured skull. She was buried in Southlawn, next to Ward's first wife. Ward was apparently so distraught that he sold the farm and left town the following year. A tenant was farming the property for a couple of years in the late 1940s, but the farm was then apparently abandoned. As late as the 1970s it was known locally as "Ward's Farm," and stories are still told today about the spectacular death of the local Lady Godiva, remembered as a long-haired blonde in a long white dress on a black stallion. Over time, memories of the second Mrs. Ward seem to have blended with memories of a beautiful teenager with long blonde hair who rode a black horse in the Hopper in the 1980s.

The 340-acre Lamb Farm was bought by a Harvard graduate who in 1912. He renamed it Deer Ridge Farm, and beginning about 1914 raised Guernsey cattle and Yorkshire hogs. But after a decade he gave up farming, moved to Boston, and sold the farm to Col. Prentice, who added it to his Mount Hope estate and hired a manager to run it for him. There were other smaller farms along Hopper Rd. Julius Exford raised poultry and a few dairy cows in the 1930s and '40s. Louis Rudnick, who had run a grist mill on Water St. in the 1930s and by the '50s was a major figure in Williamstown, owner of Rudnick's Cleaners on Spring St., co-founder of the summer theatre in 1955, and a selectman, owned 55 acres at the corner of Bressett Road and Hopper Road. In the 40s and 50s the "Rudnick Farm" was operated by Simon Bressett, who lived in a pre-1800 house near Hopper Rd., raising string beans, cucumbers, tomatoes, and squash, and selling them locally. But most farming on the Rudnick Farm was abandoned when Bressett retired in 1957, though it was still a hayfield into the 1980s. After a fire, all that remains of the old house is a cellar hole.

Life on the farms in the Hopper was never idyllic. Farming everywhere is long, hard, and often unrewarding labor. And working with power equipment can be dangerous. It's a short growing season in the northern Berkshires. It is unlikely that any of the farmers, even the Haleys, ever made much money. At best, they were land-rich and cash-poor. The houses were without insulation and for a long time without electricity. The brook often overflowed, especially at the end of winter, when ice broke up and jammed the culverts. The roads were often muddy. Only three miles from town, the Hopper probably felt isolated: until well into the 20th century not many farmers there, apart from those who farmed as a hobby, could afford to drive into town. In his 1953 history of the town, Brooks suggests that in 1790 life in the Hopper was difficult, the houses "drafty, cold, and often damp," mud in the kitchen and filth in the barnyard. But life was probably still about the same in 1890, and maybe even as late as 1940. Today the only farming on Hopper Rd., apart from the calf operation at the old Haley Farm, is done by the Galushas, who raise corn on a 30-acre parcel with some frontage on Hopper Rd., and grow corn and hay on the Ransford land.

Hikers, Campers, and Preservationists

The Inner Hopper was known for its dramatic rugged setting as early as 1819, when a Williams geologist noted that as you approach from the west a "romantic, wild, and sublime prospect opens before you." Throughout the 19th century the Hopper was described in rapturous language as a combination of beauty and grandeur, a "gulf," a "great ravine . . . , a beautiful and awesome picture of architectural work in nature hard to be comprehended by man." Albert Hopkins called it a natural "amphitheatre." In 1899 Professor John Bascom, after whom Bascom Lodge is named, called it "the distinguishing glory of the Greylock group." Hikers were attracted, walking up the farm road from the bottom of the Hopper to the Bacon farm on Sperry Rd., and enjoying the view from Stony Ledge. In 1830 a group of Williams students and faculty cut a three-mile bridle path from Bacon's upland farm to the Greylock summit. The bridle path was reportedly cut so that college president Edward Dorr Griffin, then sixty years old and still an avid horseman, though no longer a hiker, could reach the summit. Every June – in later years it was every October – for the next hundred years large groups of students celebrated "Mountain Day" by climbing this trail and spending the night on top of Greylock.

After Stephen Bacon sold his upland acres to the town for a poor farm, the cleared land was still called "Bacon Park," and after 1869 was the site of "Camp Fern," where the Alpine Club of Williamstown, founded by Professor Albert Hopkins, set up tents for summer camping. Hopkins led weeks-long excursions, conducting campers into the woods. He claims to have "discovered" the March Cataract. After the Alpine Club disbanded, the site of its summer camp was still known as "the Campground."

The history of the Greylock Reservation is well known. 400 acres at the top of Mt. Greylock were acquired in 1885 by the Greylock Park Association, and in 1898 the state Greylock Reservation was created. The destination for most visitors was probably the summit, which could be approached from the north via what is now Notch Road, the south via Rockwell Road, or the west through the Hopper and up the old Hopper wagon road.

In the mid-1930s the 107th Company of the Civilian Conservation Corps camped on the site of the old "Campground" and worked on hiking trails. They cut the Thunderbolt Ski Trail and the Stony Ledge Trail and improved the Roaring Brook and Hopper Trails. At the same time a riding group marked the "Berkshires to the Capes Bridle Trail," which went out the Hopper Rd., turned left on the private road (later called Bressett Rd.), following the brook, and then up the Hopper Trail to Sperry Rd, and from there east to Cape Cod. A 1944 topographical map shows the trail. For one steep 200' stretch riders were advised to dismount. The bridle trail's white-over-orange blazes could still be seen as late as 1959.

"Mountain Day" was discontinued in the 1930s but Williams students continued to climb Greylock, either via the Appalachian Trail (completed in 1937) or via the Hopper Trail. The event was reintroduced in the 1980s, and soon upwards of 600 Williams undergraduates would make their way up to Stony Ledge on a sunny Friday in October.

In 1997, after the Haley family sold most of their farmland in the Hopper to the Greylock Reservation, a new trail up to Stony Ledge, the "Haley Farm Trail," was cut on the old Haley property. The new trail and new publicity about hiking on Greylock led to a significant increase in the number of hikers. In later years the Williams Outing Club maintained a lean-to on the Money Brook Trail (since removed) and built and rebuilt bridges over Money Brook. Today the hiking trails that begin from the end of Hopper Rd. – the Hopper Brook Loop, the Hopper Trail, and the Money Brook Trail (which follow old farm roads) and the newer Haley Farm Trail and the Hopper Cutoff Trail – are among the most popular on the Greylock Reservation. In 1987 three stands of old-growth red spruce high in the Hopper were put on the National Register of Natural Landmarks. Land conservation in the Hopper continues: Berkshire Natural Resources Council recently acquired the old 55-acre "Rudnick Farm" at the corner of Hopper Rd. and Bressett Rd.

Prentice and the Mount Hope Era

Beginning in 1910 E. P. Prentice bought up property in the north end of the Hopper, including the lot where Sweet's mill (and the poor farm) had been, to assemble his Mount Hope estate. And he bought up houses along the road for his increasing number of employees: married employees could live in them rent-free. He installed lattice enclosures in the back yards, all painted "Mt. Hope Green," so Mrs. Prentice would not have to see clothes drying on clotheslines. When she was taken out for a weekend or summer drive, she required employees' children to dress up, sit on the front stoop, and wave as she slowly drove by. In 1913 Prentice had a new bridge built, leading directly from Green River Rd. (where his lion gates were later installed) into his estate – a bridge that survived, until it was replaced in 2017 by the present bridge. He also built a second smaller bridge over Hopper Brook so that his vehicles could easily travel into the Hopper from his cow barn on Green River Rd. A private road led down directly from Mount Hope to the Hopper Rd., through the old Deer Ridge Farm.

Prentice in 1917 began building a large poultry department on the high ground of an 80-acre parcel at the north end of Hopper Rd. It soon had a poultry house, an incubator, and a breeding house. As chief poultryman, he hired a local farmer, Norman Bottum, who was in charge until 1945. Hubert Goodale was the lead geneticist in the breeding work. Prentice called the place "Forest Hill," but locals called it "Chicken Hill." In time it had 15 or 16 separate buildings, including a very large barn. Over the years several Hopper Rd. residents worked there, including Simon Bressett.

Work continued even after Prentice's death in 1955. In 1957, the department was still being expanded, with three new buildings, under the management of Prentice's son, J. Rock Prentice. There was a staff of 32, with 25,000 hens who laid five million eggs a year. But in 1958 the Prentices sold the operation to Hawley Poultry Farms of Batavia, NY, who reorganized it as the Mt. Hope Poultry Farm, still based in Williamstown. When Mrs. Prentice died in 1962 the Mt. Hope estate was left to Lenox Hill Hospital, and in 1963 the hospital began selling off the property. Most of it went to Williams College. In 1964 the town bought 3.5 acres at the confluence of Green River and Hopper Brook – many years later it would become Mount Hope Park. Small parcels along Hopper Rd. were offered first, at a friendly price, to former Mt. Hope employees. Larger parcels were bought by newcomers.

The chicken farm, 80 acres with 16 buildings, along with 7000 laying hens, was sold to Arbor Acres Farm, a large poultry farming operation with headquarters in Glastonbury, CT. 35,000 chickens were brought to Williamstown. Although Arbor Acres primarily sold eggs for breeding stock, it occasionally sold eggs for eating – you had to pick them up at the farm. Some Mt. Hope poultry employees stayed on, including Allan Bradbury (1919-2007), who worked as a poultryman from 1945 to 1987, ending as manager of the poultry department. Some Haley family members worked there. Arbor Acres continued in business in Williamstown until 1992, when it appears that the parent company ran into financial trouble and decided to cut expenses. Poultry operations ceased, the manager closed up the farm, and a caretaker kept the grass cut. Finally, in 2000, the property was sold to a young Williams alumnus, Bo Peabody. Most of the buildings were demolished. The big Hopper Barn near the road survives.

Rural Retreat

For nearly two centuries those who lived in the Hopper worked there – mostly as farmers, and after 1910 as employees on Prentice's Mt. Hope Estate. Since Mt. Hope was broken up after Mrs. Prentice's death the Hopper has been home to many town residents– and second-homers – who are drawn by the quiet, the privacy, and the rural setting.

During the Prentice years there was little turnover. Many families lived on Hopper Rd. for decades, including Sweets, Bressetts, and Jimmos – Raymond Jimmo worked as a maple sugarman and took care of livestock at Mt. Hope. Hopper families continued to intermarry – Jolin and Haley, Ward and Green, Bacon and Sweet, Haley and Sweet – just as they had in the 19th century. (It was also common for Hopper neighbors to quarrel with each other, especially about land.) Some continued farming, but others did not. After Hiram Bacon and his wife Bessie gave up their farm on Hopper Rd. about 1930, he ran Bacon's Garage (later the Town Garage) on Water St. Years later she ran the Cold Spring Dairy Bar, known locally as "Ma Bacon's," on Cold Spring Rd. Virginia Nicklien has lived in the Hopper since 1943, at first on Hopper Road and since 1957 on Potter Rd. She is a Jimmo. She and her husband raised seven children — one still lives on Potter Rd. and another on Green River Rd. Carl Sweet has lived on Hopper Rd. all his life.

Land on Bressett Road, site of the two Pettit farms in the 19th century, was subdivided in the early 20th century into a number of small lots. Four or five summer houses, clustered at the east end of the road, were built between 1900 and 1930. During the 1930s Williams alumnus Sanford Robinson, a New York lawyer who lived in Greenwich, owned the largest house on the road. A smaller cottage was apparently used as a weekend party house by several Williams undergraduates, including Josiah Low, Class of 1935, father of the Joe Low who later built a house on Hopper Road.

After the Prentice property was sold, new families moved in, among them the Gelheisers and the Farleys, as well as several Sprague Electric Company scientists and engineers, including Kenneth Manchester and Otto Wied. (Otto and Donna Wied are still there.) In their big barn the Manchesters kept horses, including a pony named George, on whom neighborhood kids learned to ride. Bressett Rd. was by the 1960s the site of small summer rentals — Adolph Fischer's Hopper Lodge and Cottages. In 1957 one of them was sold to Simon Bressett. (Within a few years Bressett Road was named in his honor, perhaps because he was the first full-timer on the road. His greatgrandson still lives on Bressett Rd.) In 1960 one of the larger ones was sold to Professor Clay Hunt, who taught English at Williams: he lived in town during the school year and took up summer residence in the Hopper, where he delighted in swimming naked in the pond across the road, and in putting on convivial dinners for colleagues and students. The oldest house on the road was sold in 1961 to James Westall, father of well-known real estate agent Don Westall. Fischer later sold off his cottages to other second-homers: about half of the 13 houses on Bressett Rd. today belong to summer residents.

In the early 1970s the Janes and the Frosts bought houses on Hopper Rd., and the Jolins on Bressett Rd. (All but the Frosts still live in the Hopper today.) George ("Weasel") Gelheiser, who still owns a small piece of property on Hopper Brook, fondly remembers growing up on Hopper Rd. in the '60s and '70s, riding his bike all over the unpaved roads, hiking through the hills, playing softball on summer evenings at the field behind the Farley house (now Valerie Ross's), and cooling off afterwards in Hopper Brook. In the summer teenagers rode their horses up on Deer Ridge Road. In the winter kids sledded down the hillside or a driveway on the east side of Hopper Rd. In the mid-

70s Carl Sweet, age 11, built himself a little cabin in the woods. Across the road from the Gelheisers (who lived in what was originally the one-room Hopper School) was the formidable Gladys Green Salmon – "Gladdy," who served for years as the upstairs maid for the Prentices, and even into her 70's kept a big vegetable garden and a loaded .22 next to the door to shoot the woodchucks who dared to invade it. She reportedly wielded her .22 to deter the construction crew that in 1962 was widening the Hopper Road from cutting into her front yard.

Weasel Gelheiser remembers helping plow the snow off Burchard Rd. as a teenager, up to the old house at the end of the road. It had once been part of the "Ward Farm," was abandoned in the '50s and '60s, but was bought by a real estate developer in 1974. It was suspected that he wanted to subdivide the property, but because it had no frontage on Hopper Road he tried to get the town to maintain the old Burchard Rd. When that failed, he drew up an agreement in 1976 to sell the property to Ralph and Margie Hunter, with no down payment and no transfer of title until three years of monthly payments had been completed. The house had no electricity or furnace, and was heated with a woodburning stove. The Hunters were responsible for buying fire insurance. Hunter had such difficulty making the monthly payments that in mid-December 1977 the seller legally attached the property. On Christmas morning 1977 the house burned to the ground – not, so the paper said, because of any malfunction in the stove. Fortunately the Hunters and their whole family, including five children, escaped unhurt. Six months later the owner sold the property to an abutter.

In 1977 a Williams student, for an art project, put together a book of photos of life along Hopper Rd. It is full of portraits of the local residents, both the old timers like Russell Bacon and newcomers like Peter and Marnie Frost, as well as the old houses. Starting in the 1960s the Hopper began to attract more second-homers, the first of whom was probably Ives Gammell, a well-known Boston painter, who bought 50 acres on Hopper Rd. in 1963 and in 1966 built a summer house and studio at what is now 274 Hopper Rd. with a wing for himself and rooms and studios for his students. (New York lawyer Sandy Laitman bought it in 1987 and lived there full time from 1999 until his death in 2010.) In 1966 Sanford and Evelyn Jacobson, from Stamford, Connecticut – he had worked on the Manhattan Project at Los Alamos in the 1940s – bought the old house at 430 Hopper Rd. A few years later Samuel Hartwell, another New Yorker, built and gradually expanded a big house on a large piece of land on the east-west stretch of Hopper Rd. He was married to Anne Vanderbilt, daughter of the former governor of Rhode Island. While growing up in the 1940s, she had spent summers in Williamstown on Oblong Rd. She died a few years ago, and Sam Hartwell continued to come on weekends until he died in 2020.

The big white house close to the road at 541 Hopper Rd. was bought as a second home in 1975 by Henry Senger (1924-2005), Senior Vice-President at Smith Barney in New York. His six children spent summers in the Hopper. Senger was followed in 1991 by Joe Low from Greenwich, also in the investment business, who with his wife Penny bought land on the east side of Hopper Rd., including the old "Sky Meadow," and built a lodge-style house. Although Joe died in 2014, Penny still comes to Williamstown on weekends. In 2006 Bo Peabody, who now lives in New York City, having bought the old Arbor Acres property, took down an old house on "Chicken Hill," along with most of the farm buildings, and built himself a new one, along with a pool and tennis court.

The largest properties and houses in 2019 are second homes, except for a 5600-sq.-ft. house built in 1989 at 409 Potter Rd., which belongs to a full-timer. Other full-timers will live in the house under construction on the steep hillside to the west of Hopper Rd. About 1/3 of the residents have a connection to Williams College, either as faculty, coaches, and staff, or as alumni. Houses occasionally change hands, with a recent uptick: there were three real estate sales in the last six years.

Over the past fifty years some things have changed but much else has remained pretty much the same. The residents are getting older, and there are fewer young families with children. There's more traffic – partly hikers, partly construction, partly local business. The Hopper is still vulnerable to flooding on Hopper Brook, especially in 1977 and 2005 and again with Hurricane Irene in 2011, to landslides on the Hopper side of Mt. Greylock – the most recent were in 1998 and 2005, and to fire – a house fire in 1987, barn fires in 1996 and 2005. But many of the old buildings dating from the 19th century are still standing, along with a number from the middle of the 20th century, including three along Potter Rd. Nobody in the Hopper keeps horses now. But the Hopper continues to be a pretty quiet rural retreat, where you can still see the handsome white barns of the old Deer Ridge Farm along Hopper Rd., and it's not unusual to encounter one of the slow-moving Galusha farm vehicles.

E. P. Prentice at age 90, in 1953. Courtesy of Williamstown Historical Museum.

Chapter 4

—ɯ—

E. P. PRENTICE:

Mount Hope's Polymath

The main lines of the story of the man known locally as "Colonel Prentice" and his estate at Mount Hope Farm in Williamstown are well known. Most people with an interest in local history could tell you that he married a Rockefeller, bought 1400 acres in Williamstown early in the 20th century, set up an experimental farm to breed dairy cattle and poultry, built Elm Tree House in the 1920s, and continued to maintain the farm and the estate until the 1950s.

What most people don't know is that E. P. Prentice (1863-1955) had a lot of other interests besides cattle and poultry breeding. He collected rare books, including many Latin classics printed in the 16th and 17th centuries, as well as early books on agriculture and cooking, one of them a manuscript in French from about 1700 on "The art of making ice cream." He collected touring cars, including two custom-built 1932 Marmon 16-cylinder Waterhouse phaetons, one for him and one for his wife – only 400 were built before the company went out of business in the depth of the Depression. With a chassis of 154" – that's almost 13' – they each carried seven passengers, with room on the back for luggage. He also owned ten other so-called "classic" American cars from the 1930s and early 40s, including a 1931 Pierce Arrow, a 1940 Cadillac limousine, and a big 1941 Packard convertible, with a body built by the famous Rollston Company, that he bought for his wife. He also collected antique horse-drawn carriages and sleighs, including one enclosed carriage built at the time of the French Revolution. As a young man in Chicago he collected meteorological instruments. He was an accomplished birder, and led an ornithological walk at Mt. Hope in 1929, when the party spotted 46 different species. He closely followed domestic and international politics, attending sessions of Institute of Politics in Williamstown in the mid-1920s. In the 1930s his wife hosted a series of monthly Saturday afternoon "musicales" at Mount Hope, with a famous organist, Archer Gibson, brought up from New York to play the big organ in Elm Tree House. And Prentice sponsored a small local band called the Mount Hope

Orchestra, directed by Nelson Roberts, his farm manager. (Prentice himself had musical tastes too – Gibson set to music the words of a song Prentice later wrote and published.)

I've called Prentice a "polymath" – one whose "expertise spans a number of different subject areas." What is most remarkable is the range of Prentice's writing across a range of subjects. He was well educated and widely read, especially in agricultural and political history; he wrote in response to his reading, and he published widely for more than fifty years, both with trade publishers in New York and privately. Trained as a lawyer, he enthusiastically adopted a few key ideas, gathered evidence from his reading, and vigorously advocated for them.

Although he came from an old New England family, Ezra Parmalee Prentice was born in 1863 in Davenport, Iowa (while his father was serving in the U. S. Army during the Civil War). After the war it appears that the family returned to Albany where his father had been raised and his grandfather still lived. For high school he was sent to Albany Academy, where he spent at least two years. By 1879 his family had moved to Chicago, where Prentice's father went into commercial real estate with his brother-in-law. Parmalee Prentice perhaps finished high school in Chicago, before enrolling at Amherst, where he graduated Phi Beta Kappa with the class of 1885. Like his father before him, he went to Harvard Law School (1886-87) and into the practice of law in Chicago. Young Prentice rose quickly to be General Counsel of the Illinois Steel Co. in 1893, at the age of 30, where he reportedly stayed for four years.

The next part of Prentice's life is a little obscure. He lived with his parents. He moved in high social circles – one of his young friends, Harold McCormick, wealthy son of the founder of International Harvester, married the youngest daughter of John D. Rockefeller in 1895. But Prentice did not get along with Illinois Steel's new president, J. W. Gates, who arrived that year. According to one story, the brash Gates found Prentice's formal manners irritating, and Prentice left the firm, perhaps was even fired. For a time he served as general counsel of a small railway company, but then opened his own law office, and devoted at least part of his time to scholarly legal writing, publishing articles on legal topics defending corporate interests in leading literary magazines. In 1898 he co-wrote a scholarly book on *The Commerce Clause of the Federal Constitution* which became a standard reference work.

His life changed in January 1901, when he married Alta Rockefeller, John D. Rockefeller's second daughter. Soon the Prentices moved to New York City to be closer to his wife's dominant (and domineering) father and brother – apparently his wife's idea, not his. Prentice joined the law firm of Howland & Murray, which became Murray, Howland & Prentice when Prentice brought in the Rockefellers as clients. He specialized in law governing interstate commerce, a matter of great interest to the Rockefellers, who owned Standard Oil, which operated across state lines, and helped them secure railroad discounts on the interstate transportation of petroleum via railroad-owned pipelines. The Rockefellers quickly arranged for Prentice to be elected director of several companies in which they were major stockholders.

Prentice also continued his legal writing. Shortly after muckraker Ida Tarbell published her sharply critical history of the Standard Oil Company, Prentice published his second book, *The Federal Power over Carriers and Corporations*, in 1907. One reviewer regarded it as narrowly focused, "a brief for those interested in denying to the federal government the power to regulate and control large corporations engaged in interstate transportation or trading, . . .a readable partisan account of the development of a constitutional doctrine, and not a serious contribution to the legal literature of the subject." He also published polemical articles on the topic in top law journals.

But Prentice stopped publishing legal writing about 1909 – the reasons for this are mysterious. Was he disappointed by the mixed reviews his legal scholarship received? In any case, he remained at his New York firm, which in 1911 was renamed Murray, Prentice & Howland, apparently to recognize the declining importance of the elderly Henry Howland. What role Prentice played in the firm after that date is unclear. By all accounts his relations with his Rockefeller in laws were formal rather than cordial. For advice the Rockefellers may have looked more often to Winthrop Aldrich, brother-in-law of John Jr., when he joined the firm in 1919. But Prentice remained a partner until 1924, when at the age of 61 he resigned.

By then Prentice had developed other interests. In 1910, on the occasion of his 25th reunion at Amherst, and at a time when colleges like Amherst (and Williams, and Princeton) were modernizing their curriculum to incorporate the teaching of science, Prentice wrote an "Address to Trustees of Amherst," urging that the college return to "classical" education, the kind he had received in the 1880s. The address was printed as a pamphlet and widely reported in the national press. It generated a considerable amount of editorial commentary in newspapers and magazines, including a complimentary article by Theodore Roosevelt. To add weight to his argument, Prentice promptly reprinted the editorials. The Amherst trustees eventually replied, insisting on providing "a secure foundation in science" and rejecting Prentice's advice to require Greek for admission, to limit the "outside activities" of students; to reduce the size of the student body; to set competitive exams for admission; and to devote all college resources to increasing faculty salaries. Prentice was clearly disappointed with his alma mater.

Having failed in his attempt to get Amherst to give its students a traditional "classical" education, Prentice then turned his attention to the promotion of "living Latin." (He had long been interested in Latin, and claimed to speak it fluently – his brother was a classics professor at Princeton.) In the summer of 1910 he hired a tutor to teach his seen-year-old son to read and speak Latin. Prentice reportedly insisted that his children speak Latin with him at the dinner table. (He seems to have been a difficult and demanding father.)

The tutor, a Hungarian scholar who called himself Arcadius Arvellanus, had edited a Latin newspaper in Philadelphia in the 1890s and promoted Latin as a "universal language," a rival to the newly-created Esperanto. In order to make the learning of Latin more appealing to young children, Prentice then hired Arvellanus to produce some readings that might be more interesting than Caesar's *Gallic Wars*. So beginning in 1914 Arvellanus translated, and Prentice published, a series of books called the "Mount Hope Classics." The first two, published in 1914 and 1916, were once-popular boys' adventure books that have long since been forgotten: the *Adventures of Captain Mago*, a novel about Phoenician sea explorers from the Homeric era, originally published in French in 1875, and the *Mystery of the Boule Cabinet*, a best-selling detective story from 1911. (As in other matters, Prentice's literary tastes were eccentric and eclectic.) The series went on until 1928; later stories included some better-known modern English classics, Robert Louis Stevenson's *Treasure Island* (1922) and Daniel Defoe's *Robinson Crusoe* (1928). It's not clear how many copies of these books were sold. After Prentice's death, Mrs. Prentice donated copies of them to the Williams College library. (It does not appear that they have been taken out lately.) They're also available on Amazon.

Prentice also tried his own hand at adventure stories for boys. In "A Story of Mount Hope in the Revolutionary War," Prentice invented links between Mount Hope and the American Revolution. This story begins with a man called Gardiner Hardee – Prentice has made him up, but as he would have known both "Gardiner" and "Hardee" are old family names in New England. Hardee has been living in England, but in the spring of 1775 goes to a new settlement in Massachusetts, and sends letters back to his wife in England describing a place "a little South of Williamstown in Berkshire County, Massachusetts, where he had bought land near the foot of Mount Misery on the road leading toward Hancock, or Jericho as it was then called, from South Williamstown." (Mount Misery is what we now know as Misery Mountain, part of the Taconic Ridge; Jericho is indeed the old name for Hancock; it was renamed in 1776, so Prentice is pedantically accurate). Hardee reports to his wife that his beautiful surroundings include a "great hill" which blocks the sun: this is apparently the Taconic Ridge, which in fact blocks a view of the sunset from today's Elm Tree House at Mount Hope. Hardee also reports another "little hill" which "first catches the morning light": he calls this little hill "Hope." (This is the cobble at the north end of Deer Ridge, behind Elm Tree House, which indeed is the first spot to be lit by the sun as it rises over Greylock.) Hardee the narrator is thus able to write punningly that he "lives between Hope and Misery."

And Prentice the writer is thus able to provide an alternative and completely fictional history of the origin of the name "Mount Hope." The name was in fact assigned to the property by Prentice himself, and not because the cobble on Deer Hill was locally known as Mount Hope – it wasn't – but because his grandfather's farm in Albany was called Mount Hope, and *that* Mount Hope was in turn named not by his grandfather but by the previous owner, after the well-known Mount Hope in Rhode Island. (There was also a "Mount Hope Farm" there in the 17th century– and still there today as a national historic site and wedding venue in present-day Bristol, Rhode Island).

As Prentice's story of old Mount Hope continues, Hardee's son seeks to join him in South Williamstown in late 1776, has various adventures in which he tries to warn his neighbors that the British are advancing north from Lebanon in New York state, is captured, but escapes, and is able to deliver a warning to the patriots: "The Tories are coming!" He is present at the Battle of Bennington, in August 1777, where he is reunited with his father, a surgeon tending the wounded. (Prentice again invents an alternative history: British forces were in fact nowhere near Lebanon in 1776, although a number of Williamstown men did fight at the Battle of Bennington.) Prentice was apparently so pleased with this story of a boy's adventure that he had Arcadius Arvellanus translate it into Latin, and published it in 1917 as "Mons Spes" – Latin for "Mount Hope"

By this time Prentice, who owned a big town house on West 53rd St. in New York (on land where the Museum of Modern Art is now located), had also established a presence in Williamstown. In 1906 he had rented a summer house called Taconic Farm on Lake Onota in Pittsfield, and starting in 1910, when Williamstown was still at its height as a summer colony, rented for the season a house on Bulkley St. called "Keewaydin" (summer houses had names in those days). He also started buying up old exhausted farms on Green River Rd. and by 1914 had accumulated some 1400 acres. It was soon rumored that he intended to build his own house on the property, though this would not happen for another ten years. But in 1912 he did hire a Boston landscape architect, Wayne Stiles, best known for designing golf courses – in 1927 Stiles designed the course at the Taconic Golf Club – who drew up preliminary studies of the main driveways and buildings.

Why didn't Prentice spend his summers at his grandfather's big old house in Albany? Apparently because it was not available. His father's older brother inherited the property in 1905, and used the house as a summer residence in the early 20th century. But why rent in Williamstown instead of, say, the more fashionable Lenox? Perhaps because his uncle had graduated from Williams in 1855, and his father was a sometime member of the class of 1859. (So Prentice had probably visited Williamstown during his high school years at Albany Academy.)

In any case, soon after he arrived in Williamstown Prentice, even though still employed as a corporate lawyer in New York, took up a new cause: scientific agriculture – somewhat ironic, perhaps, given his dismissal of "technical" education in science at Amherst. (Many years later, in reporting the origins of his work at Mt. Hope, he said that he started buying land in Williamstown just one month after he presented his proposal to Amherst, and only days after hearing that individual trustees were opposed to it, apparently suggesting that having been blocked in one project he quickly determined to take up another.) Perhaps he was inspired by his grandfather, also called Ezra Parmalee Prentice, who was a well-known breeder of shorthorns and Ayrshire cattle in Albany in the mid-19th century, and president of the state Agricultural Society. He soon set about recreating his grandfather's farm by raising dairy cattle and planting apple orchards. At its peak the farm had 140 cattle, 100 sheep, 1000 hogs, and 12,000 chickens. There were 1200 trees in his apple orchards; he produced 1000 gallons of maple syrup every spring. And as noted he gave to his estate the name of his grandfather's place: Mount Hope Farm. In 1916 he crated up the grand gate at his grandfather's farm, consisting of a pair of stone lions. He had the lions driven to Williamstown and installed them as the formal entrance to his property at the confluence of Green River and Hopper Brook, at what we now call Mount Hope Park. (They remained there until the 1960s.) What we think of as the main gate, fronting Green River Rd., which Prentice called the Swan Lake Gate, was in fact a secondary gate to the estate. (And Prentice installed swans on a pond nearby.)

Prentice also took an interest in food production outside the bounds of his farm. In 1917, when the U. S. entered World War I, Prentice, already 54 years old, volunteered to serve in the army, apparently thinking he could help the army supply food for the troops. (He had vigorously urged the U.S. to declare war on Germany.) But he was instead assigned to the procurement division of the Ordnance Department at Fort Benning, in Georgia, where he quickly rose to the rank of major and then colonel, and Chief of Ordnance. The *North Adams Transcript* thereafter called him "Colonel Prentice," but he rarely used the title himself.

In 1917, when the U. S. Food Administration was urging people to produce and save food, so as to help the war effort in Europe, Prentice also founded the Williamstown Food Supply Commission, which organized a program helping 300 local families to raise vegetables in vacant lots and empty land: the college donated garden plots near the old "College Farm" north of Mission Park. In 1918 he addressed an audience of Berkshire County farmers about "Raising Seed Potatoes," and calling for "volunteers" to follow his lead. The farmers were probably puzzled to hear Prentice quote Latin verses from Book 1 of Ovid's *Metamorphoses* on conditions during the world's Golden Age, before agriculture was invented.

In the 1920s Prentice's major project was the building of a grand house for his family and guests on the Mount Hope property. In 1924, the year he retired from the practice of law, he began designing Elm Tree House. His architect was James Gamble Rogers, responsible for most of the "collegiate Gothic" buildings at Yale, but not known for designing country houses. The house was "Georgian" in style, in the same red brick and white marble trim of his grandfather's 1840 brick mansion in Albany. And as in his grandfather's house, the ground floor had a number of large reception rooms for entertaining.

On the second floor were bedrooms for the family and guests, and on the third floor servants' bedrooms. The house was named after the American elms that he had planted along the driveway leading to the house. A couple of them are still there today. The grounds were adorned, as were those at his grandfather's house, with formal gardens and classical statues. The mansion was completed in 1928. While it was being built, the Prentices needed a place to stay, so they bought a big house on Cole Avenue.

But Prentice never stopped writing. As is well known, in 1918 he began publishing a series of small booklets on cattle and poultry breeding, the "Mount Hope Pamphlets." Most are short essays reprinted from specialist dairyman's trade journals. Although you might imagine that the pamphlets were written by Prentice's in-house geneticist, Hubert Goodale, it seems clear that most were probably written by Prentice himself: they display his typical style. What is less known is that Prentice himself also wrote and published a number of books on breeding cattle, beginning with *Breeding Profitable Dairy Cattle* (1935), arguing, on the basis of his reading in the history of cattle breeding and of the experiments conducted at Mt. Hope, that farmers ought to breed for milk output rather than for pure blood lines. The book attracted considerable attention, including a positive review from Henry Wallace, FDR's Secretary of Agriculture.

Prentice wrote as a scholar. He did research in the British Museum and the New York Public Library. He quoted from academic journals. He included untranslated French and German quotations. He was as interested in history as he was in farming. As he noted, "it is impossible to reach sound conclusions upon the facts of history without a knowledge of historical sources." (One of his early articles, on a famous 1864 Civil War naval battle, published in *Harper's Magazine* in 1910, presented, in the words of its subtitle, a "new view of the fight of the Alabama and Kearsarge from contemporary French sources.") He carefully footnoted those sources, and he seems to have taken pleasure in displaying his learning. But also wrote as a polemicist. Reviewers noted that he was a well-informed livestock historian who "delights in sabotaging accepted fallacies." He pressed his thesis with great vigor. The material is technical, but not dull. One early reviewer says his first book was a "stimulating discourse for the practical breeder." But Prentice was for many years unable to persuade an important part of his audience, the teachers at "agricultural colleges," who continued to argue for the importance of pure blood lines in the breeding of cattle. Still, he was pleased and proud of his good reviews, his good results at Mount Hope, his international awards, and not shy about advertising his success.

Surprisingly, Prentice never publicly acknowledged his grandfather as a significant predecessor: there is no mention of him, for example, in the chapters on shorthorns and Ayrshire cows in Prentice's *American Dairy Cattle: Their Past and Future* (1942), even though his grandfather was a noted breeder. Was Prentice suppressing the origins of his ideas, and trying to emphasize his originality, or did he think his grandfather an old-fashioned dairyman who put too much emphasis on pure breeds?

Prentice's success at Mt. Hope in breeding good milkers led him to think more comprehensively about food production on a global scale. In a book called *Farming for Famine* (1936) he turned to the problem of feeding an expanding world population. Given his taste for the study of history, he soon followed this with a book, *Hunger and History: The Influence of Hunger on Human History* (1939), that looked at the problem from a historical point of view, tracing it all the way back to Greece and Rome. The latter was published locally by Prentice himself – a letter from Prentice to the printer, enclosing his check to pay the bill, survives in the collection of the Historical Museum. The latter book was then picked up and republished in 1939 as *Hunger and History* by a New York commercial publisher. This led to reviews in academic journals. One reviewer of *Hunger and History* praised its "erudition . . [and] vivid use of language," finding the book "full of information, valuable to the social historian as well as the historian of science."

Prentice pressed on, not hesitant to repeat his arguments, and to sound an alarm that, as Malthus had said back in 1798, food production increases arithmetically but population increases geometrically. He renewed his attack with *Food, War, and the Future* (1944). This time the reception was mixed. One reviewer found "an abundance of literary references in a style of considerable charm. [Prentice] attacks with vehemence and he defends with ability." Another reviewer was severe: the new book, he said, contained a "somewhat alarmist view . . . [an] unhappy mixture of population theory, cattle breeding, and political philosophy,. . . full of non-sequiturs and verbal smoke screens . . . [and] unsupported Malthusianism."

Prentice's "political philosophy" was very conservative. He was a lifelong Republican. Like many Republicans at the time, Prentice was sharply opposed to FDR's New Deal, and included a chapter on the importance of limiting the powers of government. He was also an isolationist. And once the

U. S. got into the war in 1941, and as Germany continued to advance, he took a geopolitical and pragmatic view of what the world would look like after the war. One reviewer of *Food, War, and the Future* observed that Prentice "speaks approvingly of German rule over central Europe as the best ultimate solution of the European problem." The U. S., so Prentice argued in 1944, cannot, and should not, destroy Germany or its industrial base. Regardless of the war's outcome, it is inevitable, he thought, that Germany, not Britain, would dominate postwar Europe. The U.S., he wrote, cannot afford to maintain postwar "European outposts" – that is, military bases. In order to solve the problem of feeding the world, Prentice was ready to accept "German rule" over "subject peoples." This idea is shocking to us now, but in 1944 many American observers were already predicting that the *next* war would be against the Soviet Union. (Germany of course became an American ally soon after the war's end.) Prentice's focus, however, was not on political alliances but on the food supply.

After the war Prentice continued to worry about hunger and rising population, especially in Asia. But he was now unable to find a commercial publisher. His *Progress: An Episode in the History of Hunger?*, which he described as a continuation of his *Hunger and History*, was privately published in 1947 (3rd ed., revised, 1950). Recycling many of his favorite topics and arguments, he wondered whether material progress, which the world enjoyed in the 19th and 20th centuries, would turn out not to be continuous, a mere "episode" – an interruption or digression – in the much bigger and long-term story of hunger. He was even worried that by 1980 there would not be enough food to feed the increasing population in the U. S.

Prentice was not a voice crying in the wilderness: after the war many political economists and political scientists continued to take very seriously the issue of rising population and the ability of the world to provide the food needed to support it. It was not until the "green revolution" of the late 1960s and '70s that economists' worries about food shortages eased.

The "history of hunger," and of various human efforts to relieve it, was perhaps Prentice's central concern as a writer from the 1930s to the early 50s. But it was not his only intellectual interest. This gloomy analyst, worried about how to feed the world, was also fascinated with what goes on in the kitchen: he devotes most of his book on *Progress* to recipes. One chapter concerns the history of New England cooking. Another chapter discusses *Mrs. Gardiner's Receipts from 1763*, based on old recipes from a colonial American kitchen, and a third prints Prentice's favorite 19th-century recipes from America, Britain, and France, including some from his mother, which he reports serving at Mount Hope. Prentice apparently loved to eat.

He had continuing literary interests as well. As reviewers noticed, his books were marked with "literary references," especially to the classics, not only Ovid's *Metamorphoses* and Virgil's *Aeneid* but other minor Latin writers who by 1900 were mostly known only by classicists. Prentice owned a copy of Virgil's complete works in Latin. Virgil's famous *Georgics*, a didactic poem about farming, once well-known by poets and by gentleman farmers, might even provide a literary model for Prentice's peculiar way of writing about agriculture. Like Prentice, Virgil had combined practical advice about plowing and harvesting with a wide, long view of the advance from savagery to civilization, and saw agriculture as the basis for a prosperous state.

Prentice's literary references extended much wider – to now-obscure writers such as Origen (a 3rd-century Christian theologian), Eusebius (a 4th-century bishop), and even the 11th-century Arabic writer, Avicenna; and in English not only Samuel Johnson, Sir Walter Scott, and Henry Fielding but also Robert Boyle (the 17th-century scientist), William Cobbett (the early-19th-century political writer), and George Meredith (the late Victorian novelist). He also had a taste for poetry, formed when he was a young man: he tended to favor poets who were popular in the late 19th century, Scott, Tennyson, and A. E. Housman (whose famous *Shropshire Lad* was published in 1896). At Mount Hope he formed a "Poetry Circle" and himself wrote light verses and songs. Although Prentice struck some observers as cold and formal, even "priggish and strait-laced," he clearly had a lighter side. One of his poems is called "Grandpa Casey," in the meter of "Casey at the Bat," about the imagined latter days of the famous baseball slugger Casey, now a forgotten man, "an old gray geezer" whose "base-ball days is done." The downbeat ending of the original poem – "the band is playing somewhere, and somewhere hearts are light,/ . . . But there is no joy in Mudville – mighty Casey has struck out" – is revised in Prentice's poem, as the retired and serene Casey waits for his grandchildren to arrive on the train to visit him: "So the band is playin' here, right now,/ And here's where hearts are light." Did Prentice, his fame fading by the mid-1940s, when he was in his 80s, perhaps identify with old Grandpa Casey?

Prentice also wrote a long narrative poem, in which he returned to the topic of the imaginary history of Mount Hope Farm, this time looking back not to 1776 but a century earlier, to 1676, the time of a series of battles in Rhode Island between English settlers and the Wampanoags, a local native tribe, battles which we call "King Philip's War," after the Wampanoag chief Metacomet, whom the English called "King Philip." Given the interest in history that Prentice showed in his books on cattle breeding, it is not surprising that he was interested in the history of the land that made up his country estate. What is surprising, however, is that this scholarly man, devoted to facts and to footnotes citing "historical sources," devoted himself to *inventing* another fake history of Mount Hope.

As Prentice well knew, the Mount Hope in Rhode Island, after which is grandfather's farm was named, was originally *Montaup*, an Indian word meaning 'whatever is great and dark,' in this case a hill overshadowed by trees, a hill that was the site of the Indian village of Massasoit and Metacomet on Narragansett Bay. Prentice had also figured out that he was descended from a cousin of Capt. Thomas Prentice (c.1620-1710), a Massachusetts Bay colonist who fought in the so-called "Mt. Hope Campaign" in King Philip's War (1675-76).

On the scaffolding of these few documented facts, Prentice imagined what might have happened at the end of the war, in a poem he called "Mount Hope." In Prentice's verse narrative Philip, when he takes arms against the English colonists at "the place of his last stand, Mount Hope," is killed by an Indian friend, so that he might avoid the shame of slavery. (In fact, as Prentice knew, Philip was killed by a bounty-hunter.) In the poem Philip's friend flees north and west to Mohawk Country, even though it's hostile territory, and plans to make the Mohawks pay for their refusal to help his friend. He finds himself in what would later be Williamstown:

> On this spot stood his cabin. Here he stayed,
> Over Mount Greylock saw the rising sun,
> Over Taconic mountains saw light fade
> And twilight gather, when the day was done.

Philip's friend decides to call a nearby hill "Mount Hope" (It's apparently the same cobble at the north end of Deer Ridge, behind Elm Tree House.) But hope also fades: the friend is pursed by Mohawk avengers who kill him. It's a fanciful sad tale, whose main purpose is to back-date the naming of Prentice's

Mount Hope, establishing a direct link between the original Mt. Hope in Rhode Island and the one in Williamstown, effacing the Albany Mount Hope. And coincidentally effacing his grandfather. (Prentice also falsely claimed that he gave the name of "Indian Springs" to a spring on his property, commemorating King Philip's Spring in Rhode Island.)

To illustrate the poem, Prentice commissioned two paintings, of the sun rising over Greylock and setting over the Taconics, by Leo B. Blake, a local artist who specialized in painting Berkshire landscapes. The poem and paintings were published (privately) in a collection that he put together and called simply *Worth Considering: Miscellaneous Articles on Various Subjects*. Whether Prentice meant by his title that his reader would find these nine articles "worth considering," or whether he simply meant that he had himself found writing them *worth his time* is not clear. He may have simply printed the volume for his own pleasure. The preface ends with a bit of untranslated Latin from St. Isidore of Seville (a 6th-century archbishop), a learned joke that perhaps only he would appreciate.

What the collection shows once again is that Prentice's curiosity was wide-ranging, and that his reading voracious. In the preface he notes that the essays are "fruits of reading on various subjects." Indeed, the volume reads as if it consists of Prentice's reading notes, the miscellaneous thoughts that occurred to him as he read one volume or other of forgotten lore. (It does not appear that the book ever passed through the hands of a professional editor.) The articles include a scholarly discussion of a problem in chronology based on his reading in Gibbon's *Decline and Fall of the Roman Empire*, Virgil's *Georgics*, and a 23-volume *Universal History* published in the 18th century. Several articles are equipped with lengthy footnotes, often containing untranslated passages from French or German, and long extracts from previous writers on a topic. By contrast, there is an essay with an appreciation of the late Latin writer Petronius, and another with a rambling discussion of heroines in 19th-century novels and narrative poems. Other essays are facetious. One is called "Sausages and Harmony," a whimsical essay pretending that the name 'sausage' drives from the late Latin *sus ignotus* ('unknown pig') – a made-up folk etymology, alluding to the belief that you never know what sausage is really made of – and praising sausage for promoting "family harmony," with a recipe. (Mount Hope Farm made and sold sausage from its herd of 1000 hogs.) Another, more serious, is called "Spuds and Progress," about the history of the potato.

Prentice's last two books were privately published, suggesting that he could not interest trade houses in publishing them. But that seemed not to bother him. He revised *Worth Considering* and privately published a second edition, and then a third enlarged edition in 1946. And he kept on writing and publishing academic articles in respectable scholarly journals such as *Agricultural History* and *Political Science Quarterly* in his 80s. In 1953, when he 90 years old, he assembled three volumes of *Memoirs*, reporting the history of his family from 1630 to 1880, and then sketching the basic outlines of his own life. There is a copy of them in the collection of the Williamstown Historical Museum, and a photocopy in the college archives.

Even into old age Prentice was lean and fit, and was said to look like a much younger man. But his health in fact had begun to fail in 1951. He died in 1955, at the age of 92. In an obituary in the *New York Times* he was remembered as a lawyer and as an "expert in breeding dairy herds," and for his many published books, including the "Mount Hope Classics." (The obit got his name wrong: he was not known as "Ezra.")

Given the various accomplishments of this Mount Hope polymath over the course of his long life, what remains of enduring influence? Prentice did not succeed, as he himself knew, in persuading the Amherst trustees to adopt his suggestions for a classical curriculum and for the administration of the college. But he was probably gratified to receive an honorary degree from his alma mater in 1940, and that he was asked to be the commencement speaker at Hiram College (a small liberal arts college in Ohio) in 1941. (He also received honorary degrees from Olivet College [in 1911], the University of Nebraska, and Williams.)

His translations into Latin remain a mere curio: the Mount Hope Classics series was listed as "worthy of mention but out of print" in a 1966 bibliography of intermediate reading texts in an academic classics journal. It would have to be conceded that he was not able to have much effect on the politics and political economy of the country. The federal government continued to grow in size under FDR and his successors. With the Marshall Plan in 1948 and NATO in 1949 the U. S. in effect established not just "outposts" but a massive presence in Europe. The graduated income tax, which Prentice opposed, was not repealed in his lifetime: the top rate remained above 90% from 1944 to 1963.

Prentice's warnings about the threats of overpopulation and global hunger proved to wrong. He did not foresee the "green revolution" of the

1970s. But he did have an influence on the breeding of dairy cattle. Although his so-called breeding "index" was modified several times by agricultural experts and although experimental work at Mount Hope ended in 1962, when his wife died and his geneticist Hubert Goodale retired, Prentice's ideas were taken up by his son, Rock Prentice, who founded the American Dairy Cattle Club in 1937 (in reaction to criticism of his father's work by breed organizations) and the American Breeder Service in Chicago in 1941, which grew into ABS Global, now the largest artificial-insemination company in the world.

Prentice's major influence and lasting impact is in Williamstown itself. Mount Hope Farm had a significant impact on the local economy in the 1920s and 30s – it was the town's major employer in the 1930s – and was the largest payer of property tax as late as 1962. Although Mount Hope is no longer an experimental farm, much of the estate that he assembled has largely survived pretty much intact, now divided into large residential lots, along with farm fields and woodlots. And of course Elm Tree House itself survives, with much of its original furniture, along with many farm outbuildings. On online hiking websites the ridge overlooking the Hopper Rd. is called "E. Parmalee Prentice Mountain." Several of the paintings Mrs. Prentice owned were donated to the Clark Art Institute. Copies of many of Prentice's books can still be found in the college library. His Novachord organ is still to be heard in the 1st Baptist Church, to which Prentice's children donated it. Many artifacts from the house and farm are found in the collections of the Williamstown Historical Museum. And in May 1964, at a big "plant sale" the shrubs and flowers in his formal gardens were dug up and carried off by the carful by Williamstown gardeners, invited in when the college bought the property and decided not to maintain the gardens. Many of the annuals are still growing in Williamstown back yards.

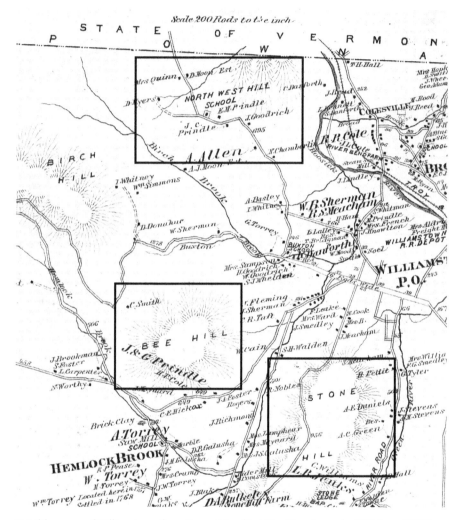

Detail from map of Williamstown, from *County-Atlas of Berkshire, Massachusetts*, by F. W. Beers (1876). Courtesy of Williams College Archives and Special Collections.

Chapter 5

—ᴍ—

THE HILLS OF WILLIAMSTOWN

Everybody knows the mountains that surround Williamstown: Greylock, Prospect, East Mtn., Berlin Mtn., South (or Brodie) Mountain. But less attention is paid to the hills closer to the town center. Many of them are shown on topographical maps: Stone Hill, Sheep Hill, Bee Hill, Buxton Hill, Birch Hill, Northwest Hill, Mason Hill, Pine Cobble. I will focus here on three of the hills, Northwest Hill and Bee Hill (both foothills in the Taconic Range) and Stone Hill (very near Bee Hill, but geologically distinct). Northwest Hill, separated from the Taconic crest by a shallow valley, is 1215' high, but because it is 600' above the nearby Hoosic River, it is the most dramatic. Bee Hill, the southeastern extension of Birch Hill, which in turn is a spur of the Taconic range, is higher (1424') but it rises only gradually. The high point on Stone Hill, really a three-mile-long ridge, is only 1145' above sea level.

Each of the three hills was settled early: a colonial road north to Pownal went over Northwest Hill; the old east-west Albany Turnpike over Bee Hill; and the old road to Pittsfield over Stone Hill. Parts of all three roads has been discontinued for maintenance or abandoned; all three are still unpaved; two have been formally designated state "Scenic Roads." Each hill was farmed and grazed for generations, but the cows and sheep are gone and the only agricultural product now is hay. Only a handful of historic houses remain: the two early-19th-century Hickox houses on Bee Hill Rd., the Mason house from c. 1880 on Northwest Hill Rd. and the former Goodrich house from c. 1850 on the north end of the road. The oldest house on Stone Hill Rd. is the 1900 Bentley Warren house, now Buxton School.

Why were these upland farms abandoned? The big answer is the decline of subsistence dairy farming in Williamstown and throughout New England, and the building of better roads that did not require climbing over a hill. But each hill has its own story of settlement and abandonment. And on all three hills much of the land has been preserved, though each in its own way.

Much of the history of these hills can be read in the landscape. If you look closely, you'll see not only old farm fields, but sunken roadbeds, crumbling stone walls, hedge rows, sheep fences, rusting farm equipment, or cellar holes, bits of metal and glass, or lilac trees, to indicate that people once spent their working lives here.

Detail from map of Williamstown, from *A Map of Williamstown from Original Surveys* by J. H. Coffin (1843). Courtesy of Williams College Archives and Special Collections.

i. Northwest Hill

Northwest Hill comprises the northwest corner of Williamstown, bounded on the east by the Hoosic River, on the west by the Taconic crest, on the south by Petersburg Rd, and on the north by the Vermont state line – although the north slopes of Northwest Hill lie in Pownal. The top of the hill is only about 3/4 of a mile from the state line. Nowadays Northwest Hill is one of the little-visited corners of Williamstown, accessible only by an unpaved road. What draws most people to the area are the trails in Hopkins Memorial Forest. But few people venture further north than the entrance to Hopkins Forest. It was not always so.

As an early town historian noted, Northwest Hill was once "very populous." In the "first division" of town land in 1754 what we think of as Northwest Hill abutted the north edge of the original house lots – which extended as far north as present-day Bulkley St. It was drained on the south side by what we now call Buxton Brook and Birch Brook, and by Ford Brook, along with smaller brooks and streams that flowed down the north and east side of the hill, into the Hoosic River. But if you didn't have access to a brook, you had to dig a shallow well, and they often ran dry in the summer. Although not as good for farming as the bottom land along the Hoosic, it was once regarded nonetheless as "pretty good upland." The south-facing lower slopes were better. Eight 100-acre lots were laid out, along with three 50-acre lots. Between the high ground and the Taconic crest was a shallow and somewhat wet valley, aligned north-south, and drained by Ford Brook: the best farm land bordered the road. (There was also good farmland on the north slopes of Northwest Hill, in Pownal, facing north.) The early farmers also owned nineteen 60-acre woodlots on the east-facing slope of the Taconics. Between the hilltop and the Hoosic River the land falls off steeply (up to a 33% grade) to the river, except for some 70 acres of flat field – the old Wire Bridge Farm.

As early as the 1765 a road was laid out to reach these lots, beginning at the west end of Main St. (where it crosses Buxton Brook), and going north up over the hill and down into Pownal. It was regarded as the "principal road" to Pownal and Bennington. (The road along the Hoosic River, today's Rt. 7, following the route of an ancient Indian trail, was narrow and hemmed in between the steep slope of Mason Hill and the Hoosic, and was regarded as dangerous.) The road was reportedly used during the Revolution by Patriots from Massachusetts going north to fight at the Battle of Bennington in 1777 and returning south with Hessian prisoners. Locals still refer to "Minuteman Rock," a large 15'-high glacial erratic by the side of the washed-out road, about 600' south of the state line. According to one old and oft-repeated story, a young woman who grew up on a farm on what is now the state line stood atop the rock in 1777 and looking north down to what is now Rt. 7 saw prisoners of war being marched back from the Battle of Bennington. According to a newer and undocumented version, a group of Minutemen spent a day atop the rock waiting to see if British redcoats were marching down from Bennington after the battle.

Other secondary roads provided access to the lots that lacked frontage on the main road. [Slide: 1843 map] One of them survives as the present route of Northwest Hill Road, which (heading north) doglegs left just past the crest of the hill. A second road, extending south from the east-west portion of Northwest Hill Road, probably followed the path of what is now the Hopkins Forest "Carriage Road." Another, continuing west where the present Northwest Hill Road turns back north, is now just a stream bed. At the end of this road, in the shallow valley between Northwest Hill and the Taconics, the road splits, one branch going south into present-day Hopkins Forest, the other going north. Here lived several families, notably the Fowlers. (Perry called it "Fowler Vale.") Several cellar holes are still to be seen in the area today. On the north branch, in a "hollow" in the Taconic slopes, lived Jacob Moon, patriarch of a poor but numerous family. All that remains of their house and barn are cellar holes. The road to "Fowler Vale" probably became a private way in 1902, when the farm was sold to a neighbor.

Further north on what is now the northern end of Northwest Hill Rd. were the Jonathan Bixby Farm, the Samuel Tyler Farm – there were several Tyler families who lived on what was called Tyler Hill – and the Pratt Farm. Silas Pratt had served as a soldier at Fort Massachusetts back in the 1740s. His house was occupied even before the Battle of Bennington. His son, William Pratt, was the "first white male child born in Williamstown."

The land was quickly cleared, right up to the top of Northwest Hill (except for the steep eastern side). Early farmers, several of whom came to Williamstown from Colchester, Connecticut in the late 18th century, included Zadock Ford, who built the house that Amos Lawrence Hopkins later bought and expanded into a mansion. Ford Brook and Ford's Glen are named after him. Joseph Tallmadge (1739-1818) bought a 50-acre lot in 1770, cleared the land and built a house at the west end of present-day Bulkley St. in what was then still thought of as "wilderness." His farm was later said to be "the best grain farm in town." He was also remembered for the potent apple brandy he used to distill, which fueled heavy drinking, gambling, and fighting that reportedly accompanied the annual "turkey shoots" conducted in nearby Ford's Glen in those days. Other early farmers were Amasa Bridges and Nathaniel Chamberlin (1759-1843), the latter settling in the neighborhood about 1790. Further up the hill were Jacob Brown and Thomas Carpenter. Carpenter's house is long gone but a photo survives in the Williamstown Historical Museum collection. Most of the original farming families remained on Northwest Hill at least until the 1820s. When the Erie Canal opened in 1825, providing good access to better farmland in western New York state, many Williamstown farmers, particularly those who tried to work rocky fields, gave up and went west. But several stayed for generations on Northwest Hill, including the Fords, the Chamberlins, the Browns, and the Pratts.

Further down the south side of Northwest Hill, on and near what is now Bulkley St., were several other early farms. The earliest was apparently the so-called "Red House Farm," lying to the west of Northwest Hill Road, originally settled by Joel Baldwin, but by 1782 owned by the Sherman family, who were still there more than a century later. On the east end of what is now Bulkley St., on Hemlock Brook, was Patrick Lally's sawmill. Further up the street was a house built as early as 1794 by Joshua Bulkeley – now the Dew House. Several other houses were built along Bulkley St. in the first half of the 19th century.

By the late 1820s the steep northern end of Northwest Hill Road had washed out so often that it was relocated less than ½ mile to the west, where the descent into Vermont was much more gradual. But the old road was apparently kept open – it appears on maps in 1843 and 1858. It was probably about this time that the schoolhouse was built, near the corner on the relocated road. A photo of it, taken about 1925, survives in the Williamstown Historical Museum. The neighborhood may have been "populous," but there were never enough people to support a church, so the farmers on Northwest Hill, who were reportedly a church-going lot, rode their wagons into town to the Congregational Church on Sunday mornings.

By about the middle of the 19th century changes were taking place on Northwest Hill. Several of the old farmers, apparently unable to make much of a living, sold their farms and moved into the village, Chamberlin to nearby Bulkley St., Bixby to adjacent "Charityville." Some remained, including the Moons and the Prindles. And some new farming families moved in, including the Goodriches, the Whitneys, and the Whitmans. In the 1870s and '80s James H. Goodrich (1834-93) was raising cattle and Merino sheep on 400 acres near the top of the hill, and also selling lumber and agricultural implements. By 1886 Edwin Goodrich (1856-1924) – from a different branch of the populous family – was farming further north on Northwest Hill Rd. He and later his sons would run that farm for nearly 80 years. Prindles, Chamberlins, and Goodriches intermarried.

The core of the house on what we still think of as the big "Mason Farm" was built about 1880, probably by Albert Allen (1832-1904), who raised Merino sheep and grew potatoes. But most of the farms on Northwest Hill remained small: only the Prindles and the Goodriches acquired more than 100 acres of land. The others were subsistence farms, and before long farmers stopped plowing and planting, finding that the silty soil was more suitable for pasture for their sheep and cattle, for hay, and for woodlots. Population declined, and the Northwest Hill schoolhouse closed in 1884: children were taken down Northwest Hill Road to the Buxton School by wagon and later by bus. By the middle of the 19th century Ford's Glen was a tamer place than in earlier decades. Children wandered down into "the Glen" on a hot summer day to drink from the "still spring" that once provided the water for Tallmadge's brandy.

Some of the farming families continued on Northwest Hill, especially on the northern slope of the hill, well into the 20th century, including the Goodriches, the Prindles, the Whitneys, and the Pratts. (The abandoned section of Northwest Hill Rd. is still regarded by neighbors as Pratt Rd.) In 1902 Edwin Goodrich expanded his acreage by buying the farm behind his. He paid $650 for a farm that had changed hands in 1867 for $2000, suggesting that the value of farmland had declined considerably over the previous 35 years. But by the 1880s, on Northwest Hill as elsewhere in Williamstown, most subsistence farms were being abandoned. Sanford Tenney began buying land in Treadwell Hollow, and Anthony Bullock was buying along Cold Spring Rd. Along came Amos Lawrence Hopkins, son of Williams College president Mark Hopkins, and an 1863 graduate of the college, who made big money in railroads and in 1887 began buying up the patchwork of old farms on Northwest Hill, and called his estate "Buxton Farms." He expanded the old Ford house into a 36-room mansion, and by 1910 had acquired more than 1600 acres of former farmland and woodlots, extending from the Hoosic River up to the crest of the Taconic Range.

But Hopkins was unable to persuade one farmer to sell: Alfred Moon (c. 1854-1924), who had bought a 100-acre farm just before Hopkins began buying, agreed to sell 40 acres of it to Hopkins in 1906, but hung on, cultivating his remaining 60 acres literally in the midst of Buxton Farms, until 1923. (And after Moon's death Lowell Primmer farmed the inholding until the mid-1950s.)

Hopkins himself was a "gentleman farmer," but Buxton Farms was also a working farm, worked by a large staff. (Unlike Mount Hope Farm, established by the Prentices just a little later, Buxton was not an experimental farm.) He had a herd of dairy cattle and over 300 sheep. There were twenty farm buildings. Along with other sheep farmers, he had to keep an eye on local dogs, who sometimes killed the sheep. In 1906 he built a carriage barn – he loved to take buggy rides along the carriage roads that he cut and maintained in his woods. He developed Ford's Glen into a sylvan retreat, damming the brook in order to form two ponds, the upper one (just upstream of Northwest Hill Rd.) for cutting ice in the winter – it long ago silted in. In 1910 he planted rows of sugar maples along Northwest Hill Road up what was called "Hopkins Hill" – they are still there today. In 1911 he relocated the road near his house a bit to the east, and rebuilt the bridge over Ford Brook as a handsome stone arch. There is a photo of the bridge in the collection of the Williamstown Historical Museum.

Meantime there were big changes on the lower slopes of Northwest Hill. The old Torrey farm on Northwest Hill Rd. immediately south of Hopkins was sold in the 1890s and converted into a summer house for a New Yorker, who renamed it "Hill Brook Farm." Along Bulkley St. a huge summer house, "Keewaydin," was built in 1890 on one old farm and a full-time residence, "Llewellyn Fields," for a wealthy young Williams alumnus in 1893 on another. In 1900 the old Joshua Bulkeley house, on the Meacham farm, was being run as an inn called Harvest Home. The owners of these mansions built coach houses for their carriages and horses, and one of the favorite "drives" of the day was to take Northwest Hill Road north up to Pownal, and to return via what we know as North St. Twelve acres of the old Meacham Farm were sold in 1911 to two men from Brooklyn, who established the Twin Oak Poultry Farm. By 1912 they had 100 hens, and were selling eggs, planning to make Twin Oak the largest chicken farm in Massachusetts. The poultry business failed, and by 1929 the property, with a large house, was bought as a summer residence.

By then Hopkins's Buxton Farms had closed too. Hopkins died in 1912, and his widow continued to run the farm until 1924, when she auctioned off the livestock and equipment, and leased some of the fields to neighboring farmers. She closed the house, and sought (without success) to sell the property, at first to a group of Williams alumni who proposed building a golf course, and in 1930 to Hopkins's young nephew, who agreed to the deal but then decided to buy a house in town. Finally, in 1933, she offered to give Buxton Farms to Williams College. The college accepted the gift without any clear idea of how it might use the land. Suggestions were offered – to develop a "Williams colony" of bungalows and summer houses for faculty and alumni, to build a ski jump for the Outing Club, to create a water supply for the college, and to develop a course of instruction in forestry for Williams students. In the end, none of these plans proved feasible, and in order to reduce its carrying costs the college deeded the entire property to the U. S. Department of Agriculture to establish an experimental forest, with the proviso that, should the government close its experimental program, the property would revert to the college.

The history of the experimental forest, fully charted in an unpublished paper by Professor Hank Art, needs only to be summarized here. The U. S. Forest Service not only sent in scientists but also a crew of CCC men, who lived on site, demolished several of the Hopkins buildings, including the big house, built a gravel road, cleared brush, and in 1940 rebuilt a bridge over Ford Brook. Scientists surveyed and mapped all 1600+ acres, set up a weather station, and divided the land into experimental plots to keep track of the annual growth of all trees within their bounds. During World War II operations at the experimental station were reduced. In 1943 four conscientious objectors worked there for $2.50 per month. After the war, experiments resumed: large-scale tree plantations were undertaken to determine which species grew the fastest. 500 Norway Spruce trees, each two years old, were planted by members of the Boys' Club near their camp. By 1967 the U. S Forest Service, consolidating its operations, concluded its research, and in 1968 the property reverted to Williams College.

Meanwhile, although a few farmers continued to work the privately held land on Northwest Hill, the focus of land use shifted toward outdoor recreation. Soon after receiving the Buxton Farms land in 1934, Williams College arranged with the local Williamstown Boys' Club to make available a tract near Ford's Glen Brook. One of Hopkins' ponds was refitted for use as a swimming pool, shelters were built, and the Boys' Club ran a summer camp on the site until 1974. Generations of young boys spent a week or more at the camp in the woods. In 1939 a summer day camp for Girl Scouts – Camp Mountain View – was set up on the old Chamberlin farm further up Northwest Hill, and in 1944 the Girl Scouts began overnight camping there, eventually running a five-week season, until the camp moved up to White Oaks Rd. in 1960. Horseback riders and skiers took advantage of the scenic unpaved road and the hilly terrain. In 1933 the Williamstown Riding Club organized a picnic ride up Northwest Hill Rd. to Pownal. In 1939 the Stony Ledge Ski Club set up an illuminated ski slope on Northwest Hill for night-time skiing. Local hunters shot partridge and deer in the fall. The Williamstown Fish & Game Protective Association met in 1950 at the Northwest Hill home of one of its members. What we know as the Mason Farm was owned for a time in the 1940s by a Williams professor, Maurice Avery. He and his wife did some small-scale farming, raising vegetables and a few cows. In 1948 Avery sold the 100-acre farm to the famous American historian Henry Steele Commager, then teaching at Columbia – he and his wife used it as a summer residence until 1951.

Over time some of the old abandoned farm fields on Northwest Hill began reverting to forest. (Many of those fields were in Hopkins Forest, and the trees were quite deliberately allowed to come back, and carefully measured as they did so.) But a few farm fields remained open. In 1950 a young Williams College graduate, Ralph C. Mason, bought the Commager farm and named it Purple Kings Farm. Mason's family ran Mason Oil Co. in town, but he and his new wife wanted to live in the country, where they dug a couple of ponds and ran a small beef cattle and sheep farm. Over time they got rid of the livestock and limited their farming to hay in the summer and maple sugaring in the winter. They also put in a grass tennis court and a one-hole golf "course." Mason ran the farm until he died in 2017. Another farmer was Harry Beals, who raised dairy cows on his fields near the Vermont line, and cut hay on the Wire Bridge Farm. Arthur and Fred Goodrich, both bachelors, operated the old family dairy farm on the northern segment of Northwest Hill Rd. into the 1960s. They were notable producers of butter and honey.

But the few farms on Northwest Hill were continuing to decline. By now the soil had been exhausted or had washed downhill. It was wet in the winter and dried up in the summer. In 1947 the old Prindle place was sold to an out-of-towner, Henry Halsted, a GM executive and a Williams College alumnus, with a son who was then in his senior year at Williams. At age 50 the elder Halsted was apparently looking ahead to building a retirement house in Williamstown. The Halsted family owned the land – on top of Northwest Hill – for almost forty years but never built on it. In the 1970s they had the woods on the land logged. Old County Road, the discontinued part of Northwest Hill Rd., was reopened in 1949, providing access from the Williamstown side to a few small cabins. One of them was owned by the young James MacGregor Burns. It burned down in 1967; a few artifacts remain.

Town dwellers also began looking for housing lots on Northwest Hill. A few new houses were built, including one in 1954 at the corner of Northwest Hill Road and what was then called "the mountain road" – i.e., evidently a narrow farm road leading to the summit of Northwest Hill. (All that remains of that house today is a cellar hole.) Before Arthur Goodrich died, he sold off some of his acreage to James Schoen, who in 1965 built a house at the point where Northwest Hill, diverted to the west, turns back north. In 1967 Alfred Whitman, a Sprague engineer, and his wife, Pansy, bought 176 acres of the old Goodrich Farm, which by then had been pretty much let go, as had the 1850 farmhouse. In 1969 they built a new house up the hill, and raised a family there.

With the advantage of 20-20 hindsight, you would think that, having established a new Center for Environmental Studies in 1967, Williams College would know exactly what to do with the re-acquired Hopkins Forest acres: an environmental research center! But in fact, as Hank Art explains, the college at first had no idea what to do with the land and buildings it now owned. The Center for Environmental Studies was still new, and the college was thinking that the recently-acquired Mount Hope property would serve very well as a kind of field station for CES. But the college did want to add to its stock of faculty housing. It made plans to subdivide 25 acres at the corner of Northwest Hill Road and Bulkley St. into twelve residential lots. The "Forest Road" development began in 1970, and the college made provisional plans for subdividing another 25 acres across Northwest Hill Road. In 1969 it sold the big house at the west end of Bulkley St. – formerly the house of the Hopkins farm manager, and too expensive for faculty housing – to Walter Beinecke, a Williams alumnus and CEO of the Sperry and Hutchinson Company. It also subdivided the old Chamberlin farm into five lots, selling one of them to Julius Hegyi, a professor in the Music Dept., in 1971. It had an opportunity to give the undevelopable land at the top of the Taconic slopes to New York State, and thought it would probably sell off the rest.

But in late 1970 Hank Art, then a newly-hired assistant professor of biology, helped persuade the college president that Hopkins Forest would be a much better field research site for the new CES than the old farm fields at Mount Hope. And the college moved quickly to make use of HMF for an interdisciplinary environmental studies course in the spring of 1971. It's now almost 50 years since that first course, and in the intervening decades the college acquired an additional 871 acres of land, including both old farm fields and woodlots between the Hoosic and the Taconic crest. Over the first fifteen years an old barn was transformed into a farm museum, the old Hopkins carriage house was converted into the Rosenburg Center, with classroom, lab, and a caretaker's apartment, a cabin was constructed for overnight camping, and a sugar house was built. Hopkins Forest is primarily a research center, but its trails are open to the public for passive recreation.

As it happens, although Hopkins Forest was "saved" in 1971, the 1970 Forest Road development was the beginning of a modest building boom on Northwest Hill Road. In 1971 Julius Hegyi built a house further up Northwest Hill Rd. In 1972 Walter Beinecke built a big house on the 96 acres he bought from the college, but in 1974 gave 68.5 of his back acres to the college, to add to Hopkins Forest. They included the irreplaceable 12-acre "Beinecke Stand" of old-growth trees, containing some of the oldest trees on the old Buxton Farms, and in Williamstown. (Beinecke's house was sold to another Williams alum, John Walsh, in 1984, who in turn sold it to Jim and Joan Hunter in1994.) Some big houses in the neighborhood changed hands in the late 1970s, bought by Williams faculty or alumni. In 1979 Charles Dew of the History Dept. bought the old Joshua Bulkeley house at 218 Bulkley St., and Bill Alden, a Williams alum, bought the old Torrey house at 91 Northwest Hill Rd.

In the last forty years several attempts have been made by real estate developers to subdivide old farms into residential lots. For one reason or another, most of the projects failed. In 1976 a young Williams graduate proposed building 38 lots on 200 acres on Pratt Rd. (the discontinued part of Northwest Hill Rd.), reached by a single access road, but the Planning Board declined to approve it. In 1979 Philip Grande, a Williamstown developer, bought 60 acres from the Goodrich brothers on the northernmost end of Northwest Hill Road, on the state line, subdivided, and sold off building lots. In the '80's and '90's several houses were built on them. In 1985 Beinecke's widow wanted to sell part of her property for three building lots near the entrance to Hopkins Forest, but the plans fell through. In the same year a landowner on Pratt Rd. sought permission to subdivide his 50-acre lot into two parcels, but the Planning Board decided not to approve, since Pratt Rd. was no longer a maintained town road. In the late 1980s Chester Soling, who in 1985 had bought the land on the top of Northwest Hill from the Halsted family, proposed subdividing the property into 40 residential lots, but when real estate prices declined he did not proceed with the plan.

But in the late '90s there was a flurry of building, this time on a larger scale. In 1993 Jim Hunter had bought nearly 200 acres on top of Northwest Hill in a foreclosure sale. He considered building a house for himself, but in 2000 he subdivided the property into seven lots, and sold six of them for $1million to Rob Miller, a Williams alum from the Class of 1987. In a land swap, Miller transferred one of the lots to Williams College for addition to Hopkins Forest in exchange for land with frontage on Northwest Hill Road — the deal stirred up some controversy. He then put in Purple Mountain Pass, an unpaved road, and quickly sold off four of the other lots, recouping almost all the purchase price, and on the one he kept for himself built a 9000 sq. ft. house. The road also leads to a second house built in 2001 by another Williams alum — it's a mere 4800 sq ft. But the two houses are set far back — the nearer one is barely visible from Northwest Hill Road in the winter months. Several of the other lots have changed hands but no other houses have been built — yet.

Ralph Mason hoped that Williams College might buy his property for a college farm, or for an addition to Hopkins Forest, but no deal went through. In 2007 the Mason farm was offered for sale for $20 million. The Masons reportedly had a lower offer, but declined to accept it. In 2016 they succeeded in selling 24 acres on the east side of Northwest Hill Road to another Williams alum, who has built a 6-bedroom (5250 sq. ft.) house, and another 60 acres on the west side of the road to yet another Williams alum who had previously bought the old Shadowbrook Farm just over the line in Pownal, where he built a big house.

Today nobody on Northwest Hill Rd. is engaged in farming. In the last seventy years the forest has taken over many of the fields, especially on the north slope of the hill. (Some of the remaining fields are still hayed.) Nobody even keeps horses. It's now a quiet residential area. A few of the residents have been in place since the 1980s, Pansy Whitman since 1967 on the old Goodrich Farm. Her son, Nick, who lives next door, cleared away the rotting farm sheds and keeps the old farm fields open, cutting them regularly: the land looks more park-like than it ever did when it was farmed. The road is still unpaved but is better maintained than it was forty years ago, and probably gets a little through traffic from Pownal. Most of the land is owned by Williams College, and makes up Hopkins Forest, the most recently acquired piece of which is 73 acres of the old Wire Bridge Farm between the hill and the river. Recently a proposal has been made to have the college put its land under permanent conservation restriction.

A small number of faculty and students conduct research in Hopkins Forest, and a pretty steady stream of town residents walk the trails. The Boys Club and Girl Scouts are gone, but the old pavilion from the boys' camp remains, and can be seen from the Hoosic River Trail. The members of the college's cross-country team and cross-country ski team can be seen running up Northwest Hill Road into Pownal, returning via the rougher ground of Pratt Rd. Mostly hidden from casual sight, cellar holes still provide traces of more "populous" settlement.

Detail from map of Williamstown, from *County-Atlas of Berkshire, Massachusetts*, by F. W. Beers (1876). Courtesy of Williams College Archives and Special Collections.

ii. Bee Hill

Arthur Latham Perry, the late 19th-century local historian, provides most of the early history of Bee Hill. He describes it as an "old-fashioned sugar loaf of gigantic size, lying on its side, base toward the southeast." Nobody these days knows what an old-fashioned sugar loaf looks like, but viewed from the southeast the hill slopes east down past what we call "Sheep Hill" to Cold Spring Rd. and Hemlock Brook, but falls steeply to the southeast from Bullock's Ledge (the base of the sugar loaf). It also falls off steeply to the southwest, as you can see if you drive or walk along Torrey Woods Rd. or the north end of Oblong Rd. Today we tend to think that, heading south, Bee Hill stops at the Taconic Trail, but in fact it slopes south down past the Taconic Trail to Hemlock Brook, Torrey Woods, and Berlin Rd. It slopes north down into Flora's Glen, which separates Bee Hill from Birch Hill, its neighbor hill to the north. To the east it slopes down to the saddle we now know as Thornliebank, before the land rises again to Buxton Hill.

The name "Bee Hill" is an old one: Perry assumes "undoubtedly" that it was given by "early settlers" who found an "abundance of wild honey" in the sugar maples that are still to be found in the woods near the top of the hill. The history of Bee Hill and its families is a combination of ordinary farming, land passed down from one generation to another, small successes and sad failures, with dramatic interruptions of desperation and a surprising number of sudden deaths and suicides.

Bee Hill Road

Bee Hill Road was laid out over the hill very early – at first running south from West Main St., to the point where Flora's Glen Brook now crosses the road, then a 90 degree turn to the west, up over the shoulder of the hill and down to the entrance of Treadwell Hollow, at first in a generally southwesterly direction and then, when it nears the top of the hill, westerly. When it reached the bottom of Bee Hill the road jogged north for a few hundred yards and turned west again, following a tributary of Hemlock Brook up to Berlin Pass. (On today's maps that last section is known as Berlin Road, but on old maps it is still called Bee Hill Road.) In 1799 Bee Hill Road was made part of the "Albany Turnpike," a through route extending from Greenfield to Troy and Albany. Why put a road, never mind a through road, over a hill? Because in the 18th century any road through a valley has to run alongside a brook, which is likely to overflow in the spring floods and wash out the road.

Other roads skirt the base of Bee Hill: on the east Cold Spring Rd. (until 1941 called Hemlock Road), laid out about 1826. On the south Torrey Woods Rd., laid out in 1830 to connect Oblong Rd. with Hemlock Rd. In Flora's Glen, on the north side of Bee Hill, farmers very early cut roads on both sides of the brook, so you could get from the farm at the bottom of the glen to the farm at the top, but those roads are now only hiking trails.

There was another important change about 1830, when it was concluded that the road from Williamstown to Albany – the old Albany Turnpike – ought to go over Petersburg Pass rather than the higher and steeper Berlin Pass. Two proposals were made – one to maintain the existing road over Bee Hill and then run a new public road up Treadwell Hollow (at the bottom of Bee Hill) to Petersburg Pass. The other proposal called for circumventing Bee Hill by extending West Main St. and Petersburg Rd. further west, over the low north shoulder of Birch Hill, and then climbing to Petersburg Pass. When a landowner in Treadwell Hollow declined to permit the road to pass through his property, the Petersburg Rd. proponents won. The result was that through traffic no longer climbed Bee Hill, and after 1830 the neighborhood became something of a backwater. But Bee Hill Rd. remained open, and continued to be the route from the village to the less-used Berlin Pass. Much travel on the road would have been by foot. As late as the 1940s it was not uncommon for residents to walk to town from the top of the road. Bee Hill itself was a local landmark and a destination for walking excursions: there was an unimpeded view of town from top of the cleared hill.

A hundred years after the Albany Turnpike was discontinued, another big through road was built: the Taconic Trail, opened in 1928, wrapping around the southern shoulder of Bee Hill and intersecting Bee Hill Rd. at that road's highest point, made Bee Hill more accessible. The part of Bee Hill Road from the new Taconic Trail down to Berlin Rd. (what came, curiously, to be called locally Bee Hill *Extension*), fell into disuse, especially since by then there were no longer any farmhouses along it. In 1962 the county ruled Bee Hill Extension a "private way," and in August 1966 maintenance of Bee Hill Extension by the town was officially discontinued. The effect has been that only a few hikers, cyclists, and hunters ever see the west side of Bee Hill.

As late as 1950 the main part of Bee Hill Road from the Taconic Trail down to Cold Spring Rd. was not plowed and was often impassable in the winter. And it was deep mud in the spring. Local papers referred to the "annual spring wash." The road washed out very badly in late March 1963. But neighbors liked it the way it was, and wanted it kept unpaved. The designation of Bee Hill Road in 1984 as a state "scenic road" was supposed to mean that the big maple trees along the road would not be removed without a public hearing . Over the years the road has been somewhat widened. Digging out the drainage ditches on either side has required cutting tree roots. In 1986 the bridge over Flora's Glen Brook washed out, not for the first time. The lower part of the road was washed out in the heavy rains and flash flood of May 2013. Now every spring the road, often badly rutted, is occasionally closed to all but local traffic.

In the late 1960s there was a proposal to put in a new road over Bee Hill, so that through traffic on Rt. 7 and Rt. 2 could bypass central Williamstown. One proposal would have carried the road north from Five Corners, just east of Rt. 7, then via a high viaduct over Cold Spring Rd., over the Rosenburg farm, and through a deep cut in Sheep Hill to reduce the grade. Another proposal would have had an interchange at the present A-Frame Bakery, a gradual ascent across the hill below Bee Hill Rd., and a bridge over Flora's Glen. In the end, after considerable discussion and protest from many residents who would have been affected, the proposals were shelved.

The Hickox Farm

The top of Bee Hill was settled soon after the village was founded. As Perry noted in 1895, it was good farm land, "very early [that is, the soil warmed enough for planting early in the spring] and very fertile." A topographical map shows that much of the land is flat, especially near the top of the hill and along Bee Hill Extension. The first owner of land on the crest of Bee Hill Rd. was Jonathan Meacham (1754-1833), one of the original settlers of Williamstown, who lived in the village, then built a log house on his Bee Hill property, but soon moved back into town. It is not certain whether or not he did much clearing of land. The next owner was Capt. Stephen Hickox (1749-1836), from Granville, MA, who served in the Revolution (including some time at the Battle of Saratoga) and arrived in Williamstown in 1781, when he bought the land from Meacham. Over the years he acquired more land. Printed sources say he had about 600 acres, but early deeds show that it was closer to 650. East-west, the farm extended about 3/4 of a mile down Bee Hill Rd. in each direction, north-south from beyond the summit of Bee Hill to more than ½ mile south of Bee Hill Rd. Over time the farm was divided among family members, and pieces sold off. Perry noted in 1895 that "four generations of the Hickox family" have lived on Bee Hill "without a break," implying that their tenure was calm and uninterrupted. A fifth generation was to succeed, but closer inspection reveals that things didn't always go well.

Clearing the land, then covered with woods, for fields and pastures, would have been a slow multi-year process, typically conducted in the winter. It has been estimated that one person could clear about one acre of land per year. In order to clear more than 100 of his acres in thirty years, he would have had to hire help. In his early years Hickox's teams of oxen reportedly dragged loads of timber, probably cut from his own land, into the village for use in building West College in 1790 and the second Meeting House in 1798. He also arranged to have 1000 apple trees planted, and built a cider mill.

In 1813, to accommodate his growing family – Hickox had three sons and five daughters, born between 1778 and 1808 – he replaced Meacham's log house with a handsome 2-story house, still standing. In about 1820 his younger son John Hickox (1781-1843) built a house on the other side of Bee Hill Rd. for *his* large family (11 children by 1820)– that house too is still standing. In 1823 Capt. Stephen Hickox, at age 74, transferred title to the farm to John and his older brother, Stephen, Jr. The two of them ran the farm together for five years, but then, apparently because John wanted to move into town, decided to divide it into two parcels.

Stephen Jr. apparently did well. Over time he bought 400 additional acres of land, realizing, perhaps, that he would eventually need to provide for his four sons. But even successful farmers have to spend money in the spring before they can sell their crops in the fall, and on several occasions he had to mortgage the farm to a neighboring landowner in order to borrow money for seed and equipment.

When Stephen Jr's sons came of age, the home farm was divided again. His first son bought his own place in 1832. One piece – west of the homestead and north of Bee Hill Rd. – was cut off for his second son, Samuel, who built a house there, perhaps shortly after he was married in 1828. The third son apparently decided to make his way elsewhere, and left home. The much younger fourth son, Chauncey, stayed on his father's farm, helping his father run it, and, when his father died in 1867, inherited it. In 1870 Chauncey was farming on 225 acres, and doing modestly well. He had 20 cows (including four milkers that yielded 300 lbs. of butter), 44 sheep (who produced 250 lbs. of wool), and 3 pigs. To feed his animals, he grew Indian corn, oats, buckwheat, and hay. He also grew potatoes. He sold a little beef and mutton, butter, wool, and timber he cut from his wood lots. He reckoned that his land was worth $11,000.

But in 1873 the country was hit with an economic "Panic" – caused by bankruptcies of overbuilt railroads, bank failures, and falling demand for farm products. A depression lasted until about 1877, and farmers in Williamstown suffered. Chauncey managed to hold on to his land, but in 1880 he estimated its value as only $6500. He still had his cows, sheep, and apple orchards, and added chickens. He now was producing 1000 lbs. of cheese. But prices for farm products had fallen. And in 1880 he decided that there might be more money in putting up summer boarders. Over the decades, his house, now nearly 70 years old, had become dilapidated. So he tore down an ell at the back of the house and built a new two-story addition, and during the 1880s was putting up city folks who wanted to spend a month in the country. He continued farming, with both cows and sheep on his back acres, which became known as "Sheep Hill." By 1890 Chauncey was 70 years old, and had only one surviving child, a daughter, Jennie (1844-1915), married to Lyman Galusha, son of the farmer next door. Lyman lived with his in-laws and took over the running of the farm – he was apparently not interested in running a boarding house – and built up a herd of Jersey cows.

Chauncey Hickox died in 1891. In 1899, his widow, "laboring under a temporary aberration of mind," either fell or jumped from a second-story window and soon died from her injuries. The farm was left to her daughter Jennie. Jennie's husband Lyman, with the help of their son George, operated the farm until he died in 1919, when it was left to their grandson Bierce Bayley. That same year George Galusha auctioned off the farm equipment and bought his own place in Granby, MA. And in 1920 the Hickox-Galusha farm on Bee Hill was offered for sale or rent.

Bayley apparently rented the farm to several different tenant farmers for a year or two at a time. In 1935 the house was divided and rooms were rented. In 1937 Bayley sold the land to his sister Beulah Bayley Thull, who lived in Albany. In 1941 she spent the summer there, renting it out during the year. The farm buildings had again fallen into disrepair – the addition to the house was by now 65 years old – and she restored them. She planned to retire to her Williamstown farm in 1951, but by 1957 her plans changed: she sold about 100 acres, on both sides of the Taconic Trail, to the state, to be added to the new Taconic Trail State Park, and the house was again for rent.

In 1960 the house was rented by Evelyn Hickox Galusha and her new husband, Dan Galusha: both had previous attachments to the house. Evelyn's first husband was a relative of Chauncey Hickox, and Dan Galusha had worked on the farm as a young man, when it belonged to his uncle, Lyman Galusha. Now, at the age of 80, Dan Galusha was doing a little farming on Bee Hill. He died there of a heart attack in 1960, while trying to control horses that had broken loose.

That proved to be the end of real farming on the old Hickox Farm. It now shrank to a 3.5 acre residential lot. In 1961 the house was sold, and sold again in 1965 to Daniel and Marcella Rauscher. She was instrumental in getting Bee Hill Rd. named a state "scenic road." The house was sold again in 2002 to future-selectman Ron Turbin, and resold in 2019. (The state-owned land behind the house is hayed every summer, but not otherwise farmed).

The Prindle Farm

Shortly after 1828, when Stephen Hickox, Jr. and his brother, John, divided up the Hickox farm, John traded his land to Col. William Waterman (1784-1858), in exchange for his tavern on the corner of Main St. and North St. in the village. (According to Danforth, his daughters were said to be "too proud to live on Bee Hill farm, and persuaded their parents to move to the village.")

Why Waterman wanted to buy a farm is not clear. Called "Colonel Waterman" because he had served in the state militia, he had long been an innkeeper, first in Adams and later in Williamstown, and was interested in politics. He served as a town selectman, county commissioners, and three terms in the state legislature. In 1850 he bought the Sand Springs (before there was a hotel on the site), and moved there with his wife. It was apparently at this time that the farm was sold to his nephew, Nathaniel Greene Waterman (1798-1876). Nathaniel Waterman was also an innkeeper and shared his uncle's interest in electoral politics. He served as a Justice of the Peace and as town selectman. He may not have had much time for farming, for he sold the farm in 1855 to Parley Prindle (1817-71). The Prindle family had been farming on nearby Birch Hill since about 1790. For several generations they also served in elective office in Williamstown and Berkshire County. Prindles would now run the Bee Hill farm for the next fifty years.

Like the Watermans, Prindle was active in politics. In 1854 he served in the state legislature and in1863 he served as a selectman. When Prindle died in

1871 his farm passed to his two sons, John F. (1851-1914) and George H. Prindle (1854-1946). The two Prindle brothers ran the farm together until 1876, when George sold his share to his brother, John, and bought River Bend Farm on North St. John Prindle came through the depression of the 1870s in pretty good shape. Perhaps he was a better farmer than Chauncey Hickox, or else he saw where money was to be made. Like Hickox, he had both sheep and cows, but his was primarily a dairy farm, producing both butter and milk – the latter could now be sold and transported in refrigerated railroad cars, patented in 1867. He reckoned that the value of his land only dropped 20% during the depression years between 1870 and 1880. By 1890 he had a milk route. In 1896 he and Dan Galusha (just downhill from him) were the two largest maple-sugar producers in town. In 1902 his farm was advertising milk, cream, and strawberries. In 1905 he harvested more than 200 barrels of apples.

John Prindle was also interested in politics. In 1898, running as a Democrat in a generally Republican district, he won election as state representative. (For that year he hired somebody to manage his farm.) But in the election the following year he lost to a Republican from Dalton. In 1902 he served as a selectman. In the same year he ran again for the state legislature and narrowly lost. He ran again in 1906 and won. Expecting to spend the winter in Boston that year, he advertised "Hillcrest Farm" and the milk route for sale, closed the farm for the winter, and rented a house in the village. He remained active in town affairs, serving as selectman in 1913. He sent a son to Williams College.

John F. Prindle died in 1914, and the farm of about 250 acres on both sides of Bee Hill Rd., next door to the Hickox-Galusha farm, with orchard, sugar bush, 30 cows, and the milk route, was sold to William F. Walsh, a New Jersey lawyer, and later a judge. He renamed it "Bee Hill Farm." Walsh, who used it as a summer residence – he lived in New Jersey in the winter – hired a local farmer to operate what he called "Bee Hill Farm." (The farmer, John Bridgeman, lived in the old house.) Walsh's farm grew apples and potatoes, and his Holsteins produced milk, which he delivered to local homes. The farm had both the old 10-room farmhouse built originally by the Hickoxes, and a more modern 9-room "bungalow" across the road, built about 1900. In 1918 Walsh decided to change his dairy herd to purebred Holsteins, and advertised to sell 10-12 Holsteins. By 1919 he was offering purebred yearlings for sale.

At first Walsh spent the summer at his farm. Beginning in 1916 his sister, Mary, and brother, John, lived there full time. Mary was apparently mentally unstable, and in 1921 at age 40 she set her bed on fire and jumped into it, and as the newspaper reported, was "almost burned to a crisp." Walsh was so distressed that he tried to sell the farm, and when he could not find a buyer he offered to rent it for the season, even offering to install electric light fixtures. In 1923 he sold his horses and farm equipment. In 1924 he again offered the land for sale – noting in his advertisement as an added inducement that the property bordered the proposed Taconic Trail. Again there was no buyer. In the fall of 1929 he tried selling just the 170 acres on the north side of the road, but his timing – just before the stock market crash – was not good. He rented out the older of the houses. His brother, John Walsh, lived in the modern house and operated the farm for him.

In 1940 Walsh finally succeeded in selling some of the farm: the old house and 18 acres on the north side of Bee Hill Rd. were bought by Anita Chace, whose sister lived in Williamstown and was about to buy an adjacent farm. Walsh retained some of the farmland, and John Walsh was still operating the milk route. But Chace, at age 47, committed suicide at her sister's house on Main St. in Williamstown in 1941 by turning on a gas range, and left the property to her mother, who lived there at least until 1946.

The farm on the north side of the road was then bought by Kenneth S. Ware, who ran it as a dairy farm for a couple of years, and lived there with his wife and two sons. But he seems not to have prospered, for in 1948 he sold 10 acres of woods to Williams College, to extend the college ski run at the Rosenburg farm, and sold the rest of the farm and equipment (but no livestock) to Daniel Primmer. Primmer restocked the farm, and milked about 20 cows. He raised feed corn for his cows on a field to the south of Bee Hill Extension. But a regional surplus of milk and a steep decline in milk prices made the venture uneconomical.

Primmer sold to Edward Wylde in 1950. Wylde raised as many as 160 Angus beef cattle until the 1970s. His daughter-in-law, Marge Wylde, fondly remembers seeing them graze on the field uphill from her house. He also raised goats. In 1973 Wylde sold off several pieces of land, and in 1986 sold a large parcel to a land trust (which held it until the state could buy it and add it to the Taconic Trail State Park), and gave the remainder (about 20 acres) to his son and daughter-in-law. They in turn sold 16 acres to George and Marabel Baker in 1991, Californians who built a large summer house. In the summer of 2019 Marge Wylde sold her house and four acres to two women from Nantucket.

Carmichael-Burns Lot

After selling the land on the north side of the road, Walsh continued to try to sell the land on the south side. It was finally sold in 1942 to the Rev. Robert Carmichael, soon to be named rector of St. John's Episcopal Church. (His wife had grown up on Bulkley St.) The Carmichaels lived there for nearly 18 years. Over the years the house was much expanded. After Carmichael moved to a church in Springfield in 1955, he kept the farm, and John Walsh acted as caretaker of his property. In 1959 Carmichael sold to the widowed mother of James MacGregor Burns. When she died in 1965 Burns inherited the property from her: Jim's former wife, Joan Burns, now lives there.

Samuel Hickox Farm

That's the story of the two big farms at the top of Bee Hill, both originally parts of the old Hickox farm. But there was also a third Hickox farm further west, on what we now call Bee Hill Extension, created back about 1830, when Stephen Hickox, Jr. gave land to his second son, Samuel. Samuel Hickox must have worked his farm on his own in the 1830s and '40s and by the late 1850s with the help of his son. In 1870 he was farming on about 140 acres, growing pretty much what his brother, Chauncey, was growing, though he seems to have specialized in producing cheese for sale. With fewer acres, his annual farm produce was worth more than Chauncey's and more than Prindle's. But the Panic of 1873 must have hit him hard, because he lost the farm: in 1876 it was owned by Harvey T. Cole, a merchant in town who was probably able to buy country acres at a fire-sale price. (Samuel Hickox and his wife then moved to Iowa to live with a daughter. It's likely that the younger Hickoxes stayed on to run the farm for him.) Cole might have been inclined to buy the farm because his wife was a daughter of Col. Waterman, and, a teenager when he bought *his* farm on Bee Hill, probably had spent time there.

In the early 1890s the Samuel Hickox farm was bought back by his young grandson, Edgar Hickox, who lived there with his wife and children, and his parents. Things didn't go well. In 1897, despondent and "temporarily insane," Edgar slit his throat, another Bee Hill suicide. His father and brothers carried on the farm for twenty more years. By then its major crop may have been apples. When Edgar's father died in 1918 the farm was sold to Sanborn Tenney, a Williamstown lawyer and real estate dealer who had already bought up much of the land in and near Treadwell Hollow. Edgar's brother, Henry

Hickox, seems to have stayed on, at least until 1920, to run the farm for him. In 1923, when Tenney died, title passed to his wife, and then, in 1941, to his son John W. G. Sanborn, a New York lawyer.

The farmhouse, on the north side of Bee Hill Extension, was vacant by 1928 and had disappeared by 1944. But the fields remained open, especially on the north side of the road, as late as 1975. The only surviving signs of the farm today are a hayfield on the south side of Bee Hill Extension, and (across the old dirt road) a big cellar hole for what was probably the farmhouse, and remains of stone walls.

There were other smaller farms on Bee Hill in the 19th century. At the east end of the road in the 1840s and '50s the Hosford family had a farm, farmhouse, and starch mill on Flora's Glen Brook. In the 1860s and '70s the farm was owned by Calvin R. Taft, the village postmaster. In 1875 Taft sold it to Alexander Shand, who was farming 40 acres in 1885. At the west end of the road, on the north side, near where it met Berlin Rd., lived Joshua Maynard (1822-95), on a small wooded lot that he must have cleared himself. On the 1850 census he is reported to be a "farmer," but it was no more than a subsistence farm. He had three children but he seems not to have prospered. By 1867 he was only a "laborer" and his wife a "servant." He held on to his land, and died twice a widower in 1895.

His son Stephen, unkindly nicknamed "Dummy," was deaf, his hearing lost in a "boyhood accident" (though it was said that "his father hit him over the head with a pitchfork"). He was not in fact dumb – he had a few words – but he never learned to read or write. He was a notable character along Bee Hill Rd., working by the day on local farms. As a young man, he was frequently in trouble with the police, accused in June 1880 of setting fire to Chauncey Hickox's 4-acre "chestnut lot," and three months later sentenced to six months in the county jail for disturbing the peace. While helping Samuel and Edgar Hickox cut ice on Flora's Glen Pond in 1897 he nearly drowned, and was restored with timely administration of whiskey. In 1898 the house he occupied, originally his father's, was destroyed by fire. (Two cellar holes remain today, one of them deep and well-preserved, but small, perhaps 13' x13'.) Thereafter he seemed to have no fixed abode, sleeping where he could, showing what the local paper called a "gypsy defiance of wind, weather, and bathing processes generally." He did odd jobs, sold berries, apples, and chestnuts door to door, and was ready to trade anything he had for something of equal value. He enjoyed his drink and "a social pipe with such as are willing to furnish the tobacco." He died at age 85 in 1937. He was still remembered by old-timers in Williamstown forty years later.

Bullock-Rosenburg Farm

Halfway down Bee Hill Rd. (as you head north toward town) was a farm on the steep hillside between Bee Hill Rd. and what was then called Hemlock Rd.: a couple of barns that may date to c. 1810 and c. 1830 survive today. On a 100-acre parcel a series of farmers raised cows, pigs, and especially sheep. One of them, in mid-century, was Marshall Prindle (1819-1906), whose brother, Parley Prindle, had a big farm up the road. Later it belonged to John A. Foster, who in 1885 was farming 153 acres on both sides of Bee Hill Road, with 11 cows and 85 sheep. In 1912 James Bullock acquired the old Foster farm. He had already bought the Shand farm on Bee Hill Rd., the John Sherman farm further north on Hemlock Rd., and the Meadowbrook Farm, further south. He called the new place "Sunnybrook Farm." He hired a farmer to run it, and raised both sheep and cows through the 1920s. Bullock built a new house at another property he called Yeadon Farm in 1924 (later the Elwal Pines Motel, and still later Mezze Restaurant). His son, Anthony, built a large house at the corner of Bee Hill Rd. and Hemlock Rd., and spent summers there in 1920s and '30s.

Beginning in 1920 the Williams Outing Club was operating a 100' ski jump on the hill on the steep hill on Bullock's Sunnybrook Farm, with a 700' vertical drop, and beginning in 1923 was sponsoring the college's Winter Carnival there. After Bullock died in 1928, Sunnybrook farm was sold in 1930 to Arthur Rosenberg, who operated a small dairy operation on it until 1985. At the north end of the farm, along Bee Hill Road, Rosenburg planted an orchard. In the winter, to bring in extra income, Rosenburg continued the relationship with the Williams College Outing Club. In 1936 he installed a 1000-foot rope tow, and ran a ski area for the college and the town until 1961. (The ski hill first became known as "Sheep Hill" in 1935.) In 1946 Williams leased about ten acres on the west side of Bee Hill Rd. for a slalom ski trail, and bought the land two years later. The rope tow was extended up the steep hill on the west side of Bee Hill Rd. (On the open Sheep Hill itself the tow poles are long gone, but in the woods above the road you can see the remains of five poles, with big metal grooved wheels to guide the rope as it returned downhill.).

Just to the north of Sunnybrook Farm was the 210-acre Sherman farm, bought by Bullock in 1891. He renamed it "Glen Farm" and hired a farmer to operate it. The farm was the site of another Bee Hill suicide. In 1894 two students stumbled on the decomposed body of a man in one of Bullock's pastures. He had shot himself in the heart, leaving a note saying that the cause was " general dissatisfaction with myself." He was first identified as M. B. Kitzinger, a 40 year-old "colored man" from St. Louis and then, by friends from New York, as Max E. Kitzinger, a young German. It was perhaps nearby Flora's Glen, regarded as an inviting and secluded place for an excursion, that attracted him to the spot. Bullock also owned the mill pond at the bottom of Flora's Glen, and determined to put it to some commercial use. In 1889 he built an ice house and cut ice from the pond. In the 1890s he developed the pond as a source of drinking water for his Greylock Hotel. After problems with the water developed, he sold the pond and dam to the town in 1896.

Anthony Bullock's house was owned after 1943 by Alex Petrie, a local businessman, who lived there with his family until he died in 1967. (The Glen Farm was leased to and operated by a local farmer, Henry George.) The house and adjacent land was then bought by Neill Megaw, a Williams professor. In the late 1960s he and his wife began the development of 19-lot Thornliebank.

Trends

Leaving aside the alarming number of suicides, over time the history of Bee Hill illustrates a number of familiar trends in land use in Williamstown and New England generally: 1) the shift from sheep to cows over the course of the 19th century; 2) the breaking up of big farms, subdivided to provide for adult sons; 3) the decline of farming, beginning in the late 19th century. Another significant trend, less familiar, is that over time, with some exceptions, agricultural land passed from owner-operators to absentee landlords: the old Hickox farm ended up in the hands of a Hickox descendant who lived in Troy; the Prindle farm was sold to a New Jersey lawyer who wanted a summer place; the Samuel Hickox farm was sold to the Tenney family who lived out of town and were happy for the land to sit idle. I conclude with a brief survey of two other trends that conflict with each other, but characterize much of the recent history of Williamstown: residential development and land conservation.

As late as the 1940s there were only three houses on Bee Hill Rd. – the two early-19th-century houses at the top of the hill, and the 1900 "bungalow." In 1948 RRR Brooks built a house at the edge of the pond where Flora's Glen

Brook crosses Bee Hill Road. Another six were built at the northern end of the road between 1958 and 1975. Three more were built in the 1990s.

Residential building at a larger scale took place in the 1970s, when the old Glen Farm was subdivided for Thornliebank. Between 1973 and 1991 Edward Wylde sold off a number of pieces of the old Prindle farm for single-family houses, including 30 wooded acres on the west side of Bee Hill Rd. sold to Donald Westall in 1986, who subdivided them into five building lots. (Houses were eventually built on two of them. One changed hands recently for more than half a million dollars.) In 1991 a 58-acre piece of the old Daniel Galusha farm on the eastern slope of Bee Hill was developed into seven building lots – on which there are now five houses. In 2008 a 19-acre tract off at the north end of Bee Hill Rd. was developed into the four-lot Flora Glen Dr. subdivision, which now has one house.

Other developments were proposed but not built. In 1988 the Williamstown Housing Partnership abandoned a plan to build affordable housing on the land that became Flora Glen Rd. In 2000 Harry Patten bid on the Rosenburg farm, with plans to subdivide it into residential lots – but he was not able to buy the property. In 2005 Charles Fox tried to develop 70 acres of steep wooded land near the top of Bee Hill Rd. for eight building lots on the proposed "Foxwood Lane." Neighbors objected that the development would overburden the scenic unpaved road. The planning board denied approval, but Fox appealed to the state land court, where he prevailed. However, the real estate market slumped and the project stalled.

Although some of the land on Bee Hill has been developed over the last 60 years for residential purposes, much more has been conserved as open space, accessible to the public. Land conservation on Bee Hill Rd. actually began in 1896, when the town of Williamstown acquired two acres of the former Glen Pond and dam. In 1941 the heirs of James Bullock gave 31 landlocked acres in Flora's Glen, on the west side of Bee Hill, to the Boy Scouts, to be called Camp Bullock. A cabin was built, and was still being used for overnight camping by Troop 60 into the 1950s. The Scouts hiked down to the camp from the Taconic Trail.

In the 1950s the state made plans to preserve old fields and woods along the Taconic Trail, beginning with a large parcel up the Trail from Bee Hill Rd., acquired from Sanford Tenney in 1955. In 1957 Beulah Thull sold 108 acres of land on both sides of the Taconic Trail, for additions to the new Taconic Trail State Park. In 1986 Edward Wylde sold two large parcels on the north side of Bee Hill Rd. to a land trust, which sold them to the state for the same purpose.

A local land trust – Williamstown Rural Lands Foundation – has also acquired land on Bee Hill Rd. for public use. In 1986 it bought one of the four-acre lots that Don Westall was selling. In 1996 it received a gift of another of the Westall lots from Jonathan Fitch, and in 1998 purchased two more. In 2000 it bought 51 acres of the former Rosenberg Farm. In 2001 it acquired a conservation restriction on 48 acres of land in Flora's Glen, belonging to John and Jid Sprague. In 2005 it was given five acres of land on Old Farm Way, and in 2015 14 acres uphill from the new Flora Glen Rd. development. Most recently, in 2017 it received a gift of 178 acres on the north side of Bee Hill Extension, the old Samuel Hickox farm, from the Tenney family. Thus, from the original Hickox farm of some 650 acres, divided over time into three separate farms, all but about 100 acres are owned by the state or a land trust.

Bee Hill today is much like Northwest Hill: it is reached by a single unpaved road; some of the old farm fields have grown in but others remain open, cut at least once a year. Most of the land has been spared from residential development, but it's important to note that very little has been put under *permanent* conservation. Northwest Hill is a little farther than Bee Hill from Spring St. and a little quieter. Its best view is westward, down over the shallow valley and up to the Taconic Crest. The best view from Bee Hill Rd. is eastward, down Sheep Hill and over the Hemlock Brook valley toward the Hopper and Mt. Greylock, and one of the finest in Williamstown.

iii. Stone Hill

Detail from map of Williamstown, williamstown.gov, showing South St. leading to Stone Hill Rd.

Stone Hill lies close to the geographical center of Williamstown. It's a narrow ridge, with two summits, 1145' and 1115', about 3000' apart, extending roughly north-south for a little over two miles. In the 18th century it served to separate the village centered on the town green (now Field Park) from the once-busy village of South Williamstown. A "military line," dividing the "north part" from the "south part," used to run over the top of Stone Hill. In 1781 a town meeting resolved to build a meeting house in the geographical center of town – on Stone Hill! – on land that had been set aside as a "Reservation." Stakes were even planted to mark the site. But the town came to its senses: the plan was soon abandoned, and a meeting house built in what is now Field Park.

Stone Hill also separates the broad Green River Valley from the steep-sided Hemlock Brook Valley. (Hemlock Brook flows generally west to east until it runs into Stone Hill, at which point it turns north.) Its boundaries are Cold Spring Road on the west, Green River Road on the east and south, and Gale Road on the north. If you include the high ground between South St. and Cold Spring Rd. and a "panhandle" extending from Scott Hill Road down to Five Corners, it comprises 2627 acres, about the same amount of land as in Hopkins Forest.

Perhaps because it isn't very high (only about 500' higher than Spring St.), is surrounded by higher mountains, and doesn't have a distinct single summit to catch the eye, we don't often look up at Stone Hill. When we do, from the east and west we see a low wooded ridge that blocks the lower part of Greylock and the Hopper or the high Taconic ridge. Looking across from Sheep Hill you may get a sense of a third "summit" north of the other two. (A glance at a topographical map will tell you it's a bump – elevation 910' – at the north end of the Stone Hill ridge, in the field above the Clark Art Institute.) When you drive south on Cold Spring Rd. past Coyote Flaco restaurant you don't sense that the steep hemlock-covered slope on your left is the northwestern edge of Stone Hill. If you were to walk into the woods a few yards beyond the treeline you would find a spring, where water emerges from the base of Stone Hill, and just south of the Cold Spring you would find yourself looking 300' straight up at a vertical cliff.

And because the top of the Stone Hill ridge is wooded, we don't often climb to its summits for the view, though for much of the town's history you could get a good western view from what was until recently called "Sunset Rocks" near the 1145' summit. In the middle of the 19th century, when most of the trees on Stone Hill – all except those on the top of the narrow rocky ridge – had been cut, there used to be a fine northern view, as evidenced by the famous 1856 lithograph by George Yeomans of Williamstown "as seen from Stone Hill."

It has been called "Stone Hill" since the earliest days of settlement: the name appears in minutes of a town meeting in 1753. But the reason for the name is not clear. One historian claims that there is or was a huge boulder on the top of the hill. But if there was ever such a boulder, it must have long since fallen. There is a large glacial erratic in a ravine on the northeast side of the ridge, but it does not seem to be prominent enough to provide the hill's name. It has also been suggested that it's because the soil is thin, and anybody who digs on Stone Hill quickly finds ledge. Geologists tell us that the hill survives as a hill because the dolomitic marble of which it is made is capped in a few places by quartzite, an unusually hard rock which prevents erosion of material underlying it. (There used to be a couple of small quarries on the slopes of the hill.) It is probably the exposed stone on the summit ridge that made early settlers refer to "Stone Hill" – to distinguish it from the *wooded* tops of Bee Hill, Birch Hill, and Northwest Hill.

Stone Hill differs from Northwest and Bee Hills in some important ways. First, although its high ground is a patch of old forest, it is not located in the northern or western outskirts of town, but is surrounded by the town itself– there has long been settlement on Cold Spring Road, Green River Road, Gale Road, and in the last forty years on the southern part of Stone Hill Road. Second, although like Northwest Hill and Bee Hill it has long been farmed – the soil has long been thought to be fertile and well limed, and the eastern and southern slopes are gentle, there are significant differences between the farms on Stone Hill and those on other town hills.

On Stone Hill consolidation of small holdings took place earlier, and since the late 19th century the land holdings on Stone Hill have been larger. By 1894 there were five large parcels, of more than 150 acres. While most farmers in town had general farms – cows and sheep, chickens and pigs, together with a vegetable garden, apple orchards, and a sugarbush – the farmers on Stone Hill tended to specialize. One early farmer acquired a reputation for his seedling potatoes. A couple of others were "market gardeners," concentrating (like today's Bill Stinson) on vegetables that could be sold in town. Several focused on breeding registered Guernseys. The hillside on the south end of Stone Hill that was part of the Mount Hope estate was devoted to orchards. By the late 19th century, when many small farms in town were being abandoned, wealthy men, usually from out of town, came in to buy up the farms on Stone Hill. Anthony Bullock and Harley Procter from Cincinnati, John B. Gale and George A. Cluett from Troy, Bentley Warren from Boston and Parmalee

Prentice and Sam Blagden from New York City all bought on Stone Hill. Some (Bullock, Gale, and Prentice) assembled large parcels by buying up several smaller farms. Others (Procter, Blagden, and Cluett) found that some large farms were available for purchase. These were not "gentleman farmers" engaging in a rich man's hobby, but men who ran their farms as a business, and hoped they would make money. In most cases the proprietors did not operate the farms themselves or make their homes there. They lived elsewhere in the winter and had summer houses in town, employing local farmers to serve as farm managers. In a few cases the Stone Hill farmers lived on their own land, and were personally involved in the day-to-day farming. Most of the Stone Hill farmers in the 20th century were college graduates, and alumni of Williams – two of them became trustees of the college. Several of the landowners became prominent local citizens, engaged in the public life of the town, two of them selectmen (Blagden and Jenks), two others leading bankers (Gale and Greene), and four of them notable philanthropists and benefactors in town (Gale, Procter, Bullock, and Cluett). Some of the Stone Hill farms prospered, and several of them – more than on Northwest Hill and Bee Hill – lasted well into the 20th century.

The best historian of Stone Hill is a Williams student, Mark Livingston, of the Class of 1972. In a term paper for an Art History course taught by Sheafe Satterthwaite in the Fall of 1970, he chose to do a land-use history of Stone Hill, together with a set of botanical and geological notes. Relying on both documentary evidence of land-transfers and observations from his own patient walks over the landscape, Livingston focused on the way fields were reverting to scrub and woods. Two years later he produced an oversized wall map which he entitled "A Portraiture of Stone Hill." Fifty years later, anybody who writes about Stone Hill today walks in Livingston's tracks.

On Stone Hill today the farm animals are gone. But most of the old farm fields are still open – more than on Northwest Hill and Bee Hill, most of them leased to local farmers who take the hay. And most of the big parcels of land have survived intact: there are currently eight larger than 50 acres. The northern part of Stone Hill Road, which once went all the way through from South St. to Scott Hill Rd., was abandoned more than fifty years ago. A major part of the history of Stone Hill is in fact the history of Stone Hill Road.

Stone Hill Road

Soon after the town was founded and the house lots laid out, Main St., North St., and South St. were cleared, South St. and North St. extending from Stone Hill to the Hoosic River. And there already was by then an old road going over Stone Hill and south to what is now Lanesboro. It's possible that this road followed an even older "Indian path" leading from South County up to the medicinal springs at what we now call Sand Springs. One 19th century source reported that there was once an "Indian camp or village" on Stone Hill, and that "relics" – presumably arrowheads – were being regularly discovered. (Some local arrowheads survive in the collection of the Williams College Museum of Art.) It's not clear whether this Indian footpath passed to the west or the east of the summits: west would have been flatter ground but east would have been a little more direct. In either case, a road that kept to the high ground on Stone Hill would be a more reliable passage than a road that followed the course of Green River or Hemlock Brook, both of which were liable to flood in the winter and spring.

In 1762 a town committee was formed to "renew the road [to Lanesboro] and to make alterations if we thought best." The committee recommended that the road should be laid out on the west side of the ridgetop. The town adopted the recommendation and surveyed the road later in 1762. At its north end the road connected to South St. At its southern end, it extended across present-day Scott Hill Rd. and continued down to present-day Five Corners. Laid out before 1765, it became part of the "old County Road," the only through-road from Pittsfield to Bennington. So it was indeed a colonial road, but the old report that President George Washington rode over Stone Hill during an August 1790 trip from Lebanon Springs to Bennington, concerning Vermont's admission to the union as the 14th state, was discredited more than a hundred years ago.

The approach to Stone Hill from the south was gradual, but the descent from the hill on the northern end was steeper, falling 300' in less than half a mile. In the spring the mud in the road was deep, or (especially in the steep northern end) badly eroded, and travel across it became almost impossible. As a consequence, in the 1820s the town laid out what are now our main north-south roads, one on the west side of Stone Hill, along Hemlock Brook, and the other on the east, along Green River. When the last segment of the Hemlock Brook Valley road was completed (today's Rt. 7), Stone Hill Road fell into disuse as a through road.

From the town's earliest years there was another way to reach Stone Hill, via what we now call Scott Hill Road and Woodcock Road. Names have changed over the years – Scott Hill used to be called Judd Hill. Scott Hill Road used to be the eastern segment of Woodcock Road, after an early settler, Nehemiah Woodcock, who lived at the intersection of Stone Hill Rd. and Woodcock Rd, what was called Woodcock's Corner. Although Scott Hill Rd. is quite steep at its eastern end, it enabled a southbound traveler along Green River Rd. to climb over Stone Hill when the road ahead – which twice crosses the river in less than half a mile – was flooded.

By the late 19th century there was another way to reach the northern end of Stone Hill, when John B. Gale cut a private road from South St. east to Water St. Gale was a Williams graduate, Class of 1842, and a wealthy retired lawyer from Troy. He acquired some notoriety in his home town by marrying his deceased wife's sister – he later wrote a short book arguing that such an "affinity" was no "bar to marriage." In Williamstown he became a leading citizen, elected a trustee of the Williamstown Savings Bank and the first president of the Williamstown National Bank. In 1881 he bought a big summer house on South St., and several years later bought three small farms at the northeast end of Stone Hill. They all had frontage and driveways on Green River Rd., and the private road he built provided him more direct access to his farms from his house. It became today's Gale Road.

Stone Hill Road continued to be used for access to the farms on Stone Hill, and the southern part of it was not difficult to maintain. But the north end remained a problem. So much so that in the 1890s one landowner, Harley Procter, who had bought two farms on Stone Hill, wanted to improve the road that led from his big house in town to his farms. He had an additional motive: his favorite sport was what was then called "driving" – taking a brisk ride through the countryside in a carriage drawn by four horses. He owned a number of carriages himself, along with a barn full of horses. Riding over Stone Hill and back via South Williamstown would constitute a scenic loop. Because the town was reluctant to spend the money on roads, Procter agreed to improve Stone Road himself, filling the gullies, grading, and resurfacing with gravel. Soon Stone Hill became a "popular drive" for horse-drawn carriages. By 1908 it was also attracting early automobiles, which frightened the horses. And some cars had difficulty descending the steep grade at the road's north end.

Procter left town in 1903, and the Stone Hill Road quickly fell into disrepair. By 1916 it was reported to be "in wretched condition." In 1930 it was said to resemble "the bed of a dry brook." In subsequent decades there was little demand to improve Stone Hill Rd. The only people who used it were farmers, hikers, and horseback riders. As late as 1950 there was only one house on the road – at the intersection of Stone Hill Rd. and Scott Hill Rd. In 1948, when the house changed hands, its new owner claimed that Stone Hill Rd. infringed on a corner of his property, and erected a fence across most of the road to prevent farm traffic from crossing it. A controversy ensued and went on for over a year: the fence was taken down, and put up again. Eventually the selectmen resurveyed the road and moved it slightly so that it no longer infringed on private property.

The town considered improving the road in 1957 but decided against. In 1959 a group calling itself the Stone Hill Trust bought 67 acres of old farmland on Stone Hill, with plans to develop it as a resort, or to subdivide it into four or five building lots. Another landowner, Walter Hoover – more on him later – who owned property fronting on Stone Hill Rd. wanted to subdivide and sell building lots, and asked the town in 1962 to rebuild the road. The town again declined, and the Stone Hill Trust sold off its land. In 1963 a town "master plan," predicting that the population of Williamstown would grow and that additional housing would be needed, suggested that if its road were improved, Stone Hill would be a good site for single-family houses. (Two new houses had been built along the southern section of Stone Hill Road in the 1950s and three more in the 1960s.)

In 1966 the town's selectmen, who had declined to spend money on the road, voted to discontinue maintenance of most of its length, from Gale Road south to what is now the northernmost of the houses. But they had to seek approval from the county commissioners. Hearings were held, and several landowners on Stone Hill opposed the selectmen's decision. Their concerns were dismissed by a vote of 2-1 as not in the public interest, and 2600' of the northern half of the road was formally "discontinued as a public way." The county commissioners' order specified that signs were to be posted warning the public not to enter the closed portion of the road. But this provision was disputed (or ignored), and it was claimed that the town retained a right of way.

Controversy died down, but a new issue arose in 1968, when the state Dept. of Public Works, responding to the problem of traffic congestion at Field Park (exacerbated since 1963 by the attraction of horse racing at the Green

Mountain track), proposed that Rt. 7 be relocated so as to bypass the center of town. In one of the two variants a four-lane highway would run northward the length of Stone Hill, just to the east of the existing Rt. 7, crossing Scott Hill Rd. between Stone Hill Rd. and Rt. 7, and then, bearing west, crossing Cold Spring Rd. at the Henry Bratcher property, just opposite Sheep Hill. Such a road, with limited access, would have plowed across farm fields and woods, though not Stone Hill Road itself. In the other variant the new highway would follow the path of Rt. 7 to Scott Hill Rd. but then cut across Stone Hill Rd. and run east, crossing Green River Rd. north of Blair Rd. Various factions emerged, pro and con. Residents on Stone Hill were strongly opposed, among them Williams professors Freeman Foote and Frank Oakley. In 1970, because of local opposition, the state DPW shelved the plans.

But before the end of the decade the old controversy about Stone Hill road came back. In 1977 two abutters, who, not permitted to develop their land, wanted to reap some economic benefit from it, and had maple trees along the road cut down. They probably remembered that in 1968 town meeting had accepted a recommendation from the Conservation Commission to harvest more than 1200 selected trees from the town-owned woodlot on Stone Hill, a vote that was overturned two years later. When the town found out about the private logging along Stone Hill Road, it sent a bill to the logger, declaring that it owned the roadway, and thus the trees. But enough uncertainty about who legally owned the road remained that the selectmen commissioned a report on the three classes of roads: accepted town ways, discontinued roads, and abandoned roads. Plans were made to have the town vote formally to "accept" Stone Hill Road at the 1978 town meeting, but the item did not appear on the warrant. The legal status of the road remained unclear.

In 1981 Walter Hoover sought permission from the Planning Board to sell five building lots along Stone Hill Rd, arguing that the town had a legal right-of-way, and petitioning the selectmen to re-open the road. A citizens group, the Stone Hill Preservation Committee, seeking to preserve Stone Hill as an "environmental and recreational center," argued that the town had no right of way, and that in any case would incur exorbitant expenses if it were to reopen and maintain the road. The road was not reopened, and Hoover soon sold his farm to Herbert Allen.

In 1987 the town again took up the matter of discontinued roads, appointing a "Special Committee on Roads" which commissioned a "Report on the Legal Status of Roads in the Town of Williamstown." The report noted that the law concerning discontinued roads, public ways, and private ways was unclear and that in the past many town actions concerning roads were procedurally improper. It recommended that the town avoid discontinuing any more roads until the legal status of a discontinued or abandoned road was clarified. It also advised that the town assume that it does *not* own the land under a discontinued public way.

After Herbert Allen in 1991 built a house on high ground, not far from Stone Hill Road, he closed off the old private farm road that led down beside his new house from Stone Hill Rd. to Green River Rd. This provoked an outcry from hikers and skiers who had used that road for years. Invoking the argument that the town had no legal right-of-way on that section of Stone Hill Rd. where he owned land on both sides of the road, Allen blocked vehicular access to the road but agreed to permit foot, bicycle, and horseback traffic – on Stone Hill Rd. but not the farm road.

As part of the 1993 project to build an underground water tank on Clark Art Institute land, a gate was put up, closing off the north end of the road. Some citizens objected. Selectmen discussed the status of Stone Hill Rd. Town counsel advised that he could not find legal grounds for declaring that the road was a "public way" – neither a formal acceptance by the town of the road nor evidence that the road had been used by the public without permission from abutters for twenty years. The Clark later removed the gate blocking Stone Hill Road, but Allen's concrete blocks remain. This seemed to leave the legal status undetermined, but a sort of truce was established: it was understood that the town did not have to maintain or plow the road, landowners with frontage on the road could not subdivide in order to develop, and traditional users, with the implicit permission of landowners, could continue to walk and hike the Stone Hill Road and trails.

Stone Hill's Farms

Who used Stone Hill Road? One of the earliest reported to have used it was Dr. Samuel Porter (1755-1822), a doctor-surgeon who lived near Woodcock's Corner on Stone Hill and traveled far and wide to tend to his patients, some of whom lived as far as Berlin, New York: to reach them after 1813 he rode south on Stone Hill Road to South Williamstown and then west over the Taconic range, via "Johnson Pass" – today's Mills Hollow Trail.

After Hemlock Road was opened all the way to Five Corners about 1830, through travelers would have stopped using Stone Hill Rd. Most of the farmers on Stone Hill in the 19th century had frontage on Green River Road or Cold Spring Road. The primary users of Stone Hill Rd. were those who lived or worked on the one big farm that lacked access to Green River Rd. or Cold Spring Rd. The farm had been laid out in 1763 by David Johnson. Johnson sold to Gurdon Bulkeley (1773-1845), who in 1828 replaced the original farmhouse with a new brick house on Stone Hill Road, built on "the very brow of the hill," just south of the summit. (At that time it appears that there was only one other house on the road.) Bulkeley's was a mixed or "general" farm. By 1840 he had moved into a house on South St., and his son, Henry G. Bulkeley (1812-79), lived on the farm and ran a school for boys there, apparently called Greenbush Academy, where he taught mathematics. By the late 1840s the farm, now being called Stone Hill Farm, was being run by Henry's youngest brother, Dan (b. 1819), known as D. A. Bulkeley, who decided to specialize in seedling potatoes. His experiments began in 1847, when each spring he selected the most promising seedlings from the previous year, and eventually produced several varieties – the Stone Hill, the Bulkeley, the Berkshire, the Monitor, the Snow Flake – which were exhibited in county fairs throughout the region and acquired a national reputation. He was still farming 300 acres in 1885. But by 1890 Dan was dead, and his son William A. Bulkeley apparently did not wish to continue farming. He sold the farm to an out-of-towner, but the buyer defaulted on his mortgage payments, and the mortgage was assigned in 1891 to another out-of-towner, Harley Procter, from Cincinnati.

Procter was in on the ground floor at Procter & Gamble – he was a son of one of the founders. When the company went public in 1890, Procter, with a 25% share in the company, retired and made plans to move to New York. Perhaps influenced by his fellow-Cincinnatian Anthony Bullock, who beginning in the 1880s had bought up land on the western edge of Stone Hill along Cold Spring Rd., Procter also began buying land in Williamstown. He acquired the old Williams Farm in 1890 (with access to Green River Rd.) and the adjacent Bulkeley Farm in 1891. (The two farms remained united through the next four changes of ownership, and remain united today.) The former consisted largely of pasture and hayfields. It bordered the L. B. Jenks farm on the south and the John B. Gale farm on the north. The Bulkeley Farm was larger, with pasture and hay fields, but also orchards and a field of rye. It abutted Bullock's Green Meadow Farm on the north, and D. B. Galusha's land on the west. This meant that Procter now owned about 400 acres on Stone Hill, extending from Green River Road to Cold Spring Rd., and from the

Gale and Bullock farms on the north nearly to Scott Hill Rd. on the south.

He let the papers know that he intended to build a summer "cottage" in town, on property he bought at the corner of Main St. and North St., and began building it in 1892. He also laid the foundation for a large barn on the Bulkeley Farm and built a water tower. On the Williams Farm he took down some old outbuildings, put up a new barn, and built an ice house. He hired a local farmer to manage the Bulkeley Farm for him and installed a local tenant farmer on the Williams Farm. In the fall of 1895, when St. John's was planning to build its church on Park St., Procter arranged to have stones from his fields on Stone Hill dug up and, in the following winter, carried by "stone boats" – heavy sledges, dragged over the snow – to the building site and stored "for use in the coming spring." Many of the fieldstones were not flat but round – which made things difficult for the builders. In the late 1890s Procter's plans for his Stone Hill farms changed: he rented the Williams farm to a wealthy young New Yorker named Sam Blagden, who had spent vacations at his parents' summer house on Bulkley St., and spent three years at Williams College.

It is likely that it was in the 1890s, now that he owned both farms, that Procter, to provide better access to his property, put in a private road from Green River Road through the Williams Farm up to the Bulkeley Farm. But this road must not have satisfied him, for as noted he also improved Stone Hill Road, the most direct route into town, at his own expense. By then it seems that Procter started losing interest in farming. In 1900 he sold the 160-acre Williams Farm to Blagden,

Soon Procter lost interest in Williamstown itself. In 1902, with a challenge gift of $10,000, he tried to get the town to raise funds to improve other roads. When the town declined to meet the challenge, Procter with his horses and carriages left town and set himself up in Lenox. In 1904 he transferred title to the Bulkeley Stone Hill Farm to his son, William Procter. William tore down the old brick house on the Bulkeley Farm to make room for a new summer house for himself, and hired a local man to serve as his farm manager. But William was as mercurial as his father: the following year, in 1905, he pulled up stakes and sold his farm to his neighbor, Sam Blagden, who thus reunited the two big farms.

Blagden, who renamed the farm "Hillside Farm," was an unlikely farmer. A couple of years after dropping out of Williams he bought a 200' coal-powered schooner, and with four friends sailed to the Caribbean and then across the Atlantic, through the Mediterranean, Scandinavia, and the British

Isles, ultimately a 10-month cruise of 30,000 miles. Shortly after returning to New York, he apparently decided to settle down. When he rented and then bought the Williams Farm, the *New York Times* reported with amusement that Blagden, apparently a well-known man about town, had "taken up quarters at Hillside Farm and has commenced amateur farming."

Blagden was actually serious about farming. He hired Fred Northup (1859-1934), who had operated Procter's farm, to manage Hillside Farm, with its small herd of cattle, dairy barns, sheep and lambs, a poultry house, and orchards. In 1901 he built a two-story annex to the farmhouse and a new 40' x 70' barn. By 1904 he decided that an enlarged farmhouse was not enough for him. Although he never married, he planned to entertain out-of-town guests, so he built a new big house, in "farmhouse style," five bedrooms on the second floor, with two wings (one a three-room apartment, the other an eight-room apartment), and professionally landscaped grounds. The *Transcript* later described it as "one of the finest dwellings in town." In 1906, after he had bought the Bulkeley/Procter Farm, he brought in a Williams professor to set up a model dairy for him. Blagden himself soon became more interested in local politics than in farming. He ran for selectman in 1906, and served for a number of terms, on and off for the next 38 years, several times as chair.

Two other wealthy men bought farms and built big houses on Stone Hill about the same time that Blagden did. In 1899 and 1900 Bentley Warren, a young Boston lawyer and a Williams graduate bought 114 acres of the old Meacham Farm that stretched from Water St. west to South St. (Meacham St. is named for the family.) In 1900 he built a large, 3-story stucco-clad summer house, set back from Gale Road, with bedrooms for his young family on the second floor and for the servants on the third. By 1902 Warren had another reason for a base in Williamstown: he became a trustee of Williams College – its president, Harry Garfield, was his classmate – and he would remain on the board for 45 years.

Although Warren had major responsibilities in Williamstown and in Boston, where he became president of the Boston Bar Association and head of the board of the Boston Symphony Ochestra, he also ran a small farm operation (with dairy barn, corn crib, poultry house and haybarn) on his Williamstown property, raising both sheep and dairy cattle. In 1921 he had the grounds landscaped by Fletcher Steele, who would go on to design the gardens at Naumkeag, a big estate in Stockbridge. And he hired Giovanni Roffinoli, an Italian emigre, to take care of the gardens and manage the farm. Over time Roffinoli dug an ice pond, planted trees, and built stone walls and walks that survive today.

Warren continued to visit his farm until 1946. When he died in 1947 the house and farm were inherited by his daughter, Ellen Geer Sangster, who as a girl had spent summers in Williamstown, and, having with her first husband founded a progressive school in New Jersey in the 1920s, moved it to Williamstown. (It is amusing to imagine dinner-table conversations between the conservative Boston brahmin lawyer who opposed the federal income tax and his daughter who founded a "progressive" school.) Buxton School has been here ever since, the main house, gate house, and barns converted to academic use. Mrs. Sangster, who served as both teacher and headmistress, lived for many years in the main house; her son's family visited her there in the 1950s.

In 1911 another wealthy young Williams alumnus bought land on Stone Hill and built a spacious summer house. He was George A. Cluett (1873-1955), Class of 1896, who happened to be a classmate of Sam Blagden. In 1908 and 1911 Cluett's father, Robert Cluett, who had built a house on Gale Rd., bought two of John B. Gale's farms and transferred title to his son, George. In 1911 the son, who lived in Troy, built a 25-room summer house across Gale Rd. from his parents' house. He hired the Frederick Law Olmsted firm to design the landscaping: the Olmsteds had worked at a number of Berkshire County estates, and beginning in 1902 produced a master plan for Williams College. Cluett, who went into the family shirt-collar business after graduating from Williams, became president of Cluett, Peabody, Inc. on the death of his father in 1919. He hired a farmer to run his Green Meadow dairy farm. Cluett raised Norwegian elkhounds. He also bred and showed Clydesdale horses, winning prizes at horse shows in Springfield and as far away as Chicago. In the early 1920s he had as many as 38 in his herd. There was a fulltime blacksmith on the farm to shoe the horses.

In 1925 his dairy herd was infected with tuberculosis, and he decided to get out of the dairy business, selling his herd and renting the barns and the fields to a local dairy farmer, Arthur Galusha. In 1929 Cluett retired from the presidency of Cluett, Peabody, and moved to Williamstown in 1930, at the age of 57. He became interested in Federal furniture and put together a major collection. From 1935 to 1946 he served as a trustee of Williams College. He continued to lease the farm to Arthur Galusha until 1937, when his tenant moved his operations to the neighboring farm.

Cluett remained on Green Meadow Farm until his death in 1955. In 1958 Cluett's heirs gave 178 acres of the property, including the house, to Williams College. The college arranged to have the Cluett barns moved down

Green River Rd. to Fairfields Farm, cleared the farmyards, laid out Cluett Drive on eleven acres in 1960, and began selling eight housing lots. In the Cluett house it established the Cluett Center for Development Economics. The college retained about 150 acres of field and woods. The big field behind the house came to be known as Kite Hill, after Williams professor Lee Hirsche, who with his art studio class designed and flew kites there on what he called Kite Day every spring from 1961 to 1975. (Hirsche lived nearby on Gale Rd.) After the Center for Development Economics moved into town in 1966, the college used the house as an alumni center, but in 1978 sold it, along with 21 acres, to David and Joyce Milne. The Milnes set up Highcroft School in the house and grounds, and ran it from 1978 to 1993. After the Pine Cobble School lost its building on Main St. in a fire, it bought the property and moved out to the old Highcroft School site and is still there: the Cluett summer house serves as the main academic building.

In the early 1930s, about the time Cluett moved fulltime to his Williamstown farm, his Williams classmate and southern neighbor, Sam Blagden, decided to give up his farm and move into town. When he sold his Hillside Farm in 1933 it was to Arthur Galusha, who had been Cluett's tenant. Galusha was already an established and very successful breeder of Guernseys. For the next fifteen years he and his sons operated what they now called Coronation Farm. (For more on Arthur Galusha, see "Thirteen Galusha Farms.")

In 1948 Arthur Galusha sold the farm with 130 head of cattle to Walter Hoover, a wealthy Vermont engineer, for the substantial sum of $100,000. Hoover hired a herdsman and continued the dairy business until 1952, when he sold his herd of Guernseys, but kept the farm, returning to his engineering work with his Hoover Transmission Company, which led in 1953 to the invention of a pulley for use in small farm vehicles. He converted his 158' x 22' calf barn into a manufacturing facility, in which he hoped to produce 150,000 pulleys a year, but had difficulty getting a zoning variance, and by 1960 abandoned the project. In the 1960s Hoover sold land on the southern end of Stone Hill Rd. for residential building lots, and in 1981, as noted, tried to sell land on the closed portion of the road. He rented one of the houses on his farm to Williams students, who threw parties in one of the barns.

In 1982 Herbert Allen bought the remainder of the property, demolished the big house that Sam Blagden had built in 1904, along with most of the farm buildings, and built a new house higher on the hill. He also restored the old Coronation Farm barns along Green River Rd., though they are no longer used for agricultural purposes. Over time Allen also bought additional property on either side of Stone Hill Road that Hoover had previously sold. He also bought the old Jenks Farm, his southern neighbor, which had been operated by the Jenks family since the middle of the 19th century, first by Lucien B. Jenks and later by his son Leland, a Williams graduate, Class of 1899, just a little behind Blagden and Cluett. Lee Jenks became a town selectman – another Stone Hill selectman! – and later went into insurance and real estate, but continued to run a successful dairy farm and market garden until 1949. When he died the farm passed to his daughter and son-in-law, Wallace Greene, who was a banker. It was Greene who sold most of the farm to Allen. He held back seven acres, including a Jenks barn, which he gave to his daughter and son-in-law in1995.

By then the other farms on Stone Hill had also ceased operations. Bullock's Meadowbrook Farm on the western edge of Stone Hill, on Cold Spring Rd., put together starting in the 1870s, was sold in 1917 to Henry Bratcher, a carpenter who bought and built up a contracting business, and did a little farming on the side. Bratcher's son (yet another long-time selectman) and daughter-in-law remained there until they died in 2011 and 2020. The only survival of the Meadowbrook Farm is the barn that Bullock built in 1896, famous in later years as the 1896 House. An old farm road on the Bratcher property, leading from Cold Spring Rd. up to Stone Hill Rd., has been closed to the public for years.

Fritz Langer's dairy farm south of Scott Hill Rd., with a collection of farm buildings at Five Corners, lasted longer. Langer bought the 225-acre Modern Dairy Farm in 1955, and continued to run it until 1980, when he sold his herd of 200 cows. He then began leasing the land to local farmers, put the property under an agricultural restriction in 1983, and finally sold in 1997 to Harry Patten's Paradise Farm Corporation. In 2010 the land was bought by Frank Lewis's Farmland Enterprises. Lewis planted thousands of apple trees, and for a few years kept farm animals, mostly as a sort of petting zoo, and ran a farm store that went out of business after only a couple of years.

Some of the farm fields on Stone Hill continued to be leased to local farmers, who grew corn, cut hay, and grazed cattle on land owned by Williams College and by Herbert Allen. Now it is only corn and hay. And some of the old fields are growing in. Wildlife – deer, coyotes, wild turkeys, and even black bears – are returning as the forest reassumes the land. But large parts of the old Bulkeley, Williams, Bullock, Gale/Cluett, and Warren farms are still kept open.

Rural Recreation

Farmers have not made use of Stone Hill Road since the days of Harley Procter. And already by his time its northern end was attracting residents of Williamstown who delighted in the sylvan scenery and the views. School groups went up on Stone Hill for picnics. Because of the shade and the views, it was in 1899 said to be a "favorite resort for summer people." In 1890, a tourist guide touted the beauties of Stone Hill, from which "the entire valley lies spread out like a picture with rich color, with harmonious light and shade." Another guide in 1915 promises that the walk over Stone Hill "takes one through beautiful woods, with rocky cliffs at some points." In the winter the northern end of the road was a good sledding hill.

One resident who especially delighted in walking up Stone Hill was Williams Professor George M. Wahl (1851-1923), who reportedly walked to Stone Hill every day to sit on a rustic birch seat to view the sunset over the Cold Spring Valley, Bee Hill, and Berlin Mountain. Wahl, born in Germany, taught German to Williams students beginning in 1892, but during the First World War he encountered hostility because of his German birth. He retired in 1917 and died in 1923. After his death, perhaps to make up for his mistreatment, his friends erected a stone bench in his memory, on the site of the old rustic seat, with stone said to have been taken from the quarry on Bentley Warren's land.

In spite of private ownership of the land on Stone Hill, hunters roamed the woods for deer, fox, and small game: in July 1921 George Cluett's grandmother, sitting on the Cluett front porch, was wounded by a bullet that was presumably fired by an out-of-season hunter. In the 1930s the Williams ski team skied up Stone Hill and down the private Bratcher road to the college's Winter Carnival at Sheep Hill. Residents on horseback used to ride along Stone Hill Road. In later decades the cross-country team occasionally runs along the road, and at one season or another you will see hikers, walkers, cross-country skiers, or photographers. Once the Clark Art Institute put in hiking trails, a favorite hike for museum visitors is the "Stone Bench Loop." And after the old trails across Stone Hill Road were improved and blazed in 2015, hikers climbing the northern end of Stone Hill Road have rediscovered the summits of Stone Hill and the grassy sward of Kite Hill, once the old Gale and Cluett farm. Stone Hill Road is also regularly approached from the south by those – mostly Williams alumni and faculty – who have moved into the seven houses built along the southern end of the road since about 1960, and who consider Stone Hill Rd. a neighborhood walk.

A walk along Stone Hill Road is also a reminder of what a 2016 Clark Art Institute exhibition on Stone Hill called "the enduring value of place" – the old farm fields still kept open on the right and the left, the road pre-dating the American Revolution, and the hill itself, once an island in Lake Bascom, still a "island" of forest in the middle of Williamstown.

An old postcard of Main St., looking east. Courtesy of Williamstown Historical Museum

Chapter 6

—⚌—

A LAYMAN'S HISTORY
OF WILLIAMSTOWN'S TREES

Old place names in Williamstown tell you that trees have long been an important part of the town's history: quite apart from street names (Elm St., Chestnut St., Walnut St., Birch Lane, Sycamore Dr., Willow Lane, Maple St., Linden St.), common in most towns in the country, we have some quite old names for neighborhoods or features of the landscape, White *Oaks*, *Hemlock* Brook, *Birch* Hill, *Pine* Cobble. Add to those some old names we no longer use – Cold Spring Rd. used to be called *Hemlock* Rd., the upper end of Henderson Rd. used to be called *Oak Hill* – along with *Elm* Tree House at Mt. Hope, The *Spruces*, *Pines* Lodge Mobile Home Park, and several motels (The *Orchards*, *Maple* Terrace, The *Willows*, and the old Elwal *Pines*). The names tell us that early settlers and more recent residents and business owners use trees to organize their spatial sense of the town's landscape.

When you look at the town's tree-lined streets and the tree-covered mountains, you might assume that trees are everywhere, and have been a constant part of Williamstown's landscape, the background and the context to the buildings and the people, but a quick look at some 19th-century lithographs reminds you that the tree cover used to be quite different: the hills surrounding the town were once cleared of trees, and, as photographs of the town before about 1950 show, Main Street was once lined with rows of elms.

And the way we think about trees has also changed over time. If you mention "trees" to visitors to Williamstown, they will think of "fall foliage," that brief and unreliable period in October when the trees – especially the sugar maples and red maples – are supposed to turn. But it was not until the late 19th century, when tourists first began to explore New England, that anybody paid much attention to leaves. Before then a few poets noticed fall colors. William Cullen Bryant, who spent a short time in Williamstown as a student, published a modest poem in 1829 on "Autumn Woods," briefly noting the "color'd landscape" of "purple and gold." Williams alumni remember Washington Gladden's "The Mountains" (1859), of which the lesser-known second verse briefly alludes to "Autumn's scarlet mantle." One exception is the traveler, Timothy Dwight, who rode through Williamstown in October 1799, who noticed with a careful eye that the "deciduous foliage" had been changed by a frost into "every tincture, from the deepest verdure of the spring though all its successive shades to the willow green; and thence through a straw colour, orange and crimson, to a reddish brown."

Apart from Dwight, the first writer to pay close attention to the color in a Berkshire fall was probably Thoreau, who published an essay on "Autumnal Tints" in the October 1862 issue of the *Atlantic Monthly*. He began the essay by remarking that "Europeans coming to America are surprised by the brilliancy of our autumnal foliage," and went on to lament that most native writers don't notice: "The autumnal change of our woods has not made a deep impression on our literature yet. October has hardly tinged our poetry." But Thoreau himself taught generations of readers to look at the "rich glow" of "painted leaves." By 1900, when Williamstown was a fashionable summer resort, the summer -colony people would typically stay through October before returning to New York for the winter, presumably to see the foliage. Still, until after World War II tourism in New England was primarily a summer phenomenon. It was not until 1955 that North Adams began its annual "Fall Foliage Festival," and not until the 1970s that tour operators companies organized a large number of "fall foliage" bus tours.

There are probably more trees in Williamstown now than at any time in the last two hundred years. Several tree species are spreading, and others declining. Change, not continuity, is the keynote. And the *rate* of change is likely to increase, as a warmer climate makes the northern Berkshires more hospitable, or less hospitable, to one species or other, and as new insects and diseases are introduced. As we try to figure out what can be done to reduce the negative consequences of global and local warming, it's worth looking at the history of Williamstown's trees since the town was founded, if only to sharpen our sense of how the present does not look like the past, and the future is not likely to resemble the present.

Before European settlers in significant numbers arrived here in the 18th century, the hills around what became Williamstown were covered with a northern hardwood forest: sugar maple, ash, and elm below an elevation of about 1300', maple, beech, and birch at higher elevations, oak and hickory still higher, and red spruce and balsam fir above 2000' on the mountain ridges. The Hoosic River Valley was fully wooded too, elm, box-elder, ash, and willow growing in flood plain from Ft. Massachusetts (in present-day North Adams) downstream to River Bend Farm on North St., and hemlock on drained slopes. From Northwest Hill the surveyor Richard Hazen in 1741 noticed beech, black birch, hemlock and bass wood. In 1746 the meadows near River Bend Farm were still covered with the "primeval forest" of "enormous pines." Timothy Dwight in 1799 saw "forests" of maple, beech, cherry birch, hemlock, and spruce.

Depending on whether the early traveler in this area focused on difficulty of access, or with the hopeful eye of the surveyor, he thought that "nearly the whole was covered with thick and impenetrable forests," or that the town was "splendidly wooded in every part." (Early settlers were interested in trees not because they were scenic, or majestic, or provided habitat or food for wildlife, or erosion control, but because they prevented you from plowing, and because you could cut them down and use them for human purposes.) The first lots were designated as "house" or "meadow" lots, and in later "divisions," beginning with the "fifth division," as "woodlots," from which settlers could harvest timber and firewood. But tree species were unevenly distributed: in the sandy soil north of the Hoosic River, and along Broad Brook, was white pine, tall, straight, and knot-free, especially valuable for building timber. In the northeast corner of the town, on the flanks of East Mountain, especially on south-facing dry uplands, was white oak, good for window frames and door sills. (There was also a stand of white oak near where Broad Brook crosses Rt. 7, which gave its name to the old White Oaks Tavern.) Hemlock was found along Hemlock Brook and Flora's Glen Brook, as well as the banks of the Green and Hoosic Rivers: it was good for tannin, used in tanning leather. Chestnut was very widely distributed: because it is resistant to rot, it was thought especially good for fence posts – but chestnut was also used to build a bridge in Flora's Glen. Red spruce was found high on Mt. Greylock and along the Taconic Crest.

Big trees could be useful to settlers as "witness trees," marking property corners, but for the most part farmers thought trees needed to be cleared to make space for a house and a barn and to open up fields. And they began cutting trees and removing stumps as soon as the lots were laid out. Most of the white pine and white oak was cut by the first quarter of the 19th century. The famous "Mills map" of 1830 shows that by then about 60% of the land in town was cleared, everywhere up to an elevation of about 2200', except on steep slopes and ridge tops. That means trees were clearcut up to Petersburg Pass (elevation: 2090') and well up the sides of Mt. Prospect, Mt. Williams, and Greylock.

Deforestation

Sawmills were set up very early on Green River, at the intersection of Broad Brook and the Hoosic River, and at the intersection of Hopper Brook and Green River. Tanneries soon followed, the first of them along Green River, to process the hemlock bark. After the peak of clearing for agriculture in about 1830, tree cutting of second-growth pine and oak continued into the late 19th century for other purposes: fuel for charcoal kilns, for railroad boilers, or for pulp. Logging continued late into the 20th century: on Mt. Fitch until 1947, in Treadwell Hollow in the 1960s, on Pine Cobble and the slopes of the Taconics in the 1970s, in the Bullock Forest Preserve in the 1980s, in the Hopper until 1991, on the town-owned Blair Lot in 1993, and on Berlin Ridge, on property now belonging to Berkshire Natural Resources Council, as late as 2000. Small-scale logging continues today, along the Mills Hollow Trail, and east of Rt. 7 in South Williamstown. Buxton School has cut trees in its woods for sawlogs and firewood. Occasionally wooded lots are clear-cut for building sites.

Logging by farmers and timber-cutters is not the only reason that trees die. Every tree has a life cycle, and even the oldest trees in New England live only a few centuries. They are also subject to several sorts of natural disturbance: avalanche, fire, windstorms, insect infestation, and fungal blight.

There were major avalanches in the Hopper in 1784 and 1823, landslides on the steep sides of Mt. Greylock which wiped out the trees and everything else in their path, and left a barren patch lasting for decades. Timothy Dwight gives two accounts of the 1784 event, which contemporaries called the "bursting of a cloud" – a downhill rush of water (probably accompanied by boulders): "A tract of about ten acres was entirely desolated of its trees, which the flood and the storm had thrown down, and which were lying in the lowest part of the tract in heaps of confusion." There were other avalanches in the Hopper in 1891, 1938, and 1990, and on the eastern side of Greylock in 1901 and 1990.

Although the Berkshires are relatively wet, and the tops of the mountains frequently shrouded in damp fog, forest fires have been destructive. There was three fires on Berlin Mt. in 1925, and trees have still not grown back on the summit a hundred years later. Recurrent fires on East Mtn. account for its bare, rocky summit. A local historian reported in 1829 that because it was "rendered almost naked by frequent fires" East Mountain used to be called "Bald Mountain." One major fire on East Mountain in April 1901 spread down as far as Cole's Grove. There was a serious fire there as recently as 1979. The most recent fire on the Taconic Crest Trail was in 2010. And in 2015 there was a serious fire in Clarksburg State Forest and up the side of the Dome. There have been no fires on Greylock since the early 1970s, but in the 19th century they were common on the drier east side of the mountain – there was one on the summit in 1884 which led to the formation of the Greylock Park Association the following year.

Windstorms can be equally destructive of trees. One such storm took down many elms in town in 1912. Another, in late July 1921, described as the "Worst Storm in 25 Years," took down 50 elms, including a number at Main and Southworth Sts., in front of an inn called "The Elms." The famous hurricane of 1938 blew down thousands of trees. In 1998 a so-called "straight-line wind event" (a sudden downburst of wind from a thunderstorm, traveling, unlike the wind in a tornado, in one direction) took down big hemlocks near the Fitch Trail off of Bee Hill Rd., and other trees on the Class of '33 Trail and at Harmon Pond. A windstorm in 2012 took out trees in the Hopkins Memorial Forest.

Insects can be devastating. The English elm beetle (now known as the European bark beetle) was found in town as early as 1901. But it was a fungus which caused the infamous Dutch Elm disease. Introduced in Boston in 1919, it began killing the elms along Main St. in Williamstown by the late 1940s. A huge elm on Main St. opposite Grundy Court was taken down in 1954: it was 85' tall, measured 4' in diameter, and was 118 years old. In the early 1960s elm trees still lined Main St. As late as 1978 the college campus still had several hundred specimen elms, and in 1982 undertook a major save-the-elms program, including removing thousands of dead trees and planting disease-resistant species. Later campaigns involved injections but these sometimes killed the trees. Big old diseased elms continued to be removed on Williams campus: in 1982 a 150-year-old elm was removed near the southeast corner of West College. Since 1988 seven more elms have been taken down on the Science Quad, including a 110-year-old tree, 40" in diameter, in 2005. In recent years the town has also had to remove elms, including big one in front of the Spirit Shop on Cole Ave. A fungus was also responsible for the chestnut blight, introduced in this country about 1907, and already common in Williamstown by 1917. American chestnut trees, with white flowers in July, were once very common in the woods around Williamstown. By one estimate, they constituted about 60% of the trees on south-facing slopes, and in the late

19th century up to 75% of the canopy, but by 1936 most of them were dead. Williamstown Rural Lands Foundation participates in a chestnut restoration program, sponsored by the American Chestnut Foundation, pinning its hopes on cross-breeding.

Tree planting

Trees have been cut down since Williamstown was founded. But early in the town's history new trees were also being planted – as ornamentals and boundary trees along town roads or defining the border of Southlawn Cemetery, est. 1769. Before the end of the 18th century Lombardy poplars were planted as an "avenue" along Main St., between West College and East College, reflecting a fashion found in towns throughout the country beginning in the 1780s. They survived into the 1840s. But poplars, fast-growing, tall, and columnar, had problems: the wood is weak, and limbs tended to break off. Beginning in 1840 they were replaced by Prof. Albert Hopkins and his Williams students, who on the annual "tree day" every year planted elms along Main St., South St., Hoxsey St., and Cole Avenue. Eventually five rows of elms stretched from Field Park east to Cole Avenue, forming a dense green canopy over the street. By the early 1940s there were an estimated 10,000 elm trees in town, along the streets, in back yards, and in the woods. Many of them survived into the 1960s. In the 1890s James Bullock planted a stand of Austrian pines on what we now know as Buxton Hill – many are still there. In 1908 Amos Lawrence Hopkins began planting a row of sugar maples along Northwest Hill Rd., and the survivors are now over a hundred years old. And in the 1960s Al Bachand began planting the spruces, which gave to the name to his upscale trailer park.

Tree planting was not just for landscaping. Farmers throughout the outlying areas planted apple trees by the hundreds, to supplement the income of their small subsistence farms, or to provide cider that might be turned into "apple jack" to warm up a cold winter evening. By about 1800 the Hickox family had planted 1000 apple trees on Bee Hill and the Prindle family another 1000 on Birch Hill. Survivors from these and other old orchards are found all over town even today. In the 1920s and 30s Col. Prentice planted 1200 apple trees on his Mount Hope Farm, and made selling apples one of the sidelines to his cow- and poultry-breeding operation. (He also planted elm trees in front of the mansion he called Elm Tree House.) The Kalarama Orchards in the northeast part of town planted apple trees, along with peach, plum, pear, and cherry trees, from 1921 into the 1960s, but the orchards are now gone. More recently the owner of Green River Farms planted a substantial dwarf apple orchard along Rt. 7, across from the high school.

The college also invested in ornamental trees. In 1912 it planted 400 red oaks in a nursery near present-day Cole Field, planning to plant a double row along Stetson Rd., to create an avenue leading to the railroad station at the north end of Cole Avenue, so that students and visitors, arriving at the train station, might then enjoy a more salubrious approach to the campus, and could avert their eyes from the unpicturesque "mill village" along Cole Avenue. In 1913 the college planted 1200 conifers and 100 beeches in the nursery. Many of the red oaks were planted on Stetson Rd., but an aerial photo from 1938 suggests that they did not form a continuous avenue.

Reforestation

The deliberate planting of trees accounts for only a small portion of the trees in Williamstown now. Most have grown up through the natural process of reforestation. In 1800, after a period of rapid clearing, it has been estimated that 33% of Williamstown was tree-covered. By 1830 the percentage was up to 40%. By mid-century is was probably higher, as small farms were abandoned. But second-growth cutting in the later 19th century, especially for fuel for wood-burning locomotives and for charcoal kilns, left tree cover in 1890 at about 34%, and from there it increased to 64% in 1953. Reforestation is more advanced in some places than others, for example, in Treadwell Hollow and parts of Hopkins Memorial Forest, which used to be farmland, and on the slopes of Greylock, once clearcut for woodpulp. More recent examples are found on Stone Hill, where a series of aerial photos shows that tree cover increased significantly from 1935 to 2015, and in the open fields along the Taconic Trail, where shrubs and trees have come back after annual brushcutting stopped.

Reforestation is the natural process, only held back by farmers, who plow every year, or cut hay, or graze horses and cattle; by landowners who cut former farm fields once or twice a year to keep them open; and by land trusts such as Williamstown Rural Lands Foundation and The Trustees of Reservations, which cut fields they own in order to preserve their "rural character." And trees will not grow in some harsh conditions, on the top of Berlin Mountain or East Mountain, for example, where the soil was burned by recurrent fires and where strong winds discourage anything more than low shrubs. As the first travelers to this region noticed, trees on the summit of Mt. Greylock don't grow tall, their growth stunted by the fierce winds and thin soil. Where trees are allowed to return, they follow standard "succession" patterns studied by biologists: first aspen, white pine, and paper birch: then red maple and red oak; then beech and hemlock; then sugar maple, as forests approach a "climax" state.

As biologists well know, forests are always changing, as individual trees produce offspring via seeds (or root sprouts), mature, and die. Trees (and communities of trees) actively compete with each other for sunlight, some species spreading, others declining. Disturbances represent a threat to some trees but an opportunity to others. Biologists are as interested in small young trees as they are in big old ones. (Landscapers are said to like best adolescent trees – not too big, not too small.) I think the rest of us – amateur tree-lovers – are particularly drawn to big or old trees. Tulip trees can live as long as 200 years, as can elms, sycamores, and red oaks. Ash trees can make it to 250, white oaks to 300, sugar maples, red spruce, and hemlocks to 400 years and more. And since the days of settlement Williamstown has had its share.

Big trees

There was once an "immense willow tree" on low ground south of West College, and probably south of Walden St. It was already huge when Williams students met under it in 1806. It was damaged by lightning in 1864, but its descendants grew up by 1900 to form a willow grove. One of the largest trees in Williamstown was a huge hemlock, cut down in 1871. It was determined, through ring-counting, to have begun growing about 1517. A section of this tree, "bound with an iron hoop," was placed by Albert Hopkins in the White Oaks Chapel, later removed, and subsequently lost. A "thick grove" of big old maples was to be seen in 1806 in what was called "Sloan's Meadow," near present-day Mission Park, and was still there a hundred years later. "Old Hickory," a hickory tree planted by Bissell Sherman on E. Main St. in 1828, in front of "old Mather Place" (at the corner of Cole and Main) to honor the election of Andrew Jackson, was still there in 1899.

When a big old tree came down, it was a big event. A huge elm tree on the Fowler farm (later owned by Elmer Sweet and then the Galushas) on Blair Rd., 160' tall, 24-27' in circumference, with three limbs more than 100' from the ground, was said by some local observers to have been hit by a fragments of a meteor in August 1892. Three months later, on Nov. 4, four days before the presidential election that brought Grover Cleveland back into the White House, the so-called "meteor elm" burst into flame: a clear sign, some people said, of something important about to happen. Professor Brainerd Mears from the college examined the tree, and opined that it had been hit by lightning, and that fire had smoldered inside the tree for three months before erupting into flame. One old-timer says he remembers seeing the stump of the tree in the 1930s.

The so-called "Stevens Pine" on the old Stevens farm on Water St., later called Pine Tree Farm, cut down in December 1924, more than 5' in diameter, and 12' in circumference, was thought to have been more than 125 years old. It was said to have been planted by the sons of the Reverend Seth Swift, first pastor of the Congregational Church, in the 1790s. When a huge willow tree, 75' tall, one stem 6' in diameter, the other 5 ½', on South St. near what is now Garfield House fell after a storm in July 1938, the event made the local paper.

Several other big old elm trees had such local fame that they also acquired names. The Hancock Elm (also called the Bryant Elm), 78" in diameter, once stood on the west side of the Hancock Road, near the town line. The tree was apparently removed in the early 1950s, when Hancock Rd. was relocated to straighten out a bend. At one time it was the oldest tree in the county. The famous "Perry Elm," planted in 1859 by Arthur Latham Perry at the site of the old Fort Massachusetts in North Adams, was often photographed. After about a hundred years the tree was seriously declining. Its felling in 1970 was the occasion for a newspaper story and photo. The "Guiden Elm" on the Guiden Farm on Oblong Rd. was cut down in the mid-1970s. In 1959, when it was still healthy, the tree was 7' in diameter, 22' in circumference.

Those trees are gone, but a number of old trees survive. There is a big elm in front of Tunnel City, and a sycamore with a diameter of 6' at the corner of Main St. and Southworth St. Many of the biggest trees are on the Williams College campus, including a line of red oaks planted in 1912 along Stetson Rd., near the college's Field House. Because they are growing in the open, and are not shaded by adjacent buildings, their crowns are lower and wider than the ten red oaks in the Freshman Quad, planted in the late 1920s, after Sage Hall was completed in 1923. Two of the oaks in the freshman quad are showing signs of decline. There used to be two big tulip trees perhaps 100' tall and 70+ years old, on the campus near Lehman Hall: one was taken down a few years ago, and the other one was taken down in 2019. Another big one grows nearby on Whitman St. A row of English elms, including some replacement trees, stands on the south side of Stetson Hall. There are five big

American elms on college property: one on the driveway leading up to the mansion at Mount Hope, one just west of the president's house, one in front of Goodrich Hall, one on the corner of West College, and one street tree on South St. Many of these trees are included in a guide to "Notable Trees in Williamstown," published in 2020.

Other big trees are found away from the campus. There is a big red oak in front of the Manton Building at the Clark Art Institute, and a beautiful maple south of the reflecting pool. There are seven big red oaks at Field Park, a giant red oak and elm at the southern end of Stone Hill Rd., a huge white oak on Bridges Rd., and old hemlocks, some more than 200 years old, in Torrey Woods and Flora's Glen, and some more than 300 years old near the old Cold Spring (on Cold Spring Rd.). There is a ring of old sugar maples near the top of Bee Hill – Perry says that the hill was named by early settlers who found honeybees in the maples. At the north end of Luce Rd. is an old bur oak, with a diameter of 67" and a circumference of about 18'. It's more than 300 years old, and is probably the "state champion" for its species. Behind the old Williams Inn (across from Field Park) are three old dwarfish Camperdown elms (the so-called "umbrella tree," low and squat), reportedly planted in the 1890s by Harley Proctor behind his mansion, at a time when they were fashionable.

Many of the oldest trees are further away from the town center. The 12-acre "Beinecke Stand" in Hopkins Memorial Forest (named after the donor of the land, Walter Beinecke), east of Northwest Hill Rd., contains its biggest and oldest trees, red oak, sugar maples, beech, and ash, some of them more than 250 years old. On the northwest slopes of Mt. Greylock are found 150 acres of old-growth red spruce, the only such stand in southern New England, some of them 120' tall and 200 years old, visible from as far away as Oblong Rd. The "flagship specimen" (the height champion, and the tallest accurately-measured red spruce in New England), 133.5' tall in 2005, fell in 2006. On the high slopes of Greylock are also found Eastern Hemlocks, some of them 170' tall and 350 years old, the tallest quaking aspen in Massachusetts, and a white ash 10 ½ ' in circumference, and as much as 275 years old. Elsewhere on Greylock are old-growth hemlocks on the Deer Hill Trail, and the state champion red spruce, accessible nearby, via the Roaring Brook Trail.

Trees Today

Many of the big, old trees of Williamstown are dying before our eyes. In 2002 there were 24 American elms on town property. In late 2018 there were maybe ten. In recent years big elms have had to be taken down on Cole Avenue, in front of the Spirit Shop, and even on Elm Street). In August 2018 an old elm in front of the '62 Center on the Williams campus was removed, and in August 2020 a huge elm on the Berkshire Quad died from Dutch Elm disease and was taken down. Elms along Ide Rd. are dying. A big maple on the college's Science Quad came down just a few years ago, and a huge willow behind the Maple Terrace Motel fell in November 2016.

Trees are affected not only by fungal disease, but also by insects: the emerald ash borer is threatening the ash trees; the woolly adelgid, which attacks hemlocks, is not yet in Williamstown but is coming this way. The Asian long-horned beetle, now being found in Worcester, attacks sugar maples, already stressed from decades of acid rain. Trees also decline from human causes: from the salt or calcium chloride we spread on roads in the winter that washes into the soil; from soil compaction caused especially by construction traffic; and from the cutting of roots required for installation of underground utility lines.

But the town, the college, and the Clark are also trying to maintain and replace trees. The town, actively replacing street trees, is substituting red maples for sugar maples. In 2017 it planted Holmstead elms on Main St. in front of Griffin Hall. But a limited budget for tree care means that the town will not be able to replace all the street trees that are removed. The college, which has about 5000 trees on its 700-acre campus is constantly replanting. For more than 25 years it has been replacing American elms with other elm species (Valley Forge elms, Liberty elms, Princeton elms). The Clark has in recent years planted 1000 trees on its campus as part of the Stone Hill Center and Clark Center projects, and plans further reforestation around the Lunder Center. Like the college, the Clark has the resources and the determination to replace diseased or dying specimen trees.

What will happen to all the dying and dead trees out in the woods? Under current policy at the Greylock Reservation, Hopkins Forest, and the Clark, dead trees will be allowed to fall and rot. On some other property dead trees can be harvested. The state currently provides some financial incentives for burning biomass to create steam. (A proposal in 2010 to build a biomass plant in Pownal met strong community opposition in Williamstown.)

Environmentalists and others worry that burning wood will increase CO_2 emissions and air pollution, and may lead to clear cutting. Loggers would like to harvest "mature" trees, encouraging younger ones to grow up and replace them. Some environmentalists argue that mature trees in fact are still growing, and are responsible for a significant part of carbon sequestration. From that point of view, it's better to let old trees grow. In fact, the more trees the better. (This point has implications for anybody who manages land – land trusts, farmers, people with woodlots, old farm fields, or even big back yards.)

Most of the biggest and oldest trees in town are on protected land – in the Greylock Reservation, and in Hopkins Forest, or on the campuses of the college and the Clark – and are thus safe from loggers. That's the good news for those who love old trees. The bad news, especially for those who like sugar maples, is that trees are also affected by human-induced climate change. Some experts predict that as the Berkshires get warmer, and some species do less well than others, our predominantly maple-birch-beech forest will gradually become an oak-hickory forest. If so, a slow farewell to reds, hello to browns.

In 2019 the Pulitzer Prize for fiction was awarded to a book called *The Overstory,* by Richard Powers. It's about a group of activists who try to stop logging of old-growth redwoods in the Pacific Northwest. But more deeply it's about the strange life of trees – how they can be said to form communities, communicating with each other and with us. As our climate inexorably changes, they may be trying to tell us something.

PART 2

THE TOWN
AND
THE COLLEGE

Portrait of *David Noble*, after William Jenyns (c. 1796). Courtesy of Williams College Museum of Art.

Chapter 7

—⚮—

ENEMIES OF THE PEOPLE:

Political Divisions in Early Williamstown

If you consult the printed histories of Williamstown during the American Revolution, you will find it said that everybody in the town at that time was a "Patriot," that is, a supporter of the Revolution. And as is well known, Williamstown men fought for the Patriot side at Bunker Hill in 1775, at White Plains in 1776, and at Bennington in 1777. Other Williamstown men, serving under then-loyal Benedict Arnold, helped capture Fort Ticonderoga in May 1775.

It is sometimes suggested that it's easy to understand why everybody was then a Patriot. Williamstown was far from the center of British colonial government in Boston. Williamstown men had a strong military tradition, going back to the attacks on Fort Massachusetts in 1746 and on the West Hoosuck blockhouse in 1756. Sturdy farmers were ready to defend their homeland.

But these arguments are fallacious. Distance from Boston cuts both ways: Boston was also the center of Patriot activity, and the small independent farmers in Berkshire County shared little with the merchants and urban professionals in Boston. Military tradition also cuts both ways. In the French and Indian War, Williamstown men fought as loyal British subjects — against the *French*. Those who fought the British at Bennington during the Revolution were primarily motivated not to promote the revolution but to defend their farms.

According to the famous estimate by John Adams, at the time the Revolution broke out 1/3 of the country were Patriots, 1/3 were Loyalists, and 1/3 were neutral or disaffected, and ready to favor either side, whichever happened to seem to be winning (and the Patriots won few victories before the fall of 1777). Adams' estimate has been revised by contemporary historians, who suggest that perhaps 20% were Loyalists, 40% Patriots, and 40% neutral. In New England, where the Revolution started, Patriots probably made up a majority.

But there was in fact a strong Tory/Loyalist presence in Berkshire County, which was geographically and culturally closer to Albany — a pro-

British city – than to Boston. The extended Williams family, still powerful and influential throughout Berkshire County in the 1770s, was Loyalist. Ephraim Williams, the man after whom the town was named, died a loyal British soldier less than twenty years earlier. His cousin, Col. Israel Williams, former military commander of British forces in western Massachusetts, was the leader of the Tory party in Berkshire County. In 1774 Israel Williams and his son, William Williams, were seized by their Hatfield neighbors and compelled to sign a statement affirming their agreement with Patriot principles. Israel Williams was called before a public meeting in Pittsfield; he and his son were later jailed.

It would have been very surprising if there weren't a few citizens in Williamstown who shared the Loyalist sentiments of the Williams family. But because many of the leading families in town quickly aligned themselves with the Patriot cause by signing up for service in the Berkshire County militia or the "Berkshire Regiment" – including the Sloans, Kelloggs, Horsfords, Simonds, Smedleys, Strattons, Blairs, and Bakers – those with Loyalist sympathies probably kept those sentiments to themselves. Loyalists tended to be professional people (lawyers, doctors, and clergymen), colonial office-holders, merchants, or large landholders, but not all Loyalists were members of the colonial elite. As historians of Loyalism have shown, there were many different reasons why a colonist might remain loyal to the colonial government, ranging from political principle to economic interest, from membership in the Church of England to abhorrence at revolutionary violence, from temperament to engagement with social networks.

David Noble

One Williamstown resident who was thought to have Loyalist leanings was David Noble. Born in New Milford, CT in 1744, Noble graduated from Yale in 1764, studied law with a Yale-trained lawyer in Pittsfield, and arrived in Williamstown in 1770, where he set up as the town's first lawyer – perhaps that is *why* he moved to town. He quickly attracted notice, and soon became one the town's leading citizens. In 1773 he was elected a representative from Williamstown to the Massachusetts state Assembly. While Noble was serving, in the spring of 1773, the Assembly discovered some private letters by Gov. Thomas Hutchinson and Lt.-Gov. Andrew Oliver, who were then at odds with many colonists resentful of British taxation ever since the Stamp Act. In one of the letters Hutchinson noted that there would have to be "an abridgement of what are called English liberties." The Assembly concluded that the two colonial officials intended "to overthrow the constitution of this government and to introduce arbitrary power" and it condemned the letters by a nearly-unanimous vote of 101-5.

On June 16 the Assembly adopted a set of "resolves" condemning Hutchinson and Oliver, and petitioned the king to remove them. But at the same time the Assembly declared its loyalty and affection for King George, reflecting the views of most colonists at the time that they wished to remain "loving" British subjects. Noble voted against the petition, because, as he said later, "I had conceived too good an opinion" of Governor Hutchinson. Since the petition was approved by a vote of 82 to 12, Noble's nay vote would have been noticed – most of the other "nays" were known Loyalists. But there is no indication that anybody in Williamstown objected at the time: Berkshire County was still little affected by the activities of the Sons of Liberty in Boston.

Hutchinson was then embroiled in controversy, stirred up by radicals determined to assert the rights of colonists. Events rapidly unfolded over the next two years, and Massachusetts quickly moved toward a break from Britain, as a quick survey will show. In December 1773 came the Boston Tea Party, and in early 1774 the British response, a set of so-called "Coercive Acts" reaffirming British control of the province. Although a Pittsfield town meeting in January 1774 condemned the men who dumped tea in Boston Harbor, there was soon substantial opposition to the Coercive Acts. In May 1774 Hutchinson was replaced as governor by General Thomas Gage. In July a Berkshire County "Congress" was held in Stockbridge: Williamstown sent three delegates. In the fall of 1774 delegates from all thirteen colonies met as a "Continental Congress" and established a "Continental Association" to resist the "Coercive Acts," which they renamed the "Intolerable Acts." They began by imposing a trade boycott. In the spring of 1775 war broke out at Lexington and Concord, and then at Bunker Hill, where the Berkshire Regiment, under Capt. Samuel Sloan of Williamstown, saw action. In late April a Massachusetts Provincial Congress was convened in Boston; Williamstown sent Samuel Kellogg as its delegate, instructing him that the townspeople were ready "to join in the common cause of American liberty, and to assist with our lives and fortunes, as occasion may require, to maintain our rights and liberties against all the hostile attempts to deprive us of our rights and liberties, made by the cruel and oppressive Acts of the British Parliament." In July 1775, George Washington, now commander in chief of the Continental army, began the siege of British-occupied Boston. On August 23 King George signed a "Proclamation of Rebellion," calling on all loyal British subjects to suppress the rebellion by the so-called "Patriots" in the colonies, but also making clear to all undecided colonists that they should abandon hope of reconciliation.

The Continental Association had also called on every town to choose Committees of Correspondence, Safety, and Inspection to enforce the trade boycott, to keep an eye on all politically suspicious persons, and to publish information about them so that "all such foes of the rights of British America may be publicly known and universally condemned as the enemies of American liberty." Those under suspicion – and there were many known Tories in Pittsfield, Lanesboro, and Hancock – were to be shunned until they agreed to recant and conform. Williamstown set up a Committee of Correspondence, chaired by Isaac Stratton. Another member was probably Samuel Kellogg. Very little is known about this Committee. No written records have been found. Earlier historians were not even able to find out who the other members were. It has been suggested that the Committee kept no records, for fear that, should the Revolution fail, its members would be subject to reprisal. It has also been suggested that, assuming the committee *did* keep records, as did, for example, the Committee of Safety in Bennington, those records were subsequently destroyed, when political circumstances changed, to protect the privacy of those, like Noble, who were accused, or the privacy of the committee members, who did the accusing.

The Williamstown Committee was probably most active in the months after the Continental Association was established in late 1774, extending through the summer of 1777, when the outcome of the Revolution was still very much in doubt, and the British offensive in the Hudson River Valley had not yet been stopped, as it was at Bennington in August 1777 and Saratoga in September and October of that year. Some towns were so enthusiastic in their monitoring of Tory/Loyalist activity that they set up separate committees of Correspondence, of Safely, *and* of Inspection. So many town committees were established that in February 1776 the new Massachusetts House of Representatives passed a law providing that there be only one committee in each town charged with inspecting, public safety, and communicating with other committees.

The state legislature increased the pressure against suspected Tory sympathizers by passing anti-Loyalist legislation, authorizing fines, confiscation of land, imprisonment, and banishment. In May 1775 it passed a law providing that those "inimical to their country" who have left a town may not sell their land. In November 1775 another law provided that the General Court might seize and sell the property of any Tory who had fled.) On October 6 the Continental Congress approved a resolution calling on local committees of safety to "arrest and secure every person . . . whose going at large may . . . endanger the safety of the colony, or the liberties of America." Clearly this new legislation would have made anybody in Williamstown with Tory sympathies very nervous.

By October 1775, and probably not by coincidence, Noble was notified by the Committee of Correspondence in Williamstown that some of his fellow townsmen, remembering his actions in the state Assembly more than two years earlier, suspected that he still harbored "Tory" sympathies and was "inimical" to his country. He was probably suspected as well because it was known that in the 1760s he had studied law under Woodbridge Little in Pittsfield – and Little was a known Tory who had fled to New York State in April 1775, and was formally "proclaimed" an enemy of the people for having secretly communicated with the British forces in New York City. (Little himself recanted and took an oath of allegiance in 1777). Noble may also have come under suspicion because Benjamin and Francis Noble of Pittsfield, neither of whom were in fact related to him, had been denounced as Tories. (Both were formally banished in 1778). Perhaps anticipating that he would be called before the Williamstown Committee of Correspondence, on October 24 Noble voluntarily made a formal declaration that because he opposed the petition to remove Governor Hutchinson, whom he now called "that arch traitor to his Country," he had "deservedly forfeited" the "good esteem" of his neighbors; he confessed that he had "committed errours," but swore that he had "ever been a cordial friend to the liberties and true interest of America, so far as I understood it, and ever have conformed myself to the advice and directions of our several Congresses, and am determined for the future to unite, according to my abilities, in the defence of our common rights and privileges." The Committee of Correspondence met two days later, and, after accepting Noble's Declaration, presented it to a town meeting for further approval.

Noble's declaration apparently satisfied his neighbors, for at a town meeting later in October 1775 they concurred with the Committee of Correspondence in accepting it. In October 1780 the 36-year-old Noble did a brief stint of military service on behalf of the Patriots. But one historian wonders "whether he ever recovered the full confidence of his fellow-citizens until the war was over, even if he did then."

In fact, Noble seems to have been fully reintegrated into civil society in Williamstown. He continued his law practice, and apparently attained enough of a county-wide reputation that in 1781 he was hired to represent a prominent man in Sheffield with good Patriot credentials who had been sued by two escaped slaves, one of them Eliza Freeman, the once-famous "Mum Bet," who sought their freedom. (Noble's client lost that case.) He also established several mercantile businesses, and became a large landholder, acquiring most of the land – some 265 acres – on either side of what is now Cole Avenue from Main St. north to the Hoosic River. He bought a big brick house at 678 Main St.

Two other Loyalists were not so lucky, probably because they fled the country during the Revolution. A 1779 law provided that the land of exiles could be confiscated. In 1769 William Krigger had bought land at the confluence of Green River and Hopper Brook and had established one of the first mills in town.

Noble was one of three trustees who were residents of Williamstown. He was named the secretary of the board. Five of the nine trustees were Yale graduates. Several had Tory leanings during the 1770s. This reflected the political sentiments of the two co-trustees: both Israel Williams and John Worthington were quite public about their Loyalist tendencies, and both were compelled to renounce their Toryism. When it came time to select trustees to establish a free school, they chose a number of like-minded men. William Williams was a Loyalist during the Revolution. Little, as we have seen, was a Tory who later took an oath of allegiance. Daniel Collins from Lanesboro was one of the most outspoken Loyalists in the county.

Noble kept his head down. During Shays' Rebellion in 1787, when some 4000 subsistence farmers in Berkshire County mounted an armed revolt to protest demands that they raise cash to pay taxes –Williamstown was sharply divided on the rebellion – Noble seems not to have staked out a public position. In 1792 he was elected moderator of town meeting, apparently signaling that he had fully won back the trust of his neighbors, and in 1795 he was named a Judge of the county Court of Common Pleas. He was briefly drawn into the controversy surrounding the contested 1796 congressional election, but quickly denied any direct involvement. When the second meeting house was built in 1797, Judge Noble and his family, who had made the second highest subscription, were assigned the front pew on the left, a place of honor. After his death in 1803 Noble was remembered as "a man of activity and enterprise, of probity and intelligence." When his estate went through probate – the file can be viewed in Registry of Probate in Pittsfield – the inventory of his assets included more than 350 acres in Williamstown.

Federalists and Republicans in 1800

The divisions that split the town in the 1770s were largely but not completely healed by the time of the election of George Washington in 1788. Everybody now claimed to be a defender of the Revolution. But during the debates about the proposed federal constitution, a new division arose between Republicans and Federalists, related to but not the same as the split between Patriots and Loyalists. Some Patriots now lined up on the Republican side, some on the Federalist side. Those – like David Noble – who had Loyalist or Tory sympathies in the early 1770s now uniformly lined up with the conservative branch of the Federalists, especially during the 1800 presidential election that pitted the Federalist incumbent, John Adams, against the Republican candidate, Thomas Jefferson.

Divisions between the two parties, both locally and nationally, were already clear in 1796, when in a very close election Adams, who had been Washington's vice-president, was elected president. His running mate was Charles Pinckney, but Pinckney did not become vice-president. Under the election rules of the day, electors had two votes, and voted for two presidential candidates. The candidate who came in second was named vice -president. Jefferson, former Secretary of State in Washington's administration, and the Republican candidate, received 68 electoral votes to Adams' 71, and was therefore elected vice -president. In that election Williamstown voted overwhelmingly for Jefferson.

Distinctions between Federalists and Republicans had begun to emerge more clearly during the first Washington administration, when one group of men, with Hamilton as their intellectual leader, wanted to strengthen the executive branch, while the Republicans, who looked to Jefferson and Madison, feared a powerful executive and defended the rights and independence of the legislative branch. Republicans claimed to be the champions of the people; Federalists were wary of what they thought the wavering judgment of an easily swayed and deluded populace. Federalists tended to admire the British political system and wanted to promote an alliance and trade with Britain; Republicans were defenders of the French Revolution.   In Williamstown many of the prominent and professional men in town were Federalists, including Samuel Sloan of South Williamstown – he owned much of what is now Sloan Rd.– and was the largest landowner in town, and "Squire" William Starkweather, who married one of Sloan's daughters; he was a Justice of the Peace and town postmaster, and owned a large house in the north part of Williamstown. Other Federalists included David Noble, the town's leading lawyer, and his son in law, Daniel Dewey, Asa Burbank (one of the town's doctors), Seth Swift, the minister of the Congregational Church, and two long-time selectmen, Levi Smedley and Nehemiah Woodcock. Ebenezer Fitch, first president of the brand-new Williams College, was a Federalist, as were most of his trustees and faculty. (Fitch also had a personal reason for favoring the Federalists: his son, Jabez Fitch, named US Marshal for Vermont in 1788, was reappointed in 1792 and again by Federalist John Adams in 1796.)

Students at the college were apparently politically fickle. One member of the Class of 1797, a future minister, lamented that during his time at Williams – the middle-1790s – "the French Revolution was very popular with almost all the inmates of College," and that, alas, a number of them adopted "infidel" principles – his dismissive term for Deists like Jefferson and French-influenced freethinkers. (Williams did not become noted for its piety until after the religious revivals of the early 19th century). At the first commencement in 1795 one graduate presented an oration on the French Revolution. But by the summer of 1798 student opinion was solidly behind Adams and his anti-French policy.

The town, including most of the small farmers, was predominantly Republican. Some of the leading citizens were also Republicans, included Tompson J. Skinner and his brother, Benjamin. They owned and operated a large building company. Thomson Skinner was a Williams trustee; his brother Benjamin, who married the daughter of Benjamin Simonds, was a deacon in the church. The town's leading doctor, William Towner, was a Republican, as was Samuel Kellogg, who had been an active Patriot during the Revolution. At least two of the larger farmers and their families were Republicans– "Squire" William Young of South Williamstown, and Absalom Blair, who married a Young – he owned a farm on what is now Blair Rd. Young Ezekiel Bacon, trained as a lawyer, came from a strong Republican family from Pittsfield.

Political divisions were promoted by regional newspapers, which in those days were even more partisan than they are today. Republicans were likely to read the *Albany Register* or the *Vermont Gazette*, published in Bennington. Federalists turned to *Andrews' Western Star*, published in Stockbridge, or the *Berkshire Gazette*, published in Pittsfield, and even subscribed to national papers published in Philadelphia, where Congress sat. Because many of these early papers are now available through online data bases, it is possible to sample the intensity of political feelings in that era. In the *Western Star* in 1798 (when political tensions were high), a reader could find the Republicans branded as "Jacobins" (after the radicals who took over the French Revolution) and described as this country's "internal enemies," and "more dangerous" than the French themselves "because suspected but by few," and as "the enemies of our peace, of our government and of our independence." In the same year a Republican reader could find in the *Vermont Gazette* the charge that the Federalists, who have never liked the Bill of Rights, fought against the British during the Revolution because they secretly hoped to "build up a nobility and aristocracy of *themselves*, in America." And they have been joined by "the whole herd of Tories" who "have never given any proof of their repentance for siding with the British." In April 1799 the *Hampshire Gazette* (a Federalist paper published in Northampton) carried a story about the arrest of an "itinerant Jacobin" found carrying papers declaring that "the officers of Government, the Clergy and Lawyers are . . . enemies of the people."

Tompson Skinner

The leading Republican in town was Tompson J. Skinner. Born in Colchester, Connecticut, in 1752 and the son of a minister, he was apparently not destined for the ministry himself, and, unlike several other eminent Williamstown men of the day, did not go to Yale, or even attend college. In any event, his father having died when Skinner was only ten, he was reportedly apprenticed to a carpenter and joiner, and learned the building trade.

He married young, arrived in Williamstown in 1775 at the age of 23, and with his younger brother, Benjamin, set up initially as a merchant and then as a carpenter and began to prosper. In 1778 the Skinner brothers built a large tavern in what was then the center of town, on the northeast corner of Main St. and North St. Skinner himself lived in a big house on the site of what is now the Milne Library. During the Revolution he served in the militia, and remained an officer after the war, rising to the rank of Major-General. (He was known thereafter as General Skinner.) Beginning in 1781 he entered Massachusetts politics, serving almost continuously for twenty years in the state assembly or the state senate. He was apparently an effective campaigner – even his political opponents conceded that he knew how to reach "the people." In 1783 and '84 he reportedly argued and voted in favor of legislation that permitted the return of exiled Tories. He was elected a delegate to the federal constitutional convention in 1788 – he voted in favor.

He also served almost twenty years (1788-2007) on the Court of Common Pleas, which met regularly in Lenox. In 1785, in recognition of his stature, he was named one of the original trustees of the Ephraim Williams donation, and was then named one of the original trustees of the Free School established in 1791 and (as noted earlier) of Williams College in 1793. He and his brother were responsible for building West College, the first college building, and the largest structure in town, in 1790. Skinner went on to be the first Treasurer of the college (1793-98), and when the town decided to build a new meeting house for the Congregational Church, Skinner's subscription of 100 pounds in 1796 was the largest amount pledged. Skinner Brothers went on to build the second meeting house as well as East College, both of them completed in 1798. In that year he could be called "the most prominent citizen in the town."

Not surprisingly, Skinner became interested in national politics. He first ran for Congress in 1788, losing to Theodore Sedgwick, a prominent lawyer in Stockbridge. Skinner ran again in 1790, 1792, and 1794, winning easily in Williamstown, but Sedgwick, drawing votes in South County, held on to his seat, though his margin of victory in 1794 was razor thin. Meanwhile, Skinner ran as a presidential elector in 1792, casting his votes for Washington and Adams. In 1796 the Congressional seat was open, Sedgwick having resigned to take appointment to an open Senate seat. Skinner took advantage of the opportunity and won the 1796 congressional election.

Although Williamstown and several other towns in North County, notably Adams and Cheshire, supported Jefferson in the presidential election that year, Skinner did not run openly as a Republican or as a supporter of Jefferson, perhaps because he knew that Federalists were strong in South County. His friends, campaigning for him, assured voters that he was a supporter of Federalist policies, and would in effect continue in the tradition of Theodore Sedgwick. They even got Williams President Fitch to publish a letter in the *Western Star*, a Federalist newspaper, certifying that to his knowledge Skinner (whom he knew well from the Williams board) in both his public and private conversation had supported the recently ratified and controversial Jay Treaty with Great Britain – a treaty favored by pro-British Federalists and opposed by pro-French Republicans.

Other letters in the *Western Star* claimed that Skinner was not really a Federalist, that he was known to admire Republican leaders and that, despite what President Fitch had certified, had been heard to declare his strong disapproval of the Jay Treaty, and to have "uniformly condemned the most prominent measures of the Federal Government" after he was elected,46 Skinner took his seat and soon revealed his Republican colors. When he lined up with the Jeffersonians, President Fitch was apparently embarrassed and chagrined for having provided Skinner any support, and Skinner's political opponents accused him of running under a "mask of Federalism."

As a congressman, Skinner was initially a close ally of Jefferson, and shared Jefferson's suspicions of the Federalists as crypto-monarchists. On January 5, 1798, while Skinner was living at Francis's Hotel in Philadelphia, where Congress was in session, he passed on to Jefferson (who also lived at Francis's) a report on "consultations" in 1787, prior to the Constitutional Convention, by Alexander Hamilton and his Federalist allies in New York and "the Eastern states", "on the subject of seizing on the powers of a government & establishing them by force." This clearly shows that Skinner in 1798 was a close ally of Jefferson. How would Skinner have heard of these conspiratorial "consultations"? Perhaps in Boston, during a session of the Massachusetts state senate while Skinner was serving there. In February Skinner voted in support of fellow-Republican Matthew Lyon, a Vermont printer, who came to blows on the floor of the House with a Connecticut Federalist.

But in the spring of 1798 an international crisis put the Republicans on the defensive. Negotiations with France to settle commercial disputes in the wake of the Jay Treaty broke off when French demands for a bribe were revealed – this was the so-called XYZ Affair. Federalists, warning of a French invasion, called for a military build-up. Skinner, remembering the many Federalist voters in Berkshire County, may have come to regret his outspoken praise of the French Republic, went home to check the political temperature. By April a local Federalist was crowing that the "Frenchified Democrats" in North County seemed to be "a little puzzled" at how to respond to French demands for money, and were not agreed "in what way to . . . vindicate the conduct of their [French] friends." On May 23 Skinner was absent from Congress, and thus did not vote with his Republican colleagues in opposing a Federalist bill authorizing the seizure of French ships.

Jefferson suspected him, along with other absent Republicans, of "desertion." Skinner was still in Williamstown in the middle of June, when four Williams students, claiming to speak for the entire student body, wrote a letter to President John Adams, expressing their condemnation of the French as atheists and imperialists, and supporting Adams as he considered going to war against France. At the suggestion of Daniel Dewey, the letter was presented to Adams by Senator Theodore Sedgwick, then serving as President pro tem of the Senate. Adams actually answered the letter, thanking the students for their support. Skinner is not recorded as speaking or voting on the controversial Alien and Sedition Acts, approved by a Federalist-dominated Congress in late June and early July. (Whether he stayed away for fear of offending either his Republican colleagues or his Federalist constituents, or whether he was tending to business at home, where Skinner Brothers was finishing up two major buildings, is not known.) By mid-July a Williamstown Federalist reported with glee to a fellow Federalist that Skinner "never in his life suffered as much mortification as he has experienced here for some weeks past – almost every man who has any pretensions to information, those particularly who live in the town street [i.e., in the big houses on Main St.], and all the officers of College, treat his political sentiments with the utmost contempt." Even if we discount this partisan rhetoric, it's pretty clear that Skinner had stirred up the Federalists to oppose him fiercely at the next election.

Skinner in fact declined to run in 1798. At county caucuses in the fall Republican leaders decided to support John Bacon, even though they thought Skinner was the best man, because Bacon, from Stockbridge, would probably run better in South County. When Federalists persuaded Sedgwick to run again for his old seat, many Republicans apparently concluded that the best way to prevent the election of a "high" Federalist like Sedgwick was to support a moderate one, the lawyer Thomas Ives, from Great Barrington. Even Republicans in Williamstown cast more votes for Ives than for the Republican candidate, but Sedgwick won big in South County, and regained his old seat. It was the high tide of the Congressional Federalists.

In May 1799 Skinner tried for state senate. Now that anti-French feeling had subsided, he campaigned as a friend of the French republic. He won easily in Williamstown but lost county-wide to a Federalist. As the 1800 election approached Skinner was out of elected office for the first time in twenty years.

Daniel Dewey

In 1800 Daniel Dewey was the most politically active and ambitious Federalist in Williamstown. Born in Sheffield, MA in 1766, he spent two years at Yale without taking a degree (not unusual in his day) and then "read law" with Theodore Sedgwick at his office in Stockbridge, and joined the bar in 1787. Perhaps it was Sedgwick, or Sedgwick's old friend and fellow-lawyer, David Noble, who suggested that Williamstown needed the services of another lawyer. Dewey arrived in Williamstown in 1790, where he boarded in Noble's house. Two years later Dewey married Noble's daughter, Mariah. He was also named town attorney. A year after that, no doubt with the support of his father-in-law, one of the original trustees of Williams, Dewey was appointed Secretary of Williams College, serving for five years, and then another five years as college treasurer (succeeding Tompson Skinner in that office).

Dewey also kept in touch with Sedgwick, who by 1796 had emerged as the leading Federalist in Berkshire County, representing the county first in Congress and then representing Massachusetts in the U.S. Senate. Eleven letters from Dewey to Sedgwick survive in the Sedgwick Family Papers at the Massachusetts Historical Society. Written from 1798 to 1806, the letters deal primarily with national and state politics, showing that Dewey was very well informed on political matters and very committed to conservative Federalist principles. It does not appear that Sedgwick had asked Dewey to serve as his eyes and ears in Williamstown. Instead, it was probably Dewey who initiated the correspondence, seeking a political patron and perhaps hoping, at age 32, to inherit the political legacy of the 52-year-old Sedgwick. The letters rarely tell Sedgwick anything he would not already have known, from his own contacts in Philadelphia or in Williamstown, where Sedgwick still served on the Williams board of trustees. Rather they serve to display that Dewey held "high" Federalist opinions, especially about the treacherous French and their American friends, the scheming, underhanded, and even seditious Republicans, whom he routinely describes (in good Federalist style) as "Democrats" or "Jacobins."

In April 1798, after the revelation of the XYZ Affair, Dewey denounced the leaders of the French republic as "a gang of abandoned Robbers, Murderers and Assassins, as ever disgraced the character of man." And he denounced their American supporters as "Frenchified Democrats" and "Demagogues." In June he told Sedgwick about the letter to President Adams, drawn up by the Williams students. (It was at Dewey's suggestion that Sedgwick himself presented the letter to Adams.) He again reported, as he had in April, that although Republican sentiment was strong in Williamstown – "I believe that no part of the United States exhibits more of the true Spirit of Sans-culotism than this corner of Massachusetts" – he was confident that honest and well-informed people were coming over to the Federalist side. (Dewey would continue these hopeful predictions even as the Federalists were swamped in the 1800 elections.) He seemed to find it inexplicable that intelligent voters might prefer the Republicans: he regards them as "uninformed and credulous," the "dupes of artful and designing men." And he took pleasure in reporting the "mortification" of Skinner at a time when anti-French sentiment was perhaps at its peak, even in Williamstown.

Dewey expressed support for the Alien and Sedition Acts, passed by the Federalist-dominated Congress on June 18, dismissing Republican complaints as "treason and sedition," and declaring that the so-called "liberty of the press" was in fact a means to disseminate "slander and licentiousness." But he also complained that he was "surrounded with Jacobins and Jacobinical newspapers, pamphlets, etc. on every side," and asked Sedgwick to send him some "good Federal papers" from Philadelphia. Dewey was pleased with the election results that fall, when Federalists regained the Berkshire County congressional seat, and his mentor Sedgwick replaced the reviled Skinner. In December he was pleased to think that Skinner, who was finishing out his term, could see "nothing very pleasing to him in prospect . . . during the present Session" of Congress, but had to acknowledge that Skinner's "partizans" in Williamstown "discover the utmost bitterness and malignity against the Government and its supporters." And by February 1799 he was a little nervous that, the fear of a French invasion having subsided, Federalist proposals to raise an army and build a navy were losing support.

The election of 1800

The story of the famous presidential election of 1800, when the Republicans ended twelve years of Federalist rule, has been often told. John Adams and Charles Pinckney again ran against Thomas Jefferson and Aaron Burr. But on this occasion Jefferson and Burr gained more electoral votes than Adams or Pinckney. Because Jefferson and Burr received the same number of votes, the election was thrown into the House of

Representatives, where Jefferson was finally elected President.

What is less well known is how Williamstown reacted to the election results. Daniel Dewey's response was not surprising. In December 1800, a week after the voting had concluded and Jefferson and Burr were tied, he wrote to Sedgwick that "should Jefferson be elected I anticipate the most serious and alarming evils to this Country." And in January 1801 he saw the forthcoming ballot in the House as a choice between two "evils." The election of Burr would "mortify" the Republicans, but "can the Government go on under the administration of a President" – the shifty Aaron Burr – " in whom no one of any party has the least confidence?" (What Dewey could not know is that Sedgwick, had been secretly lobbying fellow Federalists to vote for Burr so as to defeat the even-more-hated Jefferson.)

As it happened, the House went through 36 ballots in February before some last-minute negotiations led to a Jefferson victory on February 17. He was inaugurated a little over two weeks later. On the night of his inauguration, March 4, 1801, President Fitch of Williams College, a fierce Federalist, held a small dinner. The guests included two or three Federalists, apparently tutors at the college, along with Isabella Blair, daughter of a local Republican family. According to a story handed down in the Blair family through the 19th century, the men at the table repeated "some of the vile and foul scandals and slanders of the late campaign . . in relation to the private life of Jefferson." (Federalist writers claimed that Jefferson was both a Frenchified philosophe and a libertine.) Miss Blair, offended at their talk, declared at the table that "You may be good scholars, but you are no gentlemen."

Fitch himself had a personal stake in the outcome of the election: on the morning after the dinner, Jefferson, in one of his first official acts, removed Fitch's son as U.S. Marshal in Vermont, for "cruel conduct" toward Matthew Lyon, a Republican congressman and a printer, who had been convicted in October 1798 under the Sedition Act. (The printer was thrown into what was described in a local broadside as a loathsome prison, and treated with barbarity by the "hard-hearted savage," Marshal Fitch – described by a recent scholar as an "arch-Federalist." While in jail in Vermont in the fall of 1798, Lyon was reelected to his seat by incensed Republican voters.)

Three months later the outraged Miss Blair would have been more pleased with the celebration of the Fourth of July in Williamstown. An oration delivered by the young Republican lawyer, Ezekiel Bacon, while in the spirit of the occasion it avoided the bitter polemic that characterized the politics of that year, in an unmistakeably partisan manner made it clear that it was the followers of Jefferson who were true to the spirit of the Declaration of Independence, His election, Bacon hoped, "will heal the wounds of a bloody country."

But three months after that, at the September 2, 1801 Williams College commencement, more partisan Federalist sentiment was heard. The program included an "Oration" from one of the college tutors, "On the Emigration of Foreigners into This Country," in which the speaker declaimed vehemently against "unprincipled foreign 'Runagates'" who now held positions of influence in the U. S. , clearly pointing at Jefferson's Secretary of the Treasury, Albert Gallatin, a Swiss-born naturalized American citizen. In an "Oration on Foreign Influence," a graduating senior denounced "French Jacobins, United Irishmen, and Modern Philosophists, holding infidel and atheistic opinions," who helped decide the election of President Jefferson. And in a "Poem, on Infidel Philosophy," another new graduate somehow found it appropriate in a commencement oration to smear the "modern philosopher" as a libertine who beholds "a naked woman, displayed in all her native charms" and asserts his "claim to the same open sexual intercourse, as brutes indulge in.

Three weeks later the *Pittsfield Sun* (a Republican newspaper) printed a letter "To the President and Trustees of Williams College," from one who called himself "Cato," protesting that "the Republican part" of the commencement audience "were disgusted with the general complection of the [commencement] performances, so far as they related to politics." The orations, the letter writer complained, were "jaundiced by prejudice and embittered with the gall of party." The poem on "Infidel Philosophy," so one of the insulted ladies in the audience observed, "was not fit to be pronounced any where but in a brothel." So offensive was the language that, according to Cato, "several HUNDREDS of his hearers left the house with disgust, while he was speaking."

The Republican who wrote to the *Sun* noted that at least one of the students at the college, the son of Jefferson's Secretary of War, would have been deeply offended by the orations, and reported that he understood "that several young gentlemen, who were to have entered [the college] this very year, have on this account declined entering." Several pro-Jefferson students in fact did drop out.

The later careers of Skinner and Dewey

The election of 1800 signaled a change in national politics: no Federalist after John Adams was elected to the presidency, and the Federalists never again controlled a majority in the legislative branch. (Federalists, appointed by Washington and Adams, were still numerous in the judiciary.) Republicans, later known as Democratic Republicans, were in the ascendant, with huge majorities in both house and senate. Neither Skinner nor Dewey was a candidate in 1800. In the Berkshire County congressional election, Republican John Bacon ran again, and this time beat Federalist Ephraim Williams. (Williamstown voted overwhelmingly for Bacon, 186-44.) Perhaps because of the Republican tide, Skinner returned to politics, elected to the Governor's Council in 1801 and then running again in 1802 for the Congressional seat he had briefly held in the 1790s, this time defeating the Federalist Daniel Dewey by a margin of nearly 500 votes. A letter endorsing him as a friend of "Liberty, Virtue, Oeconomy and Peace" appeared in the new pro-Republican newspaper, the *Pittsfield Sun*. In Williamstown, he beat Dewey by 182-33, demonstrating that he had not lost the support of his fellow townspeople. In 1802 Skinner tried for a seat in the U.S. Senate, but lost to Federalist John Quincy Adams, who received major support in the Boston area. Before his congressional term was up, Skinner resigned his seat and in December 1804 accepted an appointment from Jefferson to be the U. S Marshal for Massachusetts. And in 1806, in a Republican landslide, he was elected state Treasurer. But his career did not end well. In 1808 irregularities were discovered in state accounts, and it came out that Skinner had in effect taken some $60,000 in state funds to pay off old personal debts from a 1790s property deal, and neglected to return them. Skinner retired in disgrace. The political atmosphere was still rancorous, and Federalist newspapers denounced Skinner and the Republicans in familiarly vehement terms. Within a year Skinner was dead, at age 55.

Dewey's career after 1800 also had its ups and downs. Despite the swing toward the Republicans, Dewey decided to run for political office himself as a conservative Federalist. He tried nine times for the state senate, but lost every time. In 1802 he ran for Congress, losing to Skinner. Two other Federalists also ran against him that year, splitting the vote. A Federalist newspaper also feebly claimed that stormy weather on Election Day had suppressed the Federalist turnout.

Dewey also lost to Skinner's Republican successors for the next four congressional elections. Perhaps because he was such an outspoken Federalist and so intemperate in his political opinions, he did not broaden his narrow base of support, losing in Williamstown in 1804 by 173 to 57 and 1806 by 93 to 5. Finally, in 1812, Dewey was elected to Congress, in a year when Federalists in Massachusetts benefitted from opposition to the War of 1812, which they characterized as "Mr. Madison's War." (Madison, a Republican, had succeeded Jefferson in 1808.) But even in that election he lost in Williamstown, 127-100. Like Skinner, he resigned his seat before his term was over, following in the steps of his old friend, Theodore Sedgwick, in accepting appointment by the Federalist governor to the state Supreme Court in 1814 — an appointment probably made at least in part as a reward for long and loyal service to the Federalist cause.

Although Dewey did not have much political support in Williamstown, he still had powerful and influential friends at the college. In 1803 he was elected a trustee, and in 1812 was also appointed Professor of Law. In the same year he bought a big house at 678 Main Street — on the northeast corner of Main St. and Southworth St. — it's still there today — about 500 yards west of the house where his father in law, David Noble, had lived until his death in 1803. He continued as Treasurer of the College until 1814 when he had to give up that office in order to go on the Supreme Court. But Justice Dewey did not long enjoy his reward. He died in 1815, at the age of 49.

Epilogue

Political divisions were bitter and contentious, but Williamstown was a small town, and people knew they would be running into each other every day, and had to learn to get along. Federalists in Williamstown tended to be from the economic-social elite, but as example of Jefferson himself shows, many of the Republicans were wealthy and educated, from the same social world as Federalists. This was true in Williamstown too, as can be shown by a couple of examples.

In 1792, as noted earlier, one of Federalist David Noble's daughters married the fierce Federalist Daniel Dewey. But in 1786 Noble's daughter Salome married Joshua Danforth of Pittsfield, who was a prominent Republican. And in 1803 another daughter became the second wife of Benjamin Skinner, the brother of that arch-Republican Tompson Skinner.

Dewey and Skinner, along with David Noble and Theodore Sedgwick, had to work together on the Williams College board of trustees. In 1798 Dewey and Skinner again worked together as lawyer and trustee over some local business. The Federalist Dewey drew up a second-marriage agreement between Benjamin Simonds (whose daughter was the first wife of Skinner's brother) and a local widow; her trustee in case she survived her new husband was the Republican Tompson Skinner. But the executor of Simonds' estate was the Federalist Daniel Dewey.

Perry, who comments that the bitter political divisions spilled over into social and family life, tells the story that the Federalists, reluctant to consult Republican Dr. Towner, who had a wide and respected practice, invited a Federalist, Dr. Remembrance Sheldon, to settle in town because of their strong "social prejudice against Democrats." Sheldon's practice thrived, but Perry reports that when Federalists were really sick they consulted old Dr. Towner.

Detail (head of George Chadwell) from *100 Years at Williams College* (1989), by Faith Ringgold (American: 1930-). Acrylic paint on canvas, with printed and pieced fabric. 86 3/4 x 120 in. (220.3 x 304.8 cm). Williams College Museum of Art, Williamstown, MA. (89.7). Museum purchase, John B. Turner '24 Memorial Fund, Kathryn Hurd Fund, Karl E. Weston Memorial Fund. Courtesy of Artists Rights Society.

Chapter 8

—⚉—

THE CHADWELLS OF WILLIAMSTOWN

It's not widely known that African-Americans have lived in Williamstown since the 18th century. Until about 1970, when Williams College actively began to diversify first its student body and then its faculty and staff, they rarely made up more than about 3% of the population. When local historians noticed their presence, they typically focused on notable individuals and eccentric "characters" rather than families. But there have always been extended Black families in town, and beginning in the late 19th century those families began to establish themselves and to form a nascent Black community.

One of the most remarkable of those families are the Chadwells. One of their number, George Montgomery Chadwell, was an exceptional man, graduating from Williams College in 1900 – one of the college's earliest Black graduates – and began a distinguished career as an educator. Because opportunities for African-Americans were sharply limited in a New England country town, the other members of his immediate family led much more modest lives. But they became a significant part of an emerging Black community in Williamstown in the first decades of the 20th century. Chadwell descendants have remained in Williamstown for four generations, and a number of those in the third and fourth generation, like their distinguished forebear, are college graduates.

The first Chadwells arrived in Williamstown in the 1890s. Emma, William, George, Harry, and Martha Chadwell – three brothers and two sisters – came up from Great Barrington. Their father was George William Riley Chadwell (1839-78), born in Kentucky, and probably enslaved there. During the Civil War, like many in Kentucky, he was either freed, or escaped to Union lines, and managed to go north to Massachusetts, where in January 1864 he enlisted in the 5th Massachusetts Colored Cavalry – they were Black soldiers, two thirds of them former slaves, with white officers. Back in Kentucky he may have been a groom, was probably a skilled horseman, and was trained by the army to be a cavalryman. But when his battalion was sent to Washington in May 1864 these trained Black cavalry troops were formally dismounted, and served as infantry. They took part in the siege of Petersburg in 1864 and marched victoriously into Richmond at the end of the war in April 1865.

George M. Chadwell

In 1866 George W. R. Chadwell married 18-year-old Sarah Field in Lee, Massachusetts (her home town). Their first child, William, was born in Lee in 1867. By 1869 he and his wife and child returned to Kentucky, where he probably had family, and where their second child was born, but by 1871 had come back to Lee, where they had a third child, George Montgomery Chadwell. They went on to have another five children by 1878. In that year George W. R. Chadwell died, at the age of 39. His wife remarried a man named Gardner, and the family moved to Great Barrington, perhaps because that was where Sarah Chadwell's second husband came from, perhaps because there was a significant Black community there and a new Black church. Young George Chadwell, eight years old in 1879, probably attended the integrated public schools and graduated from high school at age 18 in 1889. Somebody there must have noticed him, thought he had promise, and promoted his further education.

It's not implausible that he was encouraged by the same local men who encouraged a fellow townsman, W. E. B. DuBois, just three years older than Chadwell, who was sent to college by local churches. In 1892, at the age of 21, George was sent to Phillips Academy, Andover, where he joined the class of 1896. While at Andover he became a star athlete, playing left end on the football team in the fall – the only Black man on the squad – and running the 880 on the track team in the spring. He also developed a reputation as a skilled speaker. As one of the ten "Draper Speakers" in his class, he gave a talk on Toussaint L'Ouverture, leader of the Haitian Revolution, and another on "The Kidnapping of Anthony Burns" – Burns was a fugitive slave arrested in Boston in 1854 under the Fugitive Slave Act and forcibly returned to Virginia. He was later redeemed by abolitionists, and graduated from Oberlin. Chadwell was also one of the editors of the literary magazine.

Meanwhile, his family was dispersing. In 1893 his oldest sibling, Emma, married a man from Stockbridge and moved to Williamstown. His brother William also moved to Williamstown: he was 24 when he married a Williamstown girl, Grace Porter, in 1893. And by 1895 three more Chadwell siblings were in Williamstown, 22-year-old Harry and 17-year-old Martha, where they were joined by George, home from Andover for the summer.

After graduating from Andover in 1896, George Chadwell enrolled at Williams College. Why Williams? Probably for several reasons: 1) he was already living in Williamstown with his siblings; 2) while at Andover, he probably came to the attention of Franklin Carter, the President of Williams, who was also a trustee of Phillips Andover; 3) he was probably recommended as an athlete and a speaker by Alonzo Branch, a fellow-football-player and prize-winning speaker, a year ahead of Chadwell at both Andover and Williams. Branch was captain of the team at Williams and class president, and thus somebody whose opinion carried weight; 4) he may well have been recommended by Congregational ministers in Great Barrington, two of whom were Williams graduates.

Chadwell played left end on the Williams varsity football team for all four years. He also excelled at oratory and was selected as a speaker for the freshman class, won a "rhetorical prize" during his junior year, and was named one of the commencement speakers. George Chadwell was apparently a popular and admired man – perhaps in part because he was a star athlete, in part because he was older and more mature, having entered as a 25-year-old freshman. He was elected president of the sophomore class, and at the end of his junior year was elected to Gargoyle, the senior honor society. (More than fifty years later, when Gargoyle tapped a second Black student, Chadwell was remembered as the first.) He was Secretary and later Vice-President of the Andover Club, and was the business manager of the *Literary Monthly*. In his senior year he was elected a member of the Class Day committee.

During the school year Chadwell lived in West College, in the center of campus. His roommate was his classmate, Harrison Morgan Brown, also African-American, and a fellow Andover graduate. After his sophomore year he had a summer job as a railroad porter, one of the few jobs open to a Black man. He was not invited to join a fraternity, but he was apparently occasionally invited to dine as a guest in a fraternity house. He also took part in local Black life, serving on the committee that put on a reception for a short-lived club, through which he would have met local Black men. But it must have been difficult to be one of the very few Black students on the campus, especially since his white classmates very probably shared, consciously or unconsciously, the common prejudices of the day. One of the college clubs was a minstrel group that performed in Blackface. One of the plays put on during Chadwell's years was "The Darkey Woodcutter."

Chadwell also knew that once he left Williams, where he had a solid and secure place, he would find himself in a quite different world that offered few opportunities to an educated Black man, and he may well have looked ahead with some apprehension and bitterness. According to a possibly apocryphal story that was perhaps handed down each year to the handful of Black undergraduates at Williams, Chadwell concluded his commencement speech reviewing his Williams career by saying "Tomorrow I become a. . ." – and he uttered the n-word.

After graduation he took a job in Indianapolis teaching math in a segregated elementary school. He quickly attracted attention of the principal, W. T. B. Williams, and the school system superintendent, Calvin Kendall, who during Chadwell's first year made him a substitute principal and raised his salary. After Williams moved on, Chadwell was made principal of the McCoy School.

Chadwell kept in touch with his siblings. He spent the summer of 1901 in Williamstown. In the summer of 1903 he served as assistant to Prof. Williams in a teacher-training program at Hampton Institute in Virginia. When he returned to Indiana in the fall of 1903 he was made principal of the Frederick Douglass School – it was also segregated. Chadwell and Williams evidently remained close personal friends: in June 1904 Chadwell was best man at Williams' wedding in Detroit. The next year, 1904-05, he moved back to the McCoy School, again as principal. At the end of the summer he married a fellow schoolteacher, Edna Sweeney, whom he had known since they taught together three years earlier.

Although each of the segregated schools in Indianapolis had a Black principal, there was also a white "supervising principal" to whom the Black principal reported. In time Chadwell himself became the "supervising principal" at McCoy, the only Black supervising principal in the school system. He took a city-wide leadership role, becoming a "directing force in all of the colored schools of the city." It seemed that he was headed to a position of more importance, not only because of his talents but also because of his mentors. Kendall, his superintendent, would go on to become commissioner of education for New Jersey. W. T. B. Williams later became Dean of Tuskegee Institute in Alabama.

Chadwell spent the summer of 1908 in Detroit, with his wife and child. At the end of the summer he returned to take up his work, while his wife and child extended their stay. But on September 22, while he was playing tennis with a group of friends, he complained of feeling ill, and dropped dead, apparently of a heart attack. He was only 37 years old, younger even than his father, who had died at 39. Perhaps there was heart trouble in his family.

The local papers reported the death, noting that it was "the severest blow that the colored race of the city has suffered in recent years." And a blow as well to relations between Black and white: "There never would have been a race problem in the country if there had been more men like Chadwell among the whites as well as among the Blacks." Kendall noted that Chadwell had been "the leader of the colored teachers of the city. . . . The McCoy School, of which he had immediate charge, became one of the best schools in Indianapolis." Williams spoke of his personal qualities: "I shall miss him tremendously . . . . He has left us with an example of clean living, devotion to duty and high achievement, of lofty spirit, and of a charming, loving heart."

George Chadwell was exceptional. He was the only Black student in his graduating class at Andover. He was the first Black man on the Williams football team; he was one of two Black men in his class. And he made an unusual mark in Indianapolis, attracting considerable local attention. Why did he emerge from his modest background? Why was he able to cross the color line that divided his world? Perhaps because he was provided educational opportunities that were afforded to almost no other Black people at the time. Perhaps too because he was a talented speaker as well as an unusually talented athlete. Maybe he was regarded as a member of what W. E. B. DuBois referred to in a famous 1903 essay as the "Talented Tenth," the exceptionally talented African-Americans of the day who should be provided, so DuBois argued, with the best liberal arts education (rather than training that prepared them for a trade), so as to become the leaders of their community.

Nobody in the rest of his immediate family had such a glittering career, cut short though it was. Of his siblings, Martha was the only one who attended college. But in their much more modest way they made a mark in Williamstown. What is especially interesting about their small world is not just that it was segregated, but that, along with several other large Black families in town, it comprised a real "community," intermarrying, and attending each others picnics, weddings, and funerals. Chadwells remained in Williamstown for more than a hundred years. Several of them emerged as local leaders.

The first generation

The first Chadwell to arrive in Williamstown, Emma, was married to James S. M. Burghardt (1861-1944). He was related to W. E. B. DuBois (1868-1963). The "B" was for Burghardt – DuBois's mother was a Burghardt. James Burghardt may have been an older cousin of George Chadwell and his sister. He graduated from Stockbridge High School in 1882, evidently showing academic promise, and enrolled in the fall of 1882 at Williams, the first recorded Black student in the college's history. His expenses were to be paid by an unidentified "New York gentleman." Although apparently admitted, and expected to attend, he did not, for reasons unknown, but perhaps because it was determined that he had not met the stiff entrance requirements, which at that time included four years of Latin or Greek.

Seven years later, when Burghardt returned to Williamstown at the age of 29, he would have found few jobs open to Black men, most of whom worked as day laborers, a few as barbers, cooks, chauffeurs, or janitors. As a result, James Burghardt, a promising and ambitious student, would go on to spend more than thirty years as a janitor in several Williams College fraternities. It's worth noting that the job of janitor carried more responsibilities than the term suggests: the janitor (later called a custodian or a steward) was typically responsible for the maintenance and repair as well as the cleaning of the building. But there is no getting around the fact that this was a job with low status. A number of fraternity janitors of the day were Black. It must have been deeply disappointing and frustrating to Burghardt, as it was forty years later, when the recent college graduate Oscar Greene – a Black man who grew up in Williamstown in the 1930s – returned to town in the late 1940s and found that the only job he could get was mowing lawns or working at the A&P for $15 a week.

But Burghardt did what he could to improve working conditions. In 1904 he was elected secretary of the Building Laborers' Union. He was also interested in electoral politics. In 1903 he wrote a letter to the local paper, insisting, in response to remarks from Hernando Money, Democratic Senator from Mississippi, that Black people had "equality before the law." In 1904 he attended the county Republican nominating convention in Pittsfield. In 1905 he was elected vice-president of the recently-formed Williamstown Colored Republican Club. (The idea of a "colored Republican" club seems improbable today, but in 1905 the Republican party was still seriously thought of as "the party of Lincoln.") In the presidential election years of 1924, 1928, and 1932 he wrote long and carefully argued letters to the *North Adams Transcript* urging his fellow "colored men" to vote for the presidential candidate of the Republican Party, and not for the Democrats, who have "opposed every move that has been made for the betterment of [our] race." Just before the 1940 election, when Roosevelt (who courted southern racists in his party) ran against the moderate Republican Wendell Willkie (a champion of civil rights), the Club hosted a Willkie rally and held a meeting at Burghardt's house.

In 1933, when a North Adams-Williamstown branch of the NAACP was founded, Burghardt was elected president. In 1939 he was a member of the board of the Pittsfield Hi-Y Club, a YMCA for high school boys. He exchanged letters with his cousin, W. E. B. DuBois, who visited him in Williamstown in 1929.

For some years (1909-1919) James and Emma Burghardt lived in Bennington, where he cleaned windows and mowed lawns. In 1909 they lost two daughters to respiratory illness. In the 1920s they were back in Williamstown, where their daughter Persis graduated from Williamstown High School. In 1934 Burghardt and his wife were living on Hall St., when 35 friends gave him a surprise 73rd birthday party. When he died in 1944, he was remembered in the local paper not for having been admitted to Williams, or for serving as head of the local NAACP, or for his political activism, but as a "retired janitor."

The next oldest Chadwell in Williamstown, after Emma, was William. He and his wife Grace had seven children born here between 1893 and 1909. In 1900 he was working as a day laborer. By 1910 he too was a janitor in a Williams fraternity. And like his brother-in-law, James Burghardt, he belonged to several local organizations, including the Sons of Veterans, an integrated group whose fathers, black and white, had fought in the Civil War. He was also a charter member of the Colored Republican Club. His wife, Grace, was a member of a Black womens' Masonic group, the Order of Eastern Star. They were members of the First Congregational Church. But William and Grace apparently did not get long, and seem to have lived apart for long stretches. In his later years William worked as a gardener on Bulkley St. In his final years he reconciled with his wife, and died at the age of 85 in 1953.

The next Chadwell brother, Harry B., 22 years old when he arrived in Williamstown about 1895, and in 1899 took a job at West's Livery Stable, on North St., near the old Greylock Hotel. In 1902 he married a local girl, Sylvia

Morgan, from another large Williamstown Black family. She was a member of the Methodist church. He bounced around from one job to another: in 1903 he was working on Hoxsey St. Beginning about 1910 he again worked for more than twenty years as a janitor in several Williams fraternities. His wife, Sylvia, worked as a fraternity cook. But he owned property in town: in 1902 he and his brother George bought a house on the corner of West Main St. and Belden St. And he later owned property on E. Main St. He was also an active participant in the Black community. He was a member of the Sons of Veterans and the Colored Republican Club. Later he belonged to the St. John's Lodge of the Free and Accepted Masons in Pittsfield, another Black Masonic group. In 1909 he was chair of the Lodge's Executive Committee, and continued in a leadership role at least until 1924, when he was Treasurer. He was also a member of the St. James Lodge of the Knights of Pythias, yet another Black fraternal organization. He died in 1940.

The second generation

Some members of the next generation of Chadwells in Williamstown did not prosper. William's oldest son, George, born in 1895, worked as a chauffeur, then cleaned furnaces, and finally washed cars at Grundy's Garage on Water St. His wife, Clara, worked as a cook and housekeeper in a private house. William's next son, also called William, was in and out of trouble with the police, and in 1918, having turned 21, registered for the army, expecting to serve in the First World War. But on his way to Camp Devens, near Boston, in September 1918, he contracted the Spanish flu – the epidemic was then at its height – and died.

William's daughters did better. Lucille, born in 1893, was an entrepreneur in the restaurant business. In the 1920s she operated the Cosmo Inn on Spring St. From 1927 to 1943 she and her husband lived in Stockbridge in the summer, where they ran Lucille's Tea Room, and Williamstown in the winter, where in 1937 she re-opened the Cosmo as Lucille's Dining Room, on the second floor above the old Walden Theatre on Spring St. Much of her business came from the 40-man Williams football team, which took its training meals there. In 1938 she was put in charge of the kitchen for the Williams College training table at "Varsity House" on the campus and seems to have run it for several years. (When her appointment was reported in the student newspaper, she was said to be "the niece of the late George M. Chadwell '00." He was apparently still remembered as one of Williams's football greats.) She reportedly "took great pride" in her job, and "took a personal interest" in the players' "likes and dislikes pertaining to food." She died in 1943, with a service in the Congregational Church.

William's youngest daughter, Janette, born in 1909, went to school in Williamstown and Pittsfield, but dropped out. She did domestic work, then served as a nurse's aide at the North Adams Hospital, and later for Williams College, in both the infirmary and the Buildings & Grounds department. But in the 1940s, when she was in her 30s, she went back to school and finished her GED (the equivalent of a high school diploma) at Drury High School in North Adams. She was an active member of the First Congregational Church, and served as president of the Ecumenical Council of Churches in Berkshire County. She also belonged to the Williamstown Grange and to a Masonic order in Pittsfield. She died in 2004, at the age of 94. Her husband, Reginald Galvin, like his brothers-in-law, worked as a janitor for two college fraternities. During World War II he worked for GE in Pittsfield, and after the war for Cornish Wire on Water St.

William's third son, Leslie, lived quietly in the first part of his life, but emerged as a leader at the age of 50. Born in 1899, he lived for a time in Williamstown, but by 1918 was living in Pittsfield. In 1934 he took a janitorial job in an apartment building on Long Island. In 1937 he was living in Stockbridge, but by 1943 was back in Williamstown, finally settling in Pittsfield in 1945, but kept in touch with his Williamstown family. He was a Mason. He worked at Besse-Clarke, a downtown Pittsfield men's clothing store, retiring in 1959. In 1949 he was named president of the Berkshire branch of the NAACP. In 1950 he was a trustee of the 2nd Congregational Church in Pittsfield . He died in 1975, after a long illness.

Mary Persis Burghardt, daughter of Emma Chadwell Burghardt and James S. Burghardt, born in 1910, was apparently as good a scholar as her father was: when she graduated from Williamstown High School in 1928, she was the first Black girl to be elected to the honor society (for her academic record) and was chosen, like her Uncle George, one of the graduation speakers. Her topic was "The Music of the Negro People." She borrowed books on the subject from W. E. B. DuBois. She went on to a business college in Springfield for a year, and then transferred to the New York Academy of Business, from which she graduated in 1932.

The third generation

There were a number of Chadwells in the third generation, but most of them moved away from Williamstown. I will focus on just three who stayed in town, Marion Chadwell, Reggie Galvin, and Barbara Chadwell Hart.

George Chadwell's daughter, Marion Grace, born in 1932, was a talented singer. While still in school was performing as a soloist in local churches. She graduated from Williamstown High School, where she was president of the student council, in 1950. She worked for Sprague Electric for a year, and then went to Green Mountain Junior College. In 1952 she won a scholarship from the Williamstown Rotary. In 1953 she graduated with an A. A. degree in Music Education and went on to the University of Vermont. Later she became a music teacher in the Pittsfield Day Care Center.

Marion Chadwell's younger sister, Barbara, born in 1935, was a Girl Scout and cheerleader, and graduated from Williamstown High School in 1953. In 1960 she married Henry Hart, Jr., of the well-known local Hart family. Henry and his five siblings all attended college. Henry had spent a year at Williams as a member of the Class of 1935, and later became a successful contractor in Williamstown. He died in 1992. Barbara worked as a teacher's aide and as a Cub Scout pack leader, and participated in local politics, registering voters and serving as a poll worker. She still lives in town.

Janette Chadwell Galvin's son, Reginald C. (Reggie) Galvin, was born in 1942. He graduated from Mt. Hermon Academy, a boarding school near Greenfield, in 1961, and from U. Mass. in 1965, where he studied icthyology – the science of fish. He was also an expert fisherman. After graduation he worked for the Essex Marine Research Center in Essex, CT and in 1972 returned to Williamstown and opened the Grey Hackle Fish & Tackle Shop in Pownal. He lived with his mother at 133 North St., and then at Sweetbrook, and died in 2005.

The fourth generation

The six children of Barbara Chadwell Hart and Henry Hart, Jr. grew up on Hall St. in Williamstown. Four of them are college graduates. Timothy graduated from U. Mass in 1977. He and his brothers, Robin and Ronald, lived in Williamstown as adults for a time. Deborah graduated from Smith and Josephine from Rice, both in 1979, and Allen (who spent his high school years at Exeter) from Amherst – archrival of the college in his native Williamstown – in 1982. Both Deborah and Josephine have graduate degrees. Deborah formerly worked for Citigroup and Salomon Brothers in New York; Josephine is president of a property management company, and has a house on Oblong Rd. Allen Hart, like his great-great-uncle, George Chadwell, played football and ran track. (In his senior year Amherst beat Williams in football, 21-17.) Allen went on from Amherst to get a Ph. D. in Psychology from Harvard, and since 1996 this native son of Williamstown has been a professor and dean of students at Amherst. But the story doesn't end there: Allen's daughter Maya graduated from Williams in 2016.

The Chadwells of Williamstown were and are a remarkable family. They left a significant mark in Williamstown in the town where they spent four generations. Most of them now rest in Eastlawn Cemetery – two from the first generation, five from the second, two from the third – but a couple of Chadwells survive in town, and others have gone forth to pursue lives elsewhere. Their stories reflect both the obstacles that restricted Black lives in this town and this country, and the distinction that African-Americans achieved when they found or made opportunities. If you know where to look, you'll find their traces. In the Schow Science Library at Williams hangs a "story quilt," commissioned by the Williams College Museum or Art and made in 1989 by the award-winning artist, Faith Ringgold, to commemorate the centennial of the graduation of Gaius Bolin, the first African-American to graduate from Williams, in 1889. (That was seven years after James Burghardt spent a few weeks at Williams as a freshman.) The quilt represents one hundred years of African-Americans at Williams. On the border are images of notable African-American graduates of the college, including George Chadwell of the Class of 1900. The quilt shows that Chadwell is still remembered at Williams today as an important part of that history.

Meeting in Chapin Hall, Williams College, May 4, 1970.
Courtesy of Williams College Archives and Special Collections.

Chapter 9

—ʍ—

WILLIAMSTOWN AND VIETNAM:

The War at Home

Those who lived through the late 1960s remember that the Vietnam War sharply divided the country and led to the downfall of a president in 1968. The war also had an impact on Williamstown, especially on a decade of Williams College students who in increasing numbers protested the war, and on the local families whose sons – and in those days it was only sons – were sent to Vietnam. It divided the town; it even divided children from their parents.

About 9 million Americans were on active duty during the Vietnam period (1964-75). 2.7 million U.S. soldiers served in Vietnam. (Although cultural memories of the war are closely tied to the draft, the best estimate is that about 70% of the soldiers volunteered, and only 30% were drafted.) 58,000 died there. 150,000 - 300,000 were wounded, 98,000 of them severely or totally disabled. Another 1600 are still listed as Missing in Action. Thousands more who returned alive suffered from Agent Orange or PTSD. At least 9000 Vietnam vets, and by some estimates many thousands more, committed suicide after they came home. Some 25,000 of them joined the Vietnam Veterans Against the War, founded in 1967.

About 250 Williamstown residents served in the armed forces from 1961 to 1975. Their names are on the War Memorial in Field Park. A fraction, perhaps one third, served "in country," in Vietnam. Very few of the Williamstown boys – and they were mostly still boys, not yet 21 – who enlisted or were drafted lost their lives in Vietnam: there are three names of the dead on the Vietnam Memorial in Field Park, one of them (Tristan W. Hayes) a mistake, since he was not a Williamstown resident. 28-year-old Captain Francis Bissaillon was an Air Force pilot whose transport plane went down in 1966. The other was 20-year-old Gary Edgar Field. He was a gunner on an assault helicopter, shot down in 1970 – his body was never recovered, and he was subsequently declared dead. There is a burial stone for him in Eastlawn

Cemetery. And of the Williams College students who came to Williamstown from all over the country, only five died, all from classes who graduated in the 1960s, one in 1966, two in 1967, two in 1968.

But the war also formed (or deformed) the lives of an entire generation of young American men. Many personal and career choices were made under pressure of the draft. Many college graduates went to law school or graduate school, joined Officer Candidate School, or the Reserves, or went into the Peace Corps. Jessie Winchester, a 1966 graduate of Williams, was one of perhaps 30,000 young men who went to Canada. He went to Canada in 1967 and established a career as a folk singer. Thousands dropped out and joined the "counterculture." One Williams graduate served time in prison for firebombing an ROTC building in Hawaii in 1971. Williamstown boys who did not go on to college were certain to be drafted.

But the story of the war at home in Williamstown has never been fully told. The chapter added in 2003 to the 1953 town history says only that Williamstown "had its share of antiwar protests on and off campus," adding without comment that "in the midst of the turmoil over Vietnam," the local American Legion post celebrated its 50th anniversary. A 1990 honors thesis by a Williams history major focuses narrowly on the 1970 student strike at Williams College in response to the incursion into Cambodia, but does not attempt to tell the wider story of how the war impacted the campus and the town for nearly ten years. Now is a good time to tell a more complete story: May 2020 was the 50th anniversary of the strike.

It is important to remember that responses to the Vietnam War did not split along town/gown lines, the college community against the war and the town in support. Opinion on Williams campus was deeply divided at least until 1969 – by which time most of the campus wanted the U.S. to withdraw it troops more rapidly, though a few professors remained supporters of the Nixon administration. Opinion in town was also divided, as the letters to the editor of the local newspapers make clear.

National and international events

It may be useful to begin with a simplified timeline of the war. U.S. military advisors were in Vietnam as early as 1954, but the war did not come to national attention until the Kennedy administration. At the end of 1963 there were 16,000 military advisors in Vietnam. Escalation came by stages: the Gulf of Tonkin incident and resolution in August 1964, bombing of North

Vietnam in February 1965, and the first U.S. combat troops in Vietnam in March 1965. Within a year there were 400,000 U.S. troops there. Anti-war mass demonstrations (in New York, Washington, and San Francisco) began in April 1965.

January 1968 brought the Tet Offensive, the political turning point, when domestic sentiment turned against the war. 1968 was also the peak year for U.S. casualties: nearly 17,000 (an average of more than 325 per week). In March 1968 Lyndon Johnson declined to run again. Nixon, who said he had a "secret plan" to end the war, won the presidency that November. He promised "Vietnamization" of the war, and troops began to be withdrawn, but in May 1970 Nixon extended the bombing to Cambodia. By the time he was reelected in 1972 U.S. troop levels were down to 69,000. In January 1973 the Paris peace talks began. In March 1973 the last U.S. troops left Vietnam, but the war went on for two more years, until the U.S. evacuated Saigon in April 1975, and South Vietnam surrendered.

And here is a simplified timeline of major war-related events in Williamstown:

1964-66	Protests led by radical SDS (Students for a Democratic Society)
1967	Walkout from Williams College Convocation. Renewed SDS protests.
1969	Moratorium march to Eastlawn Cemetery
1970	Williams College student strike

Some key players

John L. Fisher (b. 1914) and his wife, **Vera I. Fisher** (b. 1916), who lived on Benlise Dr. from 1962 to 1963 and at 31 School St. from 1963 to about 1971. (In 1966 they bought the four-apartment building on School St. as an investment.) Outspoken antiwar activists, came from Berlin, and while in Germany had reportedly been members of the German Communist party in the 1930s. They emigrated to the U.S., and he later served in the U.S. Army during World War II. Fisher worked as a traveling salesman. He and his wife began writing letters to local papers about the Vietnam war and other leftist causes as early as 1963 and in 1965 organized the Berkshire Committee Against the War in Vietnam. In the early '70s the Fishers moved to Northampton.

Carlo Valone (b. 1935) was a history teacher at Mt. Greylock Regional High School. He grew up in Pittsfield, got degrees from U. Mass and Wesleyan, served in the Air Force, where he learned to speak Arabic and Chinese, and began teaching at Mt. Greylock in 1963. He was an outspoken antiwar activist. After winning a contested battle for tenure, he resigned in May 1966 and took a curriculum-development job with Xerox in West Virginia. He later lived in Williamsburg, MA.

Filmore Baker (1926-1994) was a World War II vet – he took part in the D-Day landing – who lived on Belden St. He had very little formal education, and worked as a janitor in the post office, but took a keen interest in public affairs, often writing letters to newspapers. In the early 1960s he ran repeatedly for elective office, finally being elected a selectman in 1964 and reelected in 1967, but resigned in September of that year. He ran again for selectman in 1976 but lost by a wide margin. He moved to Florida in 1985, where he died. He is buried in Southlawn Cemetery.

Frederick Schuman (1904-81) was a professor of political science at Williams. He made his reputation in the 1930s and 1940s as a scholar of international relations, writing books on Nazi Germany and the Soviet Union. By the 1950s he was a fierce critic of American foreign policy, warning against the dangers of nuclear war, and in the 1960s an outspoken opponent of the Vietnam War.

The early years

Not many Americans paid much attention to Vietnam in the early years of the war. At the time John Kennedy was killed, in November 1963, politically active citizens were paying more attention to the struggle for civil rights at home than to a war in faraway Southeast Asia. It's usually assumed that antiwar protests began on college campuses, but in Williamstown the first protest came from John Fisher, who wrote to the *North Adams Transcript* in March 1964, calling for the withdrawal of American advisors. In May 1964 a handful of Williams students attended an anti-war rally in New York City. And in July Vera Fisher wrote to the *Transcript*, enclosing a copy of her letter to Senator Wayne Morse of Oregon, in support of his speech warning of American involvement in Vietnam. In December 1964 Williams senior Steve Block founded the Williams College chapter of Students for a Democratic Society (SDS), but the group initially focused on civil rights rather than Vietnam. However, when the U.S. began bombing North Vietnam in February 1965 Block and the SDS sponsored a forum in which Williams professors Fred Schuman and Fred Greene discussed the latest U.S. actions, Schuman arguing against them and Greene broadly defending them. And after the first U.S. combat troops were sent to Vietnam in March 1965, some 150 Williams students took part in the first of what would be annual spring antiwar demonstrations in Washington.

Meanwhile, the Fishers continued their protests. John Fisher engaged in an exchange of letters with a pro-war student at North Adams State College, Fisher calling for withdrawal of troops and negotiations. And in the fall of 1965 Williamstown residents joined Williams students in a "peace march" from Williamstown to Bennington, where they found counterprotesters from the local VFW. In October Carlo Vallone, a history teacher at Mt. Greylock, and an outspoken critic of U.S. policy in Vietnam, attracted attention from both town and college by writing to the *Transcript* that the war was "completely immoral," and defending young protesters who had burned their draft cards. Several townspeople contacted the school superintendent to object to Vallone's letters, declaring that a public school teacher should not openly criticize U.S. government policy. The American Legion discussed whether it should stage a protest at the high school. The *Transcript* defended U.S. policy, but the *Eagle* editorialized in favor of Vallone's right to free speech. In November Vallone participated in a "community forum" on Vietnam at the First Congregational Church, along with fellow history teacher Baxter Richardson, Williams chaplain John Eusden, and two Williams professors. (Two town selectmen, including Filmore Baker, were invited but did not appear.) The forum drew about 140 people, as well as counterprotesters from the North Adams American Legion post. Meanwhile, most Williams College students stayed on the sidelines. Results of a survey published in the *Williams Record* in November 1965 showed that few college students had strong views about the war in Vietnam, either pro or con.

Over the next five months Vallone himself became the center of controversy, half of the Mt. Greylock faculty defending his right to speak freely, and a parents group supporting him. The school superintendent notified Vallone that he would not be recommended for tenure, but the school committee voted to disregard the superintendent's recommendation, and granted tenure. John Fisher wrote to the papers to commend the decision.

Valone's opponents then circulated a petition in town urging a reversal of the decision; one of the organizers was Filmore Baker. 500 people signed it. The school committee declined to reconsider, but Valone, apparently sensing that he faced a hostile environment, resigned at the end of the school year and left town.

The war itself was still on people's minds. On the Williams campus in December 1965 faculty circulated two petitions, both urging a negotiated settlement to the war, but one of them more supportive of U.S. policy than the other. And just before Christmas there appeared in the *Transcript* an ad, organized and paid for by John Fisher and a new organization, the Berkshire Committee Against the War in Vietnam. Entitled "An Appeal to Sanity," it called for an end to the air war, withdrawal of troops, and negotiations. It was signed by 74 local residents, including four from the Fisher family, some Williamstown residents, and some Williams College students and faculty. The ad may have had some impact. By late February the *Transcript*, which had previously editorialized in support of U.S. government policy, now declared that "better ideas" were needed, that attention needed to be paid to the "moral revulsion" in the country over the slaughter of civilians in what might well prove to be a "futile" effort. What changed the minds of the editors was probably the publication in January 1966 of the cautionary report from Senator Mike Mansfield of Montana, urging the U.S. to move quickly toward peace. The Fisher ad may have reminded the editors that there was local "moral revulsion."

But antiwar activism was still limited to a relative few, both on the Williams campus and in the town. SDS-sponsored events lapsed. A poll of Williams students in April 1966 showed that 65% supported LBJ, and that many admitted that they were not well informed about the war, even though guest speaker William Sloane Coffin attacked Vietnam policy in a campus speech on May 1, and took part in an ecumenical service focused on "Christian Responses" to the war, sponsored by college religious groups and the Williamstown Associated Ministers. Small group discussions were led by clergy, faculty and students, and "lay people from the community." When John Fisher wrote to the *Berkshire Eagle* about reports that South Vietnamese officers laughed as they killed Viet Cong, comparing U.S. policies to Hitler's, the *Eagle* replied editorially that although it opposed the war it thought the comparison unjustified.

The primary election in September 1966 showed that there was strong antiwar sentiment in town. A "peace candidate," Thomas B. Adams, ran for the Democratic nomination for U. S. Senator. Although he won only 8% of the vote statewide (13% in Berkshire County), and lost to Endicott Peabody, who in turn lost to Republican Edward Brooke in November, Adams was the leading vote-getter in Williamstown. Kurt Tauber chaired a local committee that supported his campaign. Vera Fisher, a member of Tauber's committee, was arrested and charged with distributing campaign leaflets for Adams within 150' of a polling place. (She refused to plead guilty, and when the case went to trial in November, she was found not guilty.) Later in September an incident suggested that antiwar sentiment was stronger in Williamstown than in North Adams. At the "Family Fun Day" at Noel Field in North Adams, part of the "Fall Foliage Festival," an 8-man Green Beret reserve unit was invited to demonstrate weapons, rope-climbing, and parachutes. John Eusden, spokesman for the Williamstown Associated Ministers, and some 145 others signed a paid ad in the *Transcript* the previous day, deploring "the emphasis on violence, weapons, and brutal tactics, which have been reported to be a major aspect of this year's 'Family Fun Day'." And at Noel Field fifty Williams and Bennington students picketed, distributing leaflets and waving banners with the slogans "Fall Defoliation Festival?" and "Green Berets Are Killing Children Like Yours." The *Transcript* published a letter from John Fisher, under the headline "Never Again," protesting the Green Berets' martial display.

The students were a vocal minority in the crowd at Noel Field, but antiwar sentiment was growing. Fisher's Berkshire Committee Against the War in Vietnam again published a Christmastime 1966 ad in the *Transcript*, entitled "An Appeal to the American Conscience," calling for an end to the war. This time the ad carried 136 signatures, including many from both college and town. At the end of 1966 there were 400,000 U.S. troops in Vietnam, and Williamstown had already suffered its first fatality, Capt. Francis Bissaillon.

In 1967 troops levels increased to 500,000, and in February the U.S. began bombing Haiphong Harbor. Later that month General Maxwell Taylor, former head of the Joint Chiefs of Staff and former ambassador to South Vietnam, spoke to a college crowd of 800 in Chapin Hall on the Williams campus in defense of the bombing, arguing that the U.S. should not withdraw its troops. Outside the hall 100 Williams students picketed. They were joined by local activists, including John Fisher, who held up a sign declaring "End the War in Vietnam." Also present were counterprotesters, including Filmore Baker, whose sign read

"I am a Red Blooded American – Not a Pink Pacifist." The event got full coverage in local papers. Fisher later wrote to the *Eagle*, accusing Taylor of "distortions" and "misrepresentations." He again called for and end to the bombing: "end the war, bring the troops home."

The summer of 1967 saw the formation of a new antiwar citizens group, the Northern Berkshire Action for Peace Committee. Its organizer was John Lawton, a curate at St. John's Episcopal Church, and its leaders included a dean from Williams along with three scientists from Sprague Electric Company. The committee called for an end to the bombing and a general truce. In late October it conducted a poll of residents of Williamstown, North Adams, and Adams – pollsters included both townspeople and Williams students. Results were somewhat mixed, showing that 52% of their 582-person sample were opposed to the war. (Interestingly, this was very similar to the results of a May 1967 poll of Williams students.) 72% preferred a negotiated settlement to the war over efforts to achieve total victory, but 70% either wanted the U.S. to continue bombing North Vietnam or were undecided. Surprisingly, the poll found that although Williamstown had the highest percentage against bombing, it also was the only one of the three towns in which a majority supported the war. Asked if they would vote for a presidential candidate in 1968 who would reduce U.S. involvement in the war, 45% in the three towns said yes. As a result, the Committee resolved to run a slate of antiwar candidates supporting Eugene McCarthy in the Democratic primary the following spring. And as a further result, on December 4 the Committee placed a large display ad in the *Transcript*, headed "Who Wants the War in Vietnam?", citing the results of their poll, and calling for immediate de-escalation and an end to what it called LBJ's war, signed and sponsored by 117 "friends and neighbors" of *Transcript* readers, 90% of them town rather than college (including John and Vera Fisher). College signatories included Kurt Tauber, Frank and Claire-Ann Oakley, and Dan and Mary O'Connor.

1967–1969

Opposition to LBJ was expressed more directly that fall by Williams professor Frederick Schuman, who in an open letter to John Sawyer, the college president, called Johnson a "pathological liar," a "megalomaniacal militant," and "the most dangerous man in the world today." The occasion was the Williams College Convocation on October 8, in which an honorary degree was to be awarded to Lady Bird Johnson in recognition of her environmental work.

Schuman, along with the rest of the Williams faculty, was invited to participate. On September 6 Schuman wrote to Sawyer withdrawing his previous consent to take part in Convocation, which he now saw as a "glorification of the Johnson Administration," and on October 6, two days before the Convocation, Schuman wrote to the *Williams Record*, with copies to the *Transcript* and the Eagle, to make his views crystal clear: he was especially worried that escalation would bring about a war with China. His letter aroused vigorous opposition from the editors of the *Transcript*, who deplored Schuman's "bad judgment, . . misguided zeal… and name-calling." In a letter to the *Eagle*, the head of the Pittsfield VFW attacked Schuman's views.

The presence of LBJ's wife in town aroused considerable local interest. Some 2000 people from the college and the town watched the academic procession from the Williams president's house into Chapin Hall. Some, including Filmore Baker, held up signs supporting LBJ. Others, including John Fisher, held up banners opposing him. 125 students, organized by the Williams Committee for Action and Resistance, picketed in front of Chapin Hall. Inside the hall 46 students, wearing white arms bands to signal their pro-peace sentiments, walked out when Mrs. Johnson was granted her degree and rose to speak. But when she finished, she was given a standing ovation by those who remained. Even Schuman regretted the "discourtesies" shown to her by those who walked out. The event received thorough coverage from the *Transcript* and *Eagle*, as well as the *Williams Record,* with several photographs. John Fisher wrote to the *Eagle* on October 12 and to the *Transcript* on October 17 praising the protesters for conduct he found "perfectly reasonable."

Just two weeks later one of the most famous of the Vietnam era protests took place: the march on the Pentagon in late October, reported by Norman Mailer in *Armies of the Night.* Several protesters from Williamstown played a small part in that event. The march, sponsored by the National Mobilization Committee, was planned in advance but did not receive a permit. This meant a direct challenge to the D. C. police. Forty students from Williams, together with 50 from Bennington, and a few students and teachers from Mt. Greylock Regional High School, made the trip. Several students were appointed marshals, and warnings were issued about how to respond if the police used tear gas. As the event unfolded, hundreds were arrested, including Stewart Burns, one of the Mt. Greylock students, and the son of Williams Professor James MacGregor Burns (who supported Johnson's policy). Young Stewart was fined $25 and released the next day. When his parents were contacted by a reporter from the *Transcript* and asked for a comment, they stated that they had raised their children – all four of them took part in the march on the Pentagon — to speak their minds freely.

January 1968 brought the Tet Offensive, usually cited as a political turning point, the moment when American majority opinion shifted against the war. One of those who shifted was Williams history professor Robert Waite, who in a January 13 letter to the *Williams Record* declared that "I have been mistaken about our war in Vietnam. Two years ago I generally supported U.S. policy in South East Asia. Events have proved me wrong."

Six weeks later Walter Cronkite famously announced on network television that he had concluded that the U.S. was "mired in a stalemate" and that the only way forward was through negotiations. Watching that night, Lyndon Johnson told an aide that "If I've lost Cronkite, I've lost Middle America." And less than five weeks after that he announced on national television that he would not be a candidate for president in the fall election. By then many of the more moderate of the anti-war activists both on campus and in town were devoting their energies not to protest but to electoral politics, campaigning for Eugene McCarthy and, later, for Bobby Kennedy. But John Fisher continued his public protests, leading 100 peace marchers on March 13 in Pittsfield, where they were heckled by about 60 pro-war high school students carrying signs declaring "America – Love It or Leave It," "Better Dead than Red," and "Right or Wrong, My Country." And in late April Fisher chartered a bus to take 43 residents of Williamstown, North Adams, and Pittsfield to the anti-war demonstration in New York City. In 1968 he sent at least 14 letters to local newspapers, an average of more than one a month.

In the 1968 election Humphrey carried Massachusetts easily but Nixon by a narrow margin won the national popular vote and the electoral college by a much bigger margin. In Williamstown the election proved to be the occasion for some minor violence between pro-war and anti-war activists. John Fisher, who lived near the polling station at the old Mitchell School on Southworth St., put up signs in his front yard urging voters to vote for the socialist and anti-war candidate, since, in his view there wasn't much difference on Vietnam between Nixon and Humphrey. On election day Filmore Baker accosted Fisher and tried to remove his signs. They scuffled. Baker then proceeded a short distance to the polling station, where he and a colleague found SDS members from Williams carrying similar signs, and tried to tear them up. Again a scuffle ensued, in which a student grabbed Baker and knocked him down. Police observers were on hand, but did not intervene. A second protester shouted "What the f— is going on?"and Baker then left the scene. At that point police stepped in and charged one student with assault and the other with profanity. At the police station Fisher and the students countercharged Baker with assault; he countercharged Fisher with posting an illegal sign.

The incident was reported in the local papers, complete with photographs. The *Transcript* referred to Baker and Fisher as "Williamstown's leading hawk and dove." When the case was heard at the District Court on Spring Street the courtroom was crowded with supporters of all the parties. The American Legion began raising money to pay for Baker's legal fees. Everybody pled not guilty, and a trial date was set, and then continued. Newspaper coverage also continued. In January 1969 the plaintiffs all agreed to drop charges.

For whatever reason, there was not much Vietnam-related activity in Williamstown for the first half of 1969. The Williamstown post of the American Legion commemorated the 50th anniversary of the 1919 founding of the national Legion The North Adams post of the American Legion conducted a week-long celebration. It has been speculated that many moderates were ready and willing, since Nixon had promised to reduce U.S. involvement, to cut him some slack and see what he would do about bombing and troop levels. But more engaged peace activists on the Williams campus and in the town cooperated with each other. A contingent of Williams students traveled to New York City for the annual spring antiwar demonstration in April. John and Vera Fisher helped organize the trip, taking reservations for places on the bus. Fisher wrote a long and enthusiastic account of the demonstration in a letter to the *Transcript*. A month later his son, Allen, a senior at Mount Greylock, who shared his parents' political views, was suspended for distributing an underground newspaper.

In the absence of public activity, it is difficult to determine the mood in Williamstown. But editorials in the *Eagle* and the *Transcript* suggest that local opinion was continuing to shift against the war. On Sept. 12 the *Transcript* lamented the "tired advice" that Nixon was getting from his advisors, and warned that "time is running out." Soon "Johnson's war" would become "Nixon's war." It's a "delusion," so the paper argued, to think that "military victory" is possible: the war "must be ended without further delay." On Sept. 20, after Nixon announced the withdrawal of 25,000 troops and canceled draft calls for November and December, the *Transcript* condemned what it called Nixon's "halfway measures." On the 27th its lead editorial was headlined "Nixon Can Blame Self for Lack of Support on Vietnam," and on October 1 "Nixon Should Listen to Vietnam Dissenters." The *Eagle* had turned against the war earlier than the *Transcript*. On August 29 it opined that the U.S. should cut its losses and back away from its commitment. On October 14 it argued that continuing the bombing of North Vietnam is "pointless, dangerous, and damaging to the cause of peace."

The Moratorium

The big event that year was the "Pause for Peace" march on October 15, from the college chapel to Eastlawn Cemetery, timed to coincide with the national "Moratorium" Day – when citizens all over the country were encouraged to stop "business as usual" and come together to urge that the war be speedily ended. The leaders of the national Moratorium Committee had worked in 1968 on the presidential campaigns of McCarthy and Kennedy, and sought now to use mass demonstrations, up until this point a tool of radical groups such as SDS, to mobilize public opinion and thus put pressure on the Nixon Administration. The organizer in Williamstown was a Williams senior, Joe Sensenbrenner '70. He made clear from the outset that the objective of the Moratorium was to go beyond the college campus and to seek "throughout the community as broad a base of disenchantment with the war as possible." Even the word "disenchantment" – adopted by the national organization and then by local chapters – was designed to reach a wide audience of moderates and liberals and anybody who thought the war had gone on too long and that Nixon was not moving rapidly enough to disengage from Vietnam and the Thieu-Ky government.

The event in Williamstown was carefully planned and publicized so as to attract a large turnout. The *Williams Record*, whose editor-in-chief was a strong supporter of the Moratorium, gave it enthusiastic coverage. Sensenbrenner and his local committee of faculty and students placed paid advertisements in the *Transcript* and the *Eagle*, issued press releases, quickly picked up by the local newspapers, which gave wide coverage to preparations for the community march and to plans to solicit signatures on an open letter to be sent to Nixon. He also urged participants to behave in a civil manner, to avoid violence and offensive behavior, even to dress conservatively in coat and tie, so as to demonstrate that those engaged in the march were not radicals or "hippies" or anarchists. Some faculty canceled their classes on Moratorium Day.

The *Eagle* and *Transcript* published respectful news stories and editorial support of the upcoming event. But not all opinion was favorable. On Sunday October 12 at St. John's Church in Williamstown the rector, the Rev. Lafayette Sprague, spoke from the pulpit in opposition to the Moratorium, which, he said, would "create confusion and even chaos," and urged support of government policy. One letter to the editor in the *Eagle* on October 13 insisted that the Moratorium was being organized by "the same groups of student radicals, draft dodgers, pinko intellectuals, and outright communists who did their best to force President Johnson out of office." A letter on October 14 complained about the positive coverage of the Moratorium in the *Eagle* and concluded that Russia, bent on world domination, would gain by widespread antiwar protests. A local pro-Nixon group urged that residents show their support for the U.S. government by driving with their headlights on or turning on their outdoor house lights. The head of the VFW post in North Adams warned readers that the Moratorium was being organized by a "vocal minority," and assured them that a "silent majority" completely supports U.S. government policy. Some Williams students opposed the Moratorium: one student wrote to the *Record* objecting to "precipitous withdrawal" and endorsing what he called Nixon's "middle course" of gradual withdrawal.

Plans for the Moratorium were also challenged "from the left" by antiwar activists on the Williams campus who called for "stronger action." One group, which called itself simply "The Committee," wrote to the *Record* on October 10, calling for a boycott of classes on Moratorium day, announcing that it would urge Spring St. merchants to close for the day, and arguing for confrontational tactics: don't ask for a march permit (the selectmen had in fact approved a permit by a vote of 3-1), wear what you want, continue the march even if townspeople try to block it. It closed its anonymous letter with words that some found alarming: "We will be watching you." A junior faculty member of the Moratorium Committee wrote in reply on October 14 that the purpose of the protest is to "persuade" the people of Williamstown, not to "offend" them. Professor Robert Waite, a senior member of the faculty, wrote to say that the anonymous Committee's threats were "contemptible," and reminded him of activities of the Hitler Jugend in the 1930s.

Moratorium Day began in Williamstown with a noontime service in the college chapel. Selectman and local lawyer Larry Urbano spoke, calling for "moderate means." An estimated 2000 people from the college and the town – probably more than half of them from the town – joined the march to Eastlawn Cemetery. It took place without incident, and without counterpicketing. The two bookstores on Spring St. closed for the day. An open letter, addressed to Nixon, calling for a rapid end to the war, was signed by 2100 people, including 932 students (about 75% of the student body), 108 faculty (about 85%), and about 1250 members of the local community, suggesting that on this occasion at least town and gown had come together. At the high school a number of speakers addressed the whole school body, all of them urging a rapid end to the war.

A few indications of pro-war sentiment were evident. A *Transcript* headline on Moratorium Day announced that "Moratorium Divides Town But No Incidents Reported."There was said to be an air of tension on Spring St.," and "several American flags flew and some building lights were turned on in dissent to the Vietnam Moratorium." An observer for the *Transcript* reported that at 8 am on State Rd. between Williamstown and North Adams about one car out of 50 had its headlights on; at 11:30 am, just before the march began, about three cars out of 50.

Signs indicated, then, that the community was still divided over the war. Even families were divided. At one event at Miss Hall's School in Pittsfield on the night of October 15, given extensive coverage in the next day's *Eagle*, James MacGregor Burns appeared with his son, Stewart. The elder Burns, a longtime liberal Democrat and biographer of FDR, but still a supporter of the Johnson and Nixon administration war policies, warned of the dire consequences of an immediate withdrawal of troops, and of the authoritarian North Vietnamese. Stewart, a self-described pacifist, who had not only been arrested at the Pentagon, but had burned his draft card, and faced imminent indictment, called for an immediate end to the war. At his father's funeral many years later, Stewart said that while he prioritized "social justice," his father prioritized "political freedom." He described his father as a "Cold Warrior" misinformed about "American motives and political repression in South Vietnam," but conceded that he himself was "mistaken" in thinking that the Vietnamese Communists were committed to "meeting human needs."

Local newspapers treated the Moratorium with seriousness. The *Transcript* published a photograph of the march on the front page, and editorialized in its favor: "The Vietnam Protest Comes of Age" (October 17). The *Eagle* wrote that the war was a "wretched misadventure," and that the Moratorium kept pressure on Nixon to "move toward peace." But both papers reported local dissent, reflecting the fact that support for the war was stronger in Adams and North Adams than in Williamstown. three Adams selectmen denounced the Moratorium; "opposing views" were presented at a teach-in at North Adams State College. Letters to the editors came in from both sides. John Fisher's October 15 letter was given a headline: "Anti-War Minority Now a Majority." But a letter from North Adams objected to the "thoughtless outbursts of immature children." An October 17 letter from Adams alleged that the Moratorium was "giving aid and comfort to the enemy," and constituted treason. A letter-writer to the *Eagle* (October 16) was more temperate: one could "truly want peace in Vietnam," he wrote, "and still support the administration's position, as opposed to the policy of immediate withdrawal."

The Moratorium Day was designed to be only the first of a series of monthly observances, to continue until the war policy significantly changed. The Williams Moratorium Committee began planning for a November 15 event. The march also prompted local activists on both sides to follow up. On October 30 several community members, including Joe Dewey, who ran a bookstore on Spring St., and Nancy Lawton, wife of the organizer of the North Berkshire Action for Peace Committee, sponsored a discussion at the Congregational Church on "What Way Out of Vietnam?," with speakers from the college. But the event was "sparsely attended." On the other side, the North Adams post of the American Legion organized a telephone campaign to celebrate the upcoming Veterans Day and rally support for the Nixon administration, urging people to fly the flag, leave their porch lights on, and drive with their headlights on.

Although the November Moratorium events in Williamstown lasted for three days instead of one, some momentum seems to have gone out of the local antiwar movement, perhaps because of Nixon's speech on November 3, appealing to the "silent majority" in the country to support his policy of "Vietnamization," suggesting that the administration was not going to be moved by the Moratorium, perhaps because local energies were divided when some 200 activists chose to take part in a huge mass demonstration in Washington on November 15 rather than to remain in Williamstown. It is estimated that 250,000 took part, making it the largest antiwar protest in U.S. history. The events in Williamstown were much lower-key than in October: a project to clean up vacant lots on Rt. 7 and on Cole Avenue (to demonstrate to the community that "our concerns are constructive" and that money being spent in Vietnam could be better spent at home), and informal discussions with Williams alumni in town for Homecoming. Students called off large Homecoming Weekend parties and a Shirelles concert, but the football game was played as usual. About 300 people, including local residents, took part in a candlelight procession up Spring Street, past a color guard in front of the American Legion hall, to the steps of Chapin Hall. A discussion of Nixon's November 3 speech took place at the Congregational Church, and two faculty speakers addressed students at Mt. Greylock, one (antiwar) arguing that "A Dissenter Can be a Patriot," the other (prowar) "Why We Are Fighting in Vietnam." On November 13 John Fisher organized another ad in the *Transcript*: it asked the question "Will President Nixon's Plan End the War?" and answered with a resounding "No," urging readers to support the Moratorium and write their congressman. It had 160 signatures. Pro-Nixon voices continued to be heard, but they were now a minority. On November 13 ninety-eight people signed a paid ad in the *Transcript* supporting the president. A Williams student wrote to the *Record* on November 14, claiming to represent the one-third of the student body that did not support the Moratorium.

There was no Moratorium event in Williamstown in December, organizers said, in part because students were taking final exams and in part because some committee members thought that Nixon was "pulling out troops at a faster rate than . . .expected" – on December 15 it was announced that another 50,000 would be withdrawn. (Nixon thought that troop withdrawals would cool antiwar fervor. He was apparently right on that point.) Although events sponsored by the national Moratorium Committee continued until April 1970, the local committee ceased its work. On January 15, in the middle of Winter Study, no Moratorium events were scheduled, largely because Committee leaders were out of town. When February 15 went by without local Moratorium observance, an op-ed piece headlined "Moratorium Movement Dies?" appeared in the *Record*. It quoted the former editor-in-chief, who lamented that Nixon "had given no sign of being affected" by Moratorium events, and speculated that the new draft lottery, instituted on December 1, had taken a toll. If you got a low number, you were likely to be drafted, but if you got a high number you could relax: it "has really taken a lot out of the movement."

The 1970 student strike

War-related activity in Williamstown subsided for several months, but at the end of April 1970 it burst out again, in response to Nixon's announcement of a bombing campaign in Cambodia: after the war was supposed to be winding down, it now appeared to be widening. This led to the biggest antiwar event that Williamstown has ever seen: the student strike at Williams, part of what was in effect a national student strike, beginning on May 4, the day when four students at Kent State University were killed in an anti-ROTC protest. On May 6 the faculty agreed to suspend classes for the remainder of the semester.

Much has been written about the strike: it is perhaps the best remembered protest event in Williamstown during the entire Vietnam War, so it does not need extended treatment here. What most people seem to remember is that during a mass meeting of students and faculty in Chapin Hall to decide a course of action, after a long time spent on procedural wrangling, Robert Waite stood up to declare famously "Enough of this chicken shit!" But little has been written about the impact of the strike on the town. A few points are worth making:

1) Although the strike was largely confined to the Williams campus, student organizers set up a committee on "Williamstown organization," proposing that students canvass the community to press for antiwar legislation in Congress, lead discussions in local schools, hold meetings in local churches, and encourage a special town meeting. Two Williams faculty members circulated a petition in the town protesting the invasion of Cambodia, and secured more than 1000 signatures.

2) There was no violence in Williamstown, unlike (for example), the violent crackdown on the Berkeley campus, no civil disobedience, no arrests, no confrontation between antiwar and prowar groups.

3) On May 6 students at Mt. Greylock called for a strike, but only fifty students stayed home. On May 7 three hundred people attended a community meeting in the Congregational Church to discuss the strike as a response to the widening of the war, and "most seemed friendly to the strike."

4) The *Record* published a story about local reaction, finding that opinion was divided. Several Spring St. merchants supported Nixon, and thought the strike a sign of "foolishness" and "immaturity." Other merchants placed ads in the *Record* expressing their "deep concern" about the escalation of the war and the future of America. A Mt. Greylock teacher supported the students, as did the principal. Of the four selectmen interviewed, one supported the students; another supported the war but thought the students were conducting themselves properly; two others thought the strike would not change many minds.

After an initial burst of enthusiasm, and the establishment of "Strike Central," where activities were coordinated, student engagement seemed to die down. On May 11 a strike supporter wrote to the *Record* urging that "the student commitment to peace must be maintained." (Apparently because it was *not* being maintained.) On May 12 seniors voted to hold commencement as originally scheduled. On May 13 a student who participated in the May 9 march in Washington reported a smaller crowd than at earlier demonstrations, and sensed that there was a "smell of weariness" in the air, suggesting that the antiwar movement should reconsider whether mass demonstrations were useful. On May 14 the "Pause for Peace" movement, founded on the Williams campus, working to set up a one-hour nationwide work stoppage on May 27, announced it would disband for lack of political and financial support. Some students who supported the war objected that the strike had politicized the campus, and that they themselves felt "pressure to conform." Some Black students remained uninvolved in the strike, regarding it as too narrowly focused on the war (rather than oppression at home). A day after two demonstrating students were killed at all-Black Jackson State College in Mississippi, an event little noticed at Williams, they dismissed the strike as a kind of political theatre for white students.

This judgment unfairly dismisses the political fervor that drove committed activists. But it points to the fact that, as one professor put it later, most Williams students at the time were "protected" from the war, and knew that, or way or other, they themselves would not have to serve in the war. Most of those who did not go beyond high school, including some in Williamstown, did not have this luxury. When students went home after graduation, war-related activities ceased. The strike had little or no effect on the Nixon administration. (Historians of the period are broadly agreed that nationwide campus protests in the spring of 1970 generally failed to achieve their objectives.

1970-1973

When classes at Williams resumed in the fall, the *Record* published a front page story with the headline "Students return to class; activism wanes," noting that "the sense of political urgency so evident last spring is gone." In November, on the anniversary of the second Moratorium observance, a *Record* story was headlined "Quiet on campuses contrasts with activity a year ago," and went on to say that "there is general disenchantment among student" – "disenchantment" with the war was the key word of the Moratorium – "but it hasn't translated into action. The war has decreased as an issue, and is now one of many." A student who had participated in the Moratorium a year earlier wrote to say that "many of us have turned inward," not in apathy but in pessimism that activism might accomplish anything.

Troops continued to be withdrawn, and war-related protest was only sporadic for the rest of the war. It resumed the following spring, but this time in response to two specific events: a Green Beret training exercise at the North Adams airport, and the conviction of William Calley for war crimes at My Lai. The responses served as reminders that local opinion about the war was still divided. On March 19, 105 Green Berets parachuted onto the airport in a "tactical combat training mission," aiming to "take over" the airport and then march six miles up Mt. Williams in deep snow. The event, publicized in advance, brought out some 1500-2000 people, including about 400 students from Williams and Bennington, shouting slogans and passing out leaflets, and others, including some members of the local VFW and the North Adams and Pittsfield chapters of the John Birch Society, who distributed their own leaflets. It also attracted a large crowd who just came to see the "air show." Protesters hoped to disrupt the exercise. In the end it was the wind that caused disruption, as parachutists were blown off course, and sustained casualties when they fell off roofs and from trees. The protest received thorough coverage and front-page photos in the *Williams Record*, the *Eagle,* and the *Transcript*. Some letters to the editor from local residents commended "the Green Berets' Great Show" and denounced the "pitiful actions" of a handful of "unthinking students," Another letter praised the "spirited group of peace advocates" who behaved in "a sincere and peaceable manner." A letter from Professor Kurt Tauber, co-signed by 29 others, lamented that the simulated attack brought to mind the "devastation our armies are wreaking on the people of Vietnam."

Less than two weeks later news of Calley's conviction prompted more local protests, again from both sides. A one-man "Free Calley" campaign was organized by a World War II vet, whose platoon, he said, seldom took prisoners. The *Eagle* called the court's decision a "just verdict," but published letters from those who thought Calley had been made a scapegoat, and others (including two from Williamstown) who lamented that Calley, a "confessed killer of women and children," was being hailed as a hero. Predictably, Filmore Baker wrote to the *Transcript* in defense of Calley. Just as predictably, John Fisher (along with local lawyer Larry Urbano) took part in a panel discussion, before a college audience of 90, in which the call to free Calley was firmly opposed. Fisher asserted that Johnson and Nixon should be tried as war criminals.

A year later, in the spring of 1972, antiwar protests again spiked because of another incident: escalation of the war in mid-April, when Nixon ordered the resumption of bombing of Hanoi and Haiphong, and in early May, when Nixon announced Haiphong Harbor was being mined. On May 10 a large number students and faculty – estimates ranged from 600 to 1000 – crowded into Chapin Hall, some thinking that it was time to call for another student strike. But this time the meeting was introduced by comments from President Sawyer and two faculty members. Some thought this a sign that the administration and faculty were allied with the students, others that the college had coopted the protest. When students took their turn, the meeting passed a tepid resolution calling on students to take up Sawyer's suggestion and write letters opposing the war to Congress and the White House. As the audience began trickling away, resolutions were introduced to ask the faculty for extensions on academic obligations (narrowly defeated), and to go on strike (defeated 121-166). By the time a third resolution was introduced, to endorse and continue the sit-ins that had been staged over the previous several weeks at Westover Air Force Base in Chicopee, only a handful of students remained. The *Transcript* story about the meeting was headlined "War Reaction at Williams Is Confused, Inconclusive."

Perhaps in response to the inconclusive student reaction, or to emulate faculty from Amherst who had been arrested after they staged a sit-in, fifteen junior and mid-level members of the Williams faculty traveled to Westover on May 18, tried to block the entrance to the base, were arrested for disturbing the peace, fined $10 apiece, and released. One of the participants later told me he didn't think the protesters knew what they were doing.

The protests had little effect: bombing of North Vietnam continued through October 1972. Nixon's reelection in November took more wind out of protesters' sails, as did reduction of troop levels to 69,000 by the end of the year, and the beginning of the Paris Peace talks in January 1973. The small group of Williams students who went to Washington to protest at Nixon's inauguration. reported afterward that they felt "powerless and ineffective." Defense Secretary Melvin Laird's announcement on January 27 that the military draft had ended may have meant the end of peace marches. (Some observers, including Kurt Tauber, thought that the antiwar sentiment of many students was "opportunistic" rather than principled: they did not want to be sent to Vietnam.) Even John Fisher, who had written more than 65 fierce and passionate anti-war letters to the *Transcript* and *Eagle* since 1964, had stopped sending letters about the war by late 1971. There was no further antiwar protest in Williamstown to speak of, even though the last U.S. troops would not leave Vietnam for another 14 months.

As the last troops left in late March 1973 a long story appeared in the Eagle under the headline "Williams tolls the bell for Vietnam." It noted that the college planned to install a plaque in the chapel with the names of the five alumni who died during the war, but had no records to show how many graduates had served in Vietnam, or even how many had served in the military during the Vietnam years. Already the history of the Williamstown's part in the war was being lost.

April 30, 1975, the day when the U.S. abandoned the embassy in Saigon, is usually regarded as the end of the Vietnam War. But the war has continued in cultural memory, in Hollywood movies, novels, and in books arguing why the U.S. lost the war, or whether it *really* lost the war militarily. If Vietnam has faded from conversation, it's probably because so many world crises have intervened: the fall of the Berlin Wall, 9/11, the wars in Iraq and Afghanistan, the Great Recession, never mind coronavirus. But the war has left its mark, especially on those who fought in it, or fought against it. Many of the Williamstown boys and men who fought in Vietnam now lie in Eastlawn Cemetery. Others survive, as members of the local post of the American Legion. Mike Kennedy, the local veterans' agent, worked with a number of Vietnam vets who struggled over the years with disabilities, PTSD, or with the effects of Agent Orange.

But the Vietnam War is slipping into the past. Those who were of fighting (or draftable) age in 1965 or 1970 are now in their 70s. For anybody younger than 70, Vietnam is now part of "history." The Williams professors who protested the war are now in their late 80s or 90s. At least twice a year in Williamstown, Memorial Day and Veterans Day, townspeople are all rightly invited to remember those who fought in uniform. We should also remember, perhaps on the anniversary of the October 15 Moratorium, those who fought for peace: they also served.

PART 3

THE COLLEGE

Portrait of General Ranald MacKenzie (1958), by Hananiah Harari (American; 1912-2000). Oil on canvas. 36 x 30- in. (91.2 x 76.2 cm). Williams College Museum of Art, Williamstown, MA: Gift of Ralph Perkins, Class of 1909 (58.24).

Chapter 10

—w—

THREE EPH GENERALS IN THE CIVIL WAR

Sixty Williams College undergraduates took leaves of absence to serve in the Civil War. Some 240 alumni served. 30 died – you can see their names on the wall of Thompson Chapel. Of those who served, and rose to the rank of general, two who made extraordinary contributions that attracted attention in their day are little remembered now: Ranald Slidell Mackenzie (Class of 1859) and Samuel Chapman Armstrong (Class of 1862). Over the years Williams audiences have heard about these two men, mostly about their service *after* the Civil War: perhaps it is time that they were re-introduced to Williams readers. A third Williams general in the Civil War, James A. Garfield of the Class of 1856, is better known than the other two, but again mostly for what he did after the war. His contemporaries knew of him as a war hero.

Although there is no evidence that Armstrong and Mackenzie ever met each other, their careers are curiously parallel. They each spent only two years at Williams – one arrived late, the other left early. Each compiled a distinguished academic record. They both went into the war in 1862, and rose rapidly through the ranks – to major after Gettysburg, and brevet-general by their mid-twenties. ("Brevet" means an honorary battlefield promotion.) Both were present with their regiments at Appomattox Courthouse when Lee surrendered to Grant. They were both fierce disciplinarians. Later they would both receive honorary degrees from Williams. Both died young. Until recently one of them was regarded, by the few who knew of him, as a moral exemplar, even a hero, for his work in educating African-Americans (and, later, Native Americans) at Hampton Institute, though in today's exacting political climate some would probably be made uncomfortable by his racial views. The other would be regarded with some embarrassment and disapproval as an agent of the suppression of Native Americans in the "Indian Wars" of the 1870s. Some reconstruction of their lives and military careers – each of them led regiments of Black troops – will show how this is an oversimplification. Mackenzie's assigned task was both to herd the Indians onto reservations and to protect them against the depredations of white settlers. Armstrong's view of his Black and Indian students was paternalistic:

he aimed to "civilize" them and prepare them for what would be a subordinate position in American life. Both men accomplished great things, but neither can be fairly judged by today's standards.

Several other Williams alumni rose to the rank of general in the Civil War – the most famous of them James A. Garfield, Class of 1856. He is of course better known to Williams audiences for declaring in 1871 that "The ideal college is Mark Hopkins at one end of a log and a student on the other," and for being assassinated in 1881, on his way to his Williams 25th reunion, while serving (briefly) as President of the United States. But he acquired some reputation in his own lifetime for his Civil War service. The story of his military career featured prominently in campaign biographies and in books published just after his death. He was clearly the most "political" of Williams generals, and although he was a committed Union man, with strong abolitionist sentiments, realized that an impressive wartime record might serve him well in post-war politics.

Ranald Slidell Mackenzie (1840-89)

Mackenzie spent 2 ½ years at Williams, withdrawing halfway through his junior year to transfer to West Point, where he finished at the head of his class in 1862. He was commissioned a 2nd Lieutenant in the U.S. Army Engineers – the most elite unit in the regular army. (Robert E. Lee, second in the Class of 1829, went directly into the Corps of Engineers). He served throughout the rest of the war, from Second Bull Run in 1862 to Appomattox Courthouse in 1865. In the summer of 1864, having risen to the rank of Brevet Lt.-Colonel in the regular army, he was dissatisfied with his primarily non-combat role as a bridge-builder, and asked for a battlefield command. Promoted to Colonel of the 2nd Connecticut Volunteer Artillery, he rose quickly to become Brevet Brigadier-General and Brevet Major-General, at the age of 24. Returning to the regular army at the end of the war, he was breveted Brigadier-General, one of the youngest soldiers in the history of the United States Army to reach that rank. He was wounded six times, on one occasion left for dead on the field for twenty hours, and on another insisted on remaining at his post. He lost two fingers from his right hand at Petersburg. He seems to have been a prickly and a driven man, as demanding of others as he was of himself, and was such a fierce disciplinarian that many of his men hated him.

By the end of the war Mackenzie was a battle-hardened veteran, ready to lead a regiment in the regular army. He went on to have a notable career serving in the 1870s in the "Indian Wars" in the west, working his way up from captain to colonel, in command of the 41st US Infantry and 24th Infantry (both "buffalo soldier" regiments – Black soldiers, with white officers), and most prominently of the 4th U.S. Cavalry. Instrumental in the final defeat of the Comanches on the high plains and in the canyons of the Texas Panhandle, he is commonly regarded as the most successful Indian fighter in American history, ruthless and efficient, earning both the fear and respect of his opponents, and eventually (after they "came in" to the reservations) their friendship. But his career came to a premature end: in 1875 he suffered a head injury after falling from a wagon when a horse reared, and was apparently never the same after that, displaying severe mental instability. (For the first time in his life he drank heavily, and showed interest in a woman – but the one he chose happened to have a husband already. Mackenzie never married; in his last years he brought his mother west to live with him.) Some thought he had been not only worn out but broken by the physical and mental strain of twenty years of leading men into battle. He retired from the army as a Brigadier General in 1884, and died in an asylum for the insane at the age of 49 in 1889.

Mackenzie came from Scottish stock – "Ranald" is a Scottish variant of the more-familiar "Ronald." His father spent a career in the U.S. Navy, as did two of his brothers. Ranald was the nephew of the famous John Slidell (1793-1871), a U. S. Senator from Louisiana, who later served as a diplomat for the Confederacy where he would gain controversial attention for his part in the November 1861 "Trent Affair," when the British mail ship RMS Trent, carrying Slidell and a diplomatic colleague sailing to Europe to seek support for the South, was stopped by a Union warship, and the two diplomats were seized; they were later released. Young Ranald Mackenzie grew up in Tarrytown, New York and then in Morristown, New Jersey, and according to his biographers aspired to follow his father and older brothers into a military career. But his mother's uncle, retired president of Columbia College, thought he should be a lawyer, and encouraged him to begin his preparation for the law at Williams. Why at Williams? Perhaps because one of his cousins, William Johnson Slidell, had already begun at Williams as a member of the Class of 1858. So in September of 1855, at the age of 15, Mackenzie arrived in Williamstown, the youngest member of the Class of 1859.

He was later remembered by his classmate Washington Gladden as an extremely shy lad, with a lisp, but "likeable" enough and "a good scholar." He was physically slight: in maturity he was 5' 9" and only 145 lbs. Like his cousin, he joined the Kappa Alpha Society. The only indication that he distinguished himself at Williams is that he was one of the fourteen students (out of a class of 50) selected to present an oration at the "Junior Rhetorical Exhibition." But because of a death in the family, he was unable to attend. The topic he chose – military tactics – was apparently an indication of his early military interests, but at Williams he apparently gave no other sign of the qualities that would distinguish him as a soldier – what a colleague called "indomitable will, unbelievable endurance, and unsurpassed courage." In the same year he was nominated by his uncle, Senator John Slidell, for an at-large vacancy at West Point, and as the eldest son of a military officer he was appointed. He was not to return to Williamstown, though the college was happy to maintain its connection, particularly after Mackenzie attained early distinction as a soldier. In 1863 he was restored to the rolls of the class – that is, treated as if he had completed the B. A. degree, and in 1873, when he had begun to acquire national fame as an Indian fighter, he was granted an M. A. degree.

Mackenzie has not lacked for admirers among military historians. His fame was established when Grant, at the end of his *Memoirs* (1886), called him "the most promising young officer in the army," a man who in three short years won his way from West Point to command of a corps. "This he did on his own merit and without influence" – that is, he had no political patrons, and perhaps had to live down his link to his Confederate uncle. (Grant, who had personally intervened in 1882 to get Mackenzie promoted to brigadier-general, probably recognized the grim irony of his words: in 1886, when he was writing his memoirs, he would have known of the sad end of Mackenzie's army career.) In the late 1950s Mackenzie's post-Civil War career in the west became the basis of a TV serial, "Mackenzie's Raiders." In the early 1990s he attracted two scholarly biographers, and during the war in Iraq a forward operating base 60 miles north of Baghdad was named for him. He figures prominently in the 2010 bestseller, *Empire of the Summer Moon*, Sam Gwynne's book about the rise and fall of the Comanches in the southwest. Mackenzie's Civil War career has been largely overshadowed by his subsequent service on the frontier, and in the present climate it is difficult to find the virtues of an "Indian fighter," even an incorruptible one who played by the rules. A portrait of Mackenzie, commissioned and given to the college in 1958 by an admiring alumnus, used to hang in the old Lower Reading Room of Stetson Library, and later in the Williams Club in New York City, but when the club closed in 2010 it was put into storage. On the campus today he is in effect invisible.

Samuel Chapman Armstrong (1839-1893)

Samuel Chapman Armstrong arrived in Williamstown in December 1860, less than two years after Mackenzie departed. He came from Hawaii (then still an independent kingdom), the son of a Protestant missionary, who later became Hawaii's first Minister of Public Instruction. After completing two years of collegiate study in Hawaii, he was at the age of 21 sent to Williams, in response to the wishes of his father, who revered Williams as the origin of the Protestant foreign missionary movement, and wanted his son to study under the famous evangelical leader Mark Hopkins – the elder Armstrong had met Hopkins, who served for many years on the Board for Foreign Missions.

Armstrong joined the Class of 1862, but had to make up the work of the fall term before the winter term began in mid-January. Hopkins waived his tuition fees, and even made arrangements for Armstrong to share a room in the president's house with his own son, Archibald, also a member of the Class of 1862. At first cold and lonely, Armstrong quickly adapted to college life, made a number of friends, and traveled to New York City and to the Adirondacks during vacations. Unlike Mackenzie he was outgoing and easygoing in temperament, and apparently very attractive to women – and was ready to reciprocate their interest. In his senior year he was elected president of the Philotechnian, one of the two college literary societies, and belonged to the "Missionary Band," a group of students who were preparing for a career in foreign missions. Armstrong compiled a strong academic record: he graduated fifth in his class of 54. He deeply admired Mark Hopkins as "a noble man in the highest sense of the word," "the greatest mind in New England," who made the students "think." (He would later say that "whatever good teaching I may have done has been Mark Hopkins teaching through me.") But by the time he graduated he had given up the idea of becoming a missionary, and graduated in the summer of 1862 without knowing what career he would take up.

We know a good deal about Armstrong's state of mind both at Williams and during the war because he was a prodigious letter-writer. He wrote frequently and fluently, and at length – rather loftily to his mother, teasingly to his siblings, and jauntily to his college "chum," Archie Hopkins. And those letters were preserved – many of them in the Williams College Archives – and later transcribed. (Mackenzie, by contrast, left behind almost no personal written record, only his official military reports to his superior officers, perhaps in part because – after his painful hand wound – he found it physically difficult to write, but perhaps too because he was just not a forthcoming person.)

As he left Williams Armstrong made plans for his immediate future: although he regarded himself not as an "American" but as a Hawaiian, he determined to enlist in the U. S. army, though not out of any strong political conviction. Even before commencement, he was offered a position as 2nd Lieutenant in a new regiment to be raised in New York City, but as he said he thought he could do better: and he got himself appointed senior captain of the 125th New York, a Rensselaer County regiment – after personally recruiting a company of men from Troy and environs.

Armstrong's military career began very badly: two weeks after leaving Troy, the entire 125th New York came under heavy artillery fire at Harper's Ferry, and surrendered to Stonewall Jackson. Because Jackson had to hasten off to relieve the Confederates at the then-raging Battle of Antietam, he quickly arranged for the 125th to be "paroled" – i.e., sent to a camp in Chicago under a kind of house arrest until they could be exchanged for Confederate prisoners in November 1862. Once it returned to active duty, Armstrong's regiment spent the next seven months in camp. But his letters suggest that he was discovering a new urgency about his contribution to the war effort. Looking forward to January 1, 1863, when the Emancipation Proclamation was to take effect, Armstrong wrote to his mother in December 1862 that "We are fighting for humanity and freedom." January 1, he wrote, will be "possibly the greatest day in American history . . . when the sons of Africa shall be free." The war, he now thought, was "the greatest struggle of modern times for the most sacred principles."

The regiment saw no action until the summer of 1863, when it played a significant role at Gettysburg – Armstrong himself led a part of the counterattack against Pickett's charge: his letters home vividly describe what he called his "first fight." Because his colonel was killed in the battle, all the officers moved up a rank, and Armstrong became a major. But without a company to command, he felt himself a "fifth wheel," and began looking for a new assignment.

As early as January 1863 he had tried (without success) to get an appointment to the staff of fellow-alumnus General James Garfield. Now a new opportunity presented itself.

When Lincoln decided in the spring that it was politically safe to put freed slaves to work as soldiers in the regular army, and to form Black regiments with white officers, Armstrong took the required examination and was one of the very few to pass. To serve in a Black regiment would mean moving up in rank – many white officers refused to consider leading Black troops, and even opposed the recruitment of former slaves as soldiers, so there were openings. But by the same token a soldier who agreed to lead Black troops was exposing himself to scorn from some Union supporters, and to reprisals from Confederates if he or his Black soldiers were captured. (On July 13, 1863 the Confederacy declared it would not exchange captured white officers of Black regiments: they would be court-martialed, and subject to execution. And it would not exchange Black soldiers. In reply, the Union suspended all prisoner exchanges.) Armstrong was apparently ready to face the consequences. Presumably too, given his new abolitionist convictions, he was stirred by the idea of playing a more personal role in the struggle for Black freedom. He seems to have inquired in late-summer 1863 about the possibility of raising a Black regiment of New York volunteers, and when that met political opposition, in November he accepted the assignment as Lt.-Colonel of the newly-formed 9th United States Colored Troops. (Had he not been only 24 years old he would probably have been made colonel.) As he wrote to his mother, "It will be a grand thing to have been identified with the negro movement."

At first Armstrong enjoyed his work with the 9th U. S. Colored Troops (USCT), observing with pride how his troops were being made into disciplined soldiers. He had confidence and pride in his men, though in jokey letters to Archie Hopkins he still felt free to refer to them callously as "nigs" and "darkeys." Unlike Mackenzie, he also enjoyed life in military camp: he was described by a loyal subordinate as a very "cordial"man who was "the center of the social life of the officers of his regiment." But as was not unusual, his regiment saw no front-line service – top brass were not yet convinced that Blacks would stand firm under fire – and was sent out of the way to coastal South Carolina. After a while Armstrong, even though in the absence of his colonel he was in command of the regiment, was again bored, and jealous of soldiers who were closer to the action in Virginia. But when his own regiment was sent to Virginia it was engaged in only small skirmishes, before it settled down in the trenches before Petersburg. In November Armstrong got his own regiment, the 8th USCT, and was again encouraged, if only by the promotion to colonel. But he saw little action with this regiment either, though he was present at the fall of Richmond and at the surrender at Appomattox.

Although he came out of the war as a colonel, and brevet-brigadier general of volunteers, Armstrong cannot be said to have had a brilliant career as a soldier, either in his fifteen months with the 125th New York or his 21 months with the USCT. Again unlike Mackenzie, he had few opportunities to display personal bravery, and the only bodily consequences were a broken arm and a case of malaria., which put him for a time in a war hospital. What the war did for him was to plant the seed of his future life's work as founder and first head of Hampton Institute, one of the country's oldest "historically Black colleges." It awakened his passion for the building up of the "sons of Africa." As his biographer, Robert Engs, has argued, it was serving in the USCT that convinced him that what Blacks needed was strong leadership and educational and vocational training. In a sense he was still the son of a missionary on a civilizing mission to benighted savages, whether crude farm boys from upstate New York or newly-freed slaves who as adults were painfully learning their ABC's.

Armstrong stayed in closer touch with Williams than Mackenzie did, speaking to the Boston Alumni Association in 1871, returning to Williamstown to accept his honorary degree in 1887, and again to speak in 1890. When he died in 1893 his grave at Hampton Institute was marked, so his daughter noted, "by a block of Williamstown granite at one end and Hawaiian volcano rock at the other." On the Williams campus today a dorm in the Mission complex, built in 1969, bears the name of Armstrong House.

Perhaps this suggests that Armstrong is the Civil War general Williams prefers to remember, the one it admires more, the one whose work seems to lead on to the work Williams wants its students and graduates to do. There are few recent monuments to warriors on any college campus – which may suggest that colleges today really don't know what to make of soldiers, and look for moral exemplars elsewhere. But Mackenzie held himself to very high professional standards, and behaved with exemplary courage. He effectively and efficiently carried out not his own will but the policy of the elected national government of his time, to gather the remnant of the Indian nations onto reservations and try to incorporate them – by teaching them to be farmers and sheepherders – into the white man's economy. In some respects Armstrong did the same – sought to elevate freed slaves (and Indians) through training for their role in an economy both agricultural and industrial. Armstrong's own work at Hampton was honorable – but we should not make the mistake of thinking that he looked at the great question of race in America the way that we do today. By the same token, when we realize that by today's standards Armstrong was a *racist*, we should not berate or dismiss him: by the standards of his own day he was enlightened and progressive.

James A. Garfield (1831-1881)

Like Armstrong and Mackenzie, Garfield spent only two years at Williams. Arriving in Williamstown in 1854 after spending three years at a small Ohio college, he explained later that he felt the need to "liberalize" his mind and to "break the shell of local notions." Within a month of his arrival, he heard Ralph Waldo Emerson lecture, and said he was so exhilarated that "I could not sleep that night." He quickly distinguished himself as editor of the *Williams Quarterly*, president of one of the two student literary societies (the *other* one), and president of the Mills Theological Society – Armstrong would later be a member. Like many students bound for the ministry, instead of pledging one of the Greek-letter fraternities, he joined the "Anti-Secret Society," later called the "Social Fraternity." In 1855 he prepared to argue the case against secret fraternities in a formal college debate. Like Armstrong, he was impressed with the intellectual power of Mark Hopkins, and like Armstrong, he too caught the eye of the president: Hopkins later said that at Williams Garfield "made himself a man." When he graduated in 1856 he went back to Ohio and took up a teaching position.

In the summer of 1861, having served for two years as a state senator in Ohio, and as the governor's representative in negotiations with other midwestern governors about providing troops for the Union cause, he finally received a commission as Lt.-Col. (and then Colonel) of the 42nd Ohio. (That means that with political connections he entered the Army near the top of the ranks.) After successfully leading a brigade of troops in a minor battle in Kentucky, shortly after his 30th birthday, he was promoted to Brigadier-General. In early April of 1862 he was put in charge of a brigade of four Ohio regiments and was sent to support Gen. Don Carlos Buell at Shiloh, arriving at the battlefield just after the Confederate forces had begun retreating. That summer he came down with hepatitis, and returned home to Ohio to recover. In September he was nominated as the Republican candidate for Congress from the 19th district of Ohio, a strongly Republican district, and in November he was easily elected – and thus helped Lincoln's party (with support from its Unionist Party allies) retain control of the House. But the 38th Congress was not scheduled to take its seats until December

1863, so Garfield remained in the army, awaiting further orders and hoping for a field command. By January 1863 word circulated that he would soon receive an appointment, and it was at this time that Samuel Armstrong was hoping to be able to join his staff.

As it happened, Garfield did not get another field command: in February 1863 he was appointed Chief of Staff for General William Rosecrans, head of the Army of the Cumberland, then campaigning in Eastern Tennessee. Rosecrans was a West Point graduate and an Ohio man. He was under pressure from Washington to pursue the enemy more aggressively, but chose (like Gen. George McClellan) to move cautiously. Garfield, whose strength lay in military strategy, later said that he thought of himself as Rosecrans' "alter-ego." Over the short course of his army service, he was drawn toward the radical Republicanism of Salmon P. Chase: early on he thought that the Union should give up hopes of reconciliation and should wage "total war" on a recalcitrant enemy, arming escaped Negroes – "our Black Americans," as he called them – and enrolling them in the Union army. Garfield privately agreed with Rosecrans' critics, writing to Chase, his political patron, of his impatience at Rosecrans' caution and his unwillingness to advance against the enemy. (The private letters later came to light.) There was probably a political angle to Garfield's impatience: like other Radical Republicans, and like many "political generals," he generally mistrusted West Point graduates, professional soldiers who, some thought, did not understand the threat presented to the Union by slavery, and were not determined enough to prosecute a war against troops led by their former classmates.

Garfield served with Rosecrans on the little-known Tullahoma Campaign in July 1863, a brilliant Union success, and then in September at the bloody Battle of Chickamauga, second only to Gettysburg in the total number of casualties, where his role in the Union loss, and his loyalty to Rosecrans, are still debated by historians and biographers.

When Union and Confederate forces were drawn up on either side of West Chickamauga Creek, a vaguely-written order to one of Rosecrans' brigade commanders inadvertently led to the opening of a gap in the Union lines. Confederate forces under Longstreet quickly poured through the gap and shattered the Union right. Normally it would have been Garfield as Chief of Staff who would issue his commander's orders, but in this case the unfortunate order was sent by Rosecrans himself. Even so, Garfield was suspected of pursuing his own interests. His critics claimed that when he accompanied

Rosecrans from the Chickamauga battlefield, and then advised his superior to retreat to Chattanooga, while he himself rode back to the front (a ride that was much publicized at the time), he was looking for headlines. His friends, and his most recent biographer, dispute the charges, arguing that Garfield acted properly as Chief of Staff, escorting the commanding general to safety and then returning to the battlefield , where Gen. George Thomas – the "Rock of Chickamauga" – was holding the remnants of the Union line. Garfield's objective was, he claimed, to act as Rosecrans' "eyes and ears." "Let me go to the front," he reportedly appealed to his superior: "It is dangerous, but the army and the country can better afford for me to be killed than for you." It has also been reported that it was Rosecrans who suggested that Garfield carry a message to Thomas. In any event, Garfield and an orderly rode six (or maybe eight) miles through difficult and dangerous country, evading Longstreet's sharpshooters, his horse shot out from under him, his orderly killed, and safely arrived to find Thomas holding his ground.

Historians have expressed doubt about whether "Garfield's Ride" had any military purpose or effect, but the story of it was immediately spread by a reporter who happened to be on the battlefield. It proved useful to a political campaigner, and featured prominently in a volume put together in the fall of 1880 called *Stories and Sketches of General Garfield*, where it was called "one of the gallantest acts of the war." It was still being re-told 15 years after Garfield's death, in *McClure's Magazine* for September 1895, where the story is illustrated with another drawing of the heroic young Garfield , who is quoted as saying to himself, at a particularly difficult moment, '"Now is your time; be a man, Jim Garfield."

After another promotion, to Major-General, for gallantry at Chickamauga, Garfield was still considering his options, but as his congressional colleagues were preparing to take their seats, he was persuaded by Lincoln that he would be of more service to the country in Congress – where Republicans were needed, especially those with military experience – than on the battlefield. The friends of Rosecrans muttered darkly that Garfield only resigned because Lincoln had appointed Gen. George Thomas, the hero of Chickamauga, instead of Garfield, to command the Army of the Cumberland. (This is probably unfair – Garfield would later praise Thomas as one of the best Union generals, "a colossal pillar of unchiseled granite.")

Garfield spent the next two decades in Congress. He and Samuel Armstrong became friends, and he was a member of the board at Hampton Institute for five years. He also maintained close relations with his alma mater.

He attended commencement in 1866, was granted an honorary degree in 1872, and spoke at commencement in both 1872 and 1876. (He was nominated as a trustee of the college, but declined.) Later he arranged to have his two sons, Harry and Jim, go to Williams.

When he ran for president in 1880 his Civil War record was a campaign issue, and the old stories of his conduct at the disastrous loss at Chickamauga were dug up by his political enemies. But Garfield's friends vigorously defended him, and he won his party's nomination as a compromise candidate at a deadlocked convention, defeating another Civil War general, Winfield Hancock, in the general election. After his inauguration as president in 1881, he held a reception in the White House for Williams alumni.

Garfield left more of a mark on Williams than his fellow Eph generals, and not only because of his famous remark about Mark Hopkins and the Log. He served as president of the Society of Alumni from 1871 to 1873. His son, Harry, graduated from the Class of 1885 and went on to become president of the college from 1908 to 1934. In 1935 the so-called Commons Club, a social organization, with headquarters at Currier Hall, was renamed the Garfield Club, in honor of President Harry Garfield, who had founded it in 1928 as an alternative to fraternities. Harry Garfield was a fraternity man, but may have taken an interest in forming an alternative to fraternities since his father as a student at Williams in the 1850s had declined to join a fraternity. The Garfield Club continued to be an important force on the campus until it dissolved itself in 1952, as a protest at the intransigeance of the fraternity system. One of the first scholarly treatments of Garfield was published in 1925 by Williams history professor, T. C. Smith, Professor of American History from 1903 to 1938, and a close associate of Garfield's son. When in the late 1960s the college took over from fraternities the feeding and housing of students, the old Delta Upsilon fraternity on South St. was fittingly renamed Garfield House, fitting because the DU chapter at Williams originated as the old "Social Fraternity" of which Garfield had been a member in the 1850s.

Our three Eph generals had remarkable military careers, and two of them had more remarkable careers after their military service. Remarkable too, perhaps, is that there very few others like them in the college alumni body. Williams has produced some extraordinary soldiers, several of whom won the Congressional Medal of Honor, including Charles Whittlesey (Class of 1905), who led the famous "Lost Battalion" in World War I, and William Bradford Turner (Class of 1914), whose family established in his memory the William Bradford Turner Citizenship Prize, perhaps the college's top student honor. And it has produced a few others who rose to the top ranks, including Edward B. Wheeler, Class of 1939, who went to law school after Williams, volunteered in 1941, and after a short OCS course was commissioned a 2nd Lieutenant in the Marines. By the end of the war, in which he saw heavy combat, he had risen to the rank of Major, and at war's end decided to stay in the service. Seeing combat again in Korea and Vietnam, he retired as a Major-General. Hugh G. Robinson spent his freshman year at Williams with the Class of 1953 before accepting an appointment at West Point. He graduated from there in 1954, and retired in 1983, also as a Major-General. A third was Steven Clarey, Class of 1962, who went into the U.S. Navy upon graduation from Williams, and retired as a Rear Admiral.

But almost no other Williams alumni rose to the rank of general or admiral. Perhaps it is not surprising: most of those who rise to the top of the military profession are not citizen-soldiers like Armstrong and Garfield, but professional soldiers like Mackenzie, trained like him at the military academies. (Of all those who rose throughout American history to four-star general of the Army, about 2/3 went through West Point.) Williams graduates have since the 19th century tended to go into other professions, at first the ministry and in later decades teaching, medicine, and the law. When they devote a career to public service, they are much more likely to become elected officials, or senior government advisors, or diplomats, than soldiers. Large numbers of Williams alumni performed military service, but saw that service not as their lifelong profession but as their short-term obligation as citizens, or their fate as draftees. It normally takes a long time to rise through the military ranks to the top: opportunities come more frequently during wartime – which contributed to the rise of all three Ephs in the Civil War. Furthermore, two of them had a leg up – Armstrong entering as a captain, Garfield with two legs up, mustering in as a Lt.-Colonel. The Civil War was the last American war in which most of those who fought came from volunteer forces, where advancement was more rapid than in the regular army.

Is there anything in the liberal arts that makes them antithetical to a career commitment to soldiering? Perhaps to the career commitment, though not to the short-term soldiering. If you consider only the last fifty years, resistance on college campuses across the country to the war in Vietnam (and to ROTC programs) and to the wars in the Middle East might lead one to speculate that there is something in the groves of academe that does not like war. But if you take a longer view, you can see that Williams has generally tended to align itself with the war effort during the nation's major conflicts. A monument now on the lawn in front of Griffin Hall was erected in 1868 to remember all those Williams graduates who died while fighting for the Union, and the names of all Williams alumni who have died during the country's wars have, since 1920, been chiseled in stone in Thompson *Memorial* Chapel. In the spring of 1917 three courses in "Military Arts" were introduced into the curriculum, and President Harry Garfield took a leave of absence to be national Fuel Administrator. Even before Pearl Harbor President James Phinney Baxter went to Washington for what would be four years of service with the OSS, and in 1943 the U.S. Navy established V-5 and V-12 schools on the Williams campus designed to turn out aviators and midshipmen. In a commencement address at Williams on June 4, 1972, entitled "The Citizen and the Military," historian Barbara Tuchman challenged the hastiness of students to assume that military matters are beneath their attention. At the 2008 alumni reunions, one of the more interesting and well-attended panels featured Williams alumni currently or recently serving in the military.

Remember too that the college's founder was a soldier. When his remains were dug up and brought back to Williamstown in 1920 for reinterment in the new Thompson Chapel, they were carried in a flag-draped coffin at the head of a full military parade. One of the soldiers who marched at the front of the parade was Colonel Whittlesey. The other was Colonel Archibald Hopkins, who had fought in the Civil War, and had known both Armstrong and Garfield. But even Ephraim Williams, like almost all Williams graduates, did not think of himself as before all things a soldier. The college seal notes that Williams was founded "e liberalitate e williams armigeri" – through the generosity of E[phraim] Williams, *armigeri*." "Armigeri" literally means "bearer of arms," but it does not mean "soldier": it means that his family is qualified to bear a coat of arms: "E. Williams, esquire," as we would say, or "E. Williams, gentleman." Even he, as Fred Rudolph has noted, was "not a professional soldier" but a "civilian in uniform."

That makes Armstrong and Garfield typical of the Williams warrior. Mackenzie was the outlier – and the fact that he is really a graduate of West Point seals the difference. But all three were distinguished men, and their stories of their military careers deserve to be restored to the college's institutional memory.

Bust of Tyler Dennett (c. 1954), by Elizabeth McLean-Smith. Terra cotta.
21 x 16 x 10 in. (53.3 x 40.6 x 25.4 cm). Williams College Museum of Art, Williamstown, MA:
Gift of the Class of 1904 (54.38).

Chapter 11

—꿈—

THE RESIGNATION OF TYLER DENNETT

Tyler Dennett served as president of Williams College for just three years. He resigned in June 1937, after a dispute with the Williams trustees, who decided at their meeting that month to buy the Greylock Hotel, at the corner of Main St. and North St., then closed and for sale. The trustees wanted to prevent commercial development of the property. Dennett, at a time when college finances were straitened, argued against it on the grounds that any available funds should be spent to add faculty, faculty housing, and equipment for faculty research, and that buying the property did not serve any educational purpose.

Dennett declared that it was a matter of principle, not only that money should be spent only on educational purposes but also that the college should not undertake any major step unless president and board agreed. The resignation was made verbally in the middle of a trustee meeting and then submitted in writing ten days later. At special meetings in July the board accepted the resignation and appointed James Phinney Baxter, a member of the board, as the new president.

But in his three short years at Williams, Dennett made an extraordinary mark on the college. Fred Rudolph, long-time professor of history at Williams who wrote often about the history of the college, thought that Dennett had in effect set the agenda for the next four decades: "the presidents who have succeeded him have had the job of fixing the problem that Dennett identified." Professor Charles Keller, director of admissions under Dennett, did not always agree with his boss, but thought that Dennett had done more than that. He recalled years later that Dennett "did more for Williams in three years, than most people have done in twenty-odd." In reflecting on his own twelve years as president, Jack Sawyer observed that the changes he introduced had served to "carry forward [Dennett's] essential initiatives."

Why then did Dennett's presidency only last three years? It has long been suspected that the dispute over the Greylock Hotel was just the cover story, and that Dennett was in effect forced out by trustees who were troubled by changes that he had introduced in his three years in office, and his blunt and forceful way of making them. In particular, so it has been suggested, they were disturbed that in a speech to Williams alumni in Boston in March 1937 Dennett had declared that there were "too many 'nice boys' [i.e. graduates of prep schools] at Williams" and that the college ought to try to enroll more students from public high schools, even if they were on average less prepared for college work. The speech was reported in an AP story which was printed in newspapers across the country, and, not surprisingly, aroused angry responses from Williams students and alumni (especially those who had gone to prep schools), as well as supportive responses from those who thought Dennett was doing well to try to change the mix of students at what was perceived to be a school for rich boys.

Dennett's resignation was also widely reported at the time, and much was made of his bluntness of manner and alleged intransigence. Over the decades since there have been several retrospective reports of the incident, but no clear consensus has emerged, and there has been no full account of Dennett's presidency, in part because the Dennett papers in the Williams College Archives have not been fully catalogued, and documentary evidence is scattered across several different collections of material. But from the archival record it is possible to assemble a fuller picture than has heretofore been printed. What follows is an attempt at a more complete account, based on Dennett's published speeches and reports, minutes of trustee meetings (both published and unpublished), and Dennett's private papers, especially his correspondence with trustees, alumni, and faculty.

I will here attempt to answer several old questions: was the resignation the result of a disagreement about a real estate deal? Or was it primarily a disagreement about governance between the board and its president who was also a member of the board and its presiding officer? Was it prompted by pressure from alumni who were angered by Dennett's "nice boys" speech? Was a group of conservative alumni disaffected more generally by the changes that Dennett was making to what they regarded as their college? And some new questions: was the resignation an instance of Dennett's bold and even impulsive manner, a readiness to push back sharply when opposed? Was it premeditated, or was it a sudden decision made under pressure? And did Dennett, when given time to reconsider, think that there might be a way to save his presidency?

Dennett's changes

Before turning to the events of the spring and early summer of 1937, it is important to survey the many changes that Dennett introduced to the college, beginning almost immediately after his taking office in July 1934. At his first trustees meeting in October 1934 he persuaded the trustees to create four new board committees, and made clear that he intended to balance the operating budget – which had been in deficit under his predecessor, Harry Garfield. At his induction in October he declared that the college was both a community of learning and a "business organization" that had to keep its spending within its resources. Some changes concerned student life. He announced a reorganization of student government, and transferred responsibility for discipline from a student to a faculty committee – students ratified the change. But in other respects he wanted students to take responsibility for themselves: acknowledging student sentiment, in his first academic year he announced that seniors would be permitted unlimited class cuts, were not required to attend Sunday vesper services, and did not have to take a Bible exam. Some changes concerned his senior staff: it was probably not coincidental that the college pastor resigned in January 1935. In the same month Dennett (shocked to discover that the college was accepting students as late as September, in order to "fill out the class"), brought in a new admissions director. In June 1935 he appointed a new college treasurer and in July of 1936 a new Dean of the College.

Dennett was not afraid of controversy. In early November 1934, after Roosevelt established the Federal Emergency Relief Administration, offering government aid to college students, Dennett announced in a public letter that Williams would not take FERA funds. His reason: although the college needed scholarship money, it did not want to be dependent on government funds – what the government gave in one year it might not give in the next. When FERA administrator Harry Hopkins spoke out in late November about "over-endowed" and "aristocratic" colleges (Harvard and Yale had joined Williams in declining the money), Dennett fired back at Hopkins' "demagoguery." The money might have been helpful, but for Dennett the principle was more important. It is striking that he went on to say that there were too many unemployed college graduates and that not all students enrolled in colleges were worthy of financial aid – statements that were likely to offend more people (both graduates and students) than they might please. This was perhaps a sign that Dennett planned to continue to speak out bluntly and candidly and let the chips fall where they may.

In his first year he also set out to raise scholarly standards, for both students and faculty. Early in his first year he signaled his intentions – to alumni as well as students – by publicly deploring "college loafing" and insisting that all Williams students take their academic work seriously. (Some alumni apparently thought there was no need to over-emphasize scholarship.) In his induction speech he announced that an emphasis on "small group instruction" (with a 10-to-1 faculty student ratio) would continue, but that he wanted faculty to focus on "appraisal" as well as "method," and said he did not want to hear anything more about "recitation." Proposed curricular changes, drafted by Dean of Faculty and long-time chair of the faculty Committee on Curriculum, T. C. Smith, greeted by the students in the spring of 1935 as a "liberalization" – fewer prerequisites and more course choice – turned out, when they were adopted by the faculty the following January, to make the curriculum more demanding: a double-credit senior course, a comprehensive major exam at the end of the senior year, and a beefed-up honors program.

He also wanted to strengthen the faculty. As a well-published diplomatic historian – he had published six books, including a Pulitzer-Prize winner, by the time he came to Williams – he had high expectations for scholar-teachers. In March 1935, when the faculty approved the creation of a three-member committee to advise the president on appointments, promotion, and tenure, the old "seniority" system, whereby promotion and pay raises came with length of service, was replaced by a merit system. It is often suggested that Dennett cleared out "dead wood" in the faculty – implying that he got rid of senior professors who had run out of energy. (Stories circulate that tenured faculty were called into his office and, so to speak, bluntly counseled out.) In fact, with a few exceptions (two retirees who were 70 or older), those who departed were untenured instructors and assistant professors. Twelve nontenured faculty were let go for 1935-36. and here Dennett was continuing President Garfield's practice. Over the three years of his presidency Dennett brought in 39 new men (out of a total faculty of 88) including several – George Harper, Bertrand Fox, Fred Schuman, R. R. R. Brooks, Freeman Foote, and Sam Matthews – who would become professorial mainstays for decades, as well as two long-time coaches, Clarence Chaffee and Bob Muir.

Faculty, students, and alumni were in effect put on notice that Williams would not be run in the same way it had been under Garfield.

Trustees, who approved the changes, were behind Dennett. They worked cooperatively with him on identifying the college's major needs, including several building projects: a proposed expansion to Griffin Hall, a proposed remodeling of Hopkins Hall, a new wing for Lawrence Hall, and winter sports facilities. Dennett succeeded in raising money for both the Lawrence project and squash courts.

Dennett and "nice boys"

Dennett had two more overarching concerns: first, he was worried that the student body largely consisted of boys from prep schools. In September 1933, 26.2% of the freshman came from public schools, and in September 1934 fewer than 21%. And the downward trend was continuing: over the next two years enrollment of public school graduates actually dropped further, to 18.7%. As he wrote to one alumnus in the spring of 1937, Williams has "the highest percentage of preparatory school boys of any college in the country," and he was worried that Williams might become a "class college." (In Dennett's student days – he was Class of 1904 – high school students made up about 40% of the freshman class). Dennett wanted more diversity, more heterogeneity. He also thought high school students would on the whole improve academic standards. A study he commissioned in September 1936 showed that although many high school graduates began Williams at some disadvantage they tended to catch up and outperform prep school grads by junior and senior year. They had a lower drop-out/flunk-out rate, and were over-represented on the "honor list." Seven of ten Phi Betes in 1936 (three of whom had had some private school) came from public high schools. Dennett wanted to raise the percentage of high school graduates by September 1937 to 25%.

Why had enrollment of high school students declined? Dennett thought it was not the cost of tuition: Williams did not charge more than the Ivies. And it was not for lack of scholarship money: more than two-thirds of high school applicants did not even ask for financial aid. One reason, he thought, was the recently-modified admissions requirement that applicants have four years of Latin or Greek – Williams was the last college in the country to give it up. In 1933 the requirement was reduced to three years and in May 1934 further reduced to two years, and finally ended, under Dennett, in March 1935. But Dennett thought the word had not reached high schools across the country. The most important reason, he concluded, was the college's reputation as a school for rich prep-school boys.

Dennett's second major concern, related to the first, is that campus life was dominated by fraternities, which by and large did not assign high priority to scholarship; he wanted membership in fraternities to be reduced from about 80% of the student body to about 60%. Again, things had changed since Dennett's time as a student. Fraternity membership had increased from about 52% in 1905 to about 80% when he took office. Those not admitted to fraternities, or who chose not to pledge, were invited to join the Garfield Club. But Dennett and others were concerned that the Garfield Club represented a shrinking minority of students, and that many of those who did not join fraternities felt excluded from social life on the campus. Although it was not the case that fraternity members were all prep school graduates, there was considerable overlap between public school graduates and the Garfield Club. In the fall of 1936 a faculty committee appointed by Dennett recommended that the right balance between fraternity boys and Garfield Club boys was 60-40. (Such a change would require a "new central eating place.") Fraternity students and fraternity alumni, happy with the way things were, were not pleased.

In early March 1937 Dennett attended an alumni dinner in Boston, where he made a few informal unscripted remarks about the situation on the campus. He again made the case – which he had been making since he became president – that Williams ought to, and was trying to, enroll more public high school graduates. He commented on the pedagogical advantages of heterogeneity: it's better not to have too many students of any one kind. At Williams, for example, there were "too many 'nice boys'." (He later claimed that he was using a familiar colloquial term to refer to boys with a polished social manner, and that his audience knew what he meant.) A reporter who, unbeknownst to Dennett, happened to be present, picked up the term, and an editor at his paper featured it in the headline to the reporter's story.

The story was widely reprinted, and Dennett got lots of mail, especially from alumni who had not attended the dinner and had only read the newspaper account. Dennett also exchanged letters in March and April 1937 with several trustees who did not attend and were concerned about what they read. George van Santvoord, the headmaster of Hotchkiss who (according to the misleading press report) was in effect insulted by Dennett at the dinner, wrote to say that he recognized that the newspaper story misrepresented the event. William Sidley was alarmed about press reports, but after an exchange of letters wrote in late March to Dennett say that "I am with you one hundred per cent." Lewis Perry (head of Exeter) was "entirely in sympathy" with Dennett's wish to enroll more high schools graduates, and later said that "all Williams men are behind you," but wanted Dennett to keep his emphasis on "the positive" rather than the negative. John Wilson was at first distressed about the newspaper coverage, and about Dennett's use of an "unhappy expression." But he listened to Dennett's explanations, and by mid-April wrote that "I am in full accord with you," though he urged Dennett to keep his opinions on the matter "in the family." It is perhaps significant that no exchange of letters with the most senior trustees – Bentley Warren and Henry Lefavour, both on the Executive Committee – has survived. They were probably both at the dinner, since they were both from Boston and had attended the same Boston dinner two years earlier, and did not need clarification from Dennett, but one might think they would have written if only to reassure Dennett of their confidence in him, and that Dennett might have felt nervous that they did not write.

What probably helped to reassure worried trustees (and alumni) was Dennett's speech a month later to New York alumni, where he set out to "clarify" what he had said in Boston. This time he wrote out and carefully revised his remarks, emphasizing "the positive": we want "heterogeneity" because students learn from one another; "variety of experience"; geographical distribution; economic and social distribution. We want more "self-made" and "unprivileged" boys. Trustee Frederic T. Wood wrote Dennett that night to say that it was an "excellent" speech, and that, like Dennett, he did not want Williams to be known as a "class college."

Dennett's March 8 speech sounds remarkably like the arguments in favor of "diversity" that have been heard on the Williams campus at least since the early 1990s. But it's noteworthy that while today's admissions officers talk about students of high ability from underrepresented socio-economic groups, Dennett put his emphasis on heterogeneity rather than ability. For Dennett there were also clear limits to "heterogeneity." He wanted high school graduates; he wanted boys from "unprivileged" backgrounds. But he did not think there was a place at Williams for Blacks or Jews. Although Williams had in fact enrolled small numbers of Blacks for decades, several of whom went on to achieve eminence, the numbers had declined since the last years of Garfield's presidency. By 1933-34 there was only one Black student (who was reportedly very unhappy at Williams), and by 1937 there were none, possibly because word got around that the Williams of the early 1930s was more dominated by fraternities (not welcoming to Blacks) than it had ever been. Dennett was worried that the college could not provide "favorable conditions" and that Black students who faced "social discrimination" would be unhappy. He thought Jewish students faced the same exclusion from fraternity life, and that many of "our most gifted Jewish boys" were becoming "positively bitter." The clear implication – to him – was the college ought not to enroll Jews or Blacks.

At this distance, Dennett's policy suggests blatant (or perhaps self-deceiving) racism. But we should remember that at the very moment he spoke he was making vigorous efforts to change the social circumstances on the campus, so that fraternities and prep school boys would not be so dominant; in his own mind he was perhaps making a pragmatic judgment about whether Williams was then a good "fit" for Black or Jewish students. There was probably some political calculation as well: Dennett may not have wanted "social discrimination" to draw the attention of civil rights groups. In any case, there is no evidence to suggest that in the spring of 1937 Dennett felt any pressure from trustees (or from faculty or students) to abandon his exclusionary admissions policy. It probably also helped reassure trustees that applications for admission reached record numbers in March. As Keller later put it, the families of high-school applicants were pleased to read that Williams wanted more high-school boys, and the families of prep school applicants were pleased that Williams had so many "nice boys."

But Dennett apparently did continue to feel under pressure from trustees about the "nice boys" incident. In a March 26 letter to John Wilson, Dennett reports a rumor on campus that he will be "called upon to answer before the Board of Trustees for what I said in Boston," and asks that the trustees, at their May meeting, decide "what kind of college we should be aiming at." Even after receiving a signal of Wilson's support, he wrote again three weeks later (April 14) to say he wanted to know where the board stood. He was not prepared to compromise about seeking more high school students, and was prepared to resign over it. (This sounds like raising the stakes.) And when William Sidley, who had expressed support but cautioned Dennett to be careful when speaking in public, noted that he trusted Dennett's "head and heart, and usually, but not always, your impulses." Dennett, in a letter two weeks later, was still offended: "These are, of course, very serious matters. If your feeling . . . is shared by the Board, I should not feel that it would be possible to go forward with this work. I think we should have a very frank discussion of the whole matter at the next meeting of the board." Once again it appears that Dennett was looking for a clear expression of board support and threatening to resign if he did not get it. And as it happened, at least according to the minutes of the May trustee meeting, there was no minuted discussion of the "nice boys" incident or "the kind of college we want to be." Dennett did not get what he wanted. As Sidley did not know at the time, two months later Dennett would again threaten to resign.

A difficult year

By early June 1937 it seemed that Dennett had weathered the "nice boys" episode. Alumni and student opinion, he thought, had shifted in his favor. But it had been a difficult year. The operating budget was balanced, but because of falling interest rates on invested securities, college income had continued to decline – it was $100,000 below its 1931 level. And if we look more closely it seems clear that there were simmering difficulties with all his constituencies – trustees, faculty, alumni, and students. He thought the acquisition of the old Buxton Farms in February 1934 (before he became president) was ill advised, if only because of the "carrying costs." He had yielded reluctantly to a trustee proposal in the fall of 1936 to buy the 26-acre Denison property at the foot of Spring St. He may have been lukewarm in the fall of 1936 to committing to build squash courts at a time when the college had more pressing needs. More important, there was apparently no frank discussion and official endorsement at the May 1937 trustee meeting of Dennett's plans for a more "heterogeneous" college. But there was as yet no open division between Dennett and the board.

It might be noted that on matters of national politics Dennett, a conservative Republican and a sharp critics of the New Deal, broadly agreed with the trustees. Dennett was open in his criticism of New Deal "bureaucracy" and its "public relief system." In the spring of 1937 he criticized FDR's court-packing proposal. But he also resisted calls from conservative groups for teacher loyalty oaths, and worried about the "inequitable distribution of the profits of labor," sense of entitlement on part of the rich, and the possibility of what he called a "labor war."

With the faculty there had been an ongoing tensions: many senior faculty were disaffected by the end of the seniority system (under which raises had been handed out for length of service); untenured members were unnerved because so many of their colleagues had not been reappointed. In March Dennett reported to trustee Phinney Baxter that the situation in the English Department, where he had declined to grant tenure to a long-serving assistant professor who had been at Williams since 1923, was "appalling," and that he was having difficulty finding a chair for the Romance Languages Department, where another long-serving assistant professor, at Williams since 1925, was denied tenure. And many thought that when President Garfield announced a 10% across-the-board salary cut in August 1932, there had been an implied assurance that the cut was only temporary. When a $2.4m bequest from the estate of Samuel Hopkins, arranged during Garfield's presidency, was received in 1936 and earmarked for instructional support, many faculty thought the cuts would be restored. But at its October meeting the trustees, with Dennett's support, designated the income of the gift for faculty pensions and for merit salary increases. This led to an open break from an unlikely quarter, when in early January 1937 the Dean of the Faculty, T. C. Smith, walked into Dennett's office with a report of "low morale" on the faculty, and a reminder of the implied restoration of the salary cut. Dennett told Phinney Baxter that he thought Smith, who was now organizing a "manifesto" on the matter, had "gone off the rails." Dennett sought to discourage Smith, but the latter insisted, and claimed to represent one third of the faculty. Smith presented to the trustees at their May meeting a petition for restoration of the salary cut. The board took no action, in part (it said) because the petition was unsigned, and Smith came back to the June meeting with signatures from twenty four faculty. The fact that resistance to his plan to use salary raises as a means to reshape the faculty was coming from the Dean of Faculty whom he himself had appointed must have made Dennett wonder what allies he could count on. One steady ally was Paul Birdsall, who thought Smith's "manifesto" ill-advised, and likely to "play into the hands of the Trustees who wanted to 'get' Dennett for other reasons." He conferred again with Baxter, who told him that he understood that Garfield had given "oral assurance of a general restoration" but he (Baxter) could find nothing to that effect in the minutes of trustee meetings. Dennett and the board did not feel bound by the "oral assurance," for at the June meeting they declined to restore the cuts.

While most of the regional alumni associations had expressed support for Dennett, some of the leading alumni had been a thorn in his side. (Dennett told Keller that the Williams president needed to have "the hide of a rhinoceros.") Some of them seemed to think of the college as a delightful social institution, where academics did not need to be taken too seriously. In the fall of 1936, as Dennett was planning the next convocation (then held in the middle of winter), some alumni told him that the event in the last couple of years had been "a little too intellectual." As the athletics facility project developed and three trustees contributed the funds for squash courts, a small group of sports-minded alumni insisted that a hockey rink be included in the project. They put pressure on both the president and the trustees, and by March 1937 Dennett was revealing his exasperation to at least three trustees: "I am thoroughly fed up with this effort of a few men . . . to embarrass me." The "few men" included president of the Society of Alumni, John Jay '01, and former trustee Henry R. Johnston '09 (their sons played on the Williams hockey team). In mid-April Dennett wrote to another trustee that these alums were "out to make trouble," and within two days the *Record* was passing on a rumor from a Toledo alum that Dennett would soon be leaving office. Dennett later said that he thought the alumni were the "least responsible" and the "least well informed" of his constituencies.

Finally, Dennett was fed up with the students. He was very disappointed at their hostile reaction to press reports of his Boston speech in early March, and at the "very distressing" signs of their "snobbishness" on the campus. As he put it to another trustee, "we are becoming a class college": his worst fears were being realized. He was also disturbed that the incoming editor-in-chief of the *Record* was none other than the son of Henry Johnston. Icing on the cake was perhaps the photo spread in the June 7 issue of *Life* magazine, in which Williams students were displayed lolling – with beer and dates – in the pools at "The Tubs," a swimming hole on Pownal Creek in Pownal on a Sunday afternoon picnic during houseparty weekend, the sort of publicity which would confirm the widely-held view that Williams was a school for playboys.

The Resignation

As the June 17-19 trustee meetings approached, Dennett was clearly under stress. It was, he later wrote, the "last and most difficult week" of what had been a "very fatiguing year." Not only did he have to prepare for the trustee meetings, but he had to deliver a speech to the Society of Alumni on June 19, deliver the baccalaureate sermon on June 20, and preside over commencement on June 21.

It's unclear when Dennett first learned that the trustees were considering the purchase of the Greylock Hotel. The matter was not on the agenda, but was apparently discussed at the June 17 evening meeting of the Finance Committee, at which Dennett arrived late, to find that the purchase had already been proposed. Dennett made what he later called "hurried objections" against the purchase, charging that the discussion was "hasty" and "misinformed." It came up again at the full trustee meeting the next day, where Dennett, despite his firm convictions on the matter, had not had time, he later said, to prepare a full argument against it. In response to his objection that the college would have to raise tuition to cover the cost, three trustees, including Wilson and Sidley, stepped forward to offer funds. After "considerable discussion" (according to the discreet minutes) the board, with one dissenting vote, accepted the recommendation that the college buy the hotel. Dennett must have been surprised and distressed that he was not supported by Sidley and Wilson, who had assured him in March that, at least on another matter, they were "one hundred per cent" behind him.

On Saturday morning he attended the meeting of the Society of Alumni, where his nemesis John Jay was reelected president. Dennett himself spoke, alluding angrily to the story in *Life* magazine, noting that the college wanted not fewer prep school boys but, as the *North Adams Transcript* reported, "fewer boys who would display themselves on the pages of *Life*." It was probably some consolation that retiring alumni trustee Oz Wyckoff praised Dennett and urged fellow alumni to "support whole heartedly the program of the administration."

At the second session of the full trustee meeting that afternoon the Grounds, Buildings, and Improvements Committee again reported, making other recommendations. Dennett then "offered orally his resignation" – it came, the minutes note, "without warning" and as a "distinct shock." The meeting broke up, and when it reconvened later that afternoon it appointed three of their number to confer with Dennett. The board quickly announced publicly that it had purchased the Greylock Hotel – suggesting that the trustee decision was merely a formality, and that a contract had already been drawn up. That night the three trustees asked Dennett to take time to reconsider, told him that they could not act without a formal written letter, asked him to reply by the end of the month, and proposed a special meeting of the board in New York for July 9. The next morning Dennett delivered the baccalaureate sermon to the graduating seniors, advising them that whether "the unknowable, the unexpected, and the unknown" will be a "solid wall against which we shall batter our poor heads or a gateway into a new and happy experience" depends on "our point of view." The speaker might have had his own case in mind.

Why then did Dennett resign? As we will see, there are several contemporary documents that might answer the question: Dennett's own letter of resignation; the minutes of the trustee meeting; letters from faculty responding to the event; newspaper reports; Dennett's statement to the press; and his retrospective summary in his final official act as president. More than one answer to the question is suggested. But all of these accounts must be read critically. Minutes of trustee meetings are a legal record but not a transcript of what was actually said. Some observers had incomplete knowledge; others were pursuing their own agendas. Dennett himself gave slightly differing explanations, and may have left some things unsaid.

As I have suggested, in June 1937 Dennett clearly felt he was being challenged, or at least not supported, by several constituencies. And according to the minutes of the trustee meeting, Dennett in resigning said that "he was finding the position increasingly difficult in his relations with Trustees, faculty, students and alumni." (What Dennett could not know is that for its June 21 issue the *Record* was writing an editorial praising Dennett's accomplishments over the previous three years.) He had displayed what some regarded as impulsive behavior in the recent past. Even his friends deplored his "lack of diplomacy" and his "fatal lack of tact and ability to handle men." Although known for his physical vigor and stamina, he reported to Warren that during the trustee meetings he was extremely "tired," perhaps mentally worn down with opposition, not just on the Greylock Hotel – that may have been the last straw – but on an accumulating sense that the trustees did not fully support, or fully understand, his determination to change the reputation of the college.

For the next week Dennett thought over his decision. He conferred twice with Bentley Warren. Warren told him that the issues were "not sufficiently important to bring about my resignation." Dennett let only his secretary, Kay O'Connell, and his faculty friend and supporter, Paul Birdsall, know what he was considering. Birdsall reportedly advised Dennett to stick to his guns. But on June 28 Dennett formalized his resignation, writing to Warren that his decision was "crystalized" when the board voted to buy the Greylock Hotel, suggesting that he had already been mulling the matter in his mind when he finally announced on June 19 that he was leaving. In a long letter, to which he attached a five-page memo setting out what he thought were the "facts" in the case, Dennett declared that the board's decision made clear to him that "between the Board and the President there is insufficient agreement on fundamentals to make it possible for me to go forward with confidence or with that sense of security without which leadership is impossible." Dennett firmly insisted that *he* was the "leader" and that *he* lacked "confidence" in the board's support – not, he implied, that there were grounds for any lack of confidence in *him*.

He noted a "fundamental difference with the Board on broad policies." What were those broad policy differences? Dennett devoted most of the space in his memo to the real estate issue at hand. The college is an educational institution, but in this instance a "property policy" was being "made paramount." The college had no "duty" to protect the property. It should not acquire real estate for which there is no clear academic use. (In later decades the college's sense of its "duty" on this point would change.) And he linked the matter with the reputation of the college. The deal, he said, would confirm that the board was not ready to try to alter the college's reputation as a rich boys' country club.

The board had in effect argued that while the president was in charge of education, the board itself was in charge of "non-educational policies." Dennett denied the distinction, insisting that all board policies were interrelated, and declared that the College should not buy real estate "without reference to the effect on the general plan for developing the college." He went further, and challenged the trustees on their business judgment: the college owned too much real estate (e.g., the Hopkins Farm and the Denison property), as a result of "undiscriminating" acquisitions. It was simply "not good business" to buy the Greylock Hotel. It would not be surprising if some of the trustees – several of them CEO's – took offense at an academic's suggestion about what was "good business."

But implicit too in Dennett's memo was an unresolved matter of governance. The president of the college was (and still is) a member of the governing body – defined as "the president and the trustees" – and at the time presided at its meetings. The board then had no "chairman." Instead, there was a "senior trustee" who served as chair of the board's Executive Committee. It was clear that it was the board's responsibility to hire and fire the president, but not clear how the board might adjudicate a case in which the president and the board disagreed over a matter of policy or board decision. In his induction address in October 1934 Dennett himself had addressed the question, stating that where president and trustees disagreed it would be his task to persuade them, and if he could not do so to abide by their decision. By June 1937 he saw the matter differently: now, he argued, if the board and president could not agree on a major matter, they should take no action until they came to an agreement. Did Dennett think his resignation would be accepted or refused? He hinted that he knew he was taking a calculated risk: the board might think him "obstinate and uncompromising." It appears that he was prepared to stand firm.

This was not the first time Dennett had resigned after a dispute with his colleagues and superiors. After graduating from Williams, taking a degree from Union Theological Seminary, and serving in church and missionary work, Dennett resigned from his pastorship at the Pilgrim Congregational Church in Los Angeles in 1914, reportedly in part because of "the conservatism of his Los Angeles parish." And in April 1931 he had resigned as "historical adviser" in the State Department. According to a newspaper report at the time, he did not believe "that his superiors in the state department" were "always cooperating fully." The resignation was said by some sources to be a "protest against alleged cliques in the state department and a policy of suppression of the publication of the foreign relations correspondence." It came just after Dennett returned from a six-month leave of absence, and thus was apparently not done impulsively. Perhaps Dennett in 1937 was again resigning as a form of protest from a job that he found he could not do.

But in the final sentence of his resignation letter Dennett did seem to leave the door open to further discussion. He would be "quite willing to confer with the Board [at the proposed July 9 meeting] to see whether it is possible to find a basis for a working agreement." This sentence was added on the advice of Birdsall – who clearly hoped throughout the crisis that Dennett would not resign. It's not clear what Dennett thought that "basis" might be: it was too late for the board to overturn its decision to buy the Greylock Hotel, which had been publicly announced. Perhaps it might have been the larger matter of principle.

Dennett did attend the special meeting of the board on July 9. According to the minutes of the meeting, when asked to amplify his reason for resigning, he simply cited his June 28 memo. The chair of the board's Grounds, Buildings and Improvements Committee then defended the decision to buy the Greylock Hotel. Dennett at this point must have realized that the board was not going to back down, and he declared that he "did not like the job [of president]," and found it very "wearing," causing worry and sleeplessness. But for reasons that are unclear, he then returned to principles of shared governance, and now adopted what some might think inflammatory language, and raised the stakes. The president, he said," should have an absolute veto" over board decisions, until such time as the president and the board could agree. Dennett compared it to the U. S. constitution's provision that the president has a veto over actions of the Congress, but it is notable that he apparently said nothing about how the board might "override" his veto. This does not sound like the language of a man who is seeking to remain in office. Or was he anticipating that, should his presidency somehow continue, the board and the president might disagree on other matters in the future, whether "educational or "non-educational," and the president needed veto power? The principle was no different from what he had written in his memo, but "absolute veto" was, at minimum, an undiplomatic way of putting it, and even Dennett himself later seemed to think that his choice of the term was unfortunate.

The board then went into executive session. The minutes say only that the trustees thought Dennett "temperamentally unqualified" to carry the burdens of his office, and "definitely . . . desired to be relieved of them." At no point do the minutes make reference to the "nice boys" speech, or to disaffected alumni, or even (surprisingly) to the proposed veto. They made no further reference to the Greylock Hotel. But the board unanimously accepted the resignation.

The board then quickly moved ahead to nominate Baxter (who had been its first choice back in 1934, and who had discreetly absented himself from the meeting) as Dennett's successor. Once Dennett had orally resigned, it was prudent for the board to plan for succession. But the speed with which it acted suggests that although the minutes do not show it, there must have been some prior agreement among the trustees. The meeting recessed for lunch, while Warren telephoned Baxter in Maine, receiving an indication that he would be prepared to accept the job. When the meeting resumed, a committee of three was sent to notify Dennett, and the Executive Committee was empowered to meet with Baxter in Boston on July 13. It was agreed between Warren and Dennett that the board would make no announcement about Dennett's resignation until it could formally announce the name of his successor. Dennett was asked to confer with Warren about making his own announcement. As the minutes represent it, there was no acrimony. Lewis Perry was assigned to task of drafting a resolution of thanks to Dennett.

At the July 13 meeting Baxter was again asked if he would take the job. He requested that he be given time to confer with Dennett. The committee then formally nominated Baxter, and sent a mail ballot to the other members of the board. Meantime, Professor Richard Newhall (who was perhaps informed by Dennett) sent an urgent letter to the board, asking that it defer accepting Dennett's resignation.

At this point relations between Dennett and the board took a turn for the worse. There were leaks about the resignation (either from the board or from Dennett's friends) and rumors spread in Williamstown and elsewhere that there had been alumni pressure to force Dennett's departure. They were first published in the *Springfield Republican* on July 17. Paul Birdsall thought that Dennett was being "forced out by alumni conservative and fraternity pressure." And the board said nothing to deny the rumors. This put Dennett in a bad position, and, on the same day the story appeared, apparently before conferring with Warren about any announcement, he wrote to the *New York Times* and other newspapers reporting that he had heard "innuendoes that he had been asked to quit because of alumni pressure and resentment over his desire to make the student body more heterogeneous," and confirmed that his resignation had been accepted on July 9. And he clarified his disagreements with the board, publicly insisting that there could be no distinction between "educational policies" and "non-educational policies," He also suggested that the incident had raised a key question: is the president an "employee of the board, commissioned to direct the educational affairs of the college" or the "leader, both of the faculty and the trustees"? "Employee" suggests that for him this was not just a matter of principle, but that he was personally offended to be treated as any less than *primus inter pares*. And, apparently having reconsidered his bold reference to an "absolute veto," he now reported that he had asked the board for a "suspensory veto" on board action, whereby the president could hold up (or "suspend") board action until the board had a chance to reconsider, as he put it, "to give time for further deliberation, to permit arrival at agreement on the question as to whether this proposed action fitted into a general plan."

The newspaper stories on July 19 also reported comment from Bentley Warren, who confirmed Dennett's resignation, stating that it had come as a complete surprise, and been "initiated by him, without interference by alumni or alumni groups." (Warren evaded saying whether trustees had at any point considered alumni reaction in arriving at their decision to accept the resignation.)

If Dennett was offended, so too was Bentley Warren, first, that Dennett had made an announcement to the press without first conferring with him; second, that Dennett had implied that the board wanted an "employee" rather than a "leader." On July 20 the board's Executive Committee again met with Baxter in Boston and declared him elected him as the next president. As if in response to Dennett's letter to the press, the board's July 20 announcement of Baxter's appointment added that "Dr. Dennett is under a misconception when he states that [the board] do not desire the President to be the leader of the Faculty and of its Board of Trustees. They do desire such a leader and believe that they have found him in Dr. Baxter." After this riposte, it is perhaps not surprising that the resolution of thanks to Dennett, drafted by Lewis Perry, was not brought up for adoption by the trustees.

To the question "Why did Dennett resign?" there is no simple answer. The documentary evidence is incomplete, especially concerning what was in the minds of Dennett and the trustees. And the public statements from both Dennett and the trustees conceal as much as they reveal. But it is clear that the "nice boys" speech was not a significant factor, though it raised questions for the trustees about Dennett's impulsiveness. Some alumni wanted Dennett out, but they had little or no influence on the board. Some faculty grumbled about Dennett, but senior faculty wanted him to continue in office. In any case, the trustees did not take faculty opinion into consideration. Dennett was not pushed out, nor did he feel pressure to resign. But as the June trustee meeting approached, Dennett, looking around him, although he knew he had support throughout the Williams constituencies, saw resistance or opposition on all fronts to the changes he wanted to make in the college. At the trustee meetings he realized there were serious disagreements between him and the board about the Greylock Hotel, the relationship between "educational" and "non-educational" policies, and the larger issue of governance. And as he looked ahead, he foresaw further disagreements with the trustees, and was concerned that he would not get from them the support he needed. Without documentary evidence we cannot be certain, but we can speculate that given his strongly-held convictions about how the college needed to change, it was his impatience with opposition and his stiff-necked manner that led him to insist on a veto of trustee decisions. Whether he recognized that his underlying temperament was going to make it difficult to succeed as college president is impossible to say.

But the trustees were taken by surprise by his June 19 announcement, and would probably have been relieved if he had reconsidered. (There is no evidence that they were planning to "get rid of" Dennett.) If in his memo on June 28 Dennett had not confirmed his resignation and had not raised the governance issue, he would probably have been able to continue as president. There is no clear evidence that as they went into the July 9 meeting the trustees expected to accept Dennett's resignation. If he had not announced again at that meeting, with some apparent carelessness, that he did not "like the job" and found that it wore him down, and had not asked for an "absolute veto," he could perhaps have negotiated an agreement and remained in office. For their part, the trustees did not address the disagreement with Dennett about policy or about governance, and could tell themselves that they were accepting his resignation because he was "temperamentally unqualified" and that he had made it clear to them that he did not wish to continue in office.

Aftermath

Dennett continued in office until Sept. 1, when Baxter took over. Dennett continued to correspond with Baxter through the summer, though the tone of the letters is formal on both sides. The College took possession of the Greylock Hotel on Sept. 1 – as if deferring until Dennett left office – and quickly moved to demolish the main building.

Dennett was apparently not bitter. In his President's Report for 1936-37, he wrote discreetly that he thought he had acted in accord with "opinion prevailing in the faculty as well as among alumni," but "disparity of purpose" – "disclosed," as he said, at the June trustee meetings "in a manner quite unexpected" – between the president and trustees was "such as to render the President's resignation desirable and acceptable." As he looked back, he suggested that the resignation was not long in coming, but was precipitated quite suddenly, and that it only had to do with his relations with the trustees. For his part, Baxter announced that he expected to continue Dennett's policies. Although Baxter is widely credited with continuing Dennett's campaign to strengthen the faculty, he did not address the matter of the college's reputation as a rich boys' school, or to reduce the influence of fraternities. Fraternity membership increased during the Baxter years. But so did the percentage of high school graduates in the freshman class.

Baxter led the college with firm trustee support, but the governance issue that Dennett raised was not clearly addressed until 2010, when the board's bylaws were amended to provide clearly that the board be led by a trustee serving as its chair. The college continued to invest in non-academic building projects: in Baxter's first year the college accepted a gift of $100,000 to build a faculty club – in effect a fraternity lodge for faculty and staff – on college-owned property. And in 1941 a college-owned building on Spring St. became The Log, for the use of visiting alumni. But until 1962, when Williams bought the Mt. Hope property, the college made no major acquisitions of real estate without clear academic use in mind. And in the course of Jack Sawyer's administration (1961-73) the changes to the college and its culture that Dennett wanted were largely accomplished.

The Williams Record

VOL. LIV   Z315   WILLIAMS COLLEGE   TUESDAY, APRIL 30, 1940   No. 13

William A. White Lectures Tonight At 8:30 in Jesup

Famous Author, Publisher, and Editor Will Discuss Evolution of Journalism

Last in Sidley Series

Kansan Wrote 'A Puritan in Babylon'; Has Headed His Newspaper 45 Years

William Allen White, nationally known author, journalist, and publisher, will speak in Jesup Hall at 8:30 tonight in the third and final lecture of the Sidley series. Backed by nearly half a century's experience as editor of the Emporia, Kansas *Daily and Weekly Gazette*, famous for the work Mr. White will discuss "Journalism: From Cradle to Profession to Big Business."

The Kansas writer comes to Williams at an hour's conference of the all-powerful American Newspaper Publishers Association held in New York last week. Besides being a newspaper authority he is the author of many books including *Life of Woodrow Wilson*, *Life of Calvin Coolidge* and, more recently, the best-selling *A Puritan in Babylon*.

Worked on Neutrality

Long a national figure, Mr. White was active last fall in the neutrality controversy. As chairman of the National Committee to Revise the Neutrality Law

49.6% Of Lower Classes Register In Social Sciences

Music, Astronomy Attract Three Times Their 1939 Enrollment; Math Rises

Honors Group Declines

New Major in American History and Literature Attracts 8 Sophomores

By William P. Clements, III '42

Recent spring registration for the three lower classes showed a continued trend toward the social sciences, with 49.6 percent of all course registrations made in this division, while the natural sciences continued to be second choice, with the language and literature division third. Last year's jump by the natural sciences was continued as 26.4 percent of 1941 and 1942 chose to major in this division, as compared to 25.6 per cent in 1939.

Among the most notable facts in the social science registration, which drew essentially the same enrollment as it has for the last two years, was the trend to the newly opened major in American history and literature. Though it held only tenth place in regular major registration for the class of 1942, the new major in its first year opened, it attracted nearly twice as many of the present sophomore class. Instructional candidates as did history, its closest competitor. English the thirty-nine hours

Conference Sentiment Advocates United States Entrance Into War

Conference Leaders Discuss International Relations

L. to R.: Professor Max Lerner, Senator Claude Pepper, President James P. Baxter, 3rd, Professor Frederick L. Schuman and Norman Thomas at Friday afternoon's round table.

Freshmen Credit College For Ideas On Labor, Politics

No Objection to Increase

GEORGE D. AIKEN

Conference Quotes

"The New Deal has given the farmer everything but a market and the worker everything but a permanent job."

"Industry owns labor jobs, and govern-

Students 'Afraid of Skins,' Says Schuman in Debate with Pacifist Thomas

War Dominating Issue

Interest Wanes in Panels as International Affairs Overshadow Meetings

By C. Frederick Rudolph Jr. '42

America faced the Furies in Williamstown this weekend with a despair that left little room for the optimism and hope which honored the meeting of liberals held here last May. The Williams Lecture Committee's conferences Friday and Saturday attempted only to discuss and not to solve the nation's problems, but the national leaders and educators who spoke at the six meetings had left an impression of uncertainty and gloom when the parley came to a close on Saturday night.

Except for the impassioned liberalism of Governor Aiken's address and the freshness and youthful assurance of James Carey, the C.I.O. leader, the speakers brought to the Jesup Hall round tables and Chapin Hall meetings a picture in strong contrast to last year's. It cannot be said, as was the case then, that there was one determined feeling that the problems all were able to recognize would be solved in time to preserve American democracy.

Chapter 12

—✹—

POLITICAL CULTURE AT WILLIAMS
ON THE EVE OF WORLD WAR II

Should professors bring their political views into the classroom? According to the current consensus, professors need not conceal their political opinions, but should not proselytize in their classrooms. That's not the way things were in the late 1930s and early 1940s, during the run-up to World War II when interventionists and isolationists, on the Williams campus and throughout the country, actively debated whether the U. S. should enter the war. As Arthur Schlesinger later wrote, the arguments were "more virulent" even than those in later decades over McCarthyism in the 1950s and Vietnam in the 1960s.

Some faculty at the time were quite outspoken about their politics, most notably Frederick Schuman of the Political Science Department, who taught Poli Sci 3-4 (International Relations). Schuman made no secret of his fierce anti-fascist views, his prediction that war would come, and his belief that the U.S. should enter the war against Hitler. At a conference sponsored by the Lecture Committee on April 26-27, 1940, as the German armies were sweeping into Western Europe, he feared that the Nazis would quickly win the war. He went further: he declared that the undergraduates in the audience who were opposed to the U.S. joining the war were cowards: "You're all afraid of your skins." In his Poli Sci class the next day he declined to apologize, and declared that non-interventionist students were "victims of moral blindness and intellectual confusion." Not everybody agreed with him. Many in the audience hissed. An editor of *The Williams Record*, who with his colleagues that year were inclined toward non-intervention, in a front-page editorial on May 20, 1940, criticized Schuman for presenting his "personal views and prophecies" in his political-science lecture course and for dismissing alternate views and attacking those "non-interventionists" who disagreed with him.

Not everybody agreed with the *Record* editor either. In the June 1 edition appeared a letter signed by 21 faculty colleagues, "repudiating" the editorial and defending Schuman for expressing his views in his classroom. Quoting an editorial that had appeared in the *Record* in December 1939, the signatories reaffirmed that "Professors . . . must infuse their subject with their own convictions in order to compel agreement or disagreement." The letter was signed by the recently-hired political journalist, Max Lerner, by senior faculty including Richard Newhall and Karl Weston, and a number of recently-hired junior faculty, including Donald Richmond, Robert Allen, Lane Faison, R. R. R. Brooks, Winthrop Root, and Sam Matthews, who were to go on to become eminent faculty at Williams well into the 1960s. In the same June 1 issue 132 students signed a letter to the editor, objecting to the editorial on Schuman, and endorsing faculty who made clear they had a personal stake in what they were teaching. They were in effect reaffirming what a *Record* editorial had said two years earlier: "If the undergraduates are at present gaining an unprecedented interest in contemporary affairs in the classroom, it is largely because they have high respect for those who are not only willing to state their convictions in the quiet of the classroom, but who are courageous enough to express their convictions earnestly and firmly in the public amid the sound and fury of the raucous voices of the day" (March 7, 1938). Over the decades students often voted Schuman the best teacher in the college.

During this immediately pre-war period there was a vibrant political culture on the Williams campus. The *Record* reported meetings of the Liberal Club, the Progressive Club, the International Relations Club, the Union Now Club [for a postwar federal "union" of democracies in the world], the Willkie Club, the Williams Student Union, and the Democratic Club – several of them apparently small and short-lived. Regular "round table" meetings of faculty and students – among them Jim Burns '39, editor-in-chief of the *Record*, who would go on to teach political science (and chair the department) at Williams, and his roommate Bill Gates '39, who later chaired the Economics Department – debated current events. One such roundtable took place in October 1938, a month after the Munich conference in which British Prime Minister Chamberlain agreed to let Germany take over part of Czechoslovakia. Implicitly skeptical about Chamberlain's hope that this marked "peace in our time," the roundtable included Max Lerner and Robert R. R. Brooks discussing "America and the Next War," with Gates as chair. The faculty Lecture Committee sponsored a spring conference on contemporary politics, its topics including "America Faces the 'Forties" and "America in a World at War." Faculty frequently gave talks on political affairs. Notices of new books by Williams faculty appeared in the *Record*, including a Dec. 5, 1938, report on the varying reviews of Max Lerner's *It is Later Than You Think* and a Feb. 1, 1941 survey of reviews by Fred Rudolph '42 (who later taught history at Williams) of new books by Professors Paul Birdsall and Frederick Schuman.

Outside speakers invited to campus included non-interventionists on the right and left (Herbert Agar, Rep. John Vorys of Ohio, the socialist Norman Thomas, labor leader James Carey), interventionists (Clarence Streit, the world federalist), New Dealers (Sen. Claude Pepper), leftist critics of FDR (I. F. Stone), socialists (Harold Laski, Harold Lasswell, alumnus Max Eastman '05), and industrialists (Frank W. Lovejoy, an oil company executive, and Frederick Geier '16, president of Cincinnati Milling Machine). Although Prof. Richard Newhall noted that it is "practically impossible to find any good, conservative speakers today," George Aiken, Republican and anti-FDR governor of Vermont (and an isolationist), spoke at Williams.

The faculty were mostly liberal: by 2 to 1 they favored FDR in a Fall 1940 poll. One of them, Prof. Nelson Bushnell of the English Department, gave a lecture entitled "Roosevelt for Perennial President." Another member of the English Department, Instructor Ellsworth Barnard, wrote a blistering letter to the *Record* (October 21, 1939), denouncing the repetition of "pacifist lies" in an editorial just published by the editors rejecting intervention. Many students responded to Barnard with angry letters of their own. Twenty-five years later, Barnard wrote an important biography of Wendell Willkie, who ran against FDR in 1940 and supported intervention before and after the election. Other faculty were quite outspoken leftists, including Lerner of the Poli Sci Department and Brooks, a labor historian in the Economics Department, who at the time had, as he put it later, "socialist and pacifist leanings, and Trotskyite friends." President James Phinney Baxter, though no radical, was himself quite outspoken by 1940 about his support of U.S. intervention, speaking on the same platform as Schuman and Lerner. Even if the faculty were mostly self-identified "liberals," they disagreed about whether the U.S. should get into the war. Some on the left, including Lerner and Brooks, thought the U.S. should focus on fixing American democracy and solving domestic problems. Both changed their minds by the spring of 1941 and were converted to interventionists – Brooks later wrote that the turning point for him was a public debate with Schuman.

Faculty also took public stands on political issues. Barnard repeated his vigorous argument in favor of intervention in an article entitled "Verities and the War," published in the January 1940 edition of *Harper's*. (It attracted national attention, many favorable letters in reply, and two books offers.)

In January 1941 Baxter and eight members of the History Dept, including Birdsall, sent a telegram to isolationist Sen. Burton K. Wheeler (Montana), replying to his speech on the Senate floor that the treaty of Versailles "provoked" World War II, declaring that this claim is a "distortion of history." At a May 13, 1941, mass meeting in Jesup Hall, with 450 in attendance, Baxter and five professors (Schuman, Brooks, Faison, Don Richmond, and James Bissell Pratt) argued vigorously for military intervention.

Several faculty wrote regularly for national political magazines and published book-length discussions of contemporary politics, both domestic and international. Schuman's "Nazi trilogy" (three books published in 1936, 1939, and 1941) presented a pessimistic view of the suicide of Western democracies, seeing the only hope in federation of world democratic states. Schuman also studied the Soviet Union, and argued vigorously that the way to understand Soviet foreign policy is to see that it is based not on ideology but on *realpolitik*, i.e., on producing a favorable balance of power. Lerner, a Ph. D. who had gone into political journalism at *The Nation* and *New Republic*, focused on domestic as well as international politics. Initially a New Dealer but subsequently critical of FDR, he argued for a "new," "positive," and "militant" economic democracy in books from 1938 and 1939. Birdsall's *Versailles Twenty Years After* (1941) provided an analysis of the Versailles Treaty of 1919, arguing that the best hope for the world still lay in the struggling League of Nations. Brooks, who had served as a member of the Steel Workers Organizing Committee of the Congress of Industrial Organizations (CIO) and as founder and dean of the New Haven Workers' School (weekly evening classes for trade union leaders), hired by Tyler Dennett in 1937, quickly published three books about American labor unions (1938, 1939, 1940). Soon after arriving on the campus in the fall of 1937, he told a *Record* reporter that he was admirer of John L. Lewis, leader of the United Mine Workers who would become head of the CIO the next year. In his books and his speeches on campus Brooks defended the new and controversial National Labor Relations Board (NLRB) and made clear that he was "pro-labor" and in favor of a Labor political party.

Students were mostly conservative – in a campus poll they showed a 4-1 pre-election preference (81%) for Willkie in the fall of 1940. A majority reported that their politics tended to follow those of their parents rather than their professors. But in a campus poll they supported the new Selective Service Act, passed in September 1940, by a margin of 6 to 1, even though it meant students had to register for the new draft. Student sentiment about the war sharply shifted from spring 1940 (the U.S. should stay out) to 1941 (the U.S. should intervene). While the controversial Lend-Lease program (whereby war materiel would be furnished to Great Britain) was being discussed in Congress, 537 students in March 1941 signed a telegram to Sen. Wheeler in favor of the program program, after Wheeler had declared that college student opinion was against it. An editorial by Fred Rudolph in the April 29, 1941, edition of the *Record* urged the U.S. to declare war. In a May 1941 student poll 55% favored full support of Britain, with or without a declaration of war; 28% approved all help to Britain even if it meant military involvement; only 5% wanted economic and military non-intervention.

Political activity at Williams attracted admiration from outsiders: in an essay about New England culture, Howard Mumford Jones, a Harvard professor, wrote in the April 1940 issue of the *Atlantic* that "the liveliest college faculty in the region seems to be at the moment at Williams College," going on to cite "the essays of Max Lerner." It also attracted attention in Washington. A Congressional committee (predecessor of the House Un-American Activities Committee, or HUAC) complained as early as 1937-38 of student radicalism at Williams. An inflammatory book by Carl Mote entitled *The New Deal Goose Step* (1939) claimed that Max Lerner had taken over the Political Science Department at Williams, and was taking orders from Moscow. HUAC, under its chairman Martin Dies, went after Schuman in 1943 for alleged communist affiliations.

President Baxter himself was a Republican, of the moderate internationalist branch. But he firmly protected his liberal faculty from political criticism, fending off letters by angry alumni worried, as were many conservatives in the country, that college students were being exposed to dangerous ideas and influenced by their leftist professors. Baxter politely insisted, in a carefully phrased form letter, that he would do nothing to limit Lerner's "activities outside of the campus" or his "freedom as a citizen," finessing Lerner's political activities on the campus outside his classroom.

Why did Baxter protect them? Benjamin Wurgaft, in a book on the experience of Jews at Williams, argued that Baxter firmly believed in the First Amendment, and maybe wanted to counter rumors that as a defender of the fraternity system at Williams he was at least implicitly anti-Semitic. (Lerner was known to be Jewish, but was non-observant.) Maybe Baxter also realized that Schuman and Lerner were highly respected and productive scholar/writers, and that they were bringing salutary attention to once-sleepy Williams. Schuman's lecture courses had huge enrollments. Brooks was less well known, but very productive. Perhaps Baxter thought Lerner and Schuman would balance what he described as a faculty "heavily weighted on the conservative side of the scale" (as he put it in a letter to trustee Bentley Warren). Given the strong faculty support of FDR, this may have been disingenuous.

Schuman and Brooks (and Barnard too) were hired under President Tyler Dennett, who began the upgrading of the Williams faculty that Baxter continued. Baxter, who took office as president in summer 1937 after Dennett's sudden resignation, committed to following through on Dennett's hires. Most of Baxter's other early hires – Vincent Barnett in Political Science, Robert Barrow in Music, Whitney Stoddard and Bill Pierson in Art History, Fred Stocking in English, Anson Piper in Romance Languages – were younger and more traditional in their background, three of them recent Williams graduates. Lerner, who was older and had made his name outside the academy, was an outlier, the only Jew on the faculty until 1947.

Barnard was not reappointed for 1940-41, which might lead one to think that he was fired for being outspoken. But it was not because Baxter did not protect him. Barnard had aroused opposition in the English Department after vigorously siding with a minority in the department over a significant proposed curricular change. Letters in his permanent file indicate that Baxter thought his *Harper's* article was of "high quality" and "brilliantly expressed," though Baxter himself said he did not agree with its strongly interventionist conclusions. Barnard later asked Baxter for a letter of recommendation.

The Selective Service Act passed in September 1940 required all young men from 21 to 35 to register for the draft. College students were normally permitted to complete their studies, but in the fall of 1941 more than twenty Williams students in the junior and senior class had been drafted or chosen to enlist. After Pearl Harbor enlistments jumped. In 1943 Jim Burns '39, four years out of Williams, enlisted in the Army and served for three years as a combat historian in the Western Pacific. His classmate Bill Gates served in the Navy for four years. Their classmate Jack Sawyer also enlisted in the Navy and was later assigned to OSS.

About seven months after the U.S. declared war, a number of Williams faculty – most of them too old to serve in uniform – began going on leave from the college to take up jobs in Washington. They included Brooks and Barnett (the War Production Board), Schuman (the Federal Broadcast Intelligence Service), Lerner (the Office of Facts and Figures), and Baxter himself (Office of the Coordinator of Information, forerunner of the OSS). Winthrop Root, from German, worked for the Office of War Information and later as an intelligence officer in London. In 1942 Lerner returned to the college and in 1943 left to become chief political commentator for *PM* magazine. Schuman also returned to Williams in 1943, where he resumed teaching and would go on to publish a suite of books on the Soviet Union.

Many younger faculty put on a uniform. Among them, Nelson Bushnell of the English Department served for three years as a combat intelligence officer in the Army Air Corps. William Pierson from Art History enlisted in the U. S. Navy the day after Pearl Harbor, and served on aircraft carriers in the Pacific. Lane Faison joined the Navy, worked in the OSS, and later as one of the "Monuments Men," charged with investigating the looting of art by the Nazis. Clay Hunt, recently arrived instructor in English, joined the Navy in the summer of 1942 and served on destroyers. His friend Rowland Evans, fellow instructor in English, served as a pilot in the Army Air Corps and died in a raid over Germany in February 1944, the only faculty wartime fatality.

By then the Williams campus was in effect a military training site. Beginning in January 1943 the college hosted a Naval Flight Preparatory School (the so-called V-5 program), a three-month intensive program in navigation, physics, math, and communication for 600 cadets, and beginning in May 1943 the V-12 program, to enable 460 active-duty Navy midshipmen to continue their academic studies in three accelerated 16-week terms.

More than 3700 Williams alumni and faculty served in the war, most of them young men in their 20s. Of the 118 who died, 41 were on campus in the spring of 1940 when Fred Schuman challenged them to prepare for war.

Frederick Schuman. Max Lerner. Courtesy of Williams College Archives and Special Collections.

Chapter 13

—ɷ—

FREDERICK SCHUMAN AND MAX LERNER:

Realists, Liberals, Possibilists

From 1938 to 1943 Max Lerner (1902-92) and Frederick Schuman (1904-81) were colleagues in the Political Science Department at Williams. Both were prominent, influential, and prolific mid-20th-century "realist" writers on international politics, assigning primacy to national interest over ideology or the country's ethical values. They often appeared together on the same lecture platforms at Williams. One of Lerner's early printed essays was given the form of a "letter on democracy," addressed to Schuman, in which he defines some political differences between them. The two writers continued to correspond for another twenty years – the letters are preserved in the Max Lerner Papers at Yale – arguing with and lobbying each other on both methodology and on policy. With respect to methodology, each, taking cues from Machiavelli, pursued what he regarded as tough-minded realism in politics, but each also displayed an "idealist" or even utopian side. Although they were both scholars working in academic settings for most of their careers, they were also engaged political advocates (and Schuman an activist). Both wrote for the same left/liberal magazines and audiences in a vigorous and accessible style, Schuman in the rhetorical manner of the platform speaker and Lerner in the lively fluency of the op-ed writer, and reached wide readership. They shared enemies, and aroused vehement reviews. Both were outspoken and provocative in their teaching, speaking, and writing. Both were attacked locally by conservative Williams alumni and nationally by the House Un-American Activities Committee, though neither one was ever a member of the American Communist Party, and neither was an admirer of communist ideology or political practice.

On matters of policy, they began as like-minded leftist supporters of the Popular Front and of the U. S. - Soviet Union alliance in 1941, but divided in 1948 over the presidential campaign of Henry Wallace, and over U. S. -Soviet relations, Lerner arguing for "containment" and Schuman for continuing "engagement." In time Lerner became an anti-communist "Cold

War liberal," a defender of the Vietnam War, and ultimately a Reaganite, while Schuman remained on the progressive left, an "anti-anti-communist," and a vehement critic of the U. S. role in Vietnam.

While both Schuman and Lerner maintained wide networks of correspondence, and their politics could be traced through their various interactions with many contemporaries, isolating their ongoing exchanges sharpens our focus on what brought realists together and what divided them. The ongoing relationship of Schuman and Lerner over twenty-five years has not received more than passing attention. Closer attention suggests not only that the line between "classical realism" and "ethical realism" is hard to draw, that in practice a "realist" can also be a "liberal" or an "idealist" or what Lerner liked to call a "possibilist," and that "realism" might lead to quite different policy recommendations, both domestic and international. It also suggests that the full history of realism, and especially its intersection with domestic American politics, is yet to be written.

Before the War

When Lerner joined the Political Science Department at Williams in 1938 he found himself in broad agreement with the politics of his new colleague, Fred Schuman, who had moved from the University of Chicago to Williams in 1936. As supporters of the Popular Front, they were both determined to resist fascism by means of an encompassing alliance of democrats and socialists anywhere in the world, including the Soviet Union. Both admired the Soviet economic experiments, while acknowledging the lack of political freedom in Russia. Although attacked as a Soviet apologist and a Stalinist, Schuman always insisted that he had "never been a member of any Communist or Communist front organization, nor have I ever supported or sympathized with Communist activities in the United States." Lerner too deplored the lack of freedom in the Soviet Union. But he was always more interested in and attracted to Marxist theory – as late as 1943 he would write that although the Soviets had committed a number of "errors in emphasis and calculation," those errors did not "invalidate" Marxism, which Lerner thought "the most useful and illuminating body of social thought in the world." By contrast, Schuman regarded all theory as ideology and ideology as "phraseology" – i.e., as mere words which concealed underlying political "realities." Although accused of cynicism, Schuman, from his own perspective, was simply declining to make moral judgments in the realm of international statecraft, where he thought they were inappropriate.

Schuman's disregard for Marxist thought sprang from his conviction that only *Realpolitik* could explain international politics, which was nothing but the "competitive struggle" between sovereign states for power, "as an end in itself." Schuman was interested in how states behaved. Lerner was always more interested than Schuman in *ideas*, in winning the war of ideas, in changing minds – as suggested by the titles of his books and articles, *Ideas Are Weapons*, *Ideas for the Ice Age*, "Russia and the War of Ideas." Lerner was drawn (throughout his career) to the ideas of classic political writers – Adam Smith, Machiavelli, Tocqueville, Veblen, Jefferson, Aristotle, Mill – and in introducing their work to modern audiences. And he was less an analyst than an advocate, passionately devoted to "democratic socialism," especially in the United States, which meant more "collectivism" and "economic planning" than even Roosevelt was proposing. Schuman embraced the term "liberal," but Lerner was wary that it is an outworn, or negative, or passive ideology, and preferred to think of himself as "more of a democrat."

In the run-up to war Lerner was focused primarily on American society and in promoting what he called a more "militant and disciplined" democracy. Schuman in these years was laser-focused on the threat that fascism, and especially Nazi Germany, presented to the international order. And this in turn meant that Schuman was louder and more insistent in calling for U. S. intervention after the German invasion of Poland in September 1939. When Lerner and Schuman spoke from the same platform at Williams College in May 1940, Schuman ardently advocated intervention – in the form of military aid to Britain – while Lerner was still hesitant to intervene, concerned that military action (or even economic support of Britain) would distract the U.S. from essential economic reconstruction at home.

Schuman and Lerner were in broad agreement about Soviet Russia. Both defended the first round of Soviet purge trials in 1935. Lerner signed the Open Letter to American Liberals (published in *Soviet Russia today* in March 1937) criticizing the Dewey Commission which had attacked the Moscow Trials. Schuman accepted the Soviet claims that Trotsky had committed treason, though he conceded that some of those accused in the second round of trials were probably innocent. Lerner declined to condemn them. On August 10, 1939, both Lerner and Schuman signed the Committee of 400's statement, addressed to "all active supporters of democracy and peace," attacking attempts by the Committee for Cultural Freedom to undermine the Popular Front, and defending the Soviet Union's achievements, affirming that its "political dictatorship" was only a "transitional form." Neither condemned the Nazi-Soviet pact in August 1939. Reflecting his realist views, Schuman initially regarded it as evidence of Stalin's political skill in keeping out of the coming war. Lerner agreed, but revealed some ambivalence. After the Soviets invaded Finland in November 1939, both Schuman and Lerner condemned it.

But they expressed their concern in different terms. Although he found the Soviet economic achievements impressive, in a 1937 essay Schuman sought to make clear that he "abjures both Stalinism and Trotskyism and abhors dictatorship and terrorism in all their forms." On Nazi Germany Schuman was ferociously and unequivocally condemnatory. Indeed, Schuman tended, so Lerner thought, to elide some important differences between fascism and Soviet socialism. Lerner, maintaining his focus on economics, wrote in more temperate (or evasive?) terms that the Russian Revolution did "the right economic things for the right ends through the wrong political means," while the Nazis in 1933 did "at least the partially right administrative things through the wrong political means and for catastrophically wrong ends." Lerner's primary concern was for the "democratic west," which had in his view paused in its movement toward a "democratic socialism which would do the right things in the right way for the right ends." Schuman's concern was always political and international, focused on disruptions to the state system.

With hindsight, we can see that the differences between their political views were a sign of a wider divergence later. But at the time Schuman and Lerner were prepared to overlook them, and complimented each other in print. And the differences were apparently seen by others as insignificant, a matter of emphasis or context. The two writers tended to be seen, by both friends (on the left) and foes (both on the left and the right), as closely aligned, two exemplars of the pro-Soviet Popular Front.

In the summer of 1940 both Lerner and Schuman, deploring isolationist sentiment of the American First Committee, joined the new Committee to Defend America by Aiding the Allies Lerner wanted to aid Britain economically but not (yet) militarily – "outside the limits of actual warfare if possible." But in a three-part series in *The Nation*, Lerner declined to align himself with the "interventionists." By this time, however, Schuman was advocating military intervention.

In early 1941 – after the fall of France and the Battle of Britain but before Pearl Harbor – Lerner began to draw distinctions between his own views as a "democrat" and Schuman's *Realpolitik*. The catalyst was a provocative book published in 1940 by Lawrence Dennis, the leading American fascist writer, entitled *The Dynamics of War and Revolution*. Dennis and Schuman were both "realists" – i.e., Realpolitikers – but differed on war policy: Schuman wanted the U.S. to intervene and Dennis did not. Having already forecast the end of capitalism and what he called "the coming American fascism" – he would welcome a one-party state, "some variant of an expansive totalitarian collectivism" – Dennis now argued in addition that, as Lerner put it, resistance to "Nazi military expansion" was "doomed to failure," and that the U. S. should therefore not intervene in the war. Schuman wrote to Dennis in early September 1940, conceding that it looked as if capitalism and democracy would be replaced, both in Europe and in America, by what Oswald Spengler had called "Caesarism" (an authoritarian collectivism either of the left or right), but urging that a "dynamic and revolutionary America" intervene in the war to defeat the Nazis, and try to establish "an American world imperium," even though he doubted that Americans had the political will. Intervention, though desirable, was "not within the realm of the politically possible," and thus irrelevant to realism, which, he agreed with Dennis, holds with Bismarck that "politics is the art of what is 'possible'." Dennis replied to Schuman with a defense of his views. Schuman showed the epistolary exchange to Lerner, who arranged to have the letters published (in slightly modified form) in *The Nation*, along with a reply from Lerner himself, under the title "Who Owns the Future?"

The question in effect challenged both Dennis and Schuman, and Lerner went on to argue that a "strong democratic state" might be built in America. He insisted, *pace* both Dennis and Schuman, that it made a great difference to the world whether Europe is ruled by Russian socialism or German "national socialism," thereby parting company with their realist assumption that what matters is power not ideology. To Schuman he wrote: "I cannot go along with your bland view that the differences between [socialism and fascism] are 'irrelevant'." For Lerner, ideology mattered. But he agreed with Schuman that the U. S. should intervene to send "full aid" to Britain, and should create "democratic dynamism" at home. However, while Schuman thought the U.S. did not have the will to fight, Lerner was certain that although "duped and doped" by Congress and an isolationist press, America would be willing to fight for democracy. And while he agreed with Schuman on the need for "internationalism" (a world state), he demanded that it be a "democratic world federalism." In the end he calls on Schuman to side with him, "since our ends and values are so similar," and to fight "for the world we wish to help fashion," rather than with Dennis, who seems all too ready to accept fascism both at home and abroad. For Lerner, a political commitment to democracy overrides methodological realism.

Lerner also rejected what he saw as Schuman's despair. (Schuman called it being "realistic.") At the close of his letter to Dennis, Schuman, after lamenting that the U. S. was too "decadent" to fight, resolved, in one of the rhetorical flights to which he was given, to retreat to his "ivory tower" and to await the coming of "the Ice Age," his extravagant metaphor for the end of western civilization. And at the close of *his* letter, Lerner wrote to Schuman that "you don't belong in an ivory tower," but in the heat of the fight. And he in effect replied to Schuman with his own next book, *Ideas for the Ice Age*, published ten months later, in November 1941. Its title, he wrote (without naming Schuman) was meant to reflect the "grimness of feeling" generated by "the harsh age for our civilization." His own response was not "bleakness," "despair," or "defeatism" (all of which he implicitly attributed to Schuman) but "tough-minded" confrontation of facts. The future was not foreclosed, as Schuman had implied it was, but remained open to possibilities: "the future may be totalitarian or it may be toughly and nobly democratic" (p. viii).

Wartime and Post-War

After Germany invaded the Soviet Union in June 1941 and the U. S. entered the war in December 1941, Lerner and Schuman closed ranks. Both supported an alliance with Russia, and were confident that, although there were "grave problems" to be solved, the two countries could work together after securing victory over the Nazis. Both called for a new international order, built on the foundation of the emerging "United Nations." (Both took leave from Williams to work briefly in government jobs in Washington; Lerner soon went on to write for *PM*, a left-oriented daily paper in New York City.) In February 1943, when Texas Congressman Martin Dies named Schuman, in a speech on the House floor, as a member of Communist-front organizations, and called for him to be fired, Lerner denounced Dies in his *PM* column.

By war's end Lerner had left Williams but he and Schuman read each other's political journalism and occasionally engaged in correspondence both personal and professional. By contributing repeatedly to *Soviet Russia Today*, a decidedly pro-communist monthly published by the Friends of the

Soviet Union, Schuman fed the suspicions of his critics that he was pro-Soviet, even though he firmly maintained that he was an independent observer. Lerner's *PM*, though leftist, did not follow the Communist party line, and Lerner, like Schuman, insisted on his political independence. In a six-part series of columns on the U.S. and Russia, he took a "pro-peace" position, "neither anti-Russian nor pro-Russian," opposed to red-baiters *and* to Soviet apologists, arguing that the U.S. needed to understand how the Russians look at the world, and to work through the UN for peace. He also acknowledged Russia's police state and American fears of Russian expansion, as well as Russian fears that the U.S. might use the atomic bomb against them.

Although they both deplored the red-baiting in Churchill's "Iron Curtain " speech in March 1946, and still broadly agreed about the importance of working with Russia in order to maintain peace, Lerner, as a "democrat," was having misgivings about Stalin, and was exploring another disagreement with Schuman's politics. The disagreement came out in two separate reviews in *PM* by Schuman and by Lerner, on Trotsky's posthumously-published book on Stalin.

In his review Schuman denounced Trotsky as a traitor to Russia who had cooperated with fascists, and denounced the book (completed by an editor after Trotsky's death in August 1940) as full of rage and venom, certain to provide fodder for Stalin-bashing that would encourage war-mongers. The *PM* editors printed it with a short note stating that they did not "endorse" Schuman's damning review. A week later Lerner's review was in effect a response to Schuman's. Lerner summarized Trotsky's poisonous view of Stalin's character and career, and agreed that the book is a "hymn of hate." But he asked: "Is any of this true? Are there, at least, half-truths and quarter-truths in it? I cannot say. . . If it is a fabrication. . . it is a fabrication of genius." Trotsky and Stalin had different qualities and strengths: "The historian will find in Stalin a more massive will than in Trotsky, a less intellectual but more accurate appraisal of men and forces, a steadier purpose, a more tenacious leadership of a whole people." He does not whitewash either man. Stalin was "not only astute but cunning, not only strong but ruthless." Trotsky was led into "treason." On the purge trials: "it is hard to believe" that all of the accusations against Trotsky were "fake." "I find it possible to believe a substantial part of what each accuses the other of being and doing." Lerner agreed with Schuman on the need for "close and common action between America and Russia" but disagreed that writers must judge books by their political effects: "the thinker's obligation can only be to the pursuit of truth and the spirit of free inquiry." If Trotsky's book exposed some of Stalin's failings, so be it.

But in his review Lerner did not name Schuman. In a letter written two days later, Lerner told Schuman that "I want you to know that whatever our differences – and the only crucial one [that the need for "free inquiry" trumps concerns about undesirable political effects] was the one referred to in my piece – you still have my personal affection and admiration." On the broader question of cooperation with the Soviet Union, Lerner's views were essentially those of Schuman, as published three months earlier in a new book, *Soviet Politics at Home and Abroad*. In it Schuman acknowledged that the Soviet Union was neither democratic nor egalitarian, and often totalitarian, in large part because of Western hostility, but he believed that it was not expansionist and did not seek to promote world revolution, wanted peace, and would work toward democracy. To avoid war, Schuman argued, the West should recognize a Soviet sphere of influence. Schuman's argument was broadly consistent with what Lerner had been writing in his columns and articles since the 1941 Nazi invasion of Russia.

Schuman's book was widely reviewed as a "realist" analysis, and was attacked at the time and for decades to come as an apology for Stalin. Lerner was not among the reviewers – was he reluctant to put his views on the public record? – but both he and Schuman were attacked in the same article in *Partisan Review* in the summer of 1946 for finding excuses for Soviet/Stalinist totalitarianism, and for appeasing Russia.

Both Schuman and Lerner continued to argue into 1947 for U. S. - Soviet cooperation, and (separately) deplored the announcement in March 1947 of what became known as the "Truman Doctrine," whereby the U.S. would resist Soviet influence and expansion, initially in Greece and Turkey. Lerner was much more supportive of the European Recovery Plan (now remembered as the "Marshall Plan"), first proposed on June 5, 1947, but Schuman took the view, shared by Henry Wallace and the Progressive Party, that the Plan was in effect designed primarily to promote the interests of big American business (who would sell to Europe) and to counter Soviet influence – and was thus only the economic face of the Truman Doctrine. Both Schuman and Lerner thought highly of Wallace. But their difference over the Marshall Plan was perhaps the thin end of a wedge, for Lerner, though he had no enthusiasm for Truman, had serious doubts that Wallace could win in 1948, and by the end of 1947 Schuman and Lerner were completely at odds over that point. It is notable that the break began not over how to respond to the Soviet Union, but to how to respond to the domestic political situation.

The conflict between Lerner and Schuman over Wallace's candidacy is well documented, and need only be summarized. Lerner announced in *PM* on Dec. 18, 1947 that he feared a third-party Wallace candidacy would split the Democratic vote and help Republicans win. Schuman read the editorial and wrote immediately to Lerner, declaring that he strongly disapproved: how could Lerner think Truman preferable to Dewey or Taft (considered at the time the likely Republican nominee), when in fact both Republicans, along with Truman, are equally unacceptable? But Schuman signed his letter with "Love." Lerner responded indirectly in *PM* on Dec. 28, insisting that the choice between Truman and Taft was not a choice between "Tweedledum and Tweedledee," and directly the next day, in a private letter to Schuman, clarifying that opposing Wallace did not mean supporting Truman, reaffirming his "progressive" credentials, agreeing with Schuman on current foreign policy. His views, he wrote, are "only a little less harsh than yours,", but noted that because Wallace and his Progressive Citizens of America lacked a "mass base," they would "fritter away . . . progressive energies," and damage the longer-term leftist cause.

But the battle lines were drawn. Schuman read Lerner's December 28 editorial, and on Dec. 30, before receiving Lerner's Dec. 29 letter, fired off his own angry response, declaring he would cancel his subscription to *PM* for its "base treachery to all that Progressivism stands for. I am inexpressibly shocked by your editorials. Never have you been so wrong." The letter was signed "in profound disgust and regret." After reading Lerner's Dec. 29 letter he wrote again on January 1, still angry but a little calmer: "You . . . are terribly, terribly wrong. Your articles are utterly nonsensical. . . I cannot believe that, in your heart of hearts, you mean what you are writing." You are "betraying all you and I have always stood for." But he apparently did not want an irreparable breach: he signs off touchingly with "Max, I love you, I have always respected you (until now) and all of this is a tragedy. . . May the Lord spare and keep you! As always."

In the further exchange of letters over the next two weeks the breach turned personal: Schuman wondered out loud if Lerner had yielded to pressure from the publisher. Lerner took offense. Schuman, invoking their shared politics, acknowledged that Wallace will get no more than a "thumping minority vote" but insisted that Taft or Dewey "would be infinitely less dangerous [than Truman] to all the things that you and I cherish." If either Republican is elected, his policies would be no different from Truman's, but at least liberals would be on their guard and not likely to be "bamboozled," as they would be if Truman were elected. He hoped that *PM* would eventually support Wallace. Lerner expressed some resentment and doubt about their friendship. Schuman apologized, and in effect agreed to disagree, though Schuman's language was typically hyperbolic: "You will, I suppose, continue to support that filthy, nauseating, putrid little prototype of the coming American Fascism. . . I will support Wallace."

In the end Schuman was right about Lerner's vote, though he did not know it. The exchange of letters ceased for nine months, while Lerner painstakingly laid out his ambivalence about Wallace and Truman, declining to support either the "wavering liberal" or the "bad tactician," hoping against hope that he might find another liberal Democrat – William O. Douglas and Chester Bowles were mentioned – or might be able to "liberalize" Truman. Meanwhile, Schuman fought unambivalently for Wallace, helping to draft the Progressive Party platform at the July 1948 convention where Wallace was nominated. In October Lerner, then writing for the short-lived *New York Star*, announced that, having failed to find a suitable Democrat, he would waste his vote on the Socialist Norman Thomas. Perhaps this cheered Schuman, though as Lerner admitted many years later, when he went into the voting booth he voted for Truman.

The Cold War

The Lerner-Schuman correspondence briefly resumed that fall, but for all their cordiality the letters are uneven in tone. It was Schuman rather than Lerner (who perhaps still felt wounded) who tried to start it up again. In late October, Schuman, knowing of Lerner's pro-Israel sentiments, sardonically noted that "your candidate" (Thomas) had endorsed a partition plan that would give the Negev desert to the Arabs. Having needled his old friend, Schuman insisted that "Seriously, this is all in fun. I still love you! Cheerio." Lerner conceded that he was "embarrassed" by Thomas's statement, but was pleased, though "baffled," by Schuman's "love," and later wrote to thank Schuman for sending a copy of the latest edition of *International Politics*. But Lerner's language suggests that he was trying to reconcile his politics with his feelings: "Whatever else may have passed between us, I want to tell you that my admiration for the book is undiminished." As late then as December 1948 Lerner was professing to share Schuman's realist view of international politics: the book "stands on my desk as a *vade mecum* [a handbook, literally "go with me"] for my daily journalistic writing."

This agreement also meant that Lerner was still arguing for engagement with the Russians. In a November 1948 column in the *Star* he had proposed resuming direct talks with the Soviet Union. One of his readers was Arthur Schlesinger, who wrote to Lerner to say that he was opposed to any talks, thinking that the Soviet Union would continue its "disruption" in Western Europe until it was stabilized by the Marshall Plan. Over the next several years Lerner would come to agree with Schlesinger, and with the Truman policy of "containment," his politics moving toward those of the "Cold War liberal" that he remained until the late 1960s. Schuman, although he now had some doubts about Soviet expansionism, remained the "realist" and "internationalist" that he had long been.

It was again Schuman, after another lapse in correspondence, who wrote to Lerner in May 1949, to congratulate him on his academic appointment at the newly-founded Brandeis University. He also reported that he has "greatly enjoyed, and profited from" Lerner's new book, *Actions and Passions*, a collection of his columns and essays from the past decade. But his real reason for writing appears to be to ask if Lerner thinks there might be any chance that Schuman might join him as a colleague at Brandeis: "If I thought so, I would write at once. I am weary, weary of Williams – to the point of tears and boredom, and alumni pressure to have me liquidated is constantly rising." Conservative alumni had indeed continued to write to Williams President James Phinney Baxter, protesting the presence of a "communist" on the faculty. Schuman observed gloomily that " I suppose that no other institution at all would take me," but imagined that since Brandeis had hired the leftist Lerner it might consider hiring Schuman. Given their political disagreements of the previous year, it is significant that Schuman would apparently have been happy to be Lerner's academic colleague once again.

But Lerner was perhaps not so ready for reunion. His reply to Schuman three days later offered only mild encouragement. Brandeis, he said, would be hiring "slowly," perhaps adding someone in international relations in the third year. Instead of promising to write a strong letter of endorsement, he only suggested that Schuman write to inquire: "As you know, I think you are a magnificent teacher and an eloquent writer, even when I dissent from you. I certainly think there can be no harm – and there may be a lot of good – in your writing to [the president of Brandeis] directly." Instead of saying that he will get on the phone instantly, he said he would "mention" Schuman's inquiry to the president "when I see him in a few days."

But there was no open break. Schuman remained at Williams, continuing to deliver lectures elsewhere on Soviet foreign relations and the prospects for atomic war or peace. He was perhaps more wary of Soviet expansion, but protested the founding of NATO. Lerner was at work on what would be his *America as a Civilization* (1957) – he told Schuman in May 1949 that he was still working on the first draft. It was not for some years that he was ready to have the manuscript read by colleagues, and in the fall of 1954 he asked Schuman to read the last chapter, "America as a World Power," apparently inviting that he point out where Lerner might have "gone wrong" or where the "analysis breaks down." (His request suggests that although he disagreed with Schuman on some matters, he had consulted *The Commonwealth of Man* and even borrowed from it, and still respected his opinion.)

Schuman's response was cordial and respectful, and broadly complimentary ("I am certain that this will be a great book and a very important one.") but offered some criticism. He expressed some skepticism that America is a distinct "civilization" in Toynbee's sense, a point that would be raised by some critics after the book was published. Drawing on his own expertise, Schuman asked for a sharper distinction between "realists" (among whom he lists Morgenthau, Kennan, Marshall, Lawrence Dennis, and himself) and "internationalists." And he implied, though does not say so explicitly, that Lerner wanted to be both a "realist" (i.e., unillusioned, tough-minded, pragmatic) and an "internationalist" (foreseeing that America through its moral principles could provide "world leadership" and could "inaugurate a world rule of law"). Schuman referred Lerner to chapter four of his own *Commonwealth of Man*, published two years earlier, which reviewed the prospects for world government but argued, as he now reminded Lerner, that "neither Russia nor America 'has what it takes' to fulfill the tasks performed by the great builders of Universal States in times gone by." But Schuman modestly (perhaps disingenuously) suggested that Lerner ignore this advice, since Schuman's own book, though favorably reviewed, did not sell well.

Lerner seems to have read Schuman's letter carefully, and marked two passages. But he did not follow Schuman's advice, probably reflecting the fact that he had a much more positive opinion of American "civilization" and anti-communist foreign policy than did Schuman. If he responded to Schuman, the letter has not survived. His *America as a Civilization,* published to good reviews in 1957, sold very well and his reputation reached its zenith. Schuman resumed publishing on the Soviet Union – *Russia Since 1917* (1957), *Government in the Soviet Union* (1961), and *The Cold War: Retrospect and Prospect* (1962) – but his new books attracted less attention and exerted less influence than did his work from the 1930s and 40s.

Lerner and Schuman continued to disagree, especially about foreign policy, Lerner more concerned about containment and Schuman about engagement. But again in mid-1962 Lerner asked Schuman to read the manuscript of his new book, *The Age of Overkill: a Preface to World Politics*, probably because he still regarded Schuman as one of the leading experts on international relations. Schuman responded with a lengthy and detailed critique, exposing frankly and unsparingly his deep disagreement with Lerner on matters general and detailed. Asked to read the entire manuscript, Schuman reported that, because he thought Lerner so wrong, he had to give up after reading and commenting on two of its six chapters. Lerner's book and Schuman's critique in the main recapitulate the positions each took concerning Lerner's idea of American leadership in *America as a Civilization*, but this time survey and mark their even wider differences concerning the Soviet Union and "the Communist world."

The difference between them, Schuman pointed out, is fundamental. Lerner declared that "classical world politics" – by which he means "realist" politics from Machiavelli to German "Machtpolitik" – have been "fatally undercut." Schuman, who still saw international politics as "conflicting nationalisms," thought Lerner had "preferred to restate an old thesis" ("that 'power politics' are now obsolete.")

Lerner's view had been staked out in *America as a Civilization*: that the Soviet Union and Communist leaders elsewhere have adopted a "Grand Design," "fomenting and supporting revolutions in the drive toward Communist world empire"; that the proper response is to develop a "consensus of world law" and a "world police force with a monopoly of nuclear weapons," and through the threat of military coercion to enforce "collective security." Lerner did not advocate a "world state." The system of sovereign states would remain in place, but those states would create an independent "world authority" to operate through "independent transnational agencies." Lerner had in mind a more independent UN, no longer an "international agency" that basically served the interests of the great powers, but a "transnational one."

Schuman challenged both themes. With respect to the first theme, Lerner, he wrote bluntly, was simply recycling the "prejudices," "fables," and "cliches" ("Free World," "Communist bloc") of American "Cold Warriors." Communist world empire, he insisted, was always aspirational, "not a guide to policy." Furthermore, the anti-Communists "in our time have perpetrated far greater evils than the very great evils perpetrated by Communists." And to draw the sharpest possible distinction between himself and Lerner, he declared that while Lerner is "anti-communist," Schuman insisted that he himself has "always been anti-Communist. But have also been anti-antiCommunist, ever since . . 1933." With respect to the second theme, Schuman denounced "collective security" (by whatever means) to be no more than an old "myth," and declared that the only way to achieve security was by means of a world federation of states, some form of "limited world government," *inter*-national but not "transnational," of the sort he had advocated in his *Commonwealth of Man*. (He had in fact looked forward to some form of "world unity" since the first edition of his *International Politics* in 1933).

As he had in his earlier challenges to Lerner, Schuman, ever amiable, closed with compliments and "warmest good wishes," adding that Lerner should probably "ignore altogether all the preceding comment." Lerner read the letter carefully – it is marked with numerous marginal pencil marks, suggesting that Lerner considered each of Schuman's specific suggestions. But he accepted only about a quarter of them, all corrections of minor matters of fact. If Lerner wrote back to Schuman, the letter has not survived. And at this point the Schuman-Lerner correspondence appears to have ceased.

The reasons are not difficult to imagine. Schuman had so sharply disagreed with Lerner's arguments that there appeared to be no common ground, even though both were trying to find a way beyond the East-West Cold War stalemate so that the human race might have a chance to survive. Lerner had abandoned his realist view of international politics. It would appear that by the 1960s they no longer had anything to say to each other, and that there was little they could discuss without violent disagreement, starting with the Cuban Missile Crisis in October 1962 (Lerner thought it was Kennedy's finest hour, Schuman that it was reckless endangerment) and continuing through the Vietnam War (Lerner supported at least until 1967, not turning against in until 1969, while in 1967 Schuman famously called Johnson a mass murderer).

By then Schuman had essentially concluded his writing career. In the 1970s Lerner, having meditated at the end of *The Age of Overkill* on Freud's *Beyond the Pleasure Principle* (and on the "death instinct" now revealing itself in the nuclear standoff), decided to explore the pleasure principle himself, in both his writing and his personal life in California. Lerner's politics also continued to move to the right: by 1979 he was endorsing Ronald Reagan. When Schuman died in 1981 Lerner left no comment.

Lerner was accused by his former political allies of changing with the times and of abandoning his former liberalism. He himself insisted, on some occasions, that he had always been a critic of liberalism; on other occasions he suggested that his intellectual life had gone through several phases, and conceded that he was no longer a "radical," but he avoided the terms "liberal" and "conservative," preferring to call himself a "democrat." By contrast to Lerner, Schuman stuck to his liberalism and his "realpolitik" guns throughout his long career.

Possibilist and realist

Although Lerner was wary of political labels, he liked to think of himself, particularly in his later career, as a "possibilist" (finding it useful when asked, as he occasionally was by journalists and lecture audiences, whether he was an "optimist" or a "pessimist" about the prospects for world politics.) He adapted the term as a way of distinguishing him on the one hand from "gloomy "pessimists," useful during the Cold War when Lerner was intent on celebrating the achievements and the possibilities of American democracy, even when the world worried about nuclear war. In the *Age of Overkill*, for example, he writes of a "stoic and tragic possibilism" that does not entail any "inherent doom." And it served, like "tough-minded," to distinguish him from pollyanna "optimists." It also enabled him in earlier years to argue that a better democracy was "possible" if the New Deal were pursued more vigorously, and to distinguish himself from political writers, such as Schuman and Dennis, who insisted, for example, in the dark days of 1940-41, that the victory of fascism was "inevitable." Lerner, by contrast, liked to emphasize the uncertainty of the future and, against determinism, on the persistence of human freedom.

Perhaps to disarm the charge that "possibilism" was just wishy-washy or wishful thinking – Lerner had been lampooned for his evasive ambivalence –

he tried to suggest an intellectual pedigree for his stance. As early as 1940, in his introduction to *The Prince* and *The Discourses*, Lerner, developing an idea in Machiavelli, wrote of "the socially possible." In his 1966 book on *Tocqueville and American Civilization*, he also described Tocqueville as a "possibilist."

In methodological terms, "possibilism" was also his latest attempt to split the difference between "realists" (for whom policy-makers are driven by national interests) and "idealists" (driven by "ideals" or "ideas," e.g., democracy). As early as 1939 he had attempted to find a way to blend realism with a commitment to "democracy," without being vulnerable to the charge that he was naive about the way international politics worked in practice. In that year he concluded a review of a new book on Machiavelli by arguing that although Machiavelli was properly regarded as "the father of power politics" he "did not see the whole truth about politics," and claiming that "effective pursuit of democratic objectives is equally within the scope of a strong state and an unsentimental realism about human motives." Or as he put it the next year in his introduction to and edition of Machiavelli, we can look beyond "the realm of what ought to be" (idealism) vs. "the realm of what is" (realism) toward a "third realm" of "what can be": "We can start with our democratic values, and we can start also with Machiavelli's realism about tough-minded methods. And we may yet find that an effective pursuit of democratic values is possible within the scope of a strong and militant state and an unsentimental realism about human motive." Such a realm, he suggested, might be called "humanist realism." (Rigorous theorists would say that Lerner confused a methodology with an ideology.) When in *The Age of Overkill* he again briefly distinguished "the 'realist' and the 'idealist' schools of world politics," he in effect again reveals that he wanted to have it both ways: "The 'idealists' do not reject the idea of national interest, but affirm that it can best be pursued toward goals more humane and by means more subtle than naked national power." Although Lerner's term "possibilism" has not survived in discussions of political theory, and now seems idiosyncratic, his conception of "humanist realism" has received some attention.

Schuman, by contrast, remained a "classical realist" throughout his career, focusing always on the pursuit of power by sovereign states, on what *is* rather than what *can be*; a determinist convinced that the future was inevitable, and that it was likely to be dark: a Nazi victory, the death of the West, nuclear war. As early as 1940 Schuman had argued that some actions – such as intervention in the war against Hitler – might be desirable but were simply impossible. In the *Commonwealth of Man* Schuman was hard-headed about the delusions of both the left and the right: so long as some sovereign states survive, "there can be no enduring peace, despite the prevailing delusions of the twentieth century that peace is possible through the defeat of the wicked by the virtuous, or by the organization of 'collective security' against aggressors." And as noted, his 1962 letter to Lerner reaffirmed that what Lerner regarded as *possible* he dismissed as *impossible*.

But just as Lerner the possibilist wanted to lay claim to being "tough-minded," so too Schuman the realist and dark prophet turns out to be a possibilist himself, continuing to the end of his career to express a hope for a future world government. At the end of *Commonwealth of Man*, Schuman revisits Bismarck's adage: "Politics is still the art of the possible. . . .We are left with the possibility of world government through a voluntary extension of the principles of federalism to the whole society of nations." "It is possible . . . that Man's Faith in reason and brotherhood may prevail." Schuman even distinguishes himself from "so-called 'realists'" who doubt that "inertia, fatalism, and national and ideological ethnocentrism" can be overcome: "It would be wholly premature to conclude . . . that the Parliament of Man and the Federation of the World are beyond attainment." A vision of a single human community may be "utopian" but it is "attainable, or at least imaginable." Or as he reaffirmed ten years later in his final letter to Lerner, what was essential for human survival was the "gradual evolution of the UN into a limited federal government." Pointing to an alliance of "realists" who shared this view – "Toynbee, Lippman, Kennan, Warburg, and a few others" – he declared again that "I have long regarded this prospect (and I still so regard it) as within the realm of the politically possible if enough people will work toward the goal." Indeed, it could be argued that Schuman's goal was one of two logical outcomes of his realist view (the other being "Caesarism"), and the better way out of an international "anarchy" of Hobbesian "war of all against all."

Epilogue

By the time Sanford Lakoff published his 1998 biography, Lerner's reputation had faded, and in the intervening twenty years has not yet recovered. He was by then regarded as a "Cold War liberal" who belonged to a past era; a believer in the Vietnam War until quite late in the game (and thus discussed neither a critic nor a revisionist); a celebrant of American "civilization" whose confidence came to seem dated. Perhaps too he was perceived as having gone off the rails after about 1970, with his explorations of "Eros in America." Even compared to like-minded contemporaries, Lerner is now little cited in discussions of mid-century liberalism. Despite a second edition in 1987, his *America as a Civilization* has not survived the way the comparable books of Louis Hartz, Henry Steele Commager, or Richard Hofstadter have, or the more popular Arthur Schlesinger. Perhaps with further attention to the complexities and varieties of mid-century realism, Lerner will interest future historians and political scientists.

Schuman's reputation peaked in the mid-1940s. He was eclipsed by Hans Morgenthau, whose textbook on *Politics Among Nations* (1948, 6th ed. 1985), became the "Bible" for students of international relations. Morgenthau's text book quickly outsold Schuman's, and attracted the admiration of peers. What is more, Morgenthau virtually ignored his rival. Realism attracted less attention as a methodology or theory in the years after the end of the Vietnam War and the oil crisis of 1973. But even after the revival of realism beginning with Waltz's book in 1979, Schuman was rarely discussed or even cited in books on realism from the 1950s through the 1990s. An unspoken consensus among realists regarded the leading mid-century figures as Carr, Morgenthau, and Kennan. One may speculate about the reasons for the silence about Schuman. His reputation was built on his books on Nazi Germany (which had long disappeared) and the Soviet Union (which collapsed in 1991 and about which Schuman had earlier been seen by some to be an apologist). He was known, even notorious, for his dire predictions: sometimes they turned out to be accurate (e.g, the onset of World War II), but often not. Few in the 1950s and 60s shared his enthusiasm for world government.

But with the rise of China, the resurgence of Russia, and Trump's bald assertion of American national interests, Realpolitik, as John Bew says, is "back in fashion." By the same token, Biden's hopeful appeal to what is "possible" for a country and its people to accomplish suggests that political idealism is not dead. Schuman and Lerner and the other mid-century realists — and possibilists — may once again find what Bew calls a "receptive audience."

A note on international relations scholarship since 2000

Few political scientists today discuss Schuman or Lerner. John Mearsheimer's *The Tragedy of Great Power Politics* (2001), contrasting "liberalism" (sometimes called "idealism") and "realism" as the two leading "bodies of theory" in international relations," and distinguishing three separate theories of realism, narrowly focuses a small handful of 20th-century realists: E. H. Carr, Hans Morgenthau, George Kennan, and Kenneth Waltz. Even the historians of realism look back at a select few realists, for example, Michael Smith, whose *Realist Thought from Weber to Kissinger* (1986) inserts between his titular figures only Carr, Reinhold Niebuhr, Morgenthau, and Kennan, and more recently Sean Molloy, whose realist canon in *The Hidden History of Realism* (2006) consists of Carr, Morgenthau, Waltz, and Martin Wight. One significant recent exception to this pattern is William Scheuerman, whose *The Realist Case for Global Reform* (2011) treats Schuman, beginning with his famous textbook, *International Politics*, as seriously as he does Carr, Niebuhr, and Morgenthau, as one of the "Progressive Realists" who made powerful arguments for world government.

John Bew's even more recent *Realpolitik: a History* (2016) focuses on the usual suspects, from Niebuhr to Waltz and Henry Kissinger. He devotes a few pages to Schuman, regarding him as a "classical realist," and distinguishing him from those who belong to several other "strands" of realism, including "ethical" or "humanist realism," Christian realism, neo- or structural realism, and even "liberal realism." Although he notes that political writers and political scientists have tended to use key terms loosely – in his view "realpolitik" and "realism" are related but not identical – he assumes that even though the world of international politics is messier than some theorists claim, clear distinctions can be drawn among its several strands.

Lerner the realist is not cited in John Mearsheimer's *Tragedy of Great Power Politics* (2001), or in other recent discussions of realism, perhaps because he preferred to think of himself not as a realist, but as a democrat, a liberal, a centrist, or a possibilist. But he has not been completely forgotten: Bew devotes a few pages to his writings, said (by contrast to Schuman's "classical realism") to embody "humanist realism" in his earlier writings, notably *Ideas for the Ice Age: Studies in a Revolutionary Era* (1941).

In recent years Schuman is again being cited, if only briefly– in Brian Schmidt's *The Political Discourse of Anarchy: a Disciplinary History of International Relations* (1998) and Ido Oren's *Our Enemies and Us: America's Rivalries and the Making of Political Science* (2003). Richard Ned Lebow's *The Tragic Vision of Politics: Ethics, Interests, and Orders* (2003) includes Schuman's *International Politics* among "the seminal mid-century works. " Scheuerman in 2011 and Bew in 2016 treat him substantively.

Clay Hunt. Courtesy of Williams College Archives and Special Collections.

Chapter 14

—◦m◦—

CLAY HUNT

One of the legendary teachers at Williams College – "legendary" if only because so many stories have been told about him – is Clay Hunt, Professor of English from the 1940s to the mid-1970s. Because of the impact he had on generations of students, because he was a strong influence on the shape of the English Department and the way literature was taught, reflecting strong national trends, because he often behaved in ways that would not be tolerated on today's campuses, and because several of the stories about him are at best only half-true, it's worth trying to look at Hunt, as he wanted his students to look at poems, more closely and carefully. And it's time to look now, before those stories, still being told, begin to fade: the youngest of his former students are in their early 60s, and the youngest of his former colleagues are now in their late 70s and 80s.

He was a powerful presence in the classroom, in English Department politics, and on the campus at large. In many ways he reflected an earlier Williams – when all the students were male, when the English major was based on major writers of the western tradition, when instructors were more likely to lecture than to lead a discussion, and to deliver their judgments, about the qualities of great writers and the merits of student work, with force and bluntness. Among such professors, Clay Hunt was exceptionally forceful, dominant, and influential on three decades of undergraduates, a number of whom became writers, scholars, or teachers. For Alvin Kernan, Class of 1948, who went on to a distinguished career as a teacher-scholar at Yale and academic administrator at Princeton, Hunt was "the teacher who had the greatest influence on my early education." Kernan says he found in Hunt "a rare energy of thought, intense feelings, and a conviction that knowledge was both a strenuous and almost physical pleasure. He made literature and criticism seem active and meaningful, and I followed him from one class to another, and spent my senior year in honors work with him reading modern poetry." A few years later A. R. Gurney, Class of 1952, who became an admired and successful playwright, wrote his senior thesis under Hunt's direction, and remembered him as "very influential." Kees Verheul, one of the leading writers in the Netherlands, while a young Dutch exchange student during his year at Williams in 1957-58, took Hunt's "Modern Poetry" course and learned from him a life-long "passion for poetry." Not a few alumni went on to become professors of English because of his example.

Hunt was also outspoken, and even raunchy. At times his classroom manner seemed a theatrical performance, as if he sought to wake students up and engage them by shocking them into attention. His opening gambit at the beginning of a semester, was to introduce himself to his students: "The name's Clay Hunt. Clay, as in 'lay', Hunt, as in 'c***'." (Or so an often-repeated story goes, though I have only heard one student – a graduate from the mid-1960s – confirm he actually heard Hunt utter those words in class.) As Kernan remembers Hunt from the late 1940s, he "was outrageous in everything, trying to shock his classes . . . he flushed, grimaced, and roared with laughter at his own cruel but witty sallies." Fifteen years later his manner had not changed. John Herpel '64 was a pre-med Chem major who satisfied a distribution requirement by taking Hunt's English 102. The reading for the day was Shakespeare's *Henry IV, Part I*. In Act I Falstaff complains obscurely of being "as melancholy as a gib-cat," and Prince Hal teasingly but (to a modern ear, obscurely) replies "or the melancholy of Moorditch," which Falstaff, coming right back, dismisses as a "most unsavory simile." When Hunt explained the joke – Moor Ditch was an open sewer: "That's where all the piss and shit of London went into the Thames" – Herpel was hooked: he became a Chem and English double-major.

At times Hunt's manner seemed something less calculated, reflecting his own deep and powerful engagement, a response both physical and passionate, with the writers he discussed. Kernan thought there was something "frantic" about his enthusiasm for poetry, something "uncontrollable" about his "squirming." To David Stern, Class of 1965, it looked like Hunt, as class began, was preparing for combat : "He left hand touched his chest, his head pulled back, thrusting out his chin, as if he were harnessing himself to his teaching load, or adjusting his flak jacket." William Finn, Class of 1974, author of *The Falsettos* and other plays, remembered Hunt from his "Modern Poetry" course: he was "possessed and writhing as he explicated word by word and phrase by phrase T.S. Eliot's *The Waste Land* : the tics, the growls, the maniacal breathing, the lidded eyes, his wiping himself with his handkerchief. It was as close as I'll ever see to someone having sex with text. . . . Having explained what he needed to explain, he sat back in his chair exhausted, in another world gleaming." Some students found his manner unnerving and offputting. More than one wondered whether he was on amphetamines.

Hunt concentrated in his courses on major writers from the Renaissance and the early 20th century. Eliot, Joyce, and Yeats. Shakespeare, but also John Donne, Ben Jonson, and John Milton. He also invented and taught for many years a course on Dante. He regularly taught freshmen, in English 101-102, along with upper-division seminars, as well as the required senior course. Hunt typically lectured, not unusual at the time, and did not aim to generate discussion, rarely pausing for more than a quick question. He was a brilliant lecturer, working without notes, often reading aloud from the poem or play. (He once said jokingly that he thought it was "obvious that teaching is a theatrical profession – a higher form of vaudeville, perhaps," and admitted to being a "frightful ham.") Because of his powerful delivery, his wide learning, and his equally powerful memory, he gave the impression that teaching meant closely following and responding to "the text" wherever it led him, but he in fact carefully prepared a plan for each class. As he talked, he smoked incessantly – professors could smoke in the classroom in those days. One student from the Class of 1968 remembers English 101, when students and instructor sat around the outside of a square of tables: "I sat next to him and by the end of the class my space was covered with cigarette ashes."

Many people found him intimidating. Hunt had strong opinions about what made great writers great, or less great, and did not hesitate to share those opinions with his students. (He let students in his modern poetry class know that Yeats was the greatest poet of the 20th century and that he did not think highly of the later Eliot or Auden.) Some students and colleagues thought he was dogmatic, doctrinaire, even bullying, and that they were expected to follow his line of thinking. As Hunt reportedly once said, "A good English paper states the correct interpretation and proves it is the correct interpretation." Hunt's comments on papers he regarded as weak or lazy could be brutally dismissive, and some students reacted negatively, avoiding his courses. (Hunt was also known to be a hard grader.) Others were inspired, challenged to think harder and argue better, with compelling evidence. When Hunt thought a student's interpretation was "plainly simply wrong," he said so, in lengthy and detailed interlinear comments, noting where the student had strayed from the evidence of the text. When Hunt thought a student made a good and persuasive case, even if it differed from his own view, he rewarded it with praise. As another colleague put it, he was opinionated, but loved debating about literature, and enjoyed the disputes, "win or lose."

For most of his career Hunt's students were all male, and his salty classroom language was probably designed for their ears. In the late 1950s the young wife of a married undergraduate sought to complete her Vassar English major by enrolling in one of Hunt's courses, but he declined to permit it. Through the 1960s Hunt's manner could sound like coarse locker-room talk. Boys who brought their weekend dates to his Dante class on Friday sometimes had to listen with embarrassment when Hunt salaciously advised the girls to cross their legs, so as to block the way to the "gates of Paradise." But when Williams began admitting women transfer students in 1969, Hunt adjusted, and according to several accounts was very respectful, even "gentlemanly," toward female students. Hunt clearly admired strong and smart women. In turn, they thought him "raunchy," "funny," and "irreverent," but were not offended: "He never crossed any lines . . . He inspired me. . . . I loved him dearly."

Throughout his career Hunt made a practice of getting to know his students outside of class. As early as the late 1940s he (along with his English Department colleague, Fred Stocking) invited students to his on-campus apartment in the evening to talk about poems. Daniel Kleppner '53 (who went on to become an award-winning nuclear physicist at MIT) remembers being invited while still a freshman. In later years, at year end, he invited some second-semester students to his summer house in the Hopper for beer, swimming in the pond across the road, literary talk, and an elaborate dinner he cooked himself. (Hunt was a heavy drinker, but could handle his liquor.) During spring break one year Hunt traveled to Italy with two of his undergraduates (one male, one female).

Hunt was a major figure in the lives of English majors, but he was also a major presence on the campus. He lived for many years at the Old Faculty Club at the corner of Main St. and Hoxsey St. When the Club was demolished in the spring of 1966 Hunt moved to the Stratton Road apartments. (He bought his house in the Hopper, where he did his entertaining of both colleagues and students, in the summer of 1960.) He was a regular at classical concerts in Chapin Hall, where he was an enthusiastic and even vociferous listener. Hunt had an expert's knowledge, and deeply admired Mozart and Beethoven. (He also had his strong dislikes, and passionately loathed the music of Brahms.) At intermission he would freely critique the performance, for the benefit of anybody who might be standing nearby, and even during a performance itself he did not hesitate to laugh out loud, sigh with pleasure, or grumble with disapproval. One colleague recalled Hunt "at the intermission of some concert or play . . . lecturing to all around on the exact merits of the occasion," or "stomping out, arms flailing, in the middle of some shoddy or mediocre performance, muttering imprecations by no means under his breath."

Hunt was also a familiar figure at public lectures, where he freely opined during the Q and A period. A colleague evoked the memory of Hunt "lighting into some fashionable visiting celebrity of the hour who had just made himself, in Clay's eyes, something of a boob and an insult to right reason." There are similar reports from other observers: for example, that at a lecture in the late 1960s by Robert Penn Warren, one impressionable undergraduate sitting in front of Hunt heard him grouse out loud that he "never heard such shit in my life." Some years earlier, at a lecture in 1962 by novelist William Golding about the recently-published *Lord of the Flies*, so the story goes, Hunt rose to declare that the novel was about original sin. When Golding responded that "you may think that, but it is not what I meant to say," Hunt stormed out, fuming that Golding did not understand his own book. To judge by a contemporary report in the student newspaper, the story is an exaggeration. The reporter notes that Golding himself suggested that the book was about a defect in human nature — "call it original sin, if you will." He is also reported to have said "I'm not even the best authority on this book." But the story fit Hunt's public persona.

Although students at the time probably didn't know, Hunt was also a regular at the noontime faculty swim in the old college pool. Some might have been shocked to learn that it was customary for Hunt and at least one other senior faculty member to swim in the nude – though I am told by a student from the swimming team in the '60s that this was no big deal: the swimming team routinely practiced in the nude. Hunt took things further than usual: when he invited a few students or colleagues to swim in the pond at his house in the Hopper, he made clear that swimming suits were optional, and declined to wear one himself.

Hunt was one of the few Williams faculty invited to splashy parties at Cole Porter's Williamstown house in the 1950s, where with Porter's friends he sat around the piano singing ribald parodies of Porter songs. Students and colleagues occasionally gossiped about Hunt's sexual preferences. Now and again a report would surface that Hunt found some male student or colleague attractive. (But it is well documented that he also enjoyed the company of women.) – Hunt knew that people talked, and didn't care, or even took pleasure in the idea that he was shocking conventional norms.

Hunt's Early Career

There were a lot of things about Hunt that most students did not know when they were undergraduates. He was born James Clay Hunt, Jr., on Jan. 28, 1915, in Lexington, Kentucky. Brought up in an observant Presbyterian household, he would later reject religion, but he knew well what he was rejecting. (In a panel discussion on "The Idea of 'God'" in 1961, Hunt argued that God is a "literary symbol used to express certain truths about the human condition." In the description of his famous 1970s Winter Study course on the Bible, he declared that "the religious operations of the human mind" were of "high intellectual interest, and some value" but that he himself regarded "religious belief of any kind as intellectually absurd.") His father, also James Clay Hunt, was president of the Bryant-Hunt Company, a wholesale and retail grocery business, and was 47 when the first of three children, Clay, Jr., was born. The family was financially comfortable, with a substantial house on North Broadway tended by servants. But in 1930, just after the stock market crash, Hunt's father died after a long illness, leaving Hunt's 48-year-old mother with three young children, and what must have been a substantial drop in income.

Hunt went to the University of Kentucky, in Lexington, where he graduated Phi Beta Kappa, with highest distinction, in 1934, at the age of 19. While there he would have been exposed to southern "Agrarianism." The famous *I'll Take My Stand*, a manifesto seeking to promote a "Southern way of life," an "agrarian" as opposed to a (northern) "industrial" life, was published in 1930. And he would have known regional writing, including the work of noted Kentucky writers Allen Tate, Robert Penn Warren, and Donald Davidson, and other so-called "Fugitive Poets" centered at Vanderbilt University in the 1920s. He stayed on at Kentucky for another year, and received his M.A. in 1935. He was then admitted to the Ph.D. program in English at Johns Hopkins.

At that point – it was the middle of the Depression – he and his family moved to Baltimore, so that the three children (Clay, age 20, and his two younger siblings) could live at home while they went to graduate school and college. At Hopkins the distinguished faculty included Hazelton Spencer (the senior Shakespearean, whom Hunt later remembered) and Don Cameron Allen, a Renaissance specialist. Hunt spent four years there, and began a dissertation on Elizabethan poetry. (He later claimed that he didn't think much of the teaching in graduate school.) In 1939 he took a job as an instructor at Wayne University (later called Wayne State University) in Detroit, and continued to work on his dissertation, "The Elizabethan Background of Neo-Classic Polite Verse," which he completed in 1941, when he got his degree. His faculty apparently thought very highly of it, because they accepted an essay on Elizabethan poetry, drawn from his dissertation, for the Hopkins-sponsored academic journal, *English Literary History*. At this stage in his career Hunt was primarily interested in literary history, and in particular in the relationship between the "neo-classic" poets of the early 17th century and the Elizabethans of the late 16th. In later years he was best known for teaching 20th-century writers, but in fact Hunt never abandoned his interest in Renaissance writers or in literary history.

Hunt was happy at recently-founded Wayne University, with good colleagues – one of whom was the young poet John Berryman, Hunt's exact contemporary – and interesting students. He later said that it was not unlike Williams, with small classes, except that the students worked harder. His plan was to stay on through three one-year appointments, and then, as was the standard at Wayne, come up for tenure. But after two years, in June of 1941, he got a call from Williams, which needed a last-minute replacement for an unexpected retirement. His name had been suggested by Rowland Evans, a young instructor at Williams whom Hunt had met as a fellow graduate student at Johns Hopkins. Although inclined to remain at Wayne, he went to Williamstown for an interview, and was impressed with the English Department – "good intellectually and probably better than the one at Wayne" – and its new chair, John Hawley (Jack) Roberts, along with his young colleagues Hallett Smith and Robert Allen. They all took teaching very seriously. Hunt accepted an offer, taught for academic year 1941-42, and although reappointed for a second year decided in July 1942 (eight months after Pearl Harbor), at the age of 27, to enlist in the U. S. Navy, joining many other young Williams faculty who resigned their appointments and went into the war. Hunt served four years in the navy, on destroyers, ending as a lieutenant, including one year as an instructor in Ordnance at the Midshipmen's School in New York, two years as Torpedo Officer and Asst. Gunnery Officer on the USS Hopewell, which took part in a number of battles in the western Pacific, and a year as senior instructor at the Pacific Fleet Torpedo School in Pearl Harbor, where he rewrote the standard manual on torpedo tactics into clear and plain English. In later years his students knew nothing about this. A private man who didn't talk about himself or his past, he rarely told war stories.

As a veteran, Hunt was entitled to get his job back, and returned to Williams for the 1946-47 academic year. Fred Stocking, who had taught at Williams as an instructor from 1940 to 1944, and with Ph. D. now in hand returned to Williams in 1946, became his best friend. (His old Hopkins friend Rowland Evans had been killed during the war.) Hunt later said he did not imagine he was "good enough" to stay at Williams, nor did he think Williams was a good fit for him, but he was reappointed for two three-year terms as an assistant professor, 1947-50 and 1950-53. By the early '50s, under a new chair, Robert Allen, Hunt found Williams "a very stimulating place to work." (Several of his young colleagues, including Richard Poirier and J. Hillis Miller, after spending a short time at Williams, went on to have distinguished scholarly careers elsewhere.) Among the younger men whom he liked was John (Jack) O'Neill, a fellow bachelor who also lived at the Old Faculty Club, and was Hunt's drinking and dinner partner. O'Neill, he thought, was bright and a good teacher, but not "intellectually . . . first-rate" – and he had a serious drinking problem. Hunt was brought up for tenure in the fall of 1952, and promoted to Associate Professor, to take effect in July 1953.

The early '50s was perhaps the high-water mark in the American academy of the so-called "New Criticism," particularly in classroom teaching. The term was popularized by John Crowe Ransom's 1941 book called *The New Criticism*, shifting attention from historical and biographical study of literature to the formal properties of a poem, which the critic attempted to describe in "precise" and even "scientific" terms. (One of Hunt's students in the 1960s remembers him using those very terms to describe good criticism.) One might think that it was Hunt who introduced Ransom's "New Criticism" to Williams: he would have encountered Ransom's work in the 1930s, when Ransom, at Vanderbilt, was a member of the Southern Agrarians and later of the Fugitive Poets. But it was in fact probably Stocking, who in 1945-46 was completing his dissertation on the critical theory of Ransom and his colleague Allen Tate, and who in 1940-41 had served as the junior member of the departmental committee that reorganized the required freshman English course from a survey of early major writers (Chaucer and Spenser) into a course on "critical analysis." Hunt eagerly joined in what Stocking later called the "overthrow" of the old freshman course. By the late 1940s the textbook for freshman English was the famous *Understanding Poetry* (1938, 2nd ed. 1950), by Cleanth Brooks and Robert Penn Warren" (who had been Ransom's students at Vanderbilt in the 1920s), and remained in use at least until the mid-1960s.

In the classroom Hunt, like most English teachers in those days, practiced the "formalist" criticism that Ransom, Brooks, and Warren advocated, urging students to keep their eyes on the words in "the text" and to understand how a poem was organized to achieve formal "unity." But he was no doctrinaire "New Critic." His description of his Milton course in 1972 notes that Milton's works will be interpreted "in terms of the political events of his time and of the literary and philosophical ideas of the Renaissance."

And he made plenty of room for feeling, although in so doing he took his lead from Eliot rather than Wordsworth. Poetry for him was not a "turning loose of emotion" or a "spontaneous overflow of powerful feelings" but was essentially dramatic. That meant that the critic, and especially the classroom teacher, would find the feeling in Eliot's timid Prufrock or in Yeats' "sixty-year-old smiling public man." For Hunt, a man with a big personality and yet an intensely private man, teaching was in T. S. Eliot's terms both an "escape from personality" and an "expression" of it. What students encountered was Hunt's dramatic persona.

In 1954, already tenured, Hunt published a major book with Yale University Press, *Donne's Poetry*, a series of close readings of seven poems by John Donne and a long concluding chapter defining and assessing Donne's achievement. It met with mixed reviews from Donne scholars. The book is misremembered now as if it were a "New Critical" exercise, regarding a poem as an autonomous work, considered independently of any historical or biographical context. In fact, as Hunt made clear in his preface, he did not simply do "close analysis." He also deployed "some of the techniques of historical literary scholarship . . . intellectual background . . . wider historical context" – techniques that he had applied in his Hopkins dissertation. While noting Donne's "personal reticences" – and Hunt himself was, as noted, personally reticent – he freely conjectured about the relationship between Donne the poet and Donne the man. (And speculated about the parallels between Donne and James Joyce.) And as some will be surprised to hear, Hunt argued that Donne, whose reputation was then very high, had severe "limitations" as a poet. But Hunt did not press the point in the classroom. Indeed, students were not assigned his book or expected to reproduce his interpretations. (English majors at the time were not encouraged to read literary criticism, except in upper division courses and in the honors program; they were expected to work out their own interpretations and arguments by carefully examining "the text.")

Why did Hunt not publish more? In fact, from the '40s to the early '70s his Yale book put him at the scholarly forefront of his Williams colleagues who typically spent their time and energy on their classroom teaching, and who rarely published in academic journals or university presses. (Stocking and Neill Megaw – who was primarily interested in curriculum and pedagogy – published very little, and Don Gifford's work on Joyce did not come out until the '70s. By then younger colleagues such as Larry Graver and Charles Samuels had begun publishing their scholarship.) At the time of his retirement Hunt's scholarly reputation in the academic profession still stood higher than that of any Williams colleague.

During the 1950s Hunt created his famous course on Dante, perhaps prompted to do so by Eliot's 1921 essay in praise of Dante. He also began another writing project, this time on John Milton's much-studied poem, "Lycidas." In February 1961, as part of the winter faculty lecture series, he delivered a paper on his ongoing work. By then, Nelson Bushnell having retired and Roy Lamson having left for MIT in 1958, Hunt, at 45, was the third most senior person in the department, behind chairman Robert Allen and Fred Stocking. He was promoted to full professor in 1958.

Hunt as colleague

Hunt worked hard on faculty committees, particularly in the early 1960s, in discussions leading to the adoption of the Winter Study Program. Indeed, Hunt thought he had come up with the idea, when he was chair of the Calendar Committee in December 1960, and proposed that the college reduce semesters from 14 weeks to 12, finish fall classes before Christmas, and have some kind of extended "reading period" in January. (He conceded that he had not devoted much attention to the *purpose* of the reading period.) The proposal was not adopted, but in the summer of 1962 he was part of a team of three faculty sent to a three-week conference in Colorado Springs, sponsored by the Danforth Foundation, on liberal arts curriculum. In 1962-63 he was chair of the new Committee on Educational Policy, which met with the Committee on Curriculum and developed what was later called the 4-2-4 program – under which students would take four courses in each semester and two courses in a January term. In the following year he was a member of the so-called "Committee of Three" (in fact, it had five members), which got the principle of the 4-2-4 program endorsed by the faculty. Although he was not on the 1964-65 committee charged with implementing the program, which by then had morphed into a 4-1-4, Hunt spoke influentially in favor of the proposal at the faculty meeting in the spring of 1965, when the proposal was adopted. In the early 1970s Hunt enthusiastically gave a famous Winter Study course on the Bible "as literature," and in 1975-76 served as chair of the Winter Study Committee.

During the 1960s Hunt, as one of the department's very few tenured members, played a key role on departmental search committees, interviewing candidates at the annual Modern Language Association (MLA) convention. He eagerly took his turn, along with other senior departmental colleagues, in teaching the introductory English major course, English 1-2 (later renamed 101-102). It was a "staff course," with a common syllabus across many sections. Course instructors met regularly during the semester to discuss common paper and exam topics, as well as interpretation of individual poems and plays. Hunt had strong opinions about how particular poems should be taught, and did not hesitate to advocate for them. But he did not pull rank, or condescend, and listened respectfully to counterarguments from younger colleagues.

In the mid-'60s, when Williams under President Jack Sawyer was reconsidering its curriculum, some of his English Department colleagues wanted to free instructors in 101 to devise their own reading lists. This led to a significant split in the faculty. Hunt, siding with Stocking and Allen against Gifford and Megaw, continued to argue vigorously for a common syllabus. Hunt's faction at first prevailed, but in 1968 English 102, by then a Shakespeare course, was no longer required, and by 1975, Hunt's final year of teaching, the 101 syllabus was loosened to permit instructors to assign works of their choice, so long as they chose from four specified authors. What was happening at Williams only reflected what was happening in English Departments all over the country.

The two factions also split over a loosening of the traditional sequence of required period courses, Hunt (always a literary historian), aligned with traditionalists, defending the chronological sequence, and Gifford arguing that there was no good reason that a student had to study Chaucer before studying Milton. The national trend was to abandon required "survey courses," and in this case Williams was one of the first to drop the requirement, as it did in 1970.

Hunt also had strong opinions about the merits of his colleagues and of the young untenured instructors. Fred Stocking, newly appointed chair in 1963, was pressed by Hunt (who had recommended him as chair) to re-make the department: Hunt wanted the college to decline to renew contracts of all untenured faculty. Stocking sharply objected, thinking Hunt only wanted to recruit "disciples," and their friendship suffered. His colleagues had strong opinions as well, and the department was sharply divided about recommending reappointment or tenure: one of the consequences is that from the 1950s into the late 1970s very few instructors and assistant professors were promoted. (Some younger faculty found Hunt's social manner not just eccentric but troubling. On the other hand, several assistant professors from that era report that Hunt was hospitable and friendly with younger colleagues, both those who gained tenure and those who did not.)

Hunt's tenured colleagues were wary. Stocking remembered him as "colorful" and "brilliant," with a "forceful way of talking." Hunt, he said, "could be overwhelming . . it was almost impossible to argue with him. With his powerful memory he could call up evidence to overwhelm you in any kind of argument." The younger Larry Graver agreed: he thought Hunt a "brilliant, powerful personality" who, as he put it carefully, "tended to like certain young people but dislike certain others." Don Gifford, a little less diplomatically, thought Hunt was for a time "the bane of my existence," "delightfully controversial at times, at other times irritatingly so." Even his friends conceded that he could be cruel and domineering.

By the mid-1960s, Stocking having resigned as chair, disagreements among the tenured department members – Allen, Stocking, and Hunt on one side, Gifford and Megaw on the other – were thought serious enough that in the fall of 1966 the Dean of the Faculty, John Chandler, arranged to bring in leadership from outside. The new chair, beginning in the fall of 1967, was Arthur Carr, a senior professor from the University of Michigan. Perhaps as a consequence, in the spring of 1969 Neill Megaw announced that he was leaving Williams to become chair of the English Department at the University of Texas. And according to his nephew, Hunt too thought of leaving (perhaps because he was disappointed about curricular changes or tenure decisions), but in the end decided to stay. Departmental politics were somewhat calmer, but there were still bitter tenure disputes between departmental factions in the early 1970s.

By then Hunt may have lost some influence on curriculum and tenure, but he still commanded respect for his intellect and his learning, not only from senior colleagues but also from up-and-coming junior members. Even those more devoted to published scholarship than Hunt thought appropriate for a "teaching college" deferred to the author of a Yale Press book on Donne that was still being respectfully cited by scholars.

Hunt's last years

The last ten or fifteen years of Hunt's career coincided with the Civil Rights movement and the prolonged national and local debate about Vietnam. Hunt was not notably involved in either, although not because, as is sometimes suggested, his politics reflected his southern background. In fact, Hunt said he had been happy with the "liberal" atmosphere on the Williams faculty during his time. He continued to be a divisive figure in English Department politics, but he extended his hospitality and kindness, especially to younger colleagues. He also continued to attract strong and devoted students, entertaining them at his house in the Hopper. In the summer of 1974 he loaned the house to the Williamstown Summer Theatre, which used it as the setting for a filmed version of its production of Chekhov's *The Seagull*, broadcast on public TV in New York the following January. And, as those who knew him remember, he continued to delight in making theatrically outrageous remarks in polite company, especially if they served to shock conventional pieties.

In the spring of 1976, still teaching vigorously, Hunt was diagnosed with lung cancer, and he retired early from the faculty at the end of the academic year, at the age of 61. But he remained in Williamstown, and determined that he would live his life to the end. He retained his irrepressible manner, and, ever an atheist, took an intellectual interest in the process of dying. Even while undergoing chemotherapy, he took piano lessons, as if adopting Walter Pater's advice to experience as many moments of passionate intellectual excitement as he could while there was still time. He drove his little Fiat convertible around town with the top down, in a red beret. He also determined that while he still had the energy he would complete his book on Milton. Hunt incorporated a 20-page close "analysis" of the poem, but he went well beyond "New Critical" formalism, even speculating on Milton's "state of mind." According to his nephew, the manuscript grew to an unmanageable size, reflecting the range of Hunt's intellectual interests in Renaissance neoPlatonism and Italian genre theory, and he almost abandoned the project. He realized he had to focus on his novel argument that "Lycidas," conventionally regarded as a pastoral elegy, was in fact a "fusion" of pastoral and Italianate "high lyric" descended from Dante. The manuscript was cut, and resubmitted to Yale Press in the fall of 1977.

He did not live to see it published. (It was seen through the press by a fellow Miltonist, with assistance from John Reichert, and appeared posthumously, in 1979, as *Milton and the Italian Critics*.) Hunt died at home on December 2, 1977. The program of a memorial service in the college chapel ten days later included readings from two of Hunt's favorite modern poems, Wallace Stevens's "Sunday Morning" and Yeats's "Byzantium."

> Astraddle on the dolphin's mire and blood,
> Spirit after spirit! The smithies break the flood,
> The golden smithies of the Emperor!
> Marbles of the dancing floor
> Break bitter furies of complexity,
> Those images that yet
> Fresh images beget,
> That dolphin-torn, that gong-tormented sea.

A fitting sendoff for a resolute atheist for whom Christianity provided "fresh images."

He was remembered at the February 1978 faculty meeting for his "dispassionate energy" and his "passionate intelligence," and for his characteristic intellectual manner: he was "not very tolerant . . . of everything he regarded as cant, not at all open-minded to callow opinions or shallow logic." Had he been there, Hunt himself would have snorted with pleasurable recognition.

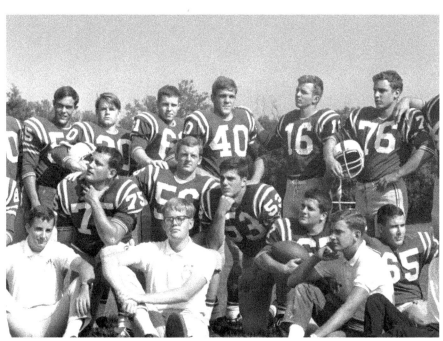

Williams College football team, Fall 1965. Rusty Powell is #56 (second row), Kirk Varnedoe #76 (third row). Courtesy of Williams College Archives and Special Collections.

Chapter 15

—ᴍ—

THE "WILLIAMS ART MAFIA"

We don't hear much new in recent years about the "Williams Art Mafia," the small group of Williams students who graduated in the 1960s and went on in the 1980s and '90s to become directors of a number of the country's major museums. But it's a topic that once attracted a lot of journalistic attention, beginning with a cover story in the glossy art-world magazine, *Art & Auction,* in November 1989, and including prominent articles in the *New York Times* over the next fifteen years. By 1989 Williams alums had in fact been in prominent positions in the museum world for several years, Jim Wood '63 as director of the Art Institute of Chicago since 1979, Earl (Rusty) Powell '66 as director of the Los Angeles County Museum of Art (LACMA) since 1980, Bob Buck '61, director of the Brooklyn Museum since 1983. A lesser-known figure, Jim Pilgrim '63, had been Deputy Director at the Metropolitan Museum in New York since 1978. Then in the late 1980s a series of Williams alums were appointed to top museum jobs: in 1987 Jack Lane '66 to become director of the San Francisco Museum of Modern Art and Kirk Varnedoe '67 to become the powerful head of painting and sculpture at the Museum of Modern Art in New York, in 1988 Roger Mandle '63 to be Deputy Director of the National Gallery of Art and Tom Krens '69 to become director of the Guggenheim. It's not often noted that all but one of them were appointed to these senior positions when they were remarkably young – still in their 30s.

And Williams alums were even more visible in the museum world for the next 20 years, after Powell moved from LACMA to head the National Gallery in 1992, Arthur Wheelock '65 curated the blockbuster Vermeer show at the National Gallery in 1995, and Lane moved from SFMoMA to head the Dallas Museum of Art in 1997. Also in the mid-1990s what might be called the second generation of the "Williams art mafia" emerged, when Michael Govan '85 was named head of the Dia Art Foundation in 1994 and Glenn Lowry '76 became head of the Museum of Modern Art in New York in 1995. Locally, Joe Thompson '81 was appointed founding director of MassMoCA in 1999. Tom Krens was especially adept at attracting attention, particularly in New York for his controversial work at the Guggenheim, and for opening the Frank Gehry-designed Guggenheim Museum in Bilbao in 1997. Williams alums continued to get top jobs in the new millennium, especially in California: in 2006 Wood, having retired from the Art Institute of Chicago, was named president of the Getty Art Trust, and Govan moved from DIA to take over at LACMA. In 2008 Mandle was appointed Executive Director of the Qatar Museums Authority.

More than thirty years have passed since the famous article in *Art & Auction*, and some of the original journalistic speculations about the "Williams art mafia" have hardened into legend, if not into fact. Now that the original members of the "mafia" have retired, most recently Powell (or died), it may be time to take another look at an old story.

It should be noted at the outset that as originally used, the term referred narrowly to a handful of museum *directors*. Varnedoe, a curator, was probably included in the 1989 *Art & Auction* article because some thought he virtually functioned as co-director of MoMA, and David Tunick '66 was probably said to be part of the group because he was a well-connected New York gallery owner. Had the article been published a few years later, it might well have included Wheelock, highly-visible curator of Dutch and Flemish Painting at the National Gallery since 1975, as well as Lowry and Govan. It should probably also be noted that the term no longer has much resonance in the larger art world. In a 2016 collection of interviews with ten active museum directors around the country (including two Williams alumni, Govan and Lowry), published by the High Museum in Atlanta, Michael Shapiro, himself a product of the Williams graduate art program, makes no reference to the "Williams Art Mafia," though in an appendix he refers to Powell and Lane. But the term is still heard around the Williams campus, occasionally at reunions, and on ephblog, and constitutes a significant part of the college's cultural history. It's worth revisiting the topic, if only to try to separate legend from fact.

According to the legend, three art history professors, Lane Faison, Whitney Stoddard, and Bill Pierson, known affectionately and facetiously in Williams circles as "the Holy Trinity," inspired wary Williams boys, who came to campus thinking there might be something unmanly about studying art. These charismatic teachers converted poli sci and econ majors into students of art. Many of these students, so it was said, were varsity athletes, and were in part persuaded to study art because their art-history teachers regularly showed up at their games. The art-history students got to know each other, and after graduating some of them went into the museum world, where they soon formed a professional network, and after a while became known, again somewhat tongue-in-cheek, as the "Williams Art Mafia."

That's a concise version of the legend, appearing first in the 1989 Judith Nathan article and then repeated in subsequent journalistic accounts in the *New York Times* and elsewhere. It makes a good story, and it is still retold today, at least in Williamstown. But to make such a good story it cherry picks from, and creatively massages, the documentable facts, focuses narrowly on the state of the art world in the late 1980s, and on a few Williams men – and they *were* all white men – who held high-profile jobs as museum directors. It leaves unanswered some crucial questions: why did Williams graduates get so many of the top directorial jobs in a short space of time? Why were they first called an "art mafia," and by whom? Why did the "mafia" emerge when it did? Is it true that Williams, for a time at least, served as more of an "incubator" for museum directors than any place else? And how did it come about that three professors at a New England college founded not by Jesuits but by Congregationalists, and long a thoroughly secular place, are still thought of as a "Holy Trinity"?

To begin with the term, "Williams Art Mafia." Nobody seems to know for certain who coined it. It may have been a jealous outsider, semi-seriously grumbling that lots of good museum jobs seemed to be going to graduates of one small college. One unsubstantiated story has it that it was Sir John Pope-Hennessy, then head of the department of European painting at the Met, and a professor at NYU's Institute of Fine Art. But it may just as likely have been the facetious remark of a Williams insider, looking around with some pride at the number of Williams alumni in senior positions at museums. If it was an outsider, the term was soon appropriated or at least accepted by Williams insiders, even though none of the Williams museum directors liked the label. But it stuck, and the neutral term "network" never caught on. "Art mafia" still makes some people at Williams wince, taken to be a sign that Williams alumni somehow "controlled" the art world in an underhanded way, as if it were the carting or gambling business, but it was never meant to be taken seriously, and in any case "mafia" had by the 1980s been applied to various fields – JFK's "Irish Mafia," "the New York literary mafia," the "atonal composers' Mafia"– to suggest a small closed group that exerted outsize influence.

Although it has been forgotten now, it probably did not pass unnoticed in the late 1980s that "art mafia" was originally a term of abuse.

When it first turned up in print, it was not linked to Williams, but to gallery owners, critics, and scholars in New York who had great influence over the world of art. In the late 1960s one New York art critic referred to young artists grousing about the "Minimal art mafia" – gallery owners who refused to show anything but minimalist art. In the early 1970s the sculptor Louise Nevelson complained bitterly, and in print, about the power wielded by the art critics Clement Greenberg (who had given her work a hostile review), Harold Rosenberg, and their peers, Michael Fried, and Rosalind Krauss, along with Henry Geldzahler, a curator at the Met who omitted her work from his high-profile 1969 exhibition of New York contemporary painting and sculpture. Ignoring the differences among them, Nevelson called them the "New York Art Mafia" and even "the Jewish art mafia." The term clearly had an edge, and expressed the resentment against insiders of an artist who thought she deserved to be on the inside.

As for the "Holy Trinity," the term, like "Williams Art Mafia" meant to be affectionate and facetious, doesn't bear close scrutiny. We are not intended to speculate about which one is the father, and who the son, never mind the Holy Ghost. The point is simply that there were *three* long-serving and equally-well-known art history professors in the Art Department at Williams College from the late 1930s to the 1970s, that they all taught in the famous introductory art history course, that they all had plenty of admirers among their students and their colleagues, and in some sense were thus all equal members of a trio, or a "trinity." The three were in fact honored as a group by the establishment in 1993 of the Faison-Pierson-Stoddard Chair in Art History. The term "Holy Trinity" was probably coined in the late 1980s, long after Faison, Pierson, and Stoddard had retired from teaching, by none other than Williams President Frank Oakley, who was given to rhetorical playfulness in his public addresses. The term caught on, and, even though the honorees disliked it, it has not been displaced by the perhaps more appropriate "triumvirate."

"Holy Trinity" was never designed to be coordinated with or to clarify "art mafia." (Don't try to figure out which one is the "don" or the "godfather.") It also obscures important distinctions among the three professors. Professor Michael Lewis some years ago pointed out significant differences: Stoddard and Pierson established scholarly reputations while Faison, who did not publish art-history scholarship, made a name for himself as a reviewer and art critic in the *Nation*. Stoddard and Faison were both Williams alumni, while Pierson's undergraduate degree was from Yale. Stoddard had been an athlete at Williams, and when he returned as a teacher was an avid sports fan, famously attending home games in all sports (Faison and Pierson did not), and in later years probably had a wider following on the campus than the other two because of his famous "Reflections on Where You Are" lectures on the campus buildings, delivered annually during what was then called "Freshman Orientation." Their teaching styles also varied – Stoddard perhaps the most entertaining, noted not just for his witty remarks in the introductory art lecture, but for what his younger colleague E. J. Johnson called "a stand-up comic's sense of timing."

They also shared a lot. All three were devoted teachers, and shared a deep interest in what Faison called "the eye," attentive visual inspection of the art object. Stoddard specialized in medieval art and Pierson in architecture, but all three had wide knowledge of the complete history of art. Although each developed a following among students, Faison is usually acknowledged to have had the most impact on the students who later became members of the "art mafia."

Focusing on the "Holy Trinity" obscures the importance of a fourth art professor, Lee Hirsche, who from 1957 until he retired early in 1985, taught studio art. Trained at Yale as a painter, he was hired by Faison to set up a studio art program at Williams, and in his early years taught all the courses – in design, painting, and a popular "Introduction to Architecture" course which proved to inspire a number of Williams students to go on to architecture school at Yale or Harvard. He shared with his colleagues on the art-history side of the Art Department a primary interest in the qualities of the visual "object" – not what it "meant" or the socio-political world it came from. All those who majored in art were required to take his basic design course, and he deserves more credit for helping to inspire Williams art major than he usually receives. By the same token, it ought to be recognized that Williams, not an art school, has produced a significant number of graduates in the 1960s who went on to become painters and architects.

"Holy Trinity" also obscures the significance of several eminent professors of art history at Williams who had established reputations as scholars and taught only briefly at the end of their academic careers in the undergraduate or graduate programs as the Robert Sterling Clark Visiting Professor, including John Pope-Hennessy, Ellis Waterhouse, George Hamilton, and Jakob Rosenberg. They too made an impact on the Williams art majors in the 1960s, particularly those going on to graduate school.

Several of the people Nathan interviewed, notably Kirk Varnedoe, suggested to her that conventional Williams "men" had to be persuaded that there was nothing unmanly about studying art. But this misrepresents the case: it may have been true just after World War II, when large numbers of veterans, focused on getting a college degree and a good job, enrolled at Williams, but by the early 1960s it was widely assumed by students that a knowledge (or at least an "appreciation") of visual art as well as classical music was a central part of the "liberal education" that Williams and other liberal arts colleges offered. In those years near the end of the all-male Williams, there were no women students flooding the art-history classrooms so as to make Williams boys think that studying art was for girls. David Tunick later recalled that at Williams there was "no stigma" attached to the study of art history. Wheelock says studying art history was not thought to be "effete." Art 201-02, "Introduction to the History of Art," was the prerequisite for all other courses in the Art major, but it also proved to be one of the most popular courses at Williams. Enrollments in the 1960s commonly exceeded 200 per semester – nearly one out of every five students on the campus. Lee Hirsche later estimated that 85% of the undergraduates took that course. So it seems unlikely that studying art history was widely regarded as unmanly. But fewer than one out of ten or twelve of those enrolled in Art 201-02 went on to be art majors.

Journalists also overstate when they say that the future members of the art mafia were converted to art history by Faison and his colleagues. It is true that Tunick and Powell (and later Lowry) started out as pre-med and switched to art history, but Wood and Wheelock always planned to go into art history. Mandle wanted to be a painter; Varnedoe arrived with a talent for drawing and an interest in studio art. Neither Buck nor Lane was an art major. Tom Krens never took an art-history course.

Was it significant that Williams alumni in the museum world played contact sports at college? *Art & Auction* put a photo of the 1965 Williams varsity football team on the cover of its "art mafia" story, implying not only that the "art mafia" was in effect a boys' club, but that Williams museum directors, hypermasculine men, began their college careers as athletes. If you look closely, however, you will see that the only students in that photo who in fact became part of the art world were Rusty Powell and Kirk Varnedoe. (Varnedoe was a starting defensive lineman, but Powell did not play much.) And as is well known, it was not unusual in the 1960s (or now) for a Williams undergraduate to play intercollegiate sports. Still, it remains remarkable that several of the Williams museum directors and senior curators were serious athletes. Arthur Wheelock '65 was a three-sport letterman, Tom Krens played varsity basketball and after graduation even played semi-pro ball in Europe, and Lowry was a downhill skier. Jim Wood once said, perhaps facetiously, that he learned as much about running a museum from playing contact sports as from anything else. (Jack Lane and Rusty Powell both said they got their best training as U.S. Navy officers). And it is at least curious that several of the "mafia" members – including Wood, Tunick, Varnedoe, and Krens – owned motorcycles, in the 1960s a distinctly gendered sign of maleness.

Did the members of the "mafia" know each other as students? Yes and no. Buck, Pilgrim, and Wood had graduated by the time Varnedoe and Krens arrived, so they could not have met until later. Powell once said that "a lot of us did not come into much contact until after we left Williams." But several would have known each other as classmates: Mandle, Pilgrim, and Wood were all members of the Class of '63, Lane, Powell, and Tunick all members of '66 (Lane and Powell were roommates.) Mandle was Tunick's Junior Advisor. Tunick and Wheelock knew Varnedoe ('67) in the art history major.

Did these alumni, when they graduated from Williams, aspire to enter the museum world? Most, but not all: Varnedoe aimed at the academic world – he was a longtime professor at Columbia and NYU; Wheelock began as a professor at the University of Maryland, and, while serving as a curator at the National Gallery, remained an academic for the rest of his career. Powell began as an academic but quickly switched to museum work. Almost all went first to graduate school in art history, getting a master's or a Ph. D. (Lane's first graduate degree was an MBA.)

Was it the undergraduate art program at Williams that prepared them for the museum world, or was it their graduate work at Harvard or NYU's Institute of Fine Art? Harvard's graduate program, in which many Williams graduates of the 1960s and 1970s enrolled, had long been productive over the decades as incubator of museum professionals. Paul Sachs' famous "museum course" (which he taught from 1921 to 1948) seeded museums all over the country with directors, from the 1930s into the 1970s, and Sachs' students formed what one of them has called "a network of museum professionals who kept in touch with one another." Varnedoe has written that while Williams prepared him to look carefully at paintings, it did not prepare him especially well for graduate school.

Did the "Holy Trinity" help their students get their first museum jobs? Yes. Faison in particular was very well connected in the New York art world: he had known the leading art critic, Clement Greenberg, very well since the late 1940s, and personally knew the curators at the Met and at MoMA. He was also still in touch with his old teachers at Harvard and Princeton. Tunick says Faison helped him get an internship at the Met. One of Lowry's first jobs was at the Sackler and Freer Gallery in Washington, hired by its director Milo Beach, who taught art history at Williams from 1969 to 1984, where he knew Lowry as an undergraduate. But it was of course not unusual then or now for professors to recommend their best students to potential employers. Paul Sachs reportedly wrote recommendations for hundreds of his students, and to good effect. And it surely did not hurt that there were well-placed Williams alums in the art world. Charles Parkhurst '35 interviewed Wheelock at the National Gallery in 1973. Krens hired Thompson and Govan; Govan says Krens was his "best mentor."

Did Williams graduates form a network once they entered the museum world? Not surprisingly, they all knew each other professionally, but as Lane said recently, when they sought to borrow paintings, hire staff, or co-sponsor exhibitions, they were no more likely to look to a museum director who happened to be a fellow Williams alum than to other museum directors: they considered above all the needs and interests of their own museums. Parkhurst, Mandle, Wheelock, and Powell of course worked together at the National Gallery, as did Varnedoe and Lowry at MoMA. But Varnedoe and Lowry are said not to have been particularly close, and parted company in 2001, when Varnedoe resigned his position and went to the Institute for Advanced Study. Varnedoe and Krens did not see eye to eye about the role of museums in promoting contemporary art. Their shared Williams connection did not keep Krens and Lowry from rivalry and competition in the art world of New York.

In fact, as has been noted, members of the Williams "mafia" are rather different from each other, Varnedoe and Wheelock scholar-curators, Powell and Lane primarily known as arts administrators, Krens a sort of entrepreneur and deal-maker. Although Williams curators and directors were not a tight-knit group, they all felt indebted to their college experience: it was the "tightness of their allegiance" not to each other but *to their Williams professors* that seems distinctive.

When did the Williams museum people begin to sense that they shared something?

Wood is quoted by Judith Dobrynzski in the *New York Times* as saying he had not thought about Williams as an "incubator" for the art world until about 1979-80 – that's when he became director at Chicago, Powell went to LACMA , and Lane was at the Carnegie Museum. (By then Mandle was director at Toledo, Buck at the Albright-Knox in Buffalo, and Jim Pilgrim Deputy Director of the Metropolitan.) Beginning in 1980 several of these directors– including Wood, Powell, Buck, and Mandle – began meeting regularly, when they started terms on the Visiting Committee of the Williams College Museum of Art. In October 1986, when Krens was director of WCMA, several of the directors, including Wood, Buck (by now at Brooklyn), and Powell, met at the reopening of the college museum. Wood, Buck, and Tunick met again, as members of the WCMA Visiting Committee, at the Art Institute of Chicago in February 1988, by which time Lane had moved to SFMoMA, Mandle to the National Galley, and Varnedoe to MoMA. It seems likely that these meetings reinforced the sense that committee members had something important in common. It's my hunch that it was during the 1988 meeting of the WCMA Visiting Committee in Chicago that somebody, observing that a handful of Williams-educated museum directors, in dark suits, had showed up in Chicago, like regional bosses gathering for a mob conference, came up with the term "Williams Art Mafia." It may even have been Lane Faison himself, who was there, and who had an impish wit.

What was the occasion for the November 1989 article? The piece, which appeared in *Art & Auction*, was originally commissioned from Judith Nathan by the *New York Times* Sunday magazine in 1988, when Krens, Varnedoe, and Lane were appointed to new jobs at the Guggenheim, MoMA, and San Francisco. (Nathan had written profiles of both Krens and Varnedoe for the weekly *New York Observer*.) But when the *Times* decided not to publish the article, apparently under some pressure from the college, Nathan found that the editors at *Art & Auction* were eager to take it: in 1989 it was still timely, since Krens was attracting further attention for his plans to open a huge museum of contemporary art in North Adams – what would eventually be MassMoCA.

And why did the core group, beginning with Jim Wood and Roger Mandle, Class of 1963, and concluding with Tom Krens, Class of 1969, emerge as leaders in the museum world when they did? Why did their equivalents not emerge, say, ten years earlier or ten years later?

Williams graduates from earlier decades had in fact attained prominence in the art world. Some had graduated even earlier than Faison '29. Gordon Washburn '23 was director of the Albright-Knox Gallery in Buffalo from 1931 to 1942, and later director of the Carnegie Museum in Pittsburgh. Edgar Richardson '25 was named Assistant Director at the Detroit Museum of Art in 1933, and then Director from 1945 until 1962. James Thrall Soby '28 became a leading art critic. In the 1940s Sam Hunter '43 quickly established a reputation as an art critic at the *New York Times* – he later served as director of the Rose Art Museum at Brandeis and ultimately as a professor of art history at Princeton. Charles Parkhurst '35 began his career as a curator at the National Gallery, served with Lane Faison as one of the "Monument Men" who recovered Nazi-looted art, and in later years was director of the Baltimore Museum of Art (1962-1970), and then Assistant Director of the National Gallery (1970-83). Other Williams grads established reputations as collectors, notably Lawrence Bloedel '23, and Soby. Another collector, Sigmund Balka '56, became a trustee of several New York-area museums, Stephen Paine '54 a trustee of the MFA in Boston.

But it remains the case that beginning about 1980 an *unusually high* number of Williams-educated men moved into directorships. No doubt it had something to do with vacancies. As Jack Lane has suggested, a number of directorships at major museums opened up in the late 1970s and early 1980s, as an older generation of museum heads retired. Lane also points to changes in museum boards, as trustees, some of them newly-monied, in the late 1970s began looking for directors with different skills, especially in attracting resources and managing a complex organization. Practical people themselves, they were interested in candidates still safely WASPy, but younger and well-rounded, even athletic, practical and pragmatic, but with advanced degrees in art history, curatorial background, and good social skills, able to talk comfortably and confidently with board members, potential patrons, and lenders. Williams grads, many with an upper-middle-class background, apparently seemed to combine the desirable qualities of the old-style museum director and the new.

Within a few years, museum boards seemed even more interested in finding an "arts administrator" than an art historian, and since the Nathan article appeared the trend toward the museum-director-as-CEO has continued and the Williams graduate (unless she has management experience) decreasingly fills the bill. As it turns out, the members of the Williams mafia were perhaps transitional figures – able to combine the qualities of connoisseur and CEO. And even in 1989 they were apparently aware that they were among the last of their kind: Nathan quotes Jim Wood as regretting "the pressure . . . to prepare oneself first as a manager and then as a connoisseur and art historian." Jack Lane told Nathan he hoped directors coming up "will not be entirely management-oriented, although there are forces in the museum profession that push things in that direction."

It has been suggested that the emergence of the "Williams art mafia" had to do with the perception that the Williams grads were safely "masculine," even "manly" or "macho." That was the view of two senior art historians – Linda Nochlin and Colin Eisler – quoted in Nathan's article. But Nochlin and Eisler may have had an agenda, implicitly arguing that women and gay men should be given opportunities to be directors. Directors of major museums at least into the '80s and '90s with a few exceptions tended, like the members of the "Williams art mafia," to be heterosexual and married white men – perhaps so that, in the minds of conservative museum trustees, they could better perform the public – social and fund-raising – duties of director. (The case was different with curators.)

Perhaps the appeal of Williams graduates also had something to do with the way art history was still being taught at Williams in the 1960s. The Williams art department famously emphasized looking closely at works of art, typically by means of slides, but in advanced courses by handling original works from the college museum, focusing on their formal properties, and then talking about what you saw in the work of art "in its own terms," in language a layman could understand. But this was generally the way the introductory art history course was being taught at Harvard and Yale in the 1960s. Within a generation, art history scholarship and teaching were to change, emphasizing the social and even political contexts in which art was created and enjoyed. Increasingly, art historians developed a technical vocabulary, and found an academic rather than a general audience. It is noteworthy that the scholars among the "Williams Art Mafia," Wheelock and Varnedoe, wrote both for professional peers and for general audiences. Varnedoe in particular was well-known for his fluent and elegant performances as a public lecturer.

As I have noted, there was something of a second "generation" of the art mafia in the 1970s and 1980s – Glenn Lowry '76, Joe Thompson '81, and Michael Govan '85. They had the benefit of learning from at least one of the "Holy Trinity" – Pierson had retired in 1973 and Faison in 1976, but Stoddard continued to teach until 1982. And they also learned from one of the best students trained by the "Trinity," E. J. Johnson '59, who began teaching at Williams in 1965. If there is a "third generation" of Williams museum professionals, they have no link to the old Williams "art mafia." They are primarily products not of the college's undergraduate art-history major, but of the Williams graduate program at the Clark Art Institute (founded in 1972): its graduates from the 1970s and 1980s went on to become Deputy Director and Senior Curator at the Baltimore Museum of Art (Jay Fisher '75), director of the High Museum in Atlanta (Michael Shapiro '76) , Deputy Director at the North Carolina Museum of Art (John Coffey '78), Deputy Director of the National Gallery (Franklin Kelly '79), former Chief Curator at the Guggenheim (Nancy Spector '84), soon-to-be-former Director of the St. Louis Art Museum (Brent Benjamin '86), and a senior curator at the Getty (James Ganz '88). Graduates from the 1990s and 2000s now in senior positions include Katy Rothkopf '91 (Director of the Marder Center for Matisse Studies at the Baltimore Museum of Art), Darsie Alexander '91 (Chief Curator at the Jewish Museum in New York), James Rondeau '94 (Director of the Art Institute of Chicago), Tom Loughman '95 (CEO of the Wadsworth Museum in Hartford), Lisa Melandri '97 (Executive Director of the Contemporary Art Museum in St. Louis), Austen Barron Bailey '99 (Chief Curator at Crystal Bridges), Brent Abbott '02 (director of collections and exhibitions at the Amon Carter Museum in Fort Worth), Alexandra Suda '05 (Director of the National Gallery of Canada), several directors of university and college museums, and a number of curators at other major museums. At the Clark, where they are taught by Williams professors and Clark curators, they get training explicitly preparing them for the museum world. In 2006 about 40% of graduates were working in museum jobs, 25% in graduate programs or academic positions, and 25% outside of art history.

But one recent development suggests that the Williams graduate program is not a pipeline to directorships, perhaps because it focuses less on the management skills that museum boards look for than on art history and curatorship, and suggests that a graduate of the Clark program who aspires to be a director may need to get further training. To provide such training, the Center for Curatorial Leadership was founded in 2008 by Agnes Gund, former president of the MoMA board, and Elizabeth Easton, a senior art historian and curator at the Brooklyn Museum. It's noteworthy that Richard Rand, a former

Clark curator, and now Associate Director at the Getty, was a fellow of the first class at the center in 2008. Olivier Meslay, now director of the Clark was a fellow in 2011, and Jay Clarke, a former Clark curator, was a fellow in 2016. Susan Cross, a curator at MassMoCA, is in the class of 2019.

The old story of the "Williams art mafia" was, as I have suggested, a story about museum directors. But as Lane Faison himself suggested, there is another story that deserves to be told, about the larger number of Williams graduates who became curators, or art dealers, art critics, heads of arts organizations, and professors of art history. Williams-educated curators are found throughout the country, from New York (where Thayer Tolles '87 and Griffith Mann '91 are curators at the Metropolitan) and Boston (where Ethan Lasser '99 is Chair of the Art of the Americas Department at the MFA) to California. Maxwell Davidson '61 ran an important gallery in New York for many years; Hiram Butler MA '79 is a prominent art dealer in Houston; Tennyson Schad '52 ran a fine-art photography gallery in New York; and Todd Weyman MA '93 is a vice-president at Swann Galleries in New York. As noted earlier, James Thrall Soby '28 and Samuel Hunter '44 were prominent art critics. Increasingly this larger group includes female graduates: Mariet Westermann '84 served as director of the prestigious Institute of Fine Arts at NYU, Laura Hoptman '83 as Executive Director of the Drawing Center in New York, and Laura Heon MA '98 Executive Director of SITE Santa Fe, a space for the exhibition of contemporary art. Faison was particularly proud of the students who followed him into the teaching of art history, including Hunter, E. J. Johnson '58, James Morganstern '58, John Hunisak '67, and Paul Tucker '72. Tucker was also one of the country's most eminent curator of exhibitions, including two blockbuster Monet shows at the MFA. A number of Williams alumni have worked in prominent positions at Christie's and Sotheby's, including Eric Widing '77, Deputy Chairman at Christie's, and Leslie Keno '79, who rose to Senior Vice President at Sotheby's before becoming an independent appraiser and antiques dealer. Greg Rubinstein (MA '85), at Sotheby's since 1990, is now Worldwide Head of Old Master & Early British Drawings. Add to these the painters and architects that Williams has produced.

Even in the top ranks of the country's leading museums Williams alumni, both male and female, continue to be a strong presence. Glenn Lowry and Michael Govan from the undergraduate program continue to lead MoMa and LACMA. Joe Thompson only just stepped back from leading

MassMoCA. From the graduate program James Rondeau directs in Chicago and Brent Benjamin until recently directed in St. Louis, Frank Kelly still serves as Deputy Director and Chief Curator at the National Gallery, and Nancy Spector has just finished a long term as Artistic Director and Chief Curator at the Guggenheim. Of the Williams graduates originally profiled in the 1989 article in *Art & Auction,* David Tunick continues to run his gallery devoted to Old Master and modern prints, and serves as president of the International Fine Print Dealers Association. Tom Krens continues to promote a proposed Extreme Model Railroad and Contemporary Architecture Museum in North Adams. It all suggests that Williams art-history graduates, thirty-five years after journalists first took notice of a "Williams Art Mafia, are in fact still highly influential, exerting a continuing impact on the broader art world disproportionate to the limited size of its student body.

Photograph of Delta Psi Lodge (St. Anthony Hall), 1897, by Alexander Davidson.
Courtesy of Williams College Archives and Special Collections.

Chapter 16

—∿∿—

AN ARCHITECTURAL HISTORY OF THE CDE BUILDING

(Formerly St. Anthony Hall)

One of the most impressive buildings on the Williams College campus is the substantial two-story stone structure on the southwest corner of Main St. and South St. that houses the Center for Development Economics (CDE). Whitney Stoddard called it "one of the most distinguished buildings on the Williams campus." Michael Lewis and E. J. Johnson call it a "masterpiece" by "one of the most brilliant architects ever to work at Williams College." The Center has been located in the building since 1966, but for eighty years before that it was known as St. Anthony Hall, the lodge of the Delta Psi fraternity. Its interior much adapted but its original exterior largely preserved, it survives as a monument from an era when Williams was what Fred Rudolph called a "gentleman's college" and most of campus social life was carried on in elegant fraternity lodges built and maintained with private money, owned not by the College but by the fraternities themselves. But in the last fifty years it has been repurposed to suit the needs of the much different Williams of today.

Antecedents

The Lambda chapter of Delta Psi fraternity was founded by Frederick Ferris Thompson (1836-99), of the Williams Class of 1856, on March 15, 1853. Thompson had begun his short college career at Columbia, where he joined the Delta Psi chapter there, but in 1852, at the age of 16, transferred to Williams – he had local connections in the area - and determined to found a new chapter of Delta Psi. By this time Williams already had five fraternities. In its first year Delta Psi enrolled 14 members.

For the first few years the chapter rented quarters in a house on West Main St. In these early days membership in the society was relatively large, and its activities were apparently social receptions and literary meetings. But it apparently wanted to build its own lodge – several other Williams fraternities had already done so. In 1860, William T. Hallett, Williams Class of 1861 and a member of Delta Psi, who went on the become an architect, produced a design for a chapter house, probably as a student exercise. Never built, it would have been a tall narrow building in Gothic revival style, with a steep roof and a tower, substantial end door surmounted by a Gothic arch, three Gothic windows above the door and on each side. The secret chapter room would probably have been in the steep-sided attic.

In the late 1860s the plans for a lodge were realized: the chapter bought a 1.5-acre lot on Park St. for $6000, and made plans to build a house. In 1868 the plans were made public and were reported in regional newspapers: it was to be a wooden frame house, "two stories high, with a Mansard roof, and when complete will cost four or five thousand dollars." (The *Chicago Republican* reported that it would cost $16,000.) In the end, it was built in 1870 for $6000, with funds provided by "a gentleman of New York whose son is a member." It in fact had three stories, not two (including a large windowed attic), with a wide 2-story piazza across the east front, a portico in the rear, and bow windows on north and south. It was painted ochre with dark trim. On the first floor Venetian doors opened into a center hall, with an arch and stairway at rear. There were four common rooms on first floor, four bedrooms on the second. The chapter room was located in the third floor attic, accessed by means of a trap door over the stairs.

The fraternity would only remain on Park St. for thirteen years, when it concluded that its lodge was too small – only four of the members could live there. By 1882 an attractive site became available at the corner of Main St. and South St., where Main St. passed over the top of the third of the town's three hills. Until 1855 it had been occupied by one of the first houses in Williamstown. In 1878 the location became even more attractive, when Cyrus W. Field gave money to the town to create Field Park, immediately in front of the site. On June 3, 1882 Delta Psi bought "the old Benjamin lot" for $6000, and in 1883 the house on Park St. was sold. It later served as the rectory for St. John's Church, and now, as Vogt House, houses the Development Office of the College.

The 1886 Stanford White building

Two-thirds of the money to build the new lodge reportedly came from Frederick Ferris Thompson, who would go on to become the most generous and important of the alumni who supported his alma mater. (It's noteworthy that his first benefaction was not to the College but to his fraternity.) The remainder of the funds reportedly came from the Field Family (Edward M. '76 and Cyrus W. Field, Jr. '79, sons of Cyrus W. Field, were both Saints) and the Fargo Family (William C. '78, James Francis '79, and Livingston W. '82 were all Saints). Thompson apparently took the lead: he hired Stanford White (1853-1906) as architect. White, who had been chief assistant to Henry Hobson Richardson from 1871 to 1877, then joined McKim and Mead, and in 1879-81 designed a town house for Thompson in New York at 283 Madison Ave. He was only 31 when he designed the chapter house for Delta Psi.

White appears to have taken inspiration from several different sources, including the interior of the house he had recently designed for Thompson, with its grand wooden staircase, wood paneling, and ceiling beams. He also seems to have in mind some of Richardson's small public libraries in eastern Massachusetts (particularly the 1882 Crane Memorial Library in Quincy), with their rusticated stone walls, steep gabled roofs, Romanesque arches, and embedded towers. White probably also looked at the chapter house for Delta Psi at Trinity College that J. C. Cady designed in 1878, with its rusticated stone walls, embedded towers (one of them hexagonal), with arrow-slit windows on the upper stories. Lewis and Johnson think White was "clearly inspired" by Cady's recently-constructed Morgan Hall (1883) on the Williams campus, with local dolomite and prominent gables.

Because White himself reportedly said the style of the building he designed was "Old English," it's plausible to assume that he was thinking of the country houses of Richard Norman Shaw, an English architect probably most associated in his own day with "Old English Style" – a term which points to the asymmetrical massing of pre-Georgian buildings in England, whether Tudor or Jacobean. ("Old English" is often regarded as part of a broader "Queen Anne Revival," of which Shingle Style is an American cousin.) But since none of Shaw's buildings resemble the Delta Psi chapter house, it's more likely that White was using the term generically. "Old English" was also used to describe the buildings of J. C. Cady.

For Delta Psi, White designed a substantial but compact 2-story rectangular building, clad in rough-cut gray stone. The basic form was perhaps modeled, as Lewis and Johnson suggest, on stone Dutch colonial houses. Its symmetry is complicated only on its front (northern) facade, composed as it is of arches on the front porch on the first floor, and a Richardsonian Romanesque arch over the entrance, interrupted by a three-story hexagonal tower. The eastern third consists of a Shingle-Style front porch, the building roof descending to form a steep front porch roof, with two wood-frame dormer windows. The western third, by contrast, is stone clad with paired recessed windows above an large inset stone, incised with the name of the fraternity – "Lambda Chapter of Delta Psi" – and the dates of the founding of the fraternity and the construction of the building – "1853 – 1886." The most prominent architectural feature is the three story hexagonal stone tower next to the entrance, that composes the middle third of the front facade, with arrow-slit windows on the third level, its flat roof topped by a Shingle-Style hexagonal cupola. It is rarely noticed that there is a lower second tower embedded at the east end of the building, round, with arrow-slit windows, and a conical cap tucked under the steep gable roof of the main part of the building. (The smaller tower contains a staircase.) For the east facade of the main block White designed a shingled triangular gable end, but for the west facade the gable end continues the stone of the first two floors, its parapet stepped in Dutch colonial revival fashion. (The parapet closely resembles the stepped gables designed by McKim, Mead, and White just two years earlier, in 1884, for the old Wolf's Head Society lodge on the Yale campus.) The stone is dolomite, cut from a quarry just south of the building site, on Cold Spring Rd. The building's roof was of slate.

It is as if White began with an idea of a simple Dutch colonial house, and varied it with elements from the Shingle and Romanesque styles. Like Richardson, he worked in several different styles, including Shingle (for which he is perhaps most known) and Romanesque (which he learned while working for Richardson). This eclecticism is in fact typical of much late-19th century American architecture.

One of the reasons that the building stands out on the Williams campus is that while echoing the grey stone of Goodrich Hall (1859), Morgan Hall (1882) and Lasell Gymnasium (1886), and the Richardsonian Romanesque of Hopkins Hall (1890), its "Old English style" makes it contrast with the predominantly Georgian architecture that became the default style on the campus beginning with the Thompson Scientific Laboratories (1892-93), the East [Berkshire] Quad (1905-08), and the Freshman Quad (1911, 1923).

The interior of White's building was dominated by the large rectangular living room, with a beamed ceiling (as in Thompson's town house), and a large central fireplace. Because of the north-facing front porch and the smallish windows on the east end, the room is somewhat dark and enclosing. It would presumably have been furnished with large and heavy pieces. Johnson and Lewis call it "magnificently intimate." Also on the first floor are an entrance hall, a vestibule, and a card room (in the tower). There were small fireplaces in each of the rooms on the tower's three levels.

A large stair hall leads to a grand U-shaped wooden stair case. Above the landing, on the back wall, was a large 5' x 8' stained-glass window depicting St. Anthony (the fraternity's patron saint) standing in the Egyptian desert. (Thompson had an interest in stained glass.) Dressed in a brown monk's robes, and surrounded by yellow glass, the figure, seen in left profile, appeared to point the way up to the fraternity's secret chapter room, then located at the head of the stairs. A dark photograph of the window appeared in a *Life* magazine cover story in 1949.

Fraternity tradition held that it was a "Tiffany window," but Williams historian Fred Rudolph said more than once that he had always heard it was by John La Farge (1835-1910). La Farge and White had collaborated on other projects. La Farge had strong links to the Delta Psi fraternity: one of his sons later became a member of Delta Psi at Penn in 1888, another at the chapter at Columbia in 1891, and a third designed the chapter house for Delta Psi at Yale in 1894. La Farge had also worked previously at Williams: he designed a memorial window for U.S. President James A. Garfield, a Williams alumnus, that was first set in Goodrich Hall in 1882. It was given by the same Cyrus W. Field who had given funds to create Field Park in front of the building, and whose two sons were recent graduates and members of Delta Psi at Williams. It seems likely that the Field family paid for the La Farge window in the Saint House.

Connected to the stair hall on the second floor are a hexagonal study in the tower and a library on the left (west). From the second-floor stairhall a narrow circular stair led up to the third level of the tower, with a bedroom in the tower and two others directly above the library. The largest space on the second floor is the chapter room, directly above the living room, but it is invisible to visitors, accessible only from the end of the living room on the first floor, through locked doors and up a staircase in the building's other tower. The chapter room was lighted by dormer windows. It had a high vaulted ceiling, and the walls and ceiling were probably decorated with fraternal symbols (reportedly an azure field with gold stars), now obscured by the drop ceiling installed in 1927. A large painting of St. Anthony hung on the east wall.

A three-story wood-frame shingled ell, projecting southward from the west end of the building, possibly part of the original construction but perhaps built shortly thereafter, provided sleeping rooms and baths for eight students. (The addition is visible in a photograph of the building, reproduced in Johnson and Lewis, probably taken in the 1880s.)

Groundbreaking for the building took place in October 1884. The building was expected to cost $24,000. On May 20, 1885 the cornerstone was laid. A private train, provided by Edward M. Field, with sleeping and dining cars, brought alumni fraternity members up from New York. By now the building was expected to cost $30,000. On March 15, 1886, the 33rd anniversary of the founding of the chapter, the new chapter house was dedicated. Again a special train brought members from New York for the event. It was now reported that the house cost $37,000. A photograph from 1897 (see p. 358) shows what the house looked like in its first years.

The fraternity's needs soon outstripped the facilities. By the 1890s a tennis court was built in the side yard. In 1898 it was announced that a "large addition" was expected to be built by an Albany contractor who had recently built a new Alpha Delta Phi house (1896) on Main St. and the Sigma Phi house (1894), along with several big private summer houses in Williamstown. But no addition was built that year.

The 1905 addition

It was built six years later. Again funded by alumni members from New York, a two -story wing was constructed off the west end of the building, projecting to the south, canted right at about 20 degrees off a right angle. Surprisingly (given the scale of the project), the name of the architect is not known. Its major space was a high-ceilinged "baronial" dining room, with paneled walls. It is flooded with light from a large Tudor leaded-glass bay window running the entire length of the west wall. (Because the wing is set at an angle, the big Tudor window is more visible from the street.) Set into the south wall was a large (63" x 38 3/4") bronze relief of the fraternity's founder, Frederick Ferris Thompson, commissioned as a memorial by his widow, and designed by Augustus Saint-Gaudens. Thompson is seen in 3/4 length, dressed in a suit and vest, hat in his left hand, an overcoat draped over his right arm, his dog in profile at the lower right. An inscription reads "Frederick Ferris Thompson Aetat LIV MDCCCXC." The still-vigorous-looking figure is apparently based on an 1890 photograph, when Thompson was 54, nine years before he died.

The wing also included a kitchen, pantry, and back hall on the first floor; a 3-room "apartment" and ladies' washroom off the main stairway on the intermediate floor; and six bedrooms and a bathroom on the second floor, in what would later be called the "Junior Wing." The old shingle-clad ell containing sleeping quarters, bathrooms, and studies, previously attached to the original building, was presumably removed and rebuilt further south, now attached to the end of the new wing.

The wing was faced on the west with compatible but darker and more rusticated limestone – the difference in color between this stone and the stone used in 1886 is clearer since all the stone was cleaned in 2019. The east wall was finished in plain stucco. Above the bay window on the west wall were three shingle-style dormers. The entire building, including the original structure, was equipped with new electrical wiring. Work began on August 9, 1904, with the clearing of trees and excavation of the site by a local contractor. The contractor for the construction was Easton, Rising & Worden, of Hoosick Falls. They had built Harley Procter's huge house across Main St. in 1891. Work was completed during the summer of 1905, and the building was ready to be occupied in the fall semester.

The 1927 addition

In 1920 a memorial plaque, designed by sculptor Harold Perry Erskine (1879-1951), Williams 1898 (and a Saint), honoring the 26 members of the several chapters of Delta Psi (including three from the Williams chapter) who died in World War I, was installed just inside the archway to the front door. In 1924 the grounds were landscaped by Boston landscape architect J. Fletcher Steele (Williams '07, and a Saint).

As early as 1924 plans were made to add another wing to the building, projecting southward from its east end. A high-profile architect was hired, Roger H. Bullard (1884-1935), who had established a reputation for designing large country houses and country clubs. (But he may actually have been chosen because as a 1907 graduate of Columbia, he was also a member of Delta Psi, and his father-in-law was head of the national fraternity). It was reported at the time that the wing, intended to provide bedrooms, studies, and bathrooms for eight additional students, would be compatible with the original building, "in the style of the Queen Anne period" (by then a more familiar term than "Old English"). Construction was to begin in 1926. "Subscriptions" were solicited from old members.

But on the morning of May 16, 1926 a fire broke out in the 3-story shingle-clad ell at the back of the building, causing damage estimated at $10,000, from fire, smoke, fire-retardant chemicals, and water. According to contemporary reports, the fire was thought to have started in a third-floor storage room. It was believed to have been caused by defective wiring. According to a story on the fire in the student newspaper, the fraternity "had previously completed plans to remodel the now useless wing this summer." The losses were "amply covered by insurance." Repairs began in July and were completed by October. The contractor, Perry Smedley of Williamstown, also constructed a new ell to replace the ell that was destroyed in the fire.

Work then proceeded on the new east wing. A two-story addition, later to be known as the "Senior Wing," it had shingled dormers and gables, with casement windows, similar to those in other Bullard houses. The northern end of the wing was aligned with the original building; the rest of it was slightly set back (serving to break up the eastern front, facing South Street) and canted left at an angle of about 10 degrees off a right angle, presumably to increase the space between the two wings and thus allow more light into the rear of the house. But a substantial part of the addition was literally underground. Bullard designed a new chapter room, two floors beneath the first floor, far grander and more elaborate, and far more secret, than the existing chapter room above the living room. It was a large 25' x 40' space, laid out like a "simplified Masonic floor plan," with an arched stone doorway, a massive wooden door, a sunken floor, a 14' beamed ceiling (echoing Stanford White's beam ceiling in the living room), with carved masks and heads under the beam ends, wood paneling on plaster walls, crown molding, 40 stalls around the perimeter for the members (with indirect lighting concealed behind them), and two high chairs for the principal officers. Up a flight of spiral stairs was an anteroom where members kept their robes and gathered before the weekly chapter meetings.

As part of the renovation project, the old chapter room became the house's "library," with a drop ceiling, though some old chapter-room decoration remains, including decorative plaster crown molding. Built-in bookshelves were added. The secret stairway in the smaller tower now became an open stairs connecting the 1st and 2nd floors of the Senior Wing.

On January 21, 1927, in the middle of the night, another fire broke out in the southwest wing. Again, it was thought to be due to defective writing, and to have started "near a provision room in the basement." This time the damage was much more severe: the ceiling of the dining room collapsed, the bay window was blown out, and the entire wing gutted. Damage, estimated at more than $31,000, was covered by insurance. The bronze relief was saved, but everything else had to be rebuilt. This time the shingle-clad ell was not rebuilt. Repairs on the southwest wing were quickly completed, as was the rest of the work on the east wing. It's likely that the cupola on top of the tower, its posts weakened or rotted by forty years of rain, was removed at this time. Students were able to move back into the building in early May 1927. The entire project, including repair and new construction, cost about $100,000.

The Center for Development Economics

The building remained much the same from 1927 until the 1960s. The basement was fitted with a mid-20th-century bar and television room, with knotty-pine paneling on the walls. As late as 1965-66 Delta Psi made full use of the house.

Beginning in 1962 fraternities at Williams were phased out, and the College sought to acquire the fraternity buildings for student housing. Delta Psi initially resisted these efforts, and in time Williams made a different approach. In 1966 the College, seeking an on-campus home for its Center for Development Economics, then located on Gale Road, leased St. Anthony Hall, and undertook renovations, designed by Russell, Gibson, and Von Dohlen, an engineering and architectural firm in Pittsfield. A new ground floor door on the east side, providing access to the old chapter room, enabled Delta Psi to continue some fraternal activities. Over the years further changes were made to make the building more suitable for academic purposes. In 1972 the College succeeded in acquiring it. In that year the old library was converted to a classroom. In 1976 parts of the chapter room were removed. Some of the changes were made to meet new building codes. In 1992 an elevator was installed, and in 1994 new mechanical systems. In 1996 stair towers were built at the ends of the two wings, at a cost of $1.24 million, to provide fire exits. These towers were faced with a grey brick, unfortunately not compatible with the stone work of the house. The front entrance arch was infilled with wood and glass, to improve heat retention. As of 2012 the building contained 24,365 square feet, and housed the CDE students aged 25 to 35, in 23 single rooms.

Many of the students came from countries in Africa and Asia where co-ed housing was considered inappropriate. By 2015 the College decided that it needed to find additional space and to provide separate housing for each sex. Platt, Byard, Dovell, and White (PBDW) Architects were brought in by the building committee to design a 2-story, 17,000 sq. ft. separate dormitory building a few yards to the south of the existing CDE building, with 30 bedrooms. (PBDW's senior partner, Samuel White, is the great-grandson of Stanford White.) The architects made significant efforts to make the new dormitory match with the iconic Stanford White building. Its two angled wings reflect the two angled wings of the old fraternity house. The dormitory is clad in a light-gray brick that is designed to harmonize with the old grey stone. Strategic placement of narrow window openings pick up the narrow windows in the old building's towers. Finally, the new building is sited in relation to the older one in order to create a semi-enclosed "courtyard," and to facilitate movement back and forth between the two buildings. Construction, supervised by Albert Cummings, was completed in December 2018. The Project Manager (from the College's Facilities Dept.) was Theresa Sawyer. Total cost of the dormitory project was $15.1 million (up from an initial budget of $11 million). It is now called Fellows Hall.

The second phase of the CDE project involved the conversion of bedrooms in the old building to offices and classrooms, the construction of a new kitchen, and the consequent switch of dining room and living room, all intended to preserve "the historic integrity of the building." The architect was Centerline Architects, from Bennington, with experience in historic renovation projects. The successful bidder was Stewart Construction, from Essex, VT, but because of slow progress in completing the renovation the College switched to Engelberth Construction, from Colchester, VT, the contractor who built the new Williams Inn. The project had a final budget of $14.2 million (up from an initial $10.5 million).

Work began in June 2018. It included an upgrading of the building envelope: stones in the walls were removed and cleaned by hand, and when replaced were repointed with carefully matched mortar. (Once the stone was cleaned, it was clear that stone in the 1905 wing was darker in color than in White's 1886 building.) Chimneys were repointed and regrouted. A cupola, built according to original plans, was reconstructed on top of the higher tower. Most of the windows were either repaired or replaced. The south facade of building – once just the largely unseen "back" of the building – was reconstructed and reclad in light-gray brick to mirror the CDE dormitory immediately to the south, and to complete the semi-enclosed "courtyard."

Inside the building changes were more substantial. Because the kitchen had long failed to meet code, it had to be substantially enlarged, and was moved from the 1905 wing to the 1927 wing. (A second self-catering kitchen for students was built adjacent to the main kitchen.) This led to a decision to move the dining room from the 1905 wing to the living room of the 1886 building, and to move living room to the better-lit old dining room. Woodwork was thoroughly cleaned. A new elevator shaft and elevator were installed to improve access and circulation. On the second floor the bedrooms and studies in the Junior and Senior Wings were reconfigured as classrooms and offices. Mechanical systems were upgraded, and mechanical space made available in the third floor of the west wing to support a new air conditioning system. Because the third floor of the tower is accessible only by a narrow circular stair, it was made off limits, except to CDE staff. Wherever possible, original interior elements from 1886, 1905, and 1927 were preserved: wood flooring, plaster walls and ceilings, wood wainscoting, wall paneling, paneled wood doors, and the grand bay window in what is now the living room.

The historical preservation consultant hired by the College recommended that the former chapter room in the sub-basement, as the largest fraternity chapter room on campus, and the best preserved, be kept intact. But because there is no fire exit – the original second exit having been closed off to create a paved entrance to the back of the house – it has been declared inaccessible except to CDE staff.

Work on the renovation project was substantially complete in March 2020, when the coronavirus closed the campus and halted construction. The final punch list was completed in the summer of 2020. The result is a spectacular renovation of a historically important building.

INDEX

This index includes proper names, places in Williamstown, and major events. Unless significant, names that appear only once are not indexed.

Aitken, Helen Jean, 11, 12
Albany Turnpike, 5, 69, 84, 84
Allen, Herbert, 2, 30, 104, 105, 110, 111
Allen, Robert, 228, 263, 264, 268
American Revolution, 19, 56, 57, 71, 85,
    113, 131, 134, 136, 137, 138, 139
Amherst College, 8, 54, 55, 56, 58, 66,
    162, 182
Armstrong, Samuel Chapman, 189, 193-97,
    198, 199, 201, 202
Arvellanus, Arcadius, 56, 58
Art, Henry (Hank), 76, 78, 79

Bacon, Ezekiel, 138, 145
Bacon, John, 142, 146, 147
Bacon Brook, 37, 41
Bacon Family (in the Hopper), 39, 41, 42,
    43, 45, 46, 48, 50
Baker, Filmore, 166, 167, 168, 169, 171,
    172-73, 182
Barnard, Ellsworth, 229, 232
Baxter, James Phinney,
    as Williams president, 202, 205, 223,
    224, 229, 230, 231, 232, 245;
    as Williams trustee, 205, 214, 220,
    221, 222
Bee Hill, 5, 69, 83-96, 99, 100, 112,
    120, 124
Bee Hill Farm, 22, 23, 31, 32, 34, 89
Bee Hill Rd., 14, 15, 20, 22, 23, 31, 34, 69,
    83-90, 93, 95, 96; Bee Hill Extension,
    85, 90, 91, 92
Beinecke, Walter, 78, 79, 124
Bennington, 71, 101, 134, 139, 157, 167,
    298; Battle of, 57, 72, 131, 134

Bennington College. 169, 171, 181
Berlin Mtn., 69, 112, 118, 121
Berlin, NY, 105
Berlin Pass, 83, 84
Berlin Rd., 83, 84, 92
Birch Hill, 69, 83, 84, 88, 99, 115, 120
Birdsall, Paul, 214, 217, 219, 221, 229, 230
Bissaillon, Francis, 163, 169
Blagden, Samuel, Jr., 29, 100, 107, 108,
    109, 110, 111
Blair, Isabella, 145
Blair Rd., 30, 31, 104, 122, 138
Bolin, Gaius, 160
Bratcher Family, 21, 25, 26, 43, 104,
    111, 112
Bressett, Simon, 44, 47, 49
Bressett Rd., 38, 44, 46, 47, 49
Brooks, R. R. R., on Bee Hill Rd., 94;
    as local historian, 9, 45;
    as professor, 208, 228, 229, 230,
    231, 232
Buck, Robert, 273, 278, 279, 281
Bulkeley Family, 73, 75, 79, 106, 107,
    108, 112
Bulkley St., 3, 10, 15, 58, 71, 72, 73, 75,
    78, 79, 91, 107, 157
Bullard, Roger H., 295, 196
Bullock, Anthony, 74, 99, 100, 106, 107;
    Anthony D., 14, 194; James, 13, 14,
    93, 94, 95, 111, 118, 120, 122
Burghardt, James S. M., 156-57, 159, 161;
    Mary Persis, 159
Burns, James M., 26, 78, 91, 171, 176, 228,
    232; Joan, 26, 91; Stewart, 220, 226
Bushnell, Nelson, 223, 229, 266

Buxton (neighborhood), 3-17
Buxton Brook, 3, 9, 11, 71
Buxton Farms, 74-75, 76, 79, 213
Buxton hill (hill), 3, 13, 69, 83, 120
Buxton Hill (house), 3, 11, 12, 15
Buxton Hill (neighborhood), 14
Buxton (private) School, 16, 69, 109, 118
Buxton School (Northwest Hill Rd.),
    3, 9, 74

Cady, J. Cleaveland, 291
Center for Development Economics
    (Williams College), 29, 110, 289-99
Chadwell Family,151-61. *See* Burghardt
    Family, Hart Family, Galvin Family.
Chamberlin, Nathaniel, 73, 74, 77, 78
Chapin Hall (Williams College), 162, 169,
    171, 178, 179, 182, 260
Civil War, 22, 41, 43, 54, 60, 151, 157,
    189-202
Clark Art Institute, 16, 43, 67, 98, 105,
    112, 113, 124, 125, 126, 284, 285
Cluett, George, 28, 29, 99, 100, 109, 110,
    111, 112
Carmichael, Robert, 91
Cold Spring Rd., 13, 20, 21, 25, 26, 43, 48,
    74, 83, 84, 98, 99, 104, 106, 111, 115,
    124, 292
Cole Avenue, 60, 119, 120, 121, 122,
    136, 177
Congregational Church, 73, 123, 138,
    140, 157, 159; and Vietnam, 167,
    177, 178, 179

Danforth, Bushnell, 7; Jonathan, 6;
    Keyes, Sr., 6, 16; Keyes, Jr., 6, 7,
    11, 16, 88; William, 11
Deans, David M., 14, 15
Delta Psi (Williams College fraternity).
    See St. Anthony Hall
DeMayo Family, 27, 31
Dennett, Tyler, 205-24. 230, 232
Dewey, Daniel, 5, 138, 142, 143-49

Dewey, Thomas E., 227, 243, 244
DuBois, W. E. B., 152, 155, 156, 157, 159
Dwight, Timothy, 116, 117, 118

East Mountain, 117, 118, 119, 121
Eastlawn Cemetery, 161, 163, 165, 174,
    176, 183
Eldridge Family, 25, 30, 34
Election of 1800, 144-55
Election of 1940, 156, 229, 230
Election of 1968, 163, 165, 170,
    172-73, 174
Eusden, John, 167, 169
Evans, Rowland, 233, 263, 264

Faison, Lane, 228, 230, 233; and
    'Williams Art Mafia', 274-75, 276,
    277, 278, 280, 281, 282, 284, 285
Field, Cyrus W., 290. 291, 293
Field, Gary Edgar, 163
Field Park, 4, 14, 15, 17, 97, 98, 103, 120,
    124, 163, 290, 293
Fisher, John, and Vietnam, 165-75, 177,
    177, 182, 183; Vera, 165, 166, 169,
    170, 173
Fitch, Ebenezer, 138, 140, 141, 145
Five Corners, 85, 98, 101, 105, 111
Flora's Glen, 83, 84, 85, 94, 95, 96, 117,
    124; Flora's Glen Brook, 83, 85, 92,
    94-95, 117
Ford, Zadock, 72, 73; Ford Brook, 83, 85,
    92, 94-95, 117; Ford's Glen, 72, 73,
    74, 75, 76
French Revolution, 53, 138, 139

Gale, John B., 99, 100, 102, 106, 107,
    109, 112
Gale Rd., 28, 98, 99, 102, 103, 108, 109,
    110, 297
Galusha Family, 19-34, 45, 51, 87, 88, 89,
    95, 106, 109, 110, 122
Galvin Family, 159, 160
Garfield, Harry, 12, 108, 207, 208, 211,

214; James A., 189, 190, 194, 197-200, 201, 202, 293
Gates, William, 228, 232
George, Arthur, 22
Gifford, Don, 266, 267, 268
Goodale, Hubert, 47, 60, 67
Goodrich Family, 11, 69, 74, 77, 78, 80
Goodrich Hall (Williams College), 124, 292, 293
Govan, Michael, 273, 274, 280, 283, 285
Graver, Lawrence, 266, 268
Green River, 31, 37, 38, 39, 48, 59, 98, 101, 118, 136
Green River Rd., 19, 23-24, 27, 29, 30, 34, 38, 47, 49, 58, 59, 98, 99, 102, 104, 105, 106, 107, 110
Greenberg, Clement, 276, 280
Greylock (Mt.). See Mount Greylock
Greylock Hotel, 94, 157; college purchases, 205, 215, 216, 217, 218, 219, 220, 222, 223
Greylock Park Association, 46, 119
Greylock Reservation, 37, 38, 43, 46, 125, 126
Griffin, Edward Dorr, 11, 45
Griffin Hall (Williams College), 125, 202, 209

Haley Family, 40, 43, 45, 46, 48
Hampton Institute, 154, 189, 196, 199
Hart Family, 160, 161
Hazen, Richard, 117
Hemlock Brook, 33, 4, 17, 20, 21, 25, 26, 73, 83, 96, 98, 101, 102, 115, 117
Hemlock Brook School, 25
Hickox Family, 20, 22-23, 31, 669, 85-88, 89, 91-93, 94, 96, 120
Highcroft School, 29, 110
Hirsche, Lee, 29. 110, 277, 278
Hoosic River, 69, 71, 74, 101, 117, 118, 136
Hoosic River Valley, 11, 116
Hoover, Walter, 29-30, 103, 104, 110, 111

Hopkins, Albert, 26, 38, 45, 46, 120; Amos Lawrence, 11, 72, 74-75, 76, 120, 122, 218; Archibald, 193, 195, 202; Mark, 74, 190, 193, 197, 200
Hopkins Hall (Williams College), 209, 292
Hopkins Memorial Forest, 3, 71, 72, 77, 78, 79, 80, 81, 98, 119, 121, 124, 125, 126
Hopper, 37-51, 96, 98, 118, 260-61, 269
Hopper Brook, 37, 38, 39, 40, 48, 49, 118, 136
Hopper Rd., 37-51, 67
Hopper School, 40, 50
Howard, Wallace, 17
Hunt, Clay, 49, 233, 257-70
Hunter Family, 16, 79, 80

"Indian," arrowheads, 101; camp, 101; path/trail, 71, 101; Indian Springs, 65; village, 101; "Wars," 189, 191, 192
Institute of Politics, 12, 53

Jenks Family, 100, 106, 111
Johnson, E. J., 277, 284, 285, 289, 291, 293, 294
Johnson, Lyndon B., 165, 170, 171, 172, 175, 176, 182

Keller, Charles, 205, 212, 214
Krens, Tom, 273, 278, 279, 280, 281, 286
Krigger Family, 39, 40, 126

La Farge, John, 293
Lane, John (Jack), 273, 274, 275, 279, 280, 281, 282, 283, 285
Lanesboro (Ma.), 101, 134, 136
Langer, Fritz, 111
Lasell Gymnasium (Williams College), 292
Lawrie Family, 7, 8-10, 11, 12, 13, 14, 15, 16
Lawton, John, 170, 177
Lerner, Max, 228-33, 235-53
Lewis, Michael, 276, 289, 291, 293, 294

Livingston, Mark, 100
Lowry, Glenn, 273, 274, 278, 279, 280, 281, 285

Mackenzie, Ranald Slidell, 188-92, 193, 195, 196, 197, 201, 202
Mandle, Roger, 273, 274, 278, 279, 280, 281
Mason Family, 69, 74, 77, 80
Masons (fraternal order), 157, 158, 159, 296
Maynard Family, 92
Meadowbrook Farm, 93, 111
Megaw, Neill, 14, 15, 94, 266, 267, 268
Moon Family, 72, 73, 75
Morgan Hall (Williams College), 292, 292
Mt. Greylock, 37, 39, 46, 51, 64, 96, 117, 118, 122, 124
Mt. Greylock Regional High School, and Vietnam, 166, 167, 171, 173, 178, 179, 180
Mount Hope Farm, 24, 37, 40, 42, 44, 47-48, 53-67, 75, 78, 79, 99, 120, 124
Mount Hope Park, 37, 38
Mt. Prospect, 37, 38, 40, 69, 117

Nathan, Judith, 275, 278, 281, 282, 283
Native Americans. *See* "Indian"
New Ashford Rd., 27, 28, 30, 38
New York Times, 66, 108, 221, 273, 275, 281, 282
Newhall, Richard, 221, 228, 229
Noble, David, 5, 6, 130, 132-37, 138, 143, 148, 149
North Adams (Ma.), 9, 10, 14, 116, 123, 157, 159, 167; and Vietnam, 166, 167, 169, 170, 172, 173, 176, 177, 181, 281, 286
North Adams Transcript, 40, 59, 157, 216
Northwest Hill, 69, 71-81
Northwest Hill Rd., 3, 69, 71-81
Northwest Hill School, 73, 74

Oakley, Frank, 104, 170, 276
Oblong Rd., 20, 22, 34, 51, 83, 84, 123, 124, 161

Paddock, Robert Lewis, 12, 16
Parkhurst, Charles, 280, 282
Perry, Arthur Latham, 38, 72, 83, 85, 86, 123, 149
Perry, Lewis, 211, 220, 222
Petersburg Pass, 84, 117
Pierson, William, 232, 233, 274, 276, 277, 284
Pine Cobble, 69, 115, 118
Pine Cobble School, 28, 29, 110
Pittsfield (Ma.), 32, 40, 58, 69, 101, 166, 171, 172, 176; and Chadwell Family, 156, 157, 158, 159, 160; in the 18th century, 132, 133, 134, 135, 137, 138, 139, 148
Pittsfield Sun, 146-47
Porter, Cole, 4, 11-13, 14, 16, 261
Porter, Dr. Samuel, 105
Potter, William, 41
Potter Brook, 37
Potter Rd., 38, 41, 43, 49, 51
Powell, Earl (Rusty), 272, 273, 274, 278, 279, 280, 281
Pownal (Vt.), 15, 22, 69, 71, 75, 77, 80, 81, 125, 160, 215
Prentice, E. Parmalee, 10, 11, 23, 24, 39, 40, 42, 43, 44, 47-48, 49, 50, 52-67
Primmer Family, 75, 90
Prindle Family, 20, 24, 73, 74, 77, 88-90, 91, 93, 94, 95, 120
Procter Family, Harley, 99, 100, 102, 103, 106-07, 108, 112, 295; William, 107

Richardson, Henry Hobson, 291, 292
Ringgold, Faith, 150, 161
Rockefeller Family, 53, 54, 55
Roffinoli, Giovanni, 108
Rosenburg, Arthur, 85, 90, 93-94, 95
Rosenburg Center (Williams College), 79

Rudolph, Frederick, as student, 228, 231;
  as Williams historian, 202, 205,
  289, 293

St. Anthony Hall (Delta Psi), 17, 289-99.
Saint-Gaudens, Augustus, 294
Samuels, Charles, 266
Sangster, Ellen Geer, 109
Sawyer, John E.,170, 171, 182, 205, 224,
  232, 267
schoolhouses. See Buxton School; Hemlock
  Brook School; Hopper School;
  Northwest Hill School
Schuman, Frederick, 166, 167, 170, 171,
  208, 227-33, 235-54
Scott Hill Rd., 98, 100, 101, 102, 103, 104,
  107, 111
Sedgwick, Theodore, 140, 142, 143, 144,
  145, 148, 149
Sensenbrenner, Joseph, 174
Shapiro, Michael, 274, 284
Sheep Hill, (south of Bee Hill), 23, 69, 87;
  (west of Cold Spring Rd.), 23, 83, 85,
  94, 96, 98, 104, 112
Sherman, John, 13, 73, 93
Sidley, William, 211, 212, 213, 216
Simonds, Benjamin, 4, 5, 6, 38, 132,
  138, 149
Skinner, Benjamin, 138, 139, 148, 149;
  Tompson, 138, 139-42, 143, 144,
  147-48, 149
Sloan, Samuel, 122, 132, 133, 138
Smith, Philip and Susan, 5, 16
Smith, T. C., 200, 208, 214
Soby, James Thrall, 282, 285
Southlawn Cemetery, 44, 120, 166
Sperry Rd., 38, 41, 45, 46
Sprague, John and Jid, 15, 96
Sprague Electric Co., 10, 15, 49, 78, 160,
  170, 175
Spring St., 4, 7, 10, 31, 37, 44, 96, 98,
  158, 213, 224; merchants and Vietnam,
  175, 176, 177, 179

Steele, Fletcher, 108, 295
Stocking, Fred, 232, 260, 264, 266,
  267, 268
Stoddard, Whitney, 232, 274, 276, 277,
  284, 289
Stone Hill, 22, 43, 69, 97-113, 121
Stone Hill Rd., 34, 69, 97, 101-05, 106,
  107, 110, 111, 112, 113, 124
Stony Ledge, 37, 38, 41, 45, 46, 77
Sweet Family, 20, 30, 31, 39, 40, 43, 47,
  48, 49, 50, 122
Sweet's Corners, 24, 38, 39, 40, 41
Swift, Rev. Seth, 123, 138

Taconic Golf Club, 10, 68
Taconic Range (Crest), 57, 64, 65, 69,
  71, 72, 74, 78, 79, 96, 98, 105,
  117, 118, 119
Taconic Trail (Rt. 2), 20, 25, 83, 84, 87,
  90, 95, 121
Taconic Trail State Park, 23, 88, 90
Tauber, Kurt, 169, 170, 181, 183
Tenney, Sanford, 74, 91, 92, 94, 95, 96
Thompson, Frederick F., 289, 290, 291,
  292, 293, 294
Thompson, Joseph, 273, 280, 283, 285
Thompson Memorial Chapel
  (Williams College) 174, 175, 183,
  189, 202, 270
Thompson Scientific Laboratories
  (Williams College), 292
Thornliebank, 5, 13-15, 83, 94, 95
Thull, Beulah Bailey, 23, 87, 95
Torrey Woods, 83, 124
Torrey Woods Rd., 20, 83, 84
Treadwell Hollow, 37, 74, 83, 84, 91,
  118, 121
trees, 14, 31, 43, 59, 70, 76, 77, 79, 85,
  86, 98, 104, 108, 111, 115-26
Tunick, David, 274, 278, 279, 280,
  281, 286

Valone, Carlo, 166, 167, 168

Varnedoe, J. Kirk T., 272, 273, 274, 278, 279, 280, 281, 283

Vietnam War, 163-84, 201, 202, 227, 236, 248, 251, 252, 269

Wahl, George, 112

Waite, Robert G. L., 172, 175, 179

Walsh, John, 89, 90, 91; William, 89, 90, 91

Warren, Bentley, on Stone Hill, 69, 99, 108, 109, 112; Williams trustee, 211, 217, 220, 221, 222, 232

Warren, Robert Penn, 261, 262, 265

Waterman Family, 88, 91

West College (Williams College), 86, 119, 120, 122, 124, 140, 153

West Main St., 3-17, 83, 84, 158, 289

Westlawn Cemetery, 4, 5, 6, 7, 16

Wheelock, Arthur, 273, 274, 278, 279, 280, 283

Whelden Family, 5, 6, 7, 12, 16

White, Stanford, 290-94, 296, 298

Whitman Family, 74, 78, 80

Whittlesey, Charles, 201, 202

Williams College Archives, 2, 66, 68, 70, 82, 162, 193, 206, 226, 234, 256, 272, 288

Williams College buildings. *See* Center for Development Economics; Chapin Hall; Goodrich Hall; Griffin Hall; Hopkins Hall; Lasell Gymnasium; Morgan Hall; Thompson Memorial Chapel; Thompson Scientific Laboratories, West College,

Williams College presidents. *See* Baxter, James Phinney; Dennett, Tyler; Fitch, Ebenezer; Garfield, Harry; Griffin, Edward Dorr; Hopkins, Mark; Oakley, Frank; Sawyer, John E.

Williams, Ephraim, Jr., 132m 140, 202; Ephraim (Federalist), 147; Israel, 132, 136; William, 132, 136

Williams Farm, 106, 107, 108

Williams Record, 215, 217, 226, 227, 228, 229, 230, 231; and Vietnam War, 167, 171, 172, 174, 175, 178, 179, 180, 181

Williamstown High School, 157, 159, 160

Williamstown Historical Museum, 5, 12, 13, 20, 25, 52, 66, 67, 73, 75, 114

Williamstown Rural Lands Foundation, 23, 30, 96, 120, 121

Wilson, John, 211, 212, 216

Wood, James, 273, 274, 278, 279, 281, 283

Woodcock, Nehemiah, 102, 138

Woodcock Corner, 102, 105; Woodcock Rd., 102

World War I, 59, 112, 158, 201, 295

World War II, 17, 76, 116, 159, 165, 166, 182, 227-33, 240-42, 252, 278

Wylde, Edward, 90, 95

Yeomans, George, 98

CPSIA information can be obtained
at www.ICGtesting.com
Printed in the USA
FSHW022211220621
82590FS